The
War of
Atonement

To those whose self-sacrifice
saved their country

The War of Atonement

Chaim Herzog

New Introduction by Brigadier General (IDF ret.) Michael Herzog

FRONTLINE BOOKS

A Greenhill Book

Published in 1998 and 2003 by Greenhill Books, Lionel Leventhal Limited
www.greenhillbooks.com

This edition published in 2018 by

Frontline Books
An imprint of
Pen & Sword Books Ltd
Yorkshire, S70 2AS

ISBN: 978-1-52671-371-1

Publishing History
The War of Atonement was first published by Weidenfeld and Nicolson, London,
in 1975 and was reproduced complete and unabridged, with an Introduction
by Michael Herzog, in 1998 by Greenhill Books. Michael Herzog has updated
his Introduction for this 2018 Frontline paperback edition. Maps are by Carta,
Jerusalem, and photographs are courtesy of the Israel Government Press Office, and
are reproduced from the original edition.

For more information on our books, please visit
www.frontline-books.com, email info@frontline-books.com
or write to us at the above address.

Printed and bound by CPI Group (UK) Ltd, Croydon, CR0 4YY

Contents

	Introduction by Brigadier General (IDF ret.) Michael Herzog	xi
	Foreword	xix
1	The New Strategic Concept	1
2	In Search of Solutions	13
3	The Tangled Web	32
4	Eyes Have They But They See Not	40
5	Like a Wolf on the Fold	55
6	The Onslaught (North)	78
7	The Holding Action	96
8	The Epic of the 7th Brigade	106
9	The Counter-Attack	116
10	The Break-in	128
11	The Onslaught (South)	146
12	On the Bar-Lev Line	170
13	An Opportunity Lost	182
14	Decision in the Desert	197
15	The Crossing	208
16	On the Other Side	231
17	The Air and Naval War	251
18	Lessons and Implications	270
	Index	293

Maps

Deployment of Forces, Saturday 6 October (North)   70

Maximum Syrian Penetration, Sunday 7 October   102

Israeli Counter-Attack Reaches Purple Line, Wednesday 10 October   119

The Break Through   131

Deployment of Forces, Saturday 6 October (South)   152

Israeli Attack on Egyptian Bridgeheads, 7 & 8 October   186

The Israeli Crossing   213

Israeli Advance West of the Canal and Cease-Fire Line   236

The Naval Theatre   265

Illustrations

Between p. 140 and p. 141

Maj.-Gen. Dan Laner

Brig.-Gen. Moshe (Mussa) Peled

Generals Dayan and Hofi with troops

Maj.-Gen. Hofi, Lieut.-Gen. Bar Lev and Maj.-Gen. Mordechai Hod

Maj.-Gen. Benjamin Peled

Maj.-Gen. (Raful) Eytan

Rear Admiral Benjamin Telem

Israeli armour in the Golan Heights

Syrian tanks

General Adan (Bren), General Elazar and General Magen

General Adan (Bren) consulting with a Brigade Commander

Generals Gonen, Elazar and Weizman

Maj.-Gen. (Albert) Mandler briefing the Chiefs-of-Staff

Colonel (now Brigadier) Danny Matt

Maj.-Gen. Ariel Sharon

Isreali troops near Ismailia

Breach in the Isreali rampart on the Suez Canal

Israeli tanks

Addendum

List of Correct Names and Numbers of IDF Units

The original edition of *The War of Atonement* (1975) contained names of Israeli commanders and numbers of IDF units modified by the author due to censorship considerations. These considerations no longer apply. This addendum provides the correct names (in alphabetic order) and numbers, including reference to the context in which they appear in the book.

The Northern Front (Syria)

Name/number and context in the original edition	Correct name/number
Lt. Col. Amos (a battalion commander joining the 7th Brigade and leading the offensive into Syria)	Amos Katz
Lt. Col. Avi (commander, 7th Battalion/7th Brigade)	Avigdor Kehalani (77th Battalion)
Col. Avigdor (commander, 7th Brigade)	Avigdor (Yanush) Ben-Gal
Avner (company commander, Barak Brigade)	Avner Landau
Bats (commander, the 1st Battalion/7th Brigade, killed in the Golan Heights)	Lt. Col. Meshulam Rates (71st Battalion)
Lt. Col. Dan (commander, 2nd Battalion/79th Brigade)	Ran Gottfried (679th Brigade)
Maj. Dov (intelligence officer, Barak Brigade)	Moshe Tzurich
Maj. Dov Pesach (deputy commander, 2nd Battalion/Barak Brigade)	Danny Pesach
Eli (company commander, 7th Brigade in the Rafid junction)	Eli Geva
Lt. Col. Elisha (paratroop battalion commander who retook the Syrian Hermon)	Elisha Shalem
Maj. Hanan (signals officer, Barak Brigade)	Hanan Schwarz
Lt. Col. Hezi (paratroop battalion commander who participated in the Mt Hermon battle)	Hezi Shelah
Lt. Col. Josh (commander, 5th Battalion/7th Brigade)	Yoss Eldar (75th Battalion)
Brig. Gen. Man (Raful's deputy)	Menahem Aviram
Captain Meir, 'Tiger' (company commander, 7th Brigade)	Meir Zamir

Lt. Col. Mir (tank battalion commander fighting in El Al junction   Maj. Yossi Amir

Brig. Gen. Moshe (Dan Laner's deputy)   Moshe Brill
(Bar Kokhva)

Lt. Col. Oded (commander, 3rd Battalion/7th Brigade)   Oded Erez (53rd Battalion)

Col. Ori (commander, 79th Reserve Brigade)   Ori Or (679th Brigade)

Lt. Col. Piniye (deputy commander, District Brigade)   Piniye Kupperman

Col. Ran (commander, 17th Reserve Brigade)   Ran Sarig (179th Brigade)

Maj. Shmulik (Yossi Ben-Hana's deputy)   Shmulik Askarov

Lt. Col. Uzi (deputy commander 17th Brigade, lost eyesight and an arm)   Uzi Mor (battalion commander, 179th Brigade)

Lt. Col. Yair (commander, 4th Battalion/Barak Brigade)   Yair Nafshi (74th Battalion)

Lt. Col. Yossi (battalion commander wounded in Tel Shams)   Yossi Ben-Hanan

The Southern Front (Egypt)

Lt. Col. Ami (tank battalion commander, Sharon's Division)   Ami Morag

Lt. Col. Amir (tank battalion commander, Gaby's Brigade)   Amir Yaffe

Col. Amnon (tank brigade commander)   Amnon Reshef

Lt. Col. Amram (commander, 7th Battalion)   Amram Mitzna (79th Battalion)

Col. Arieh (tank brigade commander, Bren's division)   Arieh Keren

Lt. Col. Arik (Danny Matt's deputy)   Arik Achmon

Col. Avraham (tank brigade commander subordinate to Albert)   Avraham Bar'am

Col. Dan (tank brigade commander subordinate to Albert)   Dan Shomron

Lt. Col. Dan (paratroop battalion commander, Danny Matt's Brigade)   Dan Ziv

Brig. Gen. David (Bren's deputy)   Dov (Dovik) Tamari

Lt. Col. Ehud (tank battalion commander, Gabi's Brigade, Bren's Division, who helped the paratroops in the Chinese Farm)   Ehud Barak

Lt. Col. Eitan (Amnon Reshef's deputy)   Eitan Arieli

Lt. Col. Emmanuel (tank battalion commander in Amnon's Brigade)   Emmanuel Sakel

Col. Gaby (tank brigade commander)   Gaby Amir

Col. Haim (tank brigade commander, Sharon's Division)   Haim Erez

Lt. Col. Itzik (paratroop battalion commander, fighting in the Chinese Farm)   Itzik Mordechai

Brig. Gen. Jackie (Sharon's deputy)   Yaacov (Jackie) Even

Lt. Col. Nathan (commander, reserve paratroop battalion, who fought under Amnon's Brigade)   Nathan Shunari

Lt. Col. Natke (tank brigade commander under Bren's Division)   Natke Nir

Col. Pinhas (commander, Northern Line Brigade at the outbreak of the war)   Pinhas Noy (Alush)

Brig. Gen. Pino (Albert's deputy)   Baruch Har'el (Pinko)

Brig. Gen. Sasoon (commander, northern force)   Sasson Itzhaki

Col. Tuvia (tank brigade commander, Sharon's division)   Tuvia Raviv

Col. Uzi (commander, paratrooper brigade, who fought in the Chinese Farm)	Uzi Yairi
Lt. Col. Uzi (tank battalion commander, Dan Shomron's Brigade)	Uzi Lanzner
Lt. Col. Uzi (tank brigade commander, Sharon's division)	Uzi Ben-Itzhak
Lt. Col. Yomtov (tank battalion commander)	Yomtov Tamir
Lt. Col. Yossi (paratroop battalion commander wounded at the town of Suez)	Yossi Yoffe
Lt. Col. Zvi (paratroop battalion commander, Danny Matt's Brigade)	Zviki Nur

Introduction

By Brigadier General (IDF ret.) Michael Herzog

THE OCTOBER 1973 Arab-Israeli War (known in Israel as the Yom Kippur War, as it broke out on Yom Kippur, the Day of Atonement, which is the holiest day in the Jewish calendar) was a breaking point and watershed in the history of the Arab-Israeli conflict. It was the last multi-front comprehensive war waged between Israel and its Arab neighbours, although the Middle East was still to witness further serious outbreaks of Arab-Israeli violence and military confrontations.

This book was written soon after the war, in 1974, and was first published in 1975. Its title, 'War of Atonement', reflects not only the date the war broke out, but conveys the deep sense of regret and soul searching in Israel following the war, over the failure to anticipate or prevent the conflict and the heavy price paid in fighting it.

In producing his account, the author, my late father, relied on all the relevant evidence that was then available. He conducted comprehensive interviews with Israeli leaders (with whom he was personally acquainted), army officers and ordinary soldiers; he toured the battlefields, and studied a large number of books and articles that had already been published. In writing the book, he gave expression to his vast experience as a soldier, general and intelligence expert as well as a military and political analyst and commentator. In fact, the book has become a classic on the history and wars of the Middle East, been translated into numerous languages, taught in military academies, and gained international recognition and praise.

Over four decades have now passed since the war, and the political environment in which we live has undergone great change. The world is no longer bi-polar as it was during the Cold War; Israel and Egypt, the largest and most important of the Arab states, have been party to a peace agreement for nearly four decades; Israel and Jordan have been party to a peace agreement for over twenty years; and Israel and its other neighbours have embarked upon a brittle peace process, fraught with crises and violent eruptions. In recent years, the Middle East has experienced unprecedented upheavals, releasing destructive energies carried by extreme Islamists, and paving the way for the Islamic Republic of Iran to emerge as a regional power and leader of the camp of enemies of peace with Israel. This, in turn, has led to the development of close, quiet relations between Israel and some of its Arab neighbours, including some with whom it has no formal relations – a development of historic irony. Finally, the technology and art of war have taken on a somewhat different face.

Nevertheless, in hindsight it seems that the book has lost none of its validity as a military history with relevant contemporary lessons. On the contrary, on reading it again, it seems like a wine that has improved with age. A huge quantity of material on the War of Atonement has been published in the interceding years, including the memoirs of some of the leaders who were involved (such as Anwar Sadat, Golda Meir and Moshe Dayan), the versions of senior military commanders (such as the book by Saad-a-Din Shazali, the Egyptian Chief of Staff during the war), the protocols of Israeli leadership debates before and during the war, and other first-hand materials. This has added details that were previously unknown, and testimony of historical weight. Nevertheless, in the final analysis this does not impair the validity of the picture painted in this book, but rather reinforces it. The book has withstood the test of time and continues to excel in its ability to portray a comprehensive, yet sharp and accurate picture, integrating tactical, operative and strategic outlooks in a broad analytical perspective.

The seeds of the War of Atonement were sown in the Six Day War, which preceded it in 1967. Israel's brilliant military victory gave rise to a delusion of power on the Israeli side and a deep sense of humiliation on the Arab side. In a tragic turn of events, the War of Atonement restored a measure of balance to this picture and thereby constituted an important milestone in the process of transition from war to peace. The Arab side won back a degree of pride by daring to instigate a military confrontation with Israel and scoring an initial success, despite ultimately suffering a military defeat. At the same time, the war sobered the Arab world's long-standing belief that it could ultimately defeat Israel by armed force, since it could not have hoped for a better start to the war than it achieved in 1973. On the Israeli side, the war demonstrated both the limits of force and the risks of conceit, complacency and stagnation. Indeed, just a few years after the war, President Sadat came to Jerusalem, and Israel and Egypt, after so bitterly shedding each other's blood, signed a formal peace agreement. Four decades have since elapsed, during which time not a soldier has fallen in an Egyptian-Israeli military confrontation.

As the book well describes, President Sadat planned the War of Atonement as a model previously unknown in the area, namely as a military initiative with limited military goals (albeit a fully-fledged war in terms of the means used), aiming to motivate a diplomatic process in the wake of the military shockwaves. The Egyptian offensive, therefore, was planned in careful detail only in its initial stages, but not beyond them. In vehement dispute with his Chief of Staff, Sadat therefore also refused to pull his forces back from the east bank of the Suez Canal in the face of Israel's crossing to its west bank in a pincer movement. Sadat's army suffered a military defeat, but, ultimately, aided by the USA, the Egyptian leader was able to gain diplomatic success, from which he later advanced towards full peace in exchange for all the territory lost by Egypt in 1967. On the other hand, Israel gained an impressive military victory, bearing in mind it was initially taken by surprise, but had to pay a considerable diplomatic price, alongside the heavy loss of life and the serious damage to public morale.

The War of Atonement put under severe scrutiny Israel's security doctrine, which had first been shaped back in the days of David Ben-Gurion, Israel's first Prime Minister, and had prevailed ever since. This doctrine was designed to provide an answer to the fundamental reality of the few against the many: to Israel's difficulty in keeping a large regular army on its borders and of withstanding a protracted war as well as the possibility of a simultaneous Arab offensive on several fronts. The Israeli concept of security was therefore based on the fundamental elements of deterrence (relying also, as a secondary layer, on American backing), early warning, air supremacy to provide a brake and response in the face of a surprise attack, a sophisticated organization of reserve units capable of being rapidly mobilised and reaching the front in time (due to early warning), taking the battle into enemy territory, and striving for as rapid and decisive a victory as possible.

The Arab coalition carefully studied this concept before the war and took pains to design a plan to neutralise Israel's advantages and target its weaknesses. They placed an emphasis on achieving surprise, splitting the Israeli forces, adhering to an anti-tank and anti-aircraft umbrella, exacting as heavy a price as possible (in terms of losses and the debilitation of forces) and creating a cloak of Arab solidarity by using the oil weapon.

The first pillar of Israel's security doctrine that failed was deterrence. Israeli political and military leaders believed so strongly in the power of Israel's deterrence that they came to consider it a permanent feature in Israel's strategic landscape and therefore dismissed any evidence that it might be weakening. This led to the failure of the second pillar, that of early warning. In the War of Atonement another chapter of intelligence failures was written – something of an Israeli Pearl Harbor. The author, who was one of the founders of Israel's military intelligence and twice stood at its head, analyses in the book the possible source of the Israeli intelligence services' failure to warn of impending war. He rightly identifies the Israeli defence establishment's conceit and complacency and its underestimation of the enemy as the major weaknesses.

Years later, the head of Israel's military intelligence at the time of the war, Major General Eli Zeira, published his detailed version of the role played by intelligence prior to the war, trying to clear himself of the stain of failure. His version gave rise to an intense methodological debate in regard to the essence of early warning. Zeira claimed that intelligence had done its duty by supplying the leaders, before the war, with a complete and accurate intelligence picture of the enemy armies' preparations, deployment and capabilities, coupled with the implication that the enemy armies were ready enough to go to war. In Zeira's opinion, based on the classic Israeli security doctrine, this presentation of the enemy's capabilities was such as to oblige the heads of state and the army to decide upon a series of measures to prepare for all eventualities. On the other hand, they ought not to have relied on the intelligence appraisal of the enemy leaders' *intentions*, since that was, by nature, a dangerous and slippery slope. Zeira therefore concludes that intelligence should not be blamed for its failure to appraise the enemy intent correctly.

Major General Zeira's case was dismissed by many, including the author. They claim, and I believe rightly so, that the responsibility of the political and military leaders does not absolve the intelligence community of its duty to appraise the other side's intentions properly. Each echelon bears its own autonomous responsibility. Intelligence, by its nature, should not merely supply facts and figures and summarise capabilities, but just as importantly, it should also supply an insight into trends and intentions, with all the inherent difficulty involved. This is a timeless lesson.

The intelligence warning (and with it the last prospect of deterrence) having failed, the Israeli decision-makers suddenly realised that war was imminent, and found themselves in a dilemma about whether or not to make a pre-emptive strike. The source material that has since been published about the first morning of the war (including testimony from the aide-de-camp to Israel's then Chief of Staff) has reinforced the picture portrayed in the book, namely that the Chief of Staff, Lieutenant General Elazar, had recommended a pre-emptive strike against Syria but this had been rejected by the political echelon, concerned that Israel would be accused of initiating the war and therefore lose the American backing essential to it. With hindsight, the author believed that this decision was right at the time. In any event, it appears that even now, given the reality of Israel's security position, such a dilemma of weighing the likely military benefit against the possible political damage can still be relevant.

As the book describes, the surprise Egyptian-Syrian offensive necessitated a desperate Israeli defensive on land and in the air. Here fundamental doctrinal and operative problems were highlighted. The Israeli ground forces were then based on a fortified line along the Suez Canal. In the years preceding the war its main aim had become blurred and to some extent it had turned in the minds of Israel's military leaders from an observation and warning line into a line of defence. The military research conducted in the years since then has strongly reinforced the conclusion that it was a mistake to emphasize static lines of defence at the expense of mobility in defined battle theatres. Indeed, the Israel Defence Forces (IDF) lacked a coherent, systemic concept of defence.

As regards the Israeli Air Force, the task with which it was confronted at the beginning of the war was an immense one. Doctrinally, it should initially have concentrated on gaining air supremacy and securing clear skies for itself. In fact, it had to split itself between that mission and assisting the ground forces, thereby impairing its own effectiveness. Nevertheless, it was, and remains, a vital and central arm in Israel's military strength, both strategically and operationally. It seems that the Arabs took into account the risk of Israeli air supremacy. They made no attempt to nullify it by means of their own air forces, realising that they would not succeed in such a mission. Instead, they tried to neutralise it by presenting the Israeli Air Force with a multiplicity of challenges, establishing a very dense air defence to accompany the ground forces, and creating a network of ground-to-ground missiles to enable and provide an answer to strikes in depth. Here too lay one element of the Israeli intelligence failure. On the basis of the information it had gathered, it assumed that the Egyptians would wait until they had equipped themselves with fighter-bombers before going to war and it misconstrued the Egyptian concept of the aerial arena.

If we analyse the developments that have occurred in the Middle East in this sphere since the War of Atonement, it would appear that the concept that guided Egypt and Syria in 1973 has merely become more entrenched over the years. The Syrian army, for example, has for decades sought to contend with Israeli air supremacy, perceived as an established fact, by a combination of air defence and ground-to-ground missile and rocket systems. In 1973, ground-to-ground missiles were only just coming on to the scene in the Middle East, but in the years since, rockets employed in huge numbers by both regular and irregular forces, have become an important military factor in the region. These are all-weather, cheap, relatively simple and easy-to-hide systems which provide a deterrent and the ability to strike deep into Israel's 'soft belly', circumventing the supremacy of the Israeli Air Force and facing Israel with serious operational and strategic dilemmas. Saddam Hussein's use of dozens of missiles against Israel in the first Gulf War in 1991, Hizbullah's use of thousands of rockets against Israeli cities in the Second Lebanon War in 2006 and Hamas's firing of thousands of rockets from Gaza in three rounds of armed conflict with Israel since 2008 – have both expressed and reinforced this trend.

The story that follows shows how, in the War of Atonement, Israel tried to apply its entrenched philosophy of moving the war into enemy territory and quickly deciding it there. However, in that war, Israel encountered numerous difficulties in implementing this philosophy, not merely because of the circumstances presented by the conflict's outbreak. The battlefield was characterized by a congested theatre saturated with forces and obstacles, giving rise to a quick burn-out of fighting forces and making manoeuvre difficult. Moreover, in the initial phases of the war the IDF split its manoeuvring efforts rather than concentrating them, to the point of bringing about the failure of its counter-offensive on the Egyptian front on 8 October 1973. These difficulties reemphasized flanking tactics, which, in the War of Atonement accounted for the essential decisive steps on both fronts by the IDF. Today, the IDF additionally emphasizes surprise operations aimed at centres of gravity in the enemy's operational and strategic rear.

Above all, these difficulties encouraged a revolutionary development in the relative strengthening of the firepower element-volume, precision and payload at the battlefront, compared with the manoeuvrability element. The development of the firepower element on both the Arab and Israeli sides has given rise to considerable controversy about the value of territory, strategic depth and manoeuvre in the modern era. The War of Atonement well demonstrated the significance of strategic depth to Israel. The Sinai Peninsula provided Israel with strategic depth against Egypt and a breathing space and room for manoeuvre to decide the war. In contrast, on the northern front the Syrian tanks fairly quickly came within ten minutes of the River Jordan and Sea of Galilee, creating a direct threat to the Israeli home front. Only the rapid mobilisation of reserve units stopped their advance. Militarily, it appears that even in an era when missiles and precision-guided munitions are multiplying and developing, and their range and precision are increasing, strategic depth, as well as the ability to manoeuvre into enemy territory, are still highly important, especially for a small and vulnerable country like Israel. While Israel has built strong firepower as well as effective counter-measures against the enemy's firepower, it would most probably still need to combine firepower with manoeuvre of formations to decide future wars.

Looking at the elements of ground warfare, the tank was the main tool in deciding the battle and though relatively less relevant to some of the up-to-date asymmetric war scenarios facing the IDF – it still remains central to its manoeuvring ground forces. However, the War of Atonement gave tremendous impetus to the development of the integrated, inter-force battle philosophy, centred on a combination of armour, infantry, air and other capabilities, and on real-time connectivity within and between service branches, combat units and intelligence assets.

Beyond all this, the story of the War of Atonement demonstrates the extent to which the human element is the key to the outcome of war. This is perhaps the main message of the book. The human decision-making behind the military campaign; the training and skill of the soldiers; their spirit, motivation, courage, initiative and perseverance; the quality of the chain of command – all determine the war's result above and beyond any weapons. Even in the era of technology, the human element still stands at the centre of the picture.

The belligerents' supporting environment is also worth consideration. Egypt and Syria based themselves on Soviet backing; certain Arab military assistance, essentially from Iraq and Jordan; and on the Arab oil weapon. Now, the USSR is no longer in existence, the Arab world is war-torn and split, the oil weapon has lost much of its might and there is a new radical axis in the region, led by Iran. For its part, Israel relied and still does rely on the backing of America, which in the 1973 war certainly contributed to its security. However, the global and regional pictures have since become far more complex, with many more shades of grey. While the American commitment to Israel's security is fundamental, unwavering and will likely come to bear in any critical challenge to Israel's national security in the foreseeable future, the extent and depth of its implementation in specific cases of war will depend on the circumstances of the time.

Despite all the changes that the Middle East has witnessed in the decades since 1973, the threat of war is still present in the Arab-Israeli context. However, the classic military challenges facing Israel are now replaced by new challenges, which necessitate changes and adaptations in Israel's traditional national security doctrine. Israel's decisive military victory in 1973 drove its enemies to seek different ways of challenging it militarily, focusing on asymmetric avenues such as non-conventional capabilities and threatening Israel's home front with terror and especially with huge numbers of rockets and missiles. The latter threats have been compounded by the emergence of heavily armed sub-state or non-state actors against the background of weakening states, who nest in civilian populated areas and employ both terror (such as suicide bombers) and military means (such as rockets) against civilians. Since the year 2000,

Israel has been forced to fight five such major asymmetric campaigns – along its northern border (the 2006 Second Lebanon War with Hezbollah), and with Palestinian armed groups (the Second Intifada beginning 2000, characterized by suicide bombers, and three rounds of armed conflict with Islamist Hamas in Gaza since 2008). And there is potential for additional, bloodier rounds, especially with Hezbollah and its arsenal of well over 100,000 rockets aimed at Israel and a plethora of additional armed Iranian proxies close to Israel's borders in the post-Islamic State era.

This type of warfare is a much more complex challenge than classic military warfare with neighbouring state armies. Because it heavily involves civilians on both sides, impacts many facets of Israel's national life and is fought also in the realm of perceptions, it requires much more than military excellence. That is why the IDF has been compelled to reinterpret its three traditional pillars of deterrence, early warning and decisive military victory – all severely challenged in the War of Atonement – in more nuanced terms, add to them a fourth pillar of defence, and emphasize elements of 'soft power' required for legitimizing the use of 'hard power.'

The story of the War of Atonement, as told in the book, is a story not only of the wisdom of war but also of its folly. This book should be of interest to those seeking to increase their knowledge of the history and theory of war, and also to the layperson seeking to broaden his or her knowledge of history in general and of the history of the Middle East in particular.

This preface should have been written by the author himself. I have assumed the task, having personally fought in the war as an infantry soldier on the Egyptian front and having continued serving in the military, but in the knowledge that nobody can really take his place. He was a unique man and gave expression to his uniqueness during a rich life, reaching the pinnacle of being President of the State of Israel. He recorded a fascinating military career as a soldier and officer in the ranks of the British Army in the war against the Nazis, in the ranks of the IDF after its establishment, and as a general and head of Israeli military intelligence. In his autobiography, *Living History*, which he managed to publish before his death, he said of himself: 'I have been many things – statesman, diplomat, businessman, commentator, lawyer, family man – but perhaps more than anything, I consider myself a soldier. If one has a great cause, I believe nothing is so noble as the willingness to fight and sacrifice for it.'

These pages are devoted with love and esteem to my late father, who was all those and far more.

Brigadier General (IDF ret.) Michael Herzog
Tel Aviv, January 2018

Foreword

FEW, IF ANY, wars have been so extensively covered by the mass media as the Yom Kippur War, and yet the story has, paradoxically enough, not really been told. How many are really familiar with the incredible battle for the Golan Heights, which could have sealed the fate of northern Israel, or of the touch-and-go Israeli crossing of the Suez Canal? For the Arabs, with their peculiar facility to create a euphoric world of make-believe, the military story of the war ends with the conclusion of the initial phases. But there was a long sequel to those opening days, in which the heavily outnumbered Israeli forces recovered, fought back with unbelievable bravery and self-sacrifice and moved over to the counter-attack. When they were halted two weeks later by the UN-imposed cease-fire, they were within artillery range of Damascus and well on the road to Cairo.

I have endeavoured to tell the full story of the war: its successes, its omissions and its failures. It is the story of an astounding Israeli victory. It is a story of special significance at a time when the Middle East echoes to the renewed sounds of sabre rattling, lending a certain measure of reality and balance to the situation. It is the story of a new type of war. It is a story which reminds the free world of the dangers threatening Western democracy.

Obviously, a book of this nature cannot encompass a description of the war in all its detail. Some formations and units have been more thoroughly portrayed than others, while some have been omitted. But this is not the story only of those who are mentioned in the narrative. It is the story of an army and an entire people in their gravest hour of challenge. The process of interviewing the many characters who grace these pages – as well as those who have been omitted – has left me with a feeling of confidence for the future. For the inherent strength and resilience of the people of Israel was revealed in the stark, grim and tragic days at the outset of the war, when, fighting back against overwhelming odds, they overcame the initial setbacks and achieved military success. I came away from this work imbued with a sense of deep humility in the face of those whose collective story I have tried to tell. No people in the world crave for peace more than the people of Israel, and yet none are more ready for self-sacrifice should the necessity arise. If this book can create even a faint question mark in the minds of the Arab world about the path of war which they have chosen in the struggle against Israel, then it will have achieved its purpose.

I was assisted at various stages in my research by Mr Amir Oren and Miss Rivka Yahalomi. I benefited greatly from the wise and firm editorial advice offered me by Miss Ina Friedman. To them and to Miss Susanne Rose, who typed the complete manuscript, I am grateful. I am above all grateful to the many who sat and recounted to me, quietly and unassumingly, a story of historic dimensions.

C. HERZOG
Zahala
February 1975

1

The New Strategic Concept

FOR THREE WEEKS in May and June 1967, the people of Israel lived through a trauma they would not easily forget. As Arab armies massed around their borders, the United Nations Emergency Force (which since the Sinai Campaign in 1956 had been dividing between the Israeli and Egyptian forces and manning the Straits of Tiran leading into the Gulf of Akaba) was ordered to withdraw by President Nasser. United Nations Secretary General U Thant – without so much as consulting the Security Council or the General Assembly – agreed to the withdrawal without demur. Egyptian forces poured into Sinai, while Jordanians and Syrians concentrated along their frontiers with Israel; Iraqi and Kuwaiti units, as well as some from other Arab countries, moved towards Israel's borders. The country was ringed by a vast Arab army – outnumbered in troops, planes and tanks. The Soviet Union took its usual cynical part in playing down this escalation in the United Nations, an escalation which according to President Nasser had been instigated to no small degree by the Soviets themselves, who had falsely advised the Syrians about the concentration of Israeli forces on their borders.

As Arab hysteria rose and the Arab media promised the Israeli population – men, women and children – destruction and annihilation in the most brutal manner, the horrors of the Nazi holocaust rose to the fore in Jewish consciousness. The Jewish people knew that these were not mere words, recalling how many nations nurtured on the tenets of Christianity had either participated in that previous bloody massacre or had looked on. And indeed the world looked on petrified, incapable of taking action.

On the morning of 5 June Israel struck – and within six days had destroyed a great part of the force which had threatened it, occupying the Sinai Peninsula, the Gaza Strip, the West Bank of the Jordan and the Golan Heights. This transformation from a potential helpless victim into a brilliant victor created a euphoria which brought about a revolutionary change of attitude in Israel. Against the background of sombre prospects a few days before, their incredible victory evoked a reaction throughout the Jewish world such as Israel had never known or experienced.

The origins of the Yom Kippur War can be found to a very considerable degree in the Six Day War, which had a profound effect on both sides to the conflict, changing in no small measure Israel's social and political life and dictating basic changes in its strategic thinking. It acted as a catalyst in the Arab world and gave rise to a complete re-evaluation of the military posture of the Egyptians, who drew conclusions from every aspect of their defeat and set about putting their military house in order with active Soviet support. The Israelis on the other hand swept under the carpet all the shortcomings that had been revealed in the war but had been overlooked in the euphoria of victory; consecrating mentally the military concepts that had emerged from the six days of war, they prepared for the next war as if it were to be the seventh day.

As a result of the armistice line in 1949, before the 1967 war Israel was living in a precarious military situation because of its lack of strategic depth in which to deploy (their deployment area in the event of war would have to be in enemy territory), and indeed this was frequently enunciated by Israeli leaders when spelling out the country's defence policy. Furthermore the very nature of Israel's borders meant danger: the Gaza Strip occupied by the Egyptians in 1948 was like a dagger poised against the main centres of population in southern Israel and along the coast; Jerusalem was divided and on a number of occasions Jordanian soldiers or local Jordanians had opened fire in the middle of the city with all that that had entailed. An advance by Jordanian troops of some 500 yards from areas along the main road to Jerusalem would have cut the main artery to the capital of Israel. Jordanian forces stationed on the hills above Kalkilyeh looked down upon Tel Aviv and its satellite cities, accommodating some 40% of Israel's population, while those stationed at Tulkarm observed the coastal city of Netanya, 10 miles away, fully aware of the fact that an armoured thrust by them across this short distance would cut the State of Israel in two at its narrow waistline. On the Golan Heights Syrian troops looked down on the Israeli villages in the Jordan Valley and harassed them with fire over the years.

This situation brought the Israeli General Staff to the conclusion that whenever the danger of military conflagration arose, Israel could not afford to permit the Arabs to take the initiative, for such an initiative could spell disaster. It was clear that the sheer momentum of an attack by the Arab forces could cut the country at Netanya or the main road to Jerusalem and overrun Israeli villages along the Gaza Strip or endanger the northern part of east Galilee. Thus any serious deterioration in the situation which might lead to war automatically obliged the Israeli General Staff to plan a pre-emptive attack.

At various periods *fedayeen* marauders had roamed about the country threatening even the very populated areas, but in 1956 *fedayeen* attacks from the Egyptian-held Gaza Strip had become intolerable and had led to a process of escalation along the front lines. Seeing war as imminently possible and taking into consideration what were thought to be favourable international circumstances, Israel had launched an attack against Egypt in the so-called Sinai Campaign. Again in 1967, when it had become evident that war was approaching, the Israeli Command had concluded that the Arabs must not be allowed to make the first move because by their sheer weight they would gain initial advantages that Israel could not afford. And so despite the very serious international political considerations which exercised both the Israeli Government and President Nasser – neither desiring to be branded as the attacker – Israel's lack of strategic option had left its forces with no alternative but to take the initiative on 5 June.

The depth afforded by the territories taken by Israel in the Six Day War gave the country for the first time in its history a strategic option. All Israeli centres of population were now removed from the Egyptian forces, and a desert barrier some 150 miles wide separated Israel from the Suez Canal, in itself a natural barrier of no mean proportions. The cities which would now be affected by the outbreak of war would not be Israeli cities but the Egyptian cities along the Suez Canal – Port Said, Ismailia, Suez – with a total population exceeding some 750,000 people. An Egyptian commander thinking of attacking Israel now would have to plan not only the very formidable task of crossing the Canal against opposition but also of developing a major attack across the Sinai Desert. Thus, it seemed to the Israelis, very heavy considerations would weigh against the renewal of hostilities against this new line.

A similarly favourable situation also obtained along the Jordanian front; the holy city of Jerusalem was now united and far removed from the Jordanian artillery which twice in twenty years had shelled it mercilessly. Instead of having to move but a few hundred yards in Jerusalem or on its approaches in order to achieve a gain or to advance a mere 10 miles in order to cut the country in two, the counter-attacking Jordanian Army would now be obliged to mount a major attack across the Jordan River and then fight its way across the Judean Desert through easily defensible mountainous terrain for a distance of some

40 miles. Even on the Syrian front the Israeli forces now had a certain, however limited, degree of depth, which made life easier for the villages in the northern Galilee and relieved them from the nightmare of incessant shelling and raising children in shelters.

The Israeli General Staff could therefore now exercise an option by either launching a pre-emptive attack if war seemed imminent or alternatively allowing the enemy the first strike – with all the international political disadvantages of such a move accruing to him – and thereafter utilizing the depth afforded by the Sinai Desert to manœuvre, concentrate and counter-attack. Furthermore, the distance from the Egyptian airfields to Israeli centres of population had increased considerably and the electronic warning time now available to Israel was some sixteen minutes instead of the four minutes before the Six Day War. This strategic situation constituted a main factor in convincing the Israeli Government and leaders of opinion that there was little danger of the renewal of hostilities in a major war against Israel.

But as these strategic advantages were discussed, sight was lost of the fact that an Egyptian-held Sinai Peninsula had been a major warning element as far as the Israeli forces were concerned: the movement of Egyptian forces into Sinai across the Suez Canal invariably sounded the alarm in Israel and allowed mobilization to be carried out in adequate time. This had occurred on a number of occasions and in particular in 1967. The eyeball-to-eyeball situation created along the Suez Canal after the Six Day War, however, with the bulk of the Egyptian Army stationed constantly in almost direct contact with the Israeli forces, removed this very important element of advance warning. It enabled the Arab forces concentrated along the Canal to move over to attack from their existing deployment in the shortest possible time.

Indeed the shortening of warning time as a result of these new frontiers was the reason for the considerably increased forces which Israel was obliged to maintain along its borders after the Six Day War. Numerous war games were conducted to test the various strategic and tactical aspects of these new defensive lines; all such games being based on the assumption of a very short warning period, with the standing army holding the attack until the reserves were mobilized within a period of some seventy-two hours.

A few weeks after the conclusion of the Six Day War, the first incidents had broken out along the Suez Canal front when the Egyptian forces which were regrouping along the west bank began to harass the Israeli forces deployed along the Canal. Fighting broke out at Ras el-Aish at the northern end of the sector between Port Said and Kantara, but the Israeli positions were makeshift and inadequate for protection. By November 1968, a year and a half after the conclusion of the war, the Egyptians, whose army had been reconstructed and re-equipped by the Soviet Union, felt strong enough to embark on a major war of attrition and in that month they launched a major artillery attack on the Israeli forces, catching them unprepared and comparatively unprotected. In one attack alone eighteen Israeli soldiers were killed. The Israeli reaction was to mount an in-depth commando operation against Najh Hamadi in the Nile Valley, destroying electricity installations and emphasizing Egypt's basic vulnerability to attack by mobile Israeli forces. The shock of this Israeli attack convinced President Nasser that he was not yet fully ready for a war of attrition and he accordingly postponed it until March 1969. During the breathing space accorded by this decision, the Israelis concentrated all their efforts to create a line that would answer the requirements of such a war.

Lieut.-Gen. Chaim Bar-Lev, the chief of staff, entrusted Maj.-Gen. Avraham ('Bren') Adan with the task of heading an interservice team to bring to the General Staff a proposal for the creation of a defensive system in Sinai. Before this team went down to Sinai, Maj.-Gen. Yeshayahu Gavish, general officer commanding the Southern Command and the commander of the victorious Israeli forces in the Sinai in the Six Day War, weighed the problems posed by the defence of Sinai. Having regard to the losses incurred as a result of the Egyptian shelling, it was obvious to him that the troops holding the line must be given adequate cover in strongpoints; the main problem facing him however was whether to keep his forces on the water line or to maintain them in depth away from it. While holding the water line in strength created a series of fixed objectives under constant observation of the Egyptians, at the same time it gave the Israeli forces the advantage of observation and an ability to deal immediately with any crossing attempt by the Egyptians. Gavish came to the conclusion that it would be advisable to hold positions on the water front, particularly at all points which were probable crossing areas, since he felt there would be no problem for the Egyptians to cross along the entire length of the Canal, and the Israelis had to be prepared to answer this possibility.

In 1968 Gavish commanded the Israeli forces in war games in which Maj.-Gen. Mordechai ('Motta') Gur, who was appointed chief of staff of the Israel Defence Forces after the Yom Kippur War, acted as the commander of the Egyptian forces. In these games Gur crossed along the entire front, advancing on all the major axes and deploying helicopter-borne forces in depth behind the Israeli front line exactly as five years later President Sadat's forces were to do. Thus already in 1968 the concept of a possible Egyptian attack had been taken into account by members of the Israeli Command.

Drawing on his experience as a member of Kibbutz Nirim near the Gaza Strip, Adan set about planning the defence of the line along the Suez Canal. He drew up the original plans for the fortifications, to be sited along the Canal

and built in such a way as to give a maximum degree of observation – good
visual observation by day and electronic observation by night – while exposing
a minimum number of troops to enemy artillery fire. He planned the individual
fortifications for a force of fifteen troops, at a distance of 7 miles one from the
other, with mobile armour patrolling between them and with artillery and
armour deployed to the rear ready to move forward and to destroy any attempt
to cross. The fortifications were conceived as a warning outpost system; they
were not seen as a line of defence, hence the limitation to fifteen troops, the
distance between them and their limited defensive facilities. Gavish accepted
Adan's plan with the proviso that at the northern end of the Canal all possible
crossing points be covered by groups of fortifications. The Israeli defence plan
based on this warning system along the Canal was brought to the General
Staff for approval. Maj.-Gen. Ariel Sharon, director of training in the General
Staff, and Maj.-Gen. Israel Tal, attached to the Ministry of Defence, opposed it.
They proposed to deploy only with armour at a certain distance from the Canal
and to control it by mobile armoured activity.

Gavish has since explained publicly his attitude to this problem. He saw
the line acting in time of war as a series of observation posts and fortifications
along all possible axes of advance, which would delay the enemy before he
came on a series of defensive infantry brigade localities with their concentrated
force of armour along the line of the passes, from the Mitla Pass in the south
to Baluza in the north. During a war of attrition and in periods of cease-fire
the fortifications would serve as observation posts (affording protection from
artillery fire during the former); as well as centres for electronic warning and
control and as bases for armoured patrols. As part of the defences along the
Canal, Gavish initiated a system of fuel installations which could be activated
from inside the fortifications to set the Canal alight.

It has always been Gavish's opinion that if the Canal was to be considered
a physical barrier, there was no option but to establish a physical presence
along it. In his view one of the main dangers which Israel would have to face
would be a sudden Egyptian move to gain a foothold, however narrow, along
the east bank followed by an attempt to achieve an immediate cease-fire by
international agreement. Furthermore, since the Israeli concept invariably
called for mounting a counter-offensive into the enemy's territory, it was
important for them to sit in force along the Canal itself and not be in a position
which would require fighting before they reached it.

In the ensuing debate there was no suggestion of leaving the Canal, but
there was an argument as to the mode of deployment, with Gen. Sharon
supporting the system of mobile defence along the Canal. Gen. Bar-Lev
decided in favour of the fortifications and the team headed by Gen. Adan

proceeded to supervise the construction of the line, which was finished on 15 March 1969. That month Nasser declared the opening of the War of Attrition and the whole system was tested out: for days on end the Egyptians employed over 1,000 artillery pieces against the Israeli forces dug in along the Canal. There is no doubt that but for these fortifications Israeli casualties would have been much heavier than they were in fact and could have reached very alarming numbers.

However the fortifications were only one element in what was later to be called the Bar-Lev line. It was not a single marginal line of defence: each fortification controlled ½–1 mile on each of its flanks and the area of some 5–6 miles between the fortifications was covered by observation points and patrols. In all the very problematic and critical fortifications – as for instance in the positions at the two extremes of the line and in isolated strongpoints – tanks were sited. To the rear there were concentrations of tanks, while platoons of them were stationed within the areas of the fortifications themselves with the ramps from which they operated sited to give enfilade fire along the Canal. Large numbers of such positions were created; these were in addition to firing ramps which were built ½–1 mile to the rear of the fortifications affording them covering fire as well as to the approaches to the Canal. On top of this a vast infrastructure of roads, underground headquarters, water and communication systems, repair facilities and stores was constructed.

When the line was established during the War of Attrition, it was standard operating procedure during an emergency for troops of the standing army or reserve parachute troops to replace all reservists in the line. The positions were brought up to full establishment of approximately thirty per position, while in isolated positions, such as the 'Quay' fortification at Port Tewfik, there would be some eighty to ninety troops. In all isolated positions and fortifications, command would be taken by an officer of field rank of major or above, usually a reservist from the parachute forces. Bar-Lev made it a practice to have reservists training in the area of the Sinai during periods of tension. On the water line he maintained a force of two armoured brigades with a third armoured brigade in reserve, adding a fourth (usually reservists training in the area) during periods of tension.

It is not possible to interpret Israel's military concepts on the eve of the Yom Kippur War without considering the effect of the War of Attrition on its thinking. The War of Attrition – initiated by Egypt in March 1969 – has been regarded as a passing event when in fact it was a major confrontation. The Egyptian forces launched the war with the declared purpose of creating a situation whereby the Suez could be crossed in strength and the Sinai reoccupied; Israel, for its part, was determined to prevent this development and to re-establish the cease-fire. In choosing to launch the War of Attrition, the Egyptians decided to take advantage of the static military situation created by the fact that both forces were ranged along the Suez Canal. This meant that Israel would not be in a position to take advantage of its undoubted superiority in manœuvre and fast-moving armoured warfare – the Suez Canal would prevent large-scale movements and would in fact protect the Egyptian forces from Israeli manœuvre. Taking shelter behind it, the Egyptians would thus initially attempt to exhaust through attrition the Israeli will to continue the fight.

The construction of the Israeli Bar-Lev line in its massive form following the Egyptian artillery barrages in October 1968 became a major consideration in their decision to commence the War of Attrition. And an analysis of these events tends only to emphasize the irony of a situation whereby Egyptian action led to the construction of the line, which in turn aroused the fears and apprehensions of the Egyptians. They saw in its construction the creation of a permanent, impregnable Israeli presence which would only perpetuate the *status quo* and limit drastically the prospects of changing the situation along the Canal. The Egyptian plan therefore was for artillery bombardment to destroy as much as possible of the line in the first stage of the War of Attrition. Once the Israeli fortifications had been destroyed to a great extent, the second stage called for a series of limited crossings by Egyptian commandos for short periods of time; the third phase called for more extensive operations in depth across the Canal, while the fourth and final stage would be a full-scale crossing operation with the object of occupying sectors of the east bank of the Canal and thus breaking the political deadlock which had set in since 1967.

An intensive bombardment of the Israeli positions was carried out during March and April 1969. In May President Nasser announced that 60% of the Bar-Lev line had been destroyed by artillery fire and that his minister of war, Mahmoud Fawzi, had advised him that the remaining 40% would soon be dealt with. (In fact the Bar-Lev line had very successfully withstood the battering it had received and had vindicated the hopes of its planners.) In mid-April Egyptian commando units began to cross the Suez Canal regularly and to attack Israeli fortified positions. This led to counter-bombardment by the Israeli forces and reprisal raids along the Egyptian line by their parachute and commando units. The fighting escalated along the Suez Canal and indeed along the Gulf of Suez, with Israeli forces attacking targets in the Gulf and inside Egypt. Israeli casualties rose alarmingly during this period, and by July they decided to commit their air power. The initiative passed to Israel and the War of Attrition became a war of counter-attrition.

During the months that followed Israeli air attacks destroyed the Egyptian SAM 2 surface-to-air missile system along the Canal and extended into the

Gulf of Suez. The Egyptians were now left without any meaningful air defence potential along the Suez front and had to abandon the third part of their original plan – crossings by army units into the Sinai – being obliged as they were to concentrate all their efforts on combating the Israeli counter-attack. In January 1970 deep-penetration raids by the Israeli Air Force began in Egypt, while at the same time Israeli forces engaged in commando activity, landing on Shadwan Island in the Gulf of Suez. At this point came a major turning point in the Middle East from an historic point of view with Nasser's secret visit to Moscow and the subsequent arrival of Soviet equipment and personnel in Egypt.

The final phase of the War of Attrition began in April 1970 when the Israeli air forces ceased raiding the Egyptian hinterland. The Soviets had taken Egyptian air space under protection and this had enabled the Egyptians to concentrate all their forces in the area of direct combat with Israel along the Suez Canal. Egyptian air and land attacks became very intense; Israeli attacks along the Canal increased. The conflict entered a ferocious phase.

It was now clear to the Egyptians that the answer to their problem was a redeployment of the surface-to-air missile system. While deployment of SAM 2 sites behind the Canal zone would affect Israeli operations over Egypt, the deployment of missiles in the Canal zone itself could create a problem for Israeli planes over the Israeli front line, where Israeli planes some 12 miles into Sinai would be within range of Egyptian missiles. This in turn would increase Egyptian ability to cross the Canal in strength. Although Israeli counter-attacks against these attempts to edge the missile system forward to the Canal were successful, their losses rose and soon they began to lose planes to the Egyptian missile defences.

Parallel to this military escalation, diplomatic moves were afoot. In July 1970 Nasser announced his acceptance of the cease-fire which was to commence on 7 August. But immediately it had come into effect, the Egyptians and the Soviets connived to move forward the missile system under its cover and to achieve the necessary military basis for an ultimate crossing of the Canal – the setting up of a missile screen which would cover the Israeli side on the east bank and neutralize their Air Force. In answer to questions at the Arab Socialist Union on 24 July 1970, President Nasser implied that he had agreed to the cease-fire for the specific purpose of moving forward the missile umbrella to the bank of the Suez Canal. And although he revealed publicly the next and final phase – the creation of a bridgehead across the Canal under cover of this missile umbrella – few paid any attention to his announcement.

For Israel the war ended with many question marks about the missile problem. For while their war of counter-attrition against the Egyptians had

had its effect, the cease-fire was certainly welcome, faced as they were with the option of continuing to squander their air power along the Canal or escalating the battle while challenging the Soviet Union. Furthermore the war had not been easy in terms of casualties, with black borders appearing every day in the Israeli press around the photographs of the troops killed the day before. It had been essentially a war of nerves and for the Israeli public, accustomed to rapid and swift results in wars with the Arabs, this was not a situation that helped morale.

It would now appear that Nasser's aim was indeed to attempt the next phase of his plans – the seizure of part of the east bank under cover of the missiles – but at this stage a number of events occurred which affected the military situation and had a direct effect on the military thinking of the Israeli leadership. On 28 September 1970 President Nasser died. He was the outstanding charismatic leader of the Arab world who had succeeded in uniting behind him the Egyptians and the Arabs in their struggle against Israel. His departure therefore meant that a major element in such a struggle – effective leadership – was now absent. Parallel to his efforts to eliminate the presence of the Western powers in the Middle East, Nasser had devoted much of his efforts to mobilizing the Arab world against Israel and had been the prime mover in an Arab anti-Israel policy. More than any other single man he had been instrumental in creating the Soviet presence in the Middle East; now he had departed, leaving behind him a country with serious internal political problems and a leadership which appeared to be utterly lacking in charisma and power.

The American response to Israel's request in September 1970 for additional arms was for the first time open and unequivocal: in view of the Arab world and of the Eastern Bloc, Congress was asked by the Nixon Administration to approve the sale to Israel of half a billion dollars' worth of the most sophisticated equipment being delivered by the United States to foreign countries. This fact was not lost on the Arabs – and certainly not on the Soviet Union – and added an additional element of confidence to Israeli thinking. A further important occurrence was the civil war in Jordan in September 1970, in which King Hussein had eliminated the Palestinian uprising, thus creating a situation in which Israel's Jordanian frontier became peaceful. The United States' unequivocal reaction to the attempted invasion of Jordan by the Syrian forces during this civil war was an encouraging factor too, demonstrating as it did American purpose in maintaining the balance in the area and in blocking Soviet expansionism. All these factors combined to create an atmosphere which in due course contributed to an obstinate unwillingness on the part of the Israeli military and political leadership to believe that a situation could exist in which the Arab world would seize military initiative and move against Israel.

On 7 August 1970 the cease-fire due to last for ninety days commenced. The Israeli command decided to take advantage of this period of grace to reconstruct those parts of the Bar-Lev line which had been damaged in the War of Attrition and to strengthen it. Gen. 'Arik' Sharon had in the meantime taken command in the south and a major construction effort was undertaken to strengthen all the positions and strongpoints along the Canal. Following a proposal put forward by him, a second line of fortifications was constructed some 5 to 7 miles to the rear, for, as he pointed out, the tanks and the artillery did not have adequate cover. Eleven such fortifications were built in addition to an infrastructure of roads and artificial barriers, such as a sand rampart (at some points 27 yards high) designed to make the east bank of the Canal impassable to armoured vehicles. Extensive minefields were laid, wire defences were erected and roads were even built over the marshy swamps in the northern sector; airfields were improved; underground headquarters were constructed and fuel tanks added. In all 2 billion Israeli pounds ($500,000,000) was spent in the whole of Sanai, of which a total of approximately 150 million Israeli pounds ($40,000,000) was spent on the fortifications.

Gen. Israel Tal was unhappy with the stepped-up construction activities and in October 1970, during the first phase of the cease-fire, expressed his reservations about the entire system for the defence of Sinai. He pointed out that the fortifications were proving to be ineffective (as in any case the Egyptians were crossing the Canal) and had become a series of fixed targets vulnerable to flat trajectory fire constantly under observation with visible supply lines which invited attack. He maintained that the fortifications were not an effective fighting unit; they could be neutralized by artillery fire and could be by-passed; at best they constituted only a shelter and the Israeli artillery was inadequate, in his view, to support them. They made a small contribution to defence, were isolated and not mutually supporting and could not prevent a water crossing by day or by night. Pointing out that of 498 Israeli casualties in Sinai between 7 January and 28 July 1970, 382 (including 62 dead) had been caused inside the fortifications or in direct relation to them, he suggested a system whereby mobile armoured forces with artillery and anti-aircraft support would be responsible for sectors with tanks in observation points along the water line. They would reinforce the fortifications which, since they already existed, would be lightly manned.

His view met with considerable opposition. Those who opposed it, including the minister of defence and the chief of staff, maintained that any attempt to hold the line without a physical presence on the ground along the Canal would be bound to encourage a creeping-forward process by the Egyptians which would ultimately place the Israeli forces in a very difficult situation (a very high percentage of the losses had been caused by ambushes, mines, missiles and artillery activity against armoured patrols and the engineering forces operating outside the fortifications). Those opposing Tal argued that his system would in the end create areas which would not be under Israeli control. Indeed, those areas which had not been held by Israeli forces along the Canal during the War of Attrition had frequently been occupied for short periods by Egyptian forces. For varying periods Egyptian forces had occupied an abandoned Israeli fortification in the area between the Firdan Bridge and north of El-Balah Island in the Suez Canal; they had frequently trained in this fortification, mined the area around it and on many occasions hoisted the Egyptian flag over it. Patrolling along the Canal frequently involved mine-clearing operations and encounters with ambushes, a situation which would become much more serious if Israeli forces were to abandon the fortifications along the Canal entirely. Indeed, there were areas, such as in the south of the Canal, where every time that Israeli forces entered, many mines had to be cleared.

With the appointment of Gen. Elazar as chief of staff in January 1972, the matter was raised again. But while he favoured the system of fortifications, a form of compromise emerged. As the period of cease-fire continued, it assumed a very concrete form and its implementation was helped both psychologically and in fact by a complete absence of hostile activity along the Canal. This inactivity tended to quieten any reservations there may have been about the reduction in the number of fortifications and troops along the Canal. It accorded with a growing feeling of security and public expressions about the excessive burden being caused by the defence budget and the necessity to look for savings. The standard of infantry in the fortifications was reduced. Wherever there was a group of fortifications, only one remained active with a minimum number of soldiers manning it (two officers, twelve fighting men and the remainder administrative for a total of twenty per fortification). Of twenty-six fortifications, some ten were closed and blocked by sand in such a manner as to require a number of weeks to activate them again; two to three men were sent by day to these abandoned fortifications in a half-track so that the Egyptians would gain the impression that they were still being manned (Egyptian soldiers would frequently stand on the other side of the Canal gesticulating mockingly and pointing at their watches to indicate that it was 6 o'clock in the evening and time for the Israelis to go home to their main fortifications). Thus, because of the compromise which no military concept could accept, the dividing line between the Bar-Lev line acting as a warning system or as a defensive system designed to block the enemy gradually became hazy and clouded. This lack of clarity was to exact its cost in the first hours of the fighting along the Canal.

2

In Search of Solutions

THE VERY MAGNITUDE and decisiveness of the Arab defeat in June 1967, with is implications to Arab pride, self-respect and honour (the importance and significance of which had never been adequately appreciated by Israeli leaders), created the inevitability of the next war. Furthermore, Nasser's resolve that 'what was taken by force, must be returned by force', was strengthened by Soviet undertakings to rebuild his forces and to make all the necessary support available to achieve this. Immediately after the 1967 war therefore he began to study with intense application the reasons for the Israeli success. In the euphoria of victory in Israel, all the divisional commanders had broadcast descriptions of their individual victories in battle. Nasser had all these broadcasts recorded. He closed himself in a room and played them back for days on end in order to try to appreciate what were the major elements that had contributed towards making the Israeli Army such an effective striking force. The Israeli military leadership – effusive as never before – left few details untold, providing anybody who was willing to sit down and study considerable food for thought.

With the aid of the Soviet Union, Nasser commenced to rebuild the Egyptian Army. This time however the reconstruction was not limited to equipment; much thought was also given to the quality of manpower and the motivation of the troops. And indeed in 1973 the Israelis were to note the marked change in the quality of the Egyptian officers and the regular army personnel – the result of a well-conceived plan to raise the standard of the Egyptian forces and to cease treating them as so much cannon fodder. For this purpose university graduates who had concluded their studies in a variety of subjects, such as engineering, agronomy and teaching, were mobilized, sent to officers' courses and kept in the army for an unspecified period of time, on the understanding that they would remain in service 'until the battle'. Many of the prisoners taken by Israel in the Yom Kippur War were highly qualified academicians who had not been allowed to pursue their professions, and had been mobilized and sent to an officers' course. The Egyptians who were thus mobilized accepted their fate, since the ultimate purpose of their mobilization – the liberation of Sinai – was explained to them as an act of patriotism, although many of them never believed that there would be 'battle'. Many of their senior officers proved to be young men in their middle thirties in the rank of colonel. Israeli officers who came into contact with Egyptian prisoners noted that the intellectual standard of the regular officer trained and educated in the regular army was superior to that of the university graduate who had been conscripted.

A most intensive political educational programme was undertaken in the Egyptian Army. Officers were encouraged to study Hebrew and learn about the adversary; every lesson that could be learnt from the Six Day War was studied, bringing about a radical change in the approach of the Egyptian forces. A monthly in Hebrew was published by Egyptian Military Intelligence giving a summary of events in Israel, teaching Hebrew for beginners, describing (for example) Israeli activities on the African continent or the history of the Israeli Air Force, and in general introducing the Egyptian soldier to the Israeli scene. The army's department for moral guidance produced a constant stream of material on the Israeli–Arab conflict, with at times marked anti-Semitic overtones.

Following the Six Day War, Nasser announced his plan to renew the fight to avenge the Egyptian defeat and to recover the lost territories, a decision that was possible only because of the Soviet Union. On 11 June 1967, as Nasser later described, the leaders of the Kremlin had cabled urging him not to give in, promising him all the support necessary in order to regain the territories that Israel had conquered. The Soviet Union, a major element in bringing on the 1967 war, was now ready to step in, make the best of a bad deal and take advantage of the Arab collapse. Weeks later towards the end of June a Soviet mission arrived in Egypt headed by the president of the Soviet Union, Nikolai Podgorny, and the Soviet chief of staff, Marshal Zakharov. The purpose of this mission was to examine the problems caused to Egypt by the war and to plan the reconstruction of the Egyptian forces. At this meeting President Nasser formally asked the Soviet Union to undertake full responsibility for the air defence of Egypt, suggesting that this defence be placed under a Soviet commander (Egypt's Air Force had been destroyed in the war, hence the urgency of the problem as the Egyptian leaders saw it). Although President Podgorny agreed to the Egyptian proposal at the time, that evening he informed Nasser that the Soviet Union could not accept responsibility for the air defence of Egypt, even under command of a Soviet general. Sadat, whom Nasser had informed about this decision by telephone, suspected at the time that the reason for the Soviet refusal was the Glasboro summit meeting, which had taken place that very day in the United States, between Premier Kosygin and President Lyndon Johnson. Later Sadat went to Moscow to renew the request, but it was turned down.

Despite their refusal to assume responsibility for the air defence of Egypt, the Soviet Union agreed to reconstruct and re-equip the Egyptian armed forces. This was effected in record time: within half a year an Egyptian Army of approximately the same size as the one that had faced Israel on the morning of 5 June was facing Israel again across the Suez Canal. This rapid resurgence was but the initiation of a process which was to create in Egypt an army ultimately numbering some 800,000 troops. As soon as adequate equipment had been received, the Egyptians commenced limited harassing operations in 1968 which later culminated in the declaration of the War of Attrition.

On 21 January 1969, in an interview published in *Al Ahram*, President Nasser stated Egypt's military policy. He was quoted as saying

> The first priority, the absolute priority in this battle, is the military front, for we must realise that the enemy will not withdraw unless we force him to withdraw through fighting. Indeed there can be no hope of any political solution unless the enemy realises that we are capable of forcing him to withdraw through fighting.

The thinking of the political and military leadership of Egypt was clarified even further two months later in an article published in *Al Ahram* on 7 March 1969 by Mohammed Hassenein Heikal, the editor of *Al Ahram* and a writer who very frequently reflected in his writing the thinking of President Nasser and later for a period of President Sadat. In this article Heikal made it clear that since the *Blitzkrieg*-type of war suited Israel because of its territory, its limited population, its state of preparedness, its standard of training and its limited resources, the Arabs must plan for a protracted war which would take into consideration their own depth in territory, their lack of sufficient preparedness, their unlimited economy and their unlimited population in which the loss of 50,000 troops would go unremarked whereas the loss of 10,000 troops by Israel would force it to ask for a cease-fire. He concluded that the future war with Israel must last from seven to eight weeks, because however much territory Israel occupied initially it would lose a war which lasted that long. Furthermore, he elaborated on the importance of the establishment of the eastern front, thus obliging Israel to face a war on two fronts.

In December 1969 American Secretary of State Mr William Rogers proposed the so-called Rogers Plan. This plan envisaged a peace treaty between Israel, Egypt and Jordan in which there would be an almost complete Israeli withdrawal from occupied territories, leaving open the questions of the Gaza Strip and Sharm el-Sheikh. While Israel was not happy with this proposal, President Nasser turned it down; the Soviet attitude to the plan, which they seemed to favour at the outset, was ambivalent. In the meantime, various proposals were being bandied about between the Israelis and the Egyptians: in May 1970 Mrs Meir, the prime minister of Israel, indicated that for true peace Israel would make concessions that might 'surprise the world'; furthermore, Israel would be willing to negotiate not only directly but through an intermediary. Nasser indicated in return that if the Israelis were to withdraw, Egypt would recognize the State of Israel. Against this background came the second Rogers Plan, which aimed at a cease-fire leading to a renewal of negotiations in which Egypt would recognize Israeli sovereignty while Israel would withdraw from occupied territories.

Nasser's reaction was at first a negative one. It is very important when considering the political developments at this stage not to lose sight of the fact that they were taking place against the background of a stepped-up War of Attrition in which both sides were sustaining heavy casualties. There is no doubt but that in the final analysis the severity of the War of Attrition was having its effect on the political decisions on both sides. President Nasser went to Moscow on 29 June 1970 and stayed until 17 July. (He was by now a very sick man and had gone to the Soviet Union for medical treatment as well as political discussions.) This Moscow visit was to have a profound effect ultimately on Soviet–Egyptian relations. According to President Sadat, in an interview published in *Al Hawadess* in Beirut on 26 April 1974, in an atmosphere of prevarication in Moscow Nasser decided in a fit of frustration, when he was seated in the conference room at the Kremlin facing the leaders of the Soviet Union, to reverse his decision and to accept the Rogers Plan.

Six months earlier during his visit to the Soviet Union in January 1970, following the Israeli bombing in depth, the Soviets had agreed to take over responsibility for the air defence of Egypt. They had furthermore acceded to the insistent demands of the Egyptians to supply them with aircraft capable of carrying out deep-penetration bombing missions in Israel; such a force they argued would in itself constitute a deterrent against Israeli bombing raids into Egypt. The Egyptians awaited the planes in addition to a Soviet-manned surface-to-air SAM missile system, but while the missiles and the crews had arrived the planes had not. Nasser had become very impatient, and, conforming to his normal practice of trying to play one side off against the other, had in his May Day speech in 1970 made overtures to President Nixon indicating a tendency to moderation. After his June visit he returned to Egypt a frustrated man. Although as a result of his treatment in the Soviet Union he looked as if he had lost twenty years, yet he was a very sick man. Sadat described how he met him at the airport, asking him what he had concluded with the Soviets. Nasser answered simply in two words, spoken in English: 'Hopeless case.' Later he added, 'I have accepted the Rogers proposals.'

Nasser saw in his success in convincing the Soviet Union to involve itself militarily in the defence of Egypt in January 1970 a tremendous step forward of very great importance and significance. But at his subsequent meeting in Moscow in June 1970 he suddenly realized that while the Soviets had sent forces to the Middle East to defend Egypt, they were not prepared to force Israel to accept an imposed solution by military means. He therefore decided that the only way to reach a solution satisfactory to Egypt would be through the Americans. In fact when Joseph Sisco, the United States assistant secretary of state, had come to Cairo in April, the first contact of a practical nature had been arranged with them. In spite of this, however, he had decided to see what he could get from the Soviets. But dissatisfied with his June visit, during the flight home he considered a political plan of action that could be developed through the Americans. He now proceeded to try to mend his fences with them.

On 28 September 1970 President Nasser died. Soviet Premier Kosygin, attended by a large entourage, rushed to Cairo and spent almost a week there in an endeavour to influence the direction of the new regime in Egypt and to strengthen the position of the group around Ali Sabri, a pro-Soviet vice-president. Another less prominent visitor at Nasser's funeral was Mr Elliot Richardson, American secretary of health, education and welfare, who quietly met President Sadat. This was to be the first of a series of American contacts with President Sadat.

Towards the end of 1970, Israeli Minister of Defence Gen. Dayan put forward a suggestion for an interim solution of the Israeli-Egyptian conflict. Israel would withdraw for a comparatively short distance from the Suez Canal, enabling the Egyptians to reopen it and permitting Egyptian civilian personnel necessary for its operation on to the east bank. Dayan reasoned that by opening the Canal a vested interest would be created for both the Egyptians and the Soviets to ensure that it would remain open. Furthermore, he believed that the demilitarization of the area on the east bank of the Canal would create a buffer area not only between the Israeli and the Egyptian forces, but also – of far greater importance – between the Israeli and Soviet forces. Contacts between President Sadat and the Americans had been developing throughout these discussions; Sadat was communicating with President Nixon and an Egyptian representative went to Washington in order to develop the idea of a partial settlement along the Canal.

Early in 1971 Sadat gave an interview to Arnaud de Borchgrave, an editor of *Newsweek*, who had become very close to him and who was to prove ultimately to be an invaluable source to Sadat's thinking. In the interview he said for the first time that he would be prepared to recognize Israel and live in peace with it. With this interview in hand de Borchgrave flew to Jerusalem and met a number of people who were impressed by this new development. He was received by Prime Minister Mrs Golda Meir and related to her the details of his interview with Sadat. Mrs Meir listened with ill-concealed impatience and stopped him in the middle saying, 'If I am not mistaken you have come to interview me, so please pose your questions.' At the end of the interview de Borchgrave said, 'Madame Prime Minister, I fear that your remarks will be out of date when they are published, because in the meantime Sadat will respond to an overture by Ambassador Jarring and will announce that he is prepared to make peace.' At that point Mrs Meir reacted sarcastically, 'That will be the day. I don't believe it will happen.' De Borchgrave flew back to New York via Zurich. At Zurich airport he was paged and called to the telephone: it was the *Newsweek* representative, relaying a request from Jerusalem that the text of the interview with Golda Meir be returned for amendment, because in the meantime Sadat had made the declaration which de Borchgrave had forecast. The fact that Mrs Meir did not amend the text, but merely brought it up to date, confirmed de Borchgrave's opinion that Mrs Meir here missed the greatest opportunity to prevent war.

On 4 February 1971 Sadat announced his proposal for a partial settlement. It had many points similar to those in Dayan's proposal but diverged on the nature of the Egyptian forces, police or military, which would be allowed to cross to the east bank. Another area of divergence was on the main issue of whether, as the Israelis maintained, the settlement would be an agreement in itself without prejudice to further negotiations for a final agreement, or, as the Egyptians maintained, it would be part of the final settlement including an advance undertaking on Israel's part for the total withdrawal of its forces from Sinai. No progress was made because of the Egyptian insistence that the Israelis undertake in advance to withdraw completely from Sinai. The next move came from Dr Gunnar Jarring, the UN Secretary General's representative, who was appointed to implement Security Council Resolution 242. He produced a proposal of his own which was very close to extreme Egyptian demands, but completely unacceptable to Israel. Following his intervention the Israeli position hardened.

For many months during 1971 negotiations continued on the issue of partial settlement but no advance was made. It is a sobering reflection on the relation of personalities to the creation of history to realize that a more able and decisive negotiator than Dr Jarring could well have achieved a breakthrough in 1971. For in the final analysis, after the 1973 war in the agreement on the disengagement of forces Egypt did agree to much of what Israel had proposed in 1971.

On 1 March 1971 President Sadat made the first of a number of secret visits to Moscow. He was accompanied by Sharawi Guma, the minister of interior, and Gen. Mahmoud Fawzi, the minister of war. Sadat was new and uncertain of himself and the two ministers accompanying him held much of the power of Egypt in their hands, especially the former who controlled the security services. During the visit Sadat raised the question of the long-range planes which had been promised to Nasser, the non-delivery of which had caused him to agree to the Rogers Plan. To Sadat's request came the reply, 'We are prepared to supply these planes to you on condition that they will not be used without prior approval from Moscow.' According to his report of the meeting, Sadat was horrified. A very sharp exchange took place. The true implications of Soviet military involvement were becoming apparent to him; and a completely new process of thought began at this point in his mind, which was to lead him to request the withdrawal of the Soviet advisers and forces from Egypt in July 1972. On his return to Egypt Sadat convened the Supreme Council of the Arab Socialist Union and recounted the story of his negotiations in Moscow, saying, 'I refused to accept the planes under such conditions because I refused to accept a situation whereby there exists on Egyptian soil a will other than that of myself and the political leadership of Egypt.'

In May 1971 American Secretary of State Rogers, accompanied by Assistant Secretary of State Sisco, came to Cairo in order to endeavour to advance the negotiations for a partial settlement (during this visit Secretary Rogers announced that he had no additional request from Egypt following Sadat's announcement in February 1971). At this meeting Sadat apparently hinted to his American visitors that certain changes might occur in Egypt, and indeed a week later, on 14 May, he eliminated his opposition, composed of the men of Nasser's inner circle, including Ali Sabri, who led the pro-Soviet elements in the leadership. This group had chosen Anwar Sadat to be president after Nasser because they considered him to be a mediocrity, an easily pliable front man who would do as they bid. As the months went on they discovered that he was not at all easy to direct and had his own views on matters of external and internal policy. Accordingly they prepared a characteristically Middle

Eastern plot to take power and overthrow him. Sadat, who kept himself well informed of the plotters' intentions, struck first. They were all arrested and subsequently brought to trial and sentenced to long prison terms.

In the Kremlin these events were viewed with considerable alarm. For the first time in years an American secretary of state had visited Cairo and now came this blow, involving as it did Ali Sabri, one of the staunch supporters of Soviet military involvement in the Middle East and in Egypt. President Podgorny was dispatched post-haste to Cairo and on arrival produced the text of the Soviet–Egyptian fifteen-year Treaty of Friendship and Co-operation. This treaty pledged Soviet support for Egypt in its struggle to become a socialist society; each of the two parties undertook not to enter in alliance or to take any action directed against the other party or to conclude any other international agreement at variance with the terms of the treaty. In their meeting with Sadat, Rogers and Sisco had implied that the United States would be prepared to do a deal at Israel's expense in return for the Egyptians doing a deal at the Soviet Union's expense. Suddenly, out of the blue, came the Soviet–Egyptian Treaty of Friendship and Co-operation to dampen the hopes of the Americans. They asked Sadat for an explanation; his reply was that Egypt was free to make its own decisions.

When the third phase of the cease-fire that had commenced on 7 August 1970 came to an end in March 1971, Sadat did not renew it as he had done twice before. For, as President Sadat announced, 1971 was to be a 'Year of Decision'.

On 6 July an additional American representative in the form of the chief of the Egyptian desk at the State Department, Mr Michael Sterner, arrived in Egypt. According to a susequent interview given to Arnaud de Borchgrave of *Newsweek* (in which Sadat's account of the negotiations between the United States and Egypt during 1971 was given in great detail), Sterner informed Sadat that President Nixon had now decided to take an active role in the Middle East crisis, although he wanted to know first if the Treaty of Friendship and Co-operation between Egypt and the Soviet Union had changed anything in the Egyptian position. Replying that the treaty had not changed anything because it was only a new frame for already existing relations, Sadat agreed to restore diplomatic relations with the United States after the first phase of an Israeli withdrawal within the framework of a partial agreement, advising Sterner that he intended to send Soviet personnel home at the end of phase one of such a withdrawal 'because I am just as keen on that as you are'.

Since nothing happened for several months, although Sisco was sent to Israel, Sadat came to the conclusion that his American approach was not paying off, so, accordingly, on 11 October 1971 he flew to Moscow for talks with the three Soviet leaders. At this meeting he managed to clear the atmosphere and at Egypt's request an arms deal was agreed on. The arms were to be delivered by the end of 1971 so that a 'decision in regard to the battle', as Sadat put it, could be made. The Egyptians were expecting deliveries of arms to start in October, but by mid-December nothing had arrived (on 8 December 1971 the India–Pakistan War had broken out and the Soviet Union found itself called upon to meet its obligations to India). Sadat notified the Soviet Union of his desire to sort the matter out by arranging immediate talks in Moscow; to his chagrin the Soviets invited him to come not in January but in February 1972.

Sadat's February visit was inconclusive; two months later, in April, he was invited again for discussions befoie President Nixon's planned summit visit to Moscow in May 1972. For the Soviet Union the situation was a delicate one. Here they were on the one hand developing a posture of détente with the United States, and on the other being pressured by Egypt to take action that was basically irreconcilable with it. At the meeting Sadat maintained that there could be no break in the log jam in the Middle East without military action although he could see that the Soviet Union was opposed to this. Nevertheless the Soviet leaders did agree that Israel had to be made aware of Egypt's strength and promised arms for this purpose. They assured Sadat that after the conclusion of the Brezhnev–Nixon talks in May they would embark on a major programme for the strengthening of Egypt's military potential. Both sides were of the opinion that since 1972 was presidential election year in the United States, and there would be no change in United States policy before the elections in November, Egypt must be ready to go to war immediately afterwards. To this, according to Sadat, the Soviets agreed.

The announcement coming out of the Nixon–Brezhnev summit meeting in Moscow referred to a mutual agreement to achieve 'a military relaxation' in the Middle East to be followed by a freezing of the situation. This to Sadat meant that Israel would be in a position of military supremacy. Furthermore, it was this reference to a military relaxation coupled with the Soviet failure to implement any of the points agreed upon at the April meeting in preparation for the coming war that prompted his decision to ask the Soviet Government to remove its forces and advisers from Egypt in July 1972. He had come to the conclusion that he could not go to war with the Soviet advisers present in Egypt and while the Soviet Government played about with him as it had done for the past year.

This move on the part of Sadat coincided with the dissatisfaction felt with the Soviet advisers in the Egyptian Army, in whose ranks pressure had mounted to dispense with their services. Their crude, gauche behaviour had created bitter antagonism. They were aloof, looking down on the Egyptian officers and treating them with faintly concealed disdain. Their whole system and

outlook was irreconcilable with that of an easy-going and friendly people, the
levantine merchants and the traders of the *souks*. Matters were not helped by
the fact that in every battalion, brigade and missile battery there sat a Soviet
adviser who submitted reports on its Egyptian commander. One can go as far
as to say that the Egyptian officers hated them, for even their religion was a
frequent subject of mockery. Egyptian prisoners related after the war how in
one brigade during a discussion in which many of the Egyptian officers criticized Soviet weapons the Soviet adviser lost his temper and said, 'If so, may
Allah give you better weapons.' There was an uproar and a call for a strike.
The matter reached the army commander and the adviser was replaced. The
bitterness aroused among the Egyptians by the Soviet behaviour was given
vivid expression in a series of articles by Mohammed Hassenein Heikal describing the reasons for the break with the Soviets. They did not appreciate,
he pointed out, that in dealing with Egypt they were dealing not with some
second-rate nation but with a people who had once led civilization and the
world.

Sadat's move against the Soviets, while arousing the apprehensions of those
elements in Egypt which favoured their presence, was received with unreserved
acclamation in the Egyptian Army. It was received with satisfaction too in
Israel, although Sadat's purpose was completely misunderstood. The various
Israeli announcements were of relief and gratification at the removal of the
Soviets from this front with Israel. Not appreciating the true reason for Sadat's
move, motives which were far removed from the true one were read into it, a
fact that contributed in no small measure to the strengthening of the 'concept'
which played such a vital part in misleading Israel.

The central guiding line of Sadat's policy remained the direct involvement
of the Americans in the Middle East dispute. At no point did he depart from
this, although he was by now becoming gradually convinced that without
military action he would not be able to set in motion effective political moves in
co-operation with the United States. He was however unwilling to bring about
a complete split with the Soviet Union. He envisaged ridding himself of
Soviet influence only so far as decision making and a growing Soviet tendency
to interfere in Egyptian policy were concerned. He wanted freedom to take
any steps he wished to take, including war, in the future; and such action would
be dependent upon maintaining an ongoing practical relationship with the
Soviet Union. Without a continuation of the massive Soviet arms deliveries,
his plans would not be very effective.

Accordingly, in October 1972, President Assad of Syria went to Moscow
and endeavoured to mediate between Egypt and the Soviet Union; shortly
afterwards he was followed by Premier Aziz Sidki of Egypt, who apparently

succeeded in convincing the Soviet leaders that there was no intention on the part of the Egyptians to rush into the arms of the United States in order to prejudice the position of the Soviet Union. They agreed to arrest the process of deterioration in the relationship between the two countries, and soon after Soviet military officers returned to Egypt. (These were in addition to those advisers and instructors who had remained after July 1972.) The Soviets had constructed an impressive war machine in Egypt and had obviously no intention of abandoning it; instead they were adapting themselves to the new situation in a characteristically pragmatic manner.

Throughout this period Sadat's personal position was becoming weaker and weaker. He had become a laughing stock in his own country with the passing of 1971, the 'Year of Decision' in which no decision was made. His specious excuses about the India–Pakistan War and other explanations for his failure to go to war were the subject of much biting humour among the wits of Cairo. His image was that of a foolish man and he headed a hesitant Egyptian society which was to a great degree demoralized and in which the credibility of the government was very low. The impression gained abroad was of a regime desperately preoccupied in an endeavour to survive from month to month. Political observers were closely examining these developments in order to evaluate what personality might emerge as an alternative to Sadat – the feeling was that he was remaining in power *faute de mieux* and the question was how long the Egyptian economy could bear a very heavy military burden and the strains of a 'no peace, no war situation'.

By agreement, renewable in March 1973 at the conclusion of five years, the Soviet Union enjoyed certain facilities for its Mediterranean fleet in Egyptian ports. The importance of these facilities, supported by an infrastructure capable of handling Soviet ships and repairing them, is obvious in the context of the growth of Soviet naval activity in the Mediterranean over the past decade. In December 1972, in accordance with the provisions of the agreement, both sides were obliged to renegotiate. Gen. Ahmed Ismail, the new Egyptian minister of war, approached the Soviet military authorities in the embassy in Cairo and advised them that Egypt intended to renew this agreement. Shortly after, at the beginning of 1973, he visited the Soviet Union as did Hafez Ismail, Sadat's adviser. These visits proved to be successful from the Egyptian point of view with the Soviet Union agreeing to the Egyptian requests for the supply of arms. The Soviets had decided to make the best of the situation and to make available the technology which the Egyptians were seeking. Immediately after Ismail's return to Egypt the material began to flow.

At the beginning of 1973 the United States Government entered into negotiations with the governments of Saudi Arabia and Kuwait for the supply to

W O—B

their air forces of Phantom fighter bombers; it was an event which passed comparatively unnoticed but which doubtless must be taken into consideration as one of the elements leading to the escalation in the area. The fact that for the first time the Americans indicated a preparedness to supply highly advanced technological equipment to Arab states, in addition to the Israelis, created a suspicion in the Soviet Union that the Americans were entering into a race in that specific field in which the Soviets considered that they had gained the upper hand and had bound many of the Arab states to them. Indeed it seems that the American negotiations with the Arabs had a certain amount of influence on the Soviet Union's own readiness to escalate and to supply equipment that had never been supplied to any country outside the Soviet Union.

For years the Egyptian leadership had lived with an obsession about Israeli air superiority, which had been brought home in the most dramatic manner in the 1967 war and which had been emphasized to an extreme degree by the deep-penetration Israeli raids in January 1970. The Egyptian military planners had all along maintained that until the Egyptian Air Force was supplied with advanced, medium-range bombers or fighter bombers such as the MIG 23, the Phantom, the Jaguar or the Mirage, which could endanger the Israeli centres of population and above all could deal with Israeli airfields, they could not embark on war. This was known in Israel and was the basis of an Israeli intelligence estimation that the Egyptians would not achieve this prerequisite until 1975, hence it was believed that war was improbable before then: the Egyptians would not be content without a bomber force adequate to deal simultaneously with all Israeli airfields. Sadat however appreciated that he could not wait until this necessary force was built up by 1975: it was doubtful from an internal point of view whether he could remain in power that long without making any move. His insistent demands on the Soviets had been for the supply of either attack planes of the type of MIG 23, which included some of the most modern Soviet technology and which in the event of war the Soviet Union feared might fall into the hands of Israel and of the West, or alternatively of medium-range surface-to-surface missiles which by their very existence on Egyptian soil could deter Israel from embarking on any bombing in depth. Gen. Ahmed Ismail's visit to Moscow in early 1973 was the turning point.

In March 1973, following the visit of a very high-level Soviet military delegation to Cairo, the Soviet Union began to ship the Scud Battlefield Support Surface-to-Surface Missile to the Egyptian Army. This missile, capable of carrying either a high-explosive warhead or a nuclear warhead, has a range of some 180 miles enabling it to engage centres of population in Israel from Egypt – the main requirement of the Egyptians before they could go to war had now been met by the Soviet Union. Sadat believed that with this deterrent in his hands he could replace the deterrent that would have been created by a medium-range bomber force and he is on record as saying that his final decision to go to war was made in April 1973 – when the first Scud missiles arrived on Egyptian soil – but in truth the final decision which led to war was made in the Kremlin by those who decided to supply the Scud to the Egyptians.

Parallel to these activities, in March 1973 (after the inauguration of President Nixon), Sadat sent Hafez Ismail, his adviser on security affairs, to Washington. The purpose of his visit was to influence the Americans to bring pressure to bear on the Israelis. Nixon, whom Ismail met, allegedly stated that he was willing to influence Israel in return for Egyptian concessions which went beyond the Rogers Plan. In view of this, Sadat reached the conclusion that there was no alternative but to go to war in order to break the stalemate. As Heikal was to explain in an interview in *Der Speigel* after the war, nobody attributed sufficient importance to the failure of Ismail's mission in Washington. There is no doubt that it played an important part in subsequent decisions.

Later that month Sadat announced that he was taking over the premiership in addition to the presidency for the purpose of preparing Egypt for total confrontation with Israel. On 9 April he gave an interview to Arnaud de Borchgrave in which he complained that during his meeting with Hafez Ismail President Nixon had refused to exert pressure on Israel and had asked for a declaration about the legitimate position of the Israeli case and for the demilitarization of Sinai.

> You Americans always use computers to solve geopolitical equations and they always mislead you. You simply forget to feed (Egyptian) psychology into the computer. Now the time has come for a decision . . . the time has come for a shock. Diplomacy will continue before, during and after the battle . . . . everything in this country is now being mobilized in earnest for the resumption of the battle – which is now inevitable . . . . the Russians are providing us now with everything that is possible for them to supply and I am now quite satisfied.

Armed with his interview de Borchgrave returned to Washington. And although he related his story to many figures in the Senate and House of Representatives and in the State Department, nobody was prepared to believe him. All were of the opinion that Sadat was bluffing. All except Dr Henry Kissinger who, according to de Borchgrave, was the only person in Washington who believed the story and who reacted seriously to Sadat's intentions. Kissinger's reaction was, 'I too expect something to happen which can be very serious', and he went on to express the opinion that in the coming war in the

Middle East oil would be a weapon. Following these two meetings with Sadat and Kissinger, de Borchgrave published his by now historic article.

Seldom has a leader of a country bent on war enunciated so clearly his intentions to the world and to all parties concerned. But while note was taken of his remarks in Israeli intelligence circles, their evaluations continued to be coloured by the assumption that Sadat could not put his threats into action until the Egyptians had solved the problem of the bomber attack force which they required. Israeli intelligence continued to maintain that this was typical of Sadat's brinkmanship; he would not go over the brink.

Perhaps Sadat's greatest success was his achievement in the Arab world. He was attacked, reviled, publicly mocked, laughed at because of the 'Year of Decision', yet he never reacted and did not quarrel with a single Arab leader. He succeeded in not being encumbered with the suspicions of his Arab brothers, a situation which surrounded Nasser all through his life. He developed relations with King Feisal of Saudi Arabia, placing the emphasis on tradition, religion and Islam, and at the same time played along with Col. Ghadafi of Libya and his idiosyncrasies. When Ghadafi offered him union, Sadat turned to King Feisal and asked him what to do: should he fall into the arms of Ghadafi, an unstable lunatic preaching against every traditional regime in the Middle East? Feisal's reaction was to draw Egypt closer and develop collaboration between their two countries.

For six years, during which attempts were made in the Arab world to mobilize the oil weapon, King Feisal maintained that war with Israel was one matter and exploiting oil as a weapon was another. Gradually however an international psychosis was built up around the problem of oil, a development that tied in with the growing financial wealth in the oil-producing states which if necessary could forgo part of the vast sums being paid as royalties, especially since more money could be received for less oil. Saudi Arabian policy was reviewed in May 1973 and gradually the coalition between Egypt and Saudi Arabia to wield the oil weapon was forged. In the course of their discussions, Sadat convinced Feisal that without the unifying force of a war it would not be possible to develop the oil weapon; and in order to create the oil weapon to further the Arab war aims, it was essential first to go to war. Feisal took along with him in this move Kuwait and the oil sheikdoms in the Persian Gulf. Israeli intelligence observed this new change in policy, but failed to link it with the military developments in the area.

In the same month, May, the Egyptian foreign minister visited Moscow. A communiqué published at the conclusion of his visit pledged Soviet support for Egyptian efforts 'to liquidate the consequences of aggression'. The possibility of military action was not ruled out. A month later however the second summit conference between President Nixon and Mr Brezhnev took place. Sadat saw the decisions taken at this conference as reflecting a desire to put the Middle East problem on ice and to incline towards a military relaxation. Nevertheless, while the summit meeting, entirely devoted towards the cause of détente, was taking place, a massive infusion of Soviet missilery and weapons into Egypt, and a crash programme to supply the Syrians with the surface-to-air missile system which they required prior to embarking on a war, was under way.

At least twice before this point, Egyptian planning for an attack on Israeli forces had been well advanced and ready for implementation. At the end of 1971 a bombing attack by fifty bombers on Sharm el-Sheikh was planned. But the India–Pakistan War broke out, so Sadat cancelled the operation on the assumption that nobody in the world would pay much attention to a war in the Middle East while a major struggle was going on in Asia. The second action was planned for October 1972. Sadat ordered his then war minister, Gen. Mohammed Sadeq, to drop a parachute brigade in the Sinai and hold a beachhead for a week to ten days. During that time the United Nations Security Council was to be called into session, Libya was to shut off oil supplies, and pressure was to be brought to bear on Washington to force Israel to withdraw from occupied Arab territories. But Gen. Sadeq objected to this operation, being unwilling to sacrifice picked troops who would certainly have been wiped out by the Israel Defence Forces. He maintained that the Egyptian home front was not ready for war and that far more comprehensive preparations for the defence of Egypt had to be undertaken before going to war.

Two months later Sadat dismissed Sadeq, a popular general in Egypt and the prime mover for ousting the Soviet advisers. According to de Borchgrave, Sadat was aware of the fact that he might not survive another defeat at the hands of the Israelis and yet he had become convinced that Egypt had little to lose by the resumption of fighting. He reasoned that should Egypt suffer a disaster, it would be a loss similar to the Vietnamese Communists' setback during the offensives of 1968 and 1972 – a military defeat but a psychological victory.

Gen. Ahmed Ismail was appointed as Sadeq's successor with instructions to prepare for war. He had taken command of the Suez front in July 1967 after the débâcle and was therefore familiar with the military problems posed by this front. He was opposed to a renewal of the War of Attrition, because it was quite obvious that Israel would not allow the Arabs to dictate the field of battle and that the Israeli reaction this time would be far greater than before. After considering a number of other possibilities, he came to the conclusion that the initial Egyptian attack must be a massive one – indeed it must be the most massive blow that the Egyptians could mount. Within a few months he was appointed commander in chief of the Arab Federation, comprising nominally Egypt, Syria and Libya, which in fact meant that he would co-ordinate the Egyptian and Syrian forces.

In analysing the problems facing him, Gen. Ismail realized that Israel had four advantages: air superiority, technological ability, a high standard of training and what he considered to be guaranteed supplies from the United States. Against this he considered that Israel suffered from a number of basic disadvantages: long lines of communication leading to a number of fronts, an inability to suffer heavy casualties because of its small population or to fight a long war because of a basic economic weakness; coupled with these were the disadvantages arising out of over-confidence and a superiority complex.

The Arabs had studied in great detail the lessons of 1967 and had analysed every point of Israeli superiority in order to produce an answer. The first conclusion they reached was that it had been a mistake to bring the Israelis to deliver the first strike in 1967; they would do it themselves in 1973. The scope and the intensity of the Israeli attack in 1967 has surprised them. This time they would throw everything they had into the initial attack. In 1967 they had failed to wage a simultaneous multi-front war, thus enabling Israel to deal with the various elements in the war at its leisure; this time they would co-ordinate the major Egyptian and Syrian offensives and use the other Arab forces, including Jordan, as a reserve. Obviously the first and foremost consideration was the supply of all the weapons necessary for the war; this was assured during Gen. Ismail's visit to Moscow and the visit of a high-level Soviet delegation to Cairo early in 1973.

Co-ordination with the Syrians began in February 1973 with Ismail's visit. For three months the Syrian front had been erupting in a series of heavy military engagements following the Israeli reactions to Palestinian terrorist activities from across the Syrian and Lebanese borders. The Israeli reaction was intense and massive. Suddenly, following an Israeli operation in January 1973, the front became quiet. There was not even a Palestinian terrorist reaction. The Israelis saw this development as one which must increase the prevailing feeling of confidence, for it was obvious to them that as a result of their activity the Syrians had been taken out of the war; in fact the motive for the quiet along the border was the Syrian preparation for war.

Meanwhile, Gen. Ismail had made a decision in principle that the Egyptian attack, when it came, would be launched along the entire front of the Suez Canal, a distance of 110 miles. Such a plan would not give the Israelis any indication as to the main thrust of the attacking forces and consequently would prevent them from concentrating against it and delay their counter-attack while they looked for the main thrust. It would furthermore answer the problem posed by Israeli air superiority, forcing them to dissipate their air power along a very wide front.

In January 1973 the Arab Defence Council worked out an overall unified plan for military and political action against Israel. In the same month President Sadat visited President Tito. (After the war the Yugoslavs explained that the overflying rights which they had granted the Soviets during the war were due to the urgings of President Sadat and not of the Soviet Union.) In February Sadat ordered a report recommending the most suitable days for the crossing of the Canal. Director of Operations Gen. Gamasy presented the report to him in handwriting, recommending three groups of days: in the second half of May, in the month of September and in the month of October.

Soon after the failure of Hafez Ismail's mission in Washington in March 1973 Minister of War Ahmed Ismail visited Damascus. Sadat now made his final decision to go to war, planning it for May of that year. (Already in January he had instructed the Egyptian chief of staff, Gen. Shazli, to plan the crossing of the Canal and to prepare other operational plans.) However in May he gave orders to postpone the attack until October. Explaining the postponement later he said:

> I planned in fact to launch the operation in May, but then the Russians set the date for the Second Summit Conference with Nixon in Washington for the month of May, and for political reasons which need not be revealed at this point I decided to postpone the date to the group of days in September or to the third group of days in October.

At that time, in May, considerable preparations for the crossing of the Canal had been made by the Egyptian Army. Israeli intelligence noted these preparations but maintained that Sadat, as was his wont, would go to the brink and then withdraw without launching a war. The Israeli chief of staff, Gen. Elazar, did not accept their evaluation of the situation and ordered a partial mobilization costing some $11 million. But the Egyptian attack did not materialize and Israeli intelligence, perhaps not specifically, declared, 'I told you so.' This vindication of their estimate in May would be a major factor in the mistaken Israeli evaluation in October.

The Egyptian war minister visited Damascus again on 8 May and frequent meetings of high-ranking Egyptian and Syrian leaders took place throughout the summer months. In June Sadat flew to Damascus for talks with Assad and by early September full details of military co-operation between the two countries had been worked out.

In the meantime feelers were thrown out to King Hussein of Jordan by the Egyptians, indicating a willingness for reconciliation. Hussein had been virtually ostracized by the rest of the Arab world following the civil war in Jordan in September 1970 and the fighting in July 1971, when the last pockets of Palestinian terrorists were wiped out. The situation was further complicated by the murder in Cairo of Wasfi Tel, the Jordanian prime minister and a close friend of King Hussein, by a group of Palestinian terrorists. Sadat did not prosecute the murderers, an omission which Hussein could not forgive. In March 1972 Hussein launched a plan for a federal Jordan, uniting Jordan with the West Bank after Israeli evacuation. This plan implied peace with Israel, and Egypt reacted by severing diplomatic relations with Jordan. It is therefore not surprising that the Egyptian feelers in early 1973 were eagerly seized upon by King Hussein (who was only too anxious to break out of his isolation in the Arab world) with the result that Jordanian envoys visited Cairo and Damascus during the summer months.

In August Sadat's personal representative, Hassan Sabri Al Khouli, visited Amman and was quoted on his return by Cairo Radio as stating that he had discussed 'the cause for which we work on all levels, namely the battle'. The appearance of Mustafa Tlas, the Syrian defence minister, in Amman on 29 August should have sounded the alarm in many places, especially in Israel, for Jordan's relations with Syria had been virtually non-existent and were at best strained and unfriendly.

On 12 September a meeting took place in Cairo between the leaders of the front-line states: Egypt, Jordan and Syria. Photographs were published of King Hussein and Presidents Sadat and Assad seated in friendly conversation. Diplomatic relations between Jordan and Egypt and Jordan and Syria were renewed, while the restoration of financial assistance from the oil states to Jordan was discussed. At this meeting Hussein was not let into the secret of the attack (he was to explain later that he had not been consulted before the outbreak of war) but was given a general indication that such an attack was planned, and that agreement with him was essential in order to guarantee the southern flank of the Syrian forces and so prevent Israel from striking at Syria through northern Jordan. His reaction was one of cautious hesitation, having regard to his unfortunate experience with his Arab allies in 1967, when he had been left in the lurch by them and as a result had lost half his kingdom. He was aware of the bitter hatred of the Palestinians towards him, but nevertheless he now released some of them from prison. It seems that in the light of all that has been published about Hussein's attitude during the war, his active intervention in the battle against Israeli territory was conditional on the prior conquest of the Golan Heights by the Syrians. As a second best and in order to protect himself from Arab criticism, during the war he committed two armoured brigades to battle within the framework of the Syrian Army.

In August Sadat had held a meeting with Yasser Arafat and the heads of the Palestine Liberation Organization in Cairo. At this meeting he told them that he had decided to go to war, asking them what their part would be and suggesting that they supply him with forces to serve along the Canal. The Palestinian leadership did not take him very seriously. After all, for years he had been talking about an imminent war and nothing had happened. They returned to Beirut, where Sadat's announcement was discussed in a nine-hour emergency session of the Executive Committee of the PLO. The meeting was informed that Sadat's ultimate purpose was to generate United States pressure on Israel. Reports of Sadat's conversation with the Palestinians leaked out and were soon the subject of amused and sceptical comment in the cafés of Beirut. On 21 September a report of the meeting appeared in the leading Beirut newspaper, *Al Nahar*. But although it was picked up and circulated throughout the world by the Associated Press, nobody paid much attention to it.

Meanwhile, throughout the summer, the two main elements which were essential in the eyes of the Arab planners and their Soviet advisers in order to launch a war were being supplied by the Soviet Union. The Egyptian and Syrian armies had received surface-to-surface missiles capable of engaging Israeli civilian targets: in Syria the FROG missile was ready for action; in Egypt the Scud missile, together with Soviet crews, was in similar readiness. Furthermore, the surface-to-air missile system which in the Soviet view would neutralize Israeli air superiority along the front line – the main Arab obsession – was being rushed to Syria in a crash programme during the months of July and August. Along the front line and on the approaches to the capital cities the Israeli Air Force would be neutralized by a surface-to-air missile system which would act as an umbrella over the advancing Arab forces, while the surface-to-surface missiles poised against targets in the centre of Israel would deter the Israeli Air Force from deep-penetration bombing attacks.

The answer to the Israeli air threat, co-ordination with Saudi Arabia for the use of oil as a weapon, co-ordination with other Arab countries in order to ensure additional reinforcements, protection of Syria's southern Jordanian flank, continuing Soviet supplies and arrangements for political support were all carefully planned. Sadat's scheme was taking concrete shape. War was certain now.

3

The Tangled Web

HAVING TAKEN the decision to go to war, President Sadat proceeded with its planning together with Gen. Ahmed Ismail. The detailed organization – entrusted to Maj.-Gen. Abdel Ghani Gamasy, appointed commander in chief of the Joint Military Command, who after the war was to become the chief of staff – was carried out within the framework of a major exercise, known as 'Granite 2', for an attack across the Canal. The operation order (subsequently updated on 25 May 1973) issued by the Egyptian Third Army forbad officers and men to visit the town of Suez or to mingle with civilians at any point alone the Canal for reasons of security. In September orders were issued under the code name 'Tahrir 41' for a major headquarters exercise to be carried out between 1 and 7 October. The subject of the exercise was to be the organization and conduct of a strategic operational attack with a breakthrough across the Suez Canal, the destruction of the enemy reserves and the conquest of the territory up to the international boundary and the Gaza Strip.

The Egyptians based their plans for the coming campaign on the numerous studies they had made of Israeli military doctrine and thinking, which had been discussed so openly and so frequently in Israel. They noted with satisfaction the over-confidence in Israel, its faith in the ever-growing technological and culture gap between itself and the Arab countries and its conviction of the inability of the Arab leadership to make a decision to attack, not to mention the lack of unity in the Arab world. During the months of preparation in the summer, everything possible was done by the Arabs to emphasize the veracity of these beliefs in the eyes of the Israelis.

Planning for the operation had been going on since the beginning of the year under Gen. Ismail. In May he visited Syria, when planning entered a more detailed phase, and on 22 May he issued instructions setting out the general concept of operation 'Badr', the joint Syrian and Egyptian attack on Israel. On 7 June additional instructions were issued. A planning and co-ordination conference took place in Alexandria in August. Here Ismail met with the chiefs of staff of the armed forces of Egypt and Syria, their chiefs of operations and other staff officers in order to decide finally whether their forces were in a position to launch an attack, to set the D day for the attack, taking into consideration all the various meteorological and other factors, and to examine closely the internal situation in Israel, the international situation and their possible effect on the coming war. It was decided that the most appropriate period would be September or October 1973.

Proposals from this meeting were brought to the attention of the political leadership, and a subsequent meeting of the operations staff decided on the tenth day of Ramadan, or 6 October, for the start of the campaign. (The tenth day of Ramadan was the day in the year 624 in which the Prophet Mohammed began preparations for the battle of Badr, which led six years later to his triumphant entry into Mecca and the start of the spread of Islam.) On the evening of 6 September Ismail issued orders to place the Syrian and Egyptian forces on an emergency basis, ready to carry out operation 'Badr' within five days of first light on 1 October. On 1 October he issued instructions for the joint air attack to take place against Israel at 2.05 pm on 6 October. On 3 October he visited Damascus together with Gen. Baha Al Din Nofal (who had staff responsibility for co-ordination between the two armies) where they met Syrian Minister of Defence Gen. Tlas and his General Staff and worked out the final details of the attack. At midday, President Hafez Assad received Ismail and confirmed that H hour for the operation would be 2.05 pm on 6 October.

Originally, at the request of the Egyptian Command, the attack had been planned for the late afternoon, when the sun would be in the eyes of the Israeli forces along the Suez Canal and when the ensuing darkness would enable the Egyptians to set up the bridges by night. The Syrians on the other hand pressed for an attack at dawn, when the sun rising from the east on their front would blind the Israeli forces. The final decision that the attack would take place at 2 o'clock in the afternoon was therefore a compromise.

For six months before the war there had been close co-ordination between the Ministry of War, the Ministry of Foreign Affairs and the Ministry of Information in Egypt in order to develop the strategic deception plan which had been evolved. Statements were issued and stories leaked to the foreign press (as for instance the story in the British press about the Soviet report on the negligent standard of maintenance in the Egyptian missile force, which rendered this arm of service almost inoperable). Sadat was later to say with an amused look on his face, 'At the same time a report reached Israel saying that the exodus of the Soviet experts rendered the Egyptian missiles valueless. . . . It could be that they relied on this evaluation. . . .' Any point, such as Arab disunity, which had been emphasized by Israeli political or military leaders in their speeches was given added emphasis. The deteriorating relations between Egypt and the Soviet Union and even between Syria and the Soviet Union found an echo in some press report which fortified the Israeli assumption.

In the meantime the Egyptian Army was preparing for the operation. Gen. Ismail launched a campaign to convince the armed forces that there was no alternative but war. An intensive programme was developed by the moral-guidance administration of the armed forces to explain the background of the war that was to come. A strong religious element was introduced into this indoctrination, which had very marked overtones of virulent anti-Semitism. Thus in the book *Instructions in Moral Guidance for the Training Year in 1969* one finds:

> Mankind has never known and will never know a brutal enemy like the Jews. They can only damage, plan conspiracies, place traps before justice and create disturbances. From their mother's womb they have the lowest form of character which they pass on from generation to generation. . . . They have spread out throughout the world in order to poison mankind. . . . They joined the conspiracy against Jesus in order to kill him [page 288].

The Egyptian plan, which was basically a very simple one, had been prepared over the years. For six years the Egyptians had not only studied closely Israeli thinking but had also followed every move along the front line. They kept a close watch on the routine along the Canal – Egyptian units along the Canal were kept in position for years – and carefully mapped out all exercises on the Israeli side. In due course the Egyptian Army had built up a clear picture of what the Israeli military reaction would be in the event of any given move made by them. An example of this meticulous preparation can be seen in the battalion which was planning to capture a strongpoint along the Canal. The soldiers of that battalion sat watching it for over three years from across the water, constructed similar fortifications on their side and planned the attack. They drew models of the position and concentrating on one sole problem, they prepared only one solution.

Minister of War Ahmad Ismail and Chief of Staff Shazli referred in their postwar summaries to their tremendous advances in scientific planning, a legacy of the Soviet instructors' emphasis on this subject. The Soviets had trained the

Egyptian Army to take a military problem, to analyse it, to find a solution, to translate that solution into a military plan, to detail the plan, to exercise it and to prepare it operationally. The Egyptians had learned to act as a modern army. For years the individual soldier was trained in his particular role in war: each unit dealt with its own problem and nothing else. One unit did nothing for three years but train in passing across a water barrier a pipe for transporting fuel; while every single day for three years bridging units would train in backing up trucks to a water barrier, stopping abruptly at the water edge, causing the elements of the PMP heavy folding-pontoon bridge on the truck to slide by momentum into the water, before they bolted together the two elements of the bridge and drove off. Twice a day during four years these units assembled and dismantled the bridge. Similarly, every day for years all operators of Sagger anti-tank missiles lined up outside vans containing simulators and went through half an hour's exercise in tracking enemy tanks with their missile. Even later, when the Israeli and Egyptian armies were ranged one against the other in a war of attrition inside Egypt on the west bank of the Suez Canal, Israeli forces noted the simulator trucks driving up every day to the front line in order to allow the troops to undergo their daily anti-tank training. This system was repeated right down the line in the army until every action became a reflex action.

The Egyptians analysed every problem which would face them on crossing, taking into consideration the limitations of the Egyptian soldier when breaking down the various functions of the army into their respective elements. They would cross the Canal with infantry. But because the infantry would be vulnerable to the Israeli armour which they knew moved forward in the event of an emergency to the banks of the Canal, the answer was a major increase in anti-tank weapons far beyond the accepted establishment in front-line units. These included RPG 7 rocket-assisted grenades with the troops, B10 and B11 recoilless weapons at battalion level and Sagger anti-tank missiles at brigade level. On many occasions the crossing operation was exercised on the Canal itself where it splits into two sections, divided by El-Balah Island, for a distance of 5 miles. (The western section of the Canal ran entirely through Egyptian territory and was ideal for this purpose.)

The Israeli rampart along the Canal made the east bank impassable for any armoured vehicles attempting to cross it. This was a major problem for the Egyptians. After high explosives were tried and failed, Egyptian engineers ultimately produced a solution whereby very high-pressure jets of water would cause the sand wall to disintegrate. The operational plans called for sixty openings on each side of the Canal and gradually the Egyptian engineers perfected the equipment, enabling them to effect such an opening within five to six hours.

Eighty units were created in order to carry out this engineering project: similar sand walls were built in Egypt and the units blasted openings twice daily and twice nightly, reconstructing the walls after each exercise. A vast earth-moving operation went on during these preparations. At the same time however – in order to hide their activities and to obtain complete observation of the Israeli side – the sand wall on the Egyptian side was raised so that it overlooked all the Israeli fortifications, strongpoints and tank ramps right back to their second line of defence.

Over a period of four months Egyptian forces gradually moved towards the Canal, but even when the date for the attack approached great care was taken to ensure that the Israelis would not notice that anything untoward was happening. The water-crossing equipment was hidden from view until as near as possible to the operation; special crates were constructed to house the equipment and hide it from inquisitive eyes; deep trenches were dug near the Canal into which the trucks drove with the equipment at night; even the movement of troops was co-ordinated in order to convince the Israelis that in fact some exercise was being carried out. For instance a brigade would move by day into the line along the Canal, carrying its equipment for crossing the Canal down to the water edge. At night only one battalion of that brigade would travel back from the Canal to the rear with full lights, creating the impression that on the completion of the training the entire force had withdrawn from the Canal.

As various problems arose in respect of the projected crossing, technical solutions were developed. It was assumed that the infantry would have to rely on its own devices for supplies during the first twelve to twenty-four hours: accordingly, each infantry soldier carried some 50 lb and at times 70 lb of weapons and ammunition. To help the infantry as they crossed the sand ramparts, a light, portable trailer on wheels was developed to be drawn by each soldier; in addition special light ladders were designed to enable them to scale the ramparts. All routes, approaches and units received distinguishing colours and coloured lights to avoid confusion at night: a driver, for instance, knew that all he had to do was follow his colour in order to remain with his unit. The planning and concentration of forces went on, with every problem being minutely examined, its solution being the subject of repeated training. No doubt was left in the minds of the officers and the men of the Egyptian Army that preparations for war were afoot. But so frequently had these exercises been carried out that the various statements promising action were viewed with a certain degree of scepticism by many of them.

The decision for the date of the attack was influenced by the fact that Arab support and world political backing for the Arab cause had reached a high point. There was little room for improvement and the next move therefore had to be a military one. The gradual erosion of Israel's position in Africa, the weakness of the leadership in Europe and the problems posed to the American administration by the Watergate affair combined to confirm Sadat in his view that this was the most advantageous time for action. The Egyptians also noted that the Israelis were by now heavily involved in their election campaign (elections to the Knesset were to take place at the end of October), which was absorbing most of the public attention in Israel. Furthermore, the Israelis would assume that Arab soldiers would not engage in military operations during the fast month of Ramadan, but 6 October – with a moonlit night during which the tide in the Suez Canal would be the most suitable for the operation – was also the Jewish fast day of Yom Kippur when alertness would be at its lowest level.

The attack was planned and prepared to the minutest degree. The general concept was based on two phases: the first phase would be the crossing of the Canal and consolidation to meet an Israeli counter-attack; the second phase would be the capture of the Mitla and Gidi passes. Considerable condemnation was expressed later of the failure of the Egyptian Army to carry out the second phase. It was the subject of bitter criticism on the part of Gen. Shazli against Sadat and Minister of War Ismail, but there is no doubt today that while the first phase was planned in every detail, the second was planned only in very broad terms. This tends to confirm the belief that the Egyptian aim was merely to gain a foothold on the east bank of the Canal in order to break the political impasse and enable the next phase to be a political one.

On 1 October the Supreme Council of the armed forces met President Sadat. To the twenty senior officers who were present Sadat said, 'I bear responsibility before history.' He appended his signature to the plan, approving the date of D day as the tenth day of Ramadan and also the plan's code name – 'The Spark'. As D day approached tension rose among the Arab military leaders on both fronts. By now Sadat had adopted a fatalistic attitude: he had made his decision and he would stick by it. It was going to be a costly one – he estimated that the crossing of the Canal would cost Egypt some 10,000 soldiers killed and he realized that his whole future was at stake. Mohammed Hassenein Heikal described a meeting with Sadat at his home in Al Gezira on Wednesday, 3 October, quoting him as follows:

It is October 3rd today and it is four in the afternoon. I believe that they will reveal our intention any moment from now and this is because our movement henceforth cannot leave any doubts in their minds as to our intentions. However whatever they do they cannot now catch up on us. Even if they know tonight, even if they decide to mobilize all their reserves and even if they think of launching a pre-emptive attack they have lost the chance to catch us up.

Sadat was basing this estimate on a careful study of the Israeli mobilization system over the years, which had led him to believe that it would be impossible for Israel to mobilize armoured formations and deploy along the Canal in less than seventy-two hours, just as it would not be possible for the entire mobilized strength of Israel to be deployed facing the Egyptian Army in under five to six days. But in assuming that the preparations which were now visible to the Israeli forces would lead it to mobilize, he overestimated his adversary.

The deception plan which was employed by the Egyptians to lull the Israelis into a sense of false security was based first and foremost on encouraging the 'concept' which the Israelis had openly adopted. And so from the outset a deception plan was worked out in great detail and developed parallel to the real plan when it moved into operation.

From January 1973 the Egyptian armed forces mobilized reservists for training and released them some twenty times; that year two major mobilization exercises of reservists released from regular service were carried out. At the end of September all three classes of reservists who had been released were mobilized, their mobilization orders including a specific instruction that they would be released by 8 October. As opposed to previous occasions – and this was noted in Israel – the civil defence organizations in Egypt and Syria were not activated, and again, as opposed to previous occasions, no atmosphere of imminent was was created. There was no attempt to prepare the population for war: indeed in his speech on the anniversary of President Nasser's death on 28 September, President Sadat ignored almost completely the question of Israel, the main theme on previous occasions. 'I have deliberately not broached the subject of the battle, because there has been enough talk. I only say that the liberation of the land as I have told you is the first and main task facing us. God willing we shall achieve this task.'

Sadat's well-conceived deception plan was designed to mislead not only the Israelis but the Americans as well. After his appointment as secretary of state, Dr Henry Kissinger called for meetings of the various Middle East foreign ministers in New York at the end of September and October. He first met most of the Arab foreign ministers collectively and with Mohammed Zayat, the Egyptian foreign minister, individually, to sound them out on whether or not they would welcome his good offices. After these meetings, Abba Eban, the Israeli foreign minister, met Dr Kissinger on 4 October. The reports he received about the situation along the borders were the same as those available in Israel: that the Egyptians were engaged in manœuvres while the Syrians had taken precautionary measures against possible Israeli attacks.

During the talk between Eban and Dr Kissinger, the question of an early war was disposed of in five minutes, both agreeing that each one's intelligence on the subject was of a reassuring character. The main point in the discussion was how to initiate the process of the negotiation. Kissinger reported that Zayat's reaction had been favourable and that he was prepared to come to Washington in November. Could Eban come too at the same time in order to work out the necessary procedures? They discussed the forthcoming Israeli elections, which would affect developments in the Middle East, and the meeting concluded with a reconfirmation that November would be a good time in which to meet, considering that, as Dr Kissinger put it at the end of the conversation, 'nothing dramatic can happen in October'. It is not clear to this day whether or not Zayat was deliberately misleading Kissinger during their meeting in the first week in October. He may have known of the planned campaign in general terms or he may not have known at all. Eban addressed the General Assembly of the United Nations on 3 October, speaking of Israel's readiness to negotiate and of territorial compromise. Zayat was marked down to address the Assembly on 4 October. For reasons that have never been explained, he cancelled his appearance and put himself down to speak on 11 October.

The main deception, however, was directed not only against Israel and the United States but against the Egyptian armed forces. In a survey carried out among the over 8,000 prisoners in Israeli hands, only one knew on 3 October that the preparations were for a real war; 95% learnt only on the morning of 6 October that the exercise in which they were engaged was in fact preparation for war and that they were about to *go* to war. The platoon of twenty assault boats in the 16th Brigade of the 16th Egyptian Infantry Division, under the command of Lieut. Abdul Laviv Ibrahim, realized that this was war only as they took their boats out of their crates and carried them down to the Canal in what they considered was part of the exercise, minutes before H hour. Of the eighteen Egyptian colonels and lieutenant-colonels in Israeli captivity, four knew on 4 October that war would break out, one was informed on 5 October and thirteen were told only on the morning of the actual day. One colonel described how at 2 o'clock on 6 October he was standing watching the Egyptian planes flying over the Third Army headquarters towards the Israeli lines. He turned to his brigadier and asked him, 'What's all this about?' 'Ask the general,' was the reply. He turned to where the general had been standing and saw him on his knees praying towards Mecca. This was his first intimation of war.

The Egyptian planners had succeeded in misleading not only the Israel Defence Forces and practically all the intelligence services in the West, but the bulk of the Egyptian Army as well!

4

Eyes Have They
But They See Not

THE NATIONAL INTELLIGENCE estimate in Israel is given by the director of Military Intelligence, since the latter is the only intelligence organization in the country with the necessary research and evaluation facilities for its preparation. The Military Intelligence Branch had grown over the years both in size and in scope, thwarting any attempt by the small research unit at the Foreign Office and by the Mossad, the Central Intelligence Collection Agency, to expand or to prepare an independent evaluation. It had produced a team of experts, soon acquiring a reputation for being the most effective intelligence service on the subject of the Middle East in the world. This was a well-earned reputation, for the organization and its personnel proved themselves time and again to be superior in their understanding of developments in the Middle East. With the growth of the number of aspects of intelligence affecting Israel throughout the world however, it soon found itself dealing with a wide gamut of subjects far beyond the realm of pure military intelligence.

Intelligence is the acquisition, collation and evaluation of information required for policy and decision making, but at no stage can or should an organization involved in such work be made responsible also for policy. In Israel however outside the military establishment there was no formal staff work in the process of decision making; there was no machinery at Cabinet level, in Parliament – or indeed in any other institution – which could achieve an evaluation of its own or check the evaluations presented by the military. Thus Military Intelligence was a vital and central factor in all decision making, although the final responsibility for evaluating the intentions of foreign governments rested at Cabinet level.

During the premiership of David Ben Gurion, officers in uniform did not appear before the Cabinet as a matter of principle. At these meetings and in the Foreign Affairs and Security Committee of the Knesset, Ben Gurion himself invariably presented the entire defence picture including intelligence. Although he was very careful about what he said to these bodies, he felt he required no partners since he accepted full personal responsibility.

When Gen. Dayan became minister of defence, he made it a matter of practice to be accompanied to the Cabinet and to the Foreign Affairs and Security Committee by the chief of staff and the director of Military Intelligence, a move that tended to eliminate the dividing line between ministerial and military responsibility. Soon these two uniformed officers began to appear at the Cabinet table as frequently as the ministers themselves. The standing of the director of intelligence, the enormous prestige of the minister of defence, no less than the fact that there was no other element in the country with the facilities or the capabilities for criticizing the Military Intelligence evaluation or bringing forward an alternative one, made the acceptance of their various estimates a foregone conclusion.

Following the ending of the War of Attrition in October 1970, the beginning of the cease-fire, the death of Nasser, the civil war in Jordan and ultimately the apparent removal of the Soviet advisers by Sadat a feeling developed in the Israeli defence establishment that a considerable period of time would elapse before the Arabs would be ready for war, a feeling that was strengthened by a lack of belief in Arab ability to wage a co-ordinated modern war and by a pervasive sense of satisfaction with the post-1967 *status quo*. Nevertheless, although a mixture of conceit and complacency tended to colour the evaluation of future developments in the area, the army continued to prepare for eventualities and adapted its planning to the general intelligence estimate that the Arabs would, by acquisition of medium-range bombers, be in a position to carry out their oft-proclaimed threat of war in 1975/6.

As time went on however and the social pressures in Israel increased, voices began to be heard urging a cut in the defence budget, particularly since it did not seem that war was around the corner. These pressures were resisted by Dayan to a great degree, although the defence budget was reduced by some 6 billion Israeli pounds for a period of five years in 1972. However, the leadership in the army, perhaps more than any other element, was aware of the danger surrounding the country. In June 1972 Maj.-Gen. Israel Tal, the vice chief of staff (acknowledged to be one of the outstanding experts on armour throughout the world), expressed the opinion that without a more dynamic political approach the Arabs would be bound to opt for military action because they would not be able to keep to the *status quo* for a long period of time. Indeed on a number of occasions between July and October 1972 Gen. Elazar had discussed the possibilities of an Egyptian attack across the Canal. He had maintained that the attack might occur at the beginning of 1973; but following the departure of the Soviets from Egypt he had changed his opinion, stating that while he did not believe the attack could happen early in 1973 he was of the opinion that it could well occur later in the year. He pointed to the presidential elections in the United States (in November 1972) as a turning point, believing that President Sadat would try to play East off against West after they had taken place (that is, early in 1973), but that as a result of frustration at his probable failure he could well decide to go to war in 1973.

On 16 April 1973 Maj.-Gen. Eli Zeira, director of Military Intelligence, later described by the Agranat Commission as 'a man of exceptionally high intellectual capabilities, who had vastly impressed both his superiors and his subordinates and was highly regarded by the government', presented the national intelligence estimate. At this time there were clear signs that the Egyptians were preparing for war in May: ground units were being moved to the Canal; during the whole of April and half of May some sixty-five tank ramps had been built along the Canal, while the main rampart along their front had been elevated to overlook the Israeli rampart; new openings had been prepared in the rampart and new descents to the water had been opened. The Egyptian civil defence was mobilized, blood donors were called for, a black-out was declared in the cities, bridges were protected and war declarations were issued while Sadat talked of the 'phase of total confrontation'. Notwithstanding these preparations, Israeli intelligence estimated that the probability of war was remote: the Egyptians had no answer to an Israeli air attack in depth; and although war *would* come at a later date, *this* time Sadat would, as was his wont, move to the brink and then withdraw. As we have seen Sadat had decided to postpone the attack until autumn, but this development, rather than acting as a warning that the attack had merely been postponed, only confirmed the intelligence estimate that Sadat would go so far before withdrawing.

Gen. Elazar however did not accept this estimate and called for partial mobilization, as noted earlier. In a number of public addresses at the time, he emphasized that while the possibility of war was low, the Israelis must take into consideration that the Egyptians were frustrated by the results of the Nixon–Brezhnev meeting and by the lack of any political advance; pressures were growing within Egypt and they could definitely constitute danger to peace.

Three possibilities faced Israel at this time: a sporadic outbreak of war, a war of attrition, or an all-out war. Elazar did not believe in the first two possibilities, considering the third as being the only probable one. As he saw it, the Egyptians would be interested in (1) renewing hostilities in order to break the *status quo* and to emphasize their unwillingness to accept the situation which had been created; (2) causing a maximum loss in life and property to Israel; (3) waging the war in such a manner that at its conclusion Egypt would have achieved an advance from a military point of view, however minimal. He felt that a few acres gained on the east bank of the Suez Canal or an advance of merely half a mile on the Golan Heights could satisfy the Arab war aims. On more than one occasion he estimated the possibility of a simultaneous mass attack by both the Egyptian and the Syrian forces.

Elazar was not the only senior officer who revealed a clear perception at the time of the possible developments in the area and who lived without any illusions about Arab intentions. During the same period Gen. Tal went on record to emphasize the importance of the oil weapon in the hands of the Arabs and to warn that in his view the advent of the surface-to-air missiles meant that the use of planes as a major delivery system would by the end of the 1970s be very limited. He also discussed at length the possible effect of a war on Israel's internal situation. On 21 May 1973 Minister of Defence Moshe Dayan issued guidelines to the General Staff, ordering it to prepare for war in the light of the threats coming from Egypt and Syria. In his directive he said, 'A renewal of war in the second half of summer must be taken into account.'

The Israeli defence concept was built on three major elements: advanced warning by Israeli intelligence of enemy movements that might indicate plans for hostile operations; the strength and capability of a standing army, together with an air force that was almost entirely a regular force, to block any development of a major thrust against Israel and hold the advancing enemy forces. Great emphasis was laid here on the role which the Israeli Air Force would play in this holding operation, while at the same time protecting the skies of Israel and enabling the third element, namely the rapid mobilization of reserves, to be carried out and their move to the front line effected efficiently and rapidly.

Israeli intelligence was in a good position to evaluate developments in the Arab world and had over the years developed an efficient collection system. Following Sadat's elevation to the presidency of Egypt there had been four periods of escalation in which it had noted major Egyptian mobilization and preparations to go to war. There had been numerous emergencies along the line and on every occasion the Israeli forces had invariably been strengthened and moved forward to the line in accordance with the operational plans existing at the time. A major mobilization involving the Egyptian home front however was less frequent.

The first major mobilization to take place during Sadat's period was at the end of the 'Year of Decision', in 1971, when the Egyptians planned a surprise bombing attack by fifty bombers on Sharm el-Sheikh (cancelled by Sadat because of the outbreak of the India–Pakistan war). During this alert there was a general mobilization of reserves, civilian vehicles and the civil defence in the cities; GHQ and all Egyptian field forces were engaged in manœuvres. General formations of tanks were advanced to the Suez Canal, as well as bridging and crossing equipment. Earth-moving activity took place along the water, positions were prepared for tanks and artillery, and the approaches to the Canal were opened up in the southern sector. The Egyptian media announced that war was inevitable, to the accompaniment of warlike statements by the leadership.

A year later a second major mobilization took place, during December 1972, when Sadat planned an operation in which a parachute brigade was to seize and hold territory in Sinai until the United Nations intervened. During this mobilization, too, manœuvres were held in the field forces, soldiers were returned from leave, work was stepped up on the ramps and fortifications along the Suez Canal, with the preparation of areas for the launching of crossing vehicles and bridging equipment, and a war atmosphere was created in the media. But neither the reserves nor the civil defence in the cities were mobilized; nor were ground units advanced to the Canal with their bridging and crossing equipment. The third and fourth periods of escalation and mobilization both took place in 1973 – in April–May and September–October.

Egyptian capability to attack Israel without advance warning existed – and indeed in the discussions which took place with members of the Cabinet in the days before the war, Gen. Zeira and his director of research, Brig.-Gen. Aryeh Shalev, acknowledged its existence, while indicating the low probability of its happening. The presence of the Egyptian Army in strength along the Canal was not in itself an indication of impending war, as this deployment had been in effect since 1969, nor, it was argued, were the signs of escalation a definitive signal, as three previous mobilizations had taken place since 1971 without the subsequent aggressive strike. The sole key to providing an advance warning now lay in the evaluation of Egyptian intention, which in effect meant estimating what the head of state in Egypt, President Sadat, might decide; and such a task could hardly be made the exclusive responsibility of the director of Military Intelligence. The mistake of all involved both in intelligence and at the policy-decision level, in the given circumstances of unusually heavy concentrations and escalation, was in not relating the simultaneous increase in capability in the north and in the south to Syrian and Egyptian intentions.

The Israeli intelligence community followed with interest the development of the major exercise in Egypt, while at the same time being somewhat concerned by the large concentration of forces in Syria, although all the indications were that Syria was simply nervous about a possible Israeli reaction to Syrian operations in retaliation for their shooting down of thirteen Syrian planes on 13 September. The assumption however was that there was no real danger from Syria because it would never attack on its own. All they saw as they looked towards Egypt, were preparations for an exercise, special precautions being taken for fear that an Israeli attack might be in the offing. There were numerous indicators that should have given rise to concern, but these were offset by perhaps twice the number of signs showing that there was no cause for alarm. Towards the end of September however information was received from various sources indicating that the Egyptians were preparing for an all-out war. In many cases the intelligence material went into details of various developments about to occur. But when these did in fact occur, they were ignored.

With the commencement of the Egyptian manœuvres, the Israeli forces along the Suez Canal noted an increased degree of activity. A growing stream of information about the Egyptian preparations along the Canal began to flow back daily from their positions. Lieut. David Abu Dirham, commanding one of the most northerly fortifications, Orkal B, some 5 miles south of Port Fuad, reported that a ship was unloading artillery, equipment and ammunition at the port. Reports came in of artillery being moved into forward positions, unoccupied surface-to-air and surface-to-surface missile positions being occupied, minefields being cleared along the Canal and Egyptian soldiers diving into the water to blow up underwater mines. The reports described improvement works on the various descents to the water, earth-moving activity, preparation of areas for crossing and for bridges and pontoons. However, as the Egyptians cleared mines at seventy points along the Canal, they laid them at others; some descents to the water were opened, others were closed. On the other hand the normal daily routine – both of soldiers and of civilians – continued without any change: Egyptian soldiers continued to fish and to wander along the banks of the Canal without helmets; civilians continued their work as if nothing untoward were happening.

As the Egyptian exercise began, the armoured division of Maj.-Gen. Avraham ('Albert') Mandler, comprising some 280 tanks, was placed on alert along the Canal. Southern Command headquarters issued instructions to ensure that all standing orders for such an alert were carried out. All mobilization systems were checked. Leaves were cancelled. Maj-.Gen. Shmuel Gonen, GOC Southern Command, who had assumed the post less than three months earlier, visited the Canal on 2 October and issued a number of orders to ensure a higher state of alert. He asked for permission to take a number of precautionary steps, but some of his requests were turned down. Orders were issued to increase guards and security around all camps in Sinai and to ensure that Operation 'Shovach Yonim', which would come into operation should the enemy move – and which had not been tested for some time – was familiar to all forces. Orders were also issued to accelerate the assembly of a preconstructed bridge – to be used in the event of an Israeli crossing of the Canal – and to place ambushes along the rampart.

On 4 October Gonen attended a General Staff meeting, which was devoted entirely to the subject of discipline in the armed forces. From Tel Aviv he travelled to Haifa, where at 1 o'clock on the morning of the 5th his command intelligence officer, Lieut.-Col. David Gedaliah, called to advise him that that night the Egyptians had worked on the ramparts until 10 o'clock.

On 7 October Albert Mandler was due to be replaced by Brig.-Gen. Kalman Magen as commander of the division holding the line along the Suez. And throughout that week the various units had been taking leave of their general. In the event Mandler did not take leave of the troops but instead made a valedictory speech in which he talked about the importance of preparedness and about the fact that he felt that war was imminent. On Friday, 5 October, with Southern Command and Mandler's division busy checking preparedness and issuing last-minute instructions, Albert met Magen, an officer with a considerable amount of combat experience, who had just completed his tour of duty as commandant of the Command and General Staff School and had returned but a few days before from a trip abroad. As the two officers discussed the transfer of command due to take place on Sunday, it became clear that it would be postponed. Brig.-Gen. Pino, Albert's deputy, very disturbed by the continuous flow of reports from the front line, suggested that Albert order all the forces out of the camps and move them forward to take up their positions in accordance with the emergency plans of 'Shovach Yonim'. But while Magen was all for it, Albert said that it was not possible: all the instructions they had been receiving were that on no account were they to arouse any suspicion on the part of the Egyptians; they were not to carry out moves that might lead to a general escalation along the front. In fact Albert had been of the clear opinion that war was imminent from Wednesday, 3 October. In order to emphasize the situation as he saw it, the division sent urgent cables to Southern Command describing every indication of preparations for war on the Egyptian side, while every evening sending a complete daily summary of all the activity noted.

According to the Agranat Commission's report, on 1 October, Lieut. Benjamin Siman Tov, the order of battle officer in Southern Command intelligence, had submitted a document to Lieut-Col. David Gedaliah, intelligence officer of Southern Command, analysing the deployment on the Egyptian side as an indication of preparations to go to war, the exercise notwithstanding.

Again on 3 October he submitted a further document pointing out a number of factors that indicated the exercise might be a cover-up for preparations for war. Gedaliah did not distribute this junior officer's evaluation, and it was omitted from the Southern Command intelligence report. In fact the director of Military Intelligence, Gen. Zeira, did not learn about Siman Tov's evaluation until March 1974, during the Agranat Commission hearings (whereupon he invited Siman Tov, who had been removed from Southern Command intelligence, to his office, heard his story and promoted him to the rank of captain).

On 5 October the division requested reinforcements, which were to include additional troops to the strongpoints along the Canal and forces for deployment in the passes some 20 miles east of it. In reply they received a signal from Southern Command headquarters, repeating a signal from GHQ, to the effect that the Egyptian exercise was nearing its conclusion and would soon be over.

Meanwhile Soviet broadcasts emphasized that the Israeli concentrations along the Syrian border were there with the intention of attacking Syria; Israeli intelligence estimated that Syrian apprehension as to the possibility of an Israeli attack had grown in the past twenty-four hours, and that the Syrian deployment was a result of their belief that for political reasons – caused by Israel's growing isolation in the world and the increased co-operation between the front-line Arab countries – Israel might launch a pre-emptive attack against Syria. Similarly, Egyptian fears of an Israeli attack were also emphasized, as was the fact that for the first time since the War of Attrition a major naval exercise in both the Mediterranean and the Red Sea was taking place.

At dawn on 5 October it was noted that the Egyptian Army along the Suez had reached a degree of emergency deployment and dispositions such as had never been observed previously by the IDF. An addition of 56 batteries of artillery, bringing the total in the forward areas up to 194, was noted. Furthermore, it was reported that all five infantry divisions were fully deployed, that all five concentration areas for bridging and crossing equipment were partially filled up and that the ramps prepared on the sand ramparts enabling tanks to fire into Sinai were occupied by platoons of tanks along the entire Canal. Mobile GSP pontoon units were identified and the move forward of additional concentrations of forces to the rear areas noticed. Reading all the various indications, the senior intelligence officer of the Israeli Navy expressed the opinion to his commanding officer early in the week that war was imminent. His appreciation was not accepted by GHQ.

On 30 September the situation had been discussed at GHQ. Gen. Tal expressed grave reservations about the soothing intelligence estimate, while Gen. Zeira maintained that the probability of war was low, explaining that the Syrian concentrations were related to the 13 September incident, when Syrian planes were shot down by Israeli planes, and that the Egyptians were simply preparing for a major exercise. But Tal was disturbed and invited Zeira and Shalev to a meeting in which he again maintained that he did not accept their evaluation. They, however, did not accept his approach.

There was one other element in the Middle East which provided indications of imminent war, involved as it was in the military developments in the area, namely the Soviet Union. Three days before the war a Soviet reconnaissance satellite was launched and proceeded to fly over areas of Sinai, the Suez Canal and the Syrian–Israeli border area in addition to the area of the Galilee. Each day its path was altered in order to take in the different sectors of Israel's two front lines.

On Wednesday morning, 3 October, President Sadat summoned the Soviet ambassador, Vinogradoff. At approximately the same time President Assad summoned the Soviet ambassador in Damascus to meet him. The two presidents indicated to the ambassadors that war was imminent, without entering into details.

On 4 October units of the Soviet fleet stationed in Alexandria and Port Said began to move out. This mass exodus strengthened the suspicions of Israeli naval intelligence. In the meantime information was received of the arrival of giant Antonov 22 Soviet planes in Cairo and Damascus and the evacuation by air of the Soviet families stationed there. The explanation of all these Soviet moves by Israeli intelligence was: either they indicated a knowledge on the part of the Soviets that war was about to break out (and the evacuation and naval withdrawal might be a Soviet move designed to deter the Egyptians from such an action, since at the end of the 'Year of Decision' in 1971, during a previous general mobilization in Egypt, Soviet vessels had evacuated the port of Port Said); or it might be that the Egyptians, together with the Syrians, had finally decided to liquidate Soviet presence in Egypt, although this did not seem very feasible.

On Saturday, 29 September two Palestinian gunmen held up at the Czech–Austrian border a train carrying Russian Jews from Moscow to Vienna. They took as hostages five Jews and an Austrian customs official and demanded facilities to fly themselves and the hostages to an Arab country. In the course of the negotiations, Bruno Kreisky, Austria's chancellor, himself a Jew, initiated a proposal to close the transit centre for Jewish immigrants in Schonau Castle near Vienna. The hostages were released and the gunmen were set free. Israel was horrified and outraged and the event dominated all the media. The Israeli Government became completely absorbed in this problem. Mrs Meir flew as scheduled to Strasbourg to address the Council of Europe and then, despite the misgivings of some of her Cabinet members, she flew to Vienna in an abortive attempt to persuade Kreisky to reconsider his decision. She returned to Israel on Wednesday, 3 October, and immediately convened a Cabinet meeting.

It is not clear to this day whether or not this operation was part of the general deception plan in order to divert Israel's attention from developments along the front. The operation was carried out by a little-known Palestinian terrorist organization but the fact that it was linked to Saika, the Palestinian guerrilla organization controlled by the Syrian Army, lends credence to the assumption that the operation was part of the general deception plan. However, whether or not it was planned, the operation certainly did contribute towards diverting government and public attention from the ominous developments along the northern and southern borders of Israel.

The Syrian situation was revealed to Mr Zeev Sharef, the Israeli minister of housing, during his visit to the Golan Heights on Wednesday, 3 October, to inaugurate a number of housing projects which had been constructed by his ministry. At the ceremonies he conversed with Gen. Hofi, GOC Northern Command, and learnt how concerned he was about the unparalleled Syrian military build-up along the front line. In the midst of his tour he was called back to Tel Aviv to a Cabinet meeting following Mrs Meir's return from Vienna to hear a full report on her discussions with Chancellor Kreisky. Not a word was said to the Cabinet about the military situation along the two frontiers however.

Before the Cabinet proper assembled, Mrs Meir's 'Kitchen Cabinet' attended a meeting which lasted over two hours in order to discuss the disturbing developments along the borders. Present at the meeting were Mrs Meir, Deputy Prime Minister Yigael Allon, Minister of Defence Moshe Dayan, Minister without Portfolio Yisrael Galili, Chief of Staff Elazar and Chief of Intelligence Research Shalev (Director of Intelligence Zeira was ill at home). Brig. Shalev presented a detailed picture of the developments along the borders, enumerating the capabilities of the enemy forces. On a number of occasions Mrs Meir asked him whether the Arab armies would be capable of launching an attack from their present dispositions. The reply was in the affirmative. For some two hours the 'Kitchen Cabinet' concentrated its discussions on the possible intentions of the Arab leadership in the light of this news. They recalled that in May intelligence had asserted that the likelihood of the Arabs going to war was not very probable. At that time the chief of staff had thought differently, although the intelligence evaluation had proved to be the correct one; this time he agreed with the intelligence evaluation that an attack was unlikely. The meeting broke up with the conclusion that the military concentrations described to them did not indicate an imminent war. It was agreed to report on the situation to the regular Cabinet meeting on Sunday, 7 October.

On Thursday evening Gen. Zeira brought the news of the evacuation of Soviet families from Egypt and Syria to the chief of staff; Zeira had been away ill for two days and this new information gave him an uncomfortable feeling.

Early on Friday morning military correspondents of the Israeli press were briefed not to exaggerate the reports coming from abroad about large Arab concentrations along the borders and to indicate that the Israel Defence Forces were taking all necessary steps in the light of the developments. That same morning however Gen. Elazar decided on a 'C' state of alert, the highest state of alert in the standing army; it was the first time that he had declared such a state of alert since he had been chief of staff.

At the same time a conference was held with the minister of defence. Gen. Zeira described the Soviet airlift, reflecting that this could indicate a final break between the Arabs and the Soviet Union, although he did not consider this as very probable. He went on to say that the Soviets were obviously aware of the fact that the possibility of a conflagration existed; it may be that they had accepted the Arab claim that Israel was about to launch an attack, which they had incidentally echoed in their broadcasts. This however seemed unlikely, because in such a case the Soviets would doubtless have approached the Americans, who in turn would have made approaches to Israel counselling moderation. There had been no American approaches, so therefore, Zeira concluded, it was conceivable that the Soviets were aware of the possibility of an Arab attack and feared for their families in the consequences of an Israeli counter-attack. Nevertheless the feeling of intelligence was that the probability of an Arab attack was very low.

The meeting broke up and moved over to the prime minister's office, where the situation was explained to Mrs Meir with the help of air photographs that showed the heavy concentrations along the front lines. The state of alert that had been announced in the armed forces was confirmed and it was decided to put the reserve mobilization centres on alert; Dayan expressed satisfaction with the preparedness moves taken by Elazar. In the face of this situation Mrs Meir decided to call a Cabinet meeting – it was Yom Kippur eve. Most of the ministers had already left for home throughout the country (seven of them lived in Jerusalem, one in Haifa, others had returned to their kibbutzim). In order not to disturb those who had already left for home, it was decided to convene only the Tel Aviv-based ministers. The failure to invite those from Jerusalem, but one hour's drive away, was later to be the subject of much cynical comment by those not invited.

At the meeting the ministers were put into the full picture. Twice in the course of his talk the chief of staff emphasized that the Arab deployment could mean either attack or defence; during his presentation Gen. Zeira emphasized this point three times. The intelligence estimate was that the probability of war was low. It was known that while ten days earlier the Americans were of the opinion that war was inevitable, their opinion now was the same as that of Israeli intelligence. The ministers were advised that the army had been placed on a full 'C' alert. During the meeting Gen. Bar-Lev sent a note to the chief of staff asking him how many tanks were deployed, receiving the reply: 300 in the south and 200 in the north. After questions were asked by the Cabinet, and detailed replies given by the director of Military Intelligence, all ministers were asked to indicate where they could be found during Yom Kippur. On the way 'out Galili turned to Shimon Peres, minister of transportation and communications, 'What do you think?' Peres replied, 'It looks as if there is going to be a war.'

Gen. Elazar had all along been convinced that he could expect adequate warning for mobilization from Military Intelligence, and an evaluation of the information that poured in during the fateful days of the first week in October vindicates his assumption. Yet after the war he was to maintain that a considerable amount of material indicating the probability of war had *not* reached him. There were, according to Elazar's testimony before the Agranat Commission, items of information on Friday morning indicating the imminence of war, yet these had not reached him until Saturday morning. Had he received this information, he maintained he would have mobilized on Friday morning. Even on Friday he still considered that he would receive adequate warning in the event of war, although two days previously, on 3 October, he had addressed the editors of the Israeli press who asked him if the regular forces would be adequate to deal with the attack should war break out. He answered that they would not; at best together with the Air Force they could prevent a collapse in the event of a complete surprise, but it was generally assumed that Israel would have adequate warning in which to mobilize the reserves.

From Thursday evening Zeira was torn by doubts, but he invariably comforted himself with the knowledge that the standing army was on alert and that its strength was considered sufficient by GHQ to be able to withstand an initial assault. In this he saw an additional insurance policy as far as the intelligence warning was concerned. On Friday, 5 October, a meeting of the General Staff took place. The intelligence picture was again presented, but the probability of war breaking out was regarded as 'the lowest of the low'. A staff conference at Southern Command which took place at 3.30 pm reviewed all the preparations which had been made and discussed all the relevant operational plans. It was decided that on the next day, half of the staff would visit the Suez front, while the other half visited other parts of the command.

That night the political and military leaders of Israel went to sleep with an uneasy feeling, but few dreamt that the country was facing an imminent attack. Had they been able to overcome their preconceived notions in time, the entire history of the next few days would have been very different.

At 4 o'clock on the morning of 6 October the strident buzz of the telephone ringing by his bedside awoke Gen. Zeira. He listened to the voice at the other end and immediately dialled three numbers, one after the other, waking the minister of defence, the chief of staff and the vice chief of staff (Gen. Tal). He recounted the information he had received – that war would break out that evening on both fronts towards sundown. Within half an hour they all met at GHQ. Somewhere along the intelligence pipeline information that the attack would take place at sunset turned into an estimate that the attack was scheduled for about 6.00 pm. This hour was soon to be given as definite.

Gen. Elazar put down his phone and immediately telephoned to Gen. Benjamin Peled, the commander of the Air Force, asking him how soon a pre-emptive attack could be launched. Peled replied, 'If you tell me go ahead now we can be ready by 11 o'clock.' Elazar decided to launch an attack against the Syrian missile system and the Syrian airfields, feeling that by so doing he would take the Syrians by surprise, disrupt their attack and thus ensure close support for his ground forces. At 5.00 am he held the first meeting with Gen. Tal and Gen. Peled and issued instructions to prepare for mobilization of reservest deployment along the front and in depth, activation of civil defence, evacuation of the villages in the Golan and preparation for a pre-emptive strike. At 5.30 he issued orders to the branch chiefs and the commanders of the Air Force and the Navy.

At 5.50 am the first meeting took place in Dayan's office. Elazar proposed general mobilization and a pre-emptive strike by the Air Force against Syria. Dayan turned down his proposal for such a strike and a discussion took place about the mobilization of reserves. At first Dayan was inclined to authorize the mobilization of only one brigade for Northern Command. He then agreed to a brigade for Southern Command, finally consenting to the mobilization of a division for each command. But although Elazar pressed for a total mobilization of the fighting forces, insisting that it was essential to mobilize forces which could undertake an immediate counter-attack, Dayan insisted on a mobilization solely for defensive purposes. Elazar maintained that it was impossible to distinguish between defence and counter-attack, asserting that the timing of the counter-attack was an integral function of defence. Dayan decided to bring the matter to the prime minister for decision, saying, 'I will suggest to Golda that we mobilize 50,000 men.' Elazar objected and insisted that his proposal for a general mobilization too be presented. Dayan agreed to bring before her both sets of proposals. Despite his difference of opinion with the minister of defence,

Elazar issued orders for the mobilization of several thousands of reserves for the ground force and the Air Force, whose mobilization was considered absolutely essential.

Orders had in the meantime been issued to the GOCs Northern and Southern Command to rush by plane to Tel Aviv. At 7.15 am Gen. Elazar held a chief of staff's conference with the GOCs Northern and Southern Command present. He issued general instructions for war, emphasizing that the first phase would be the holding operation and that all forces must be ready to move over to a counter-attack as early as possible. He recapitulated the various operational plans for defence and attack and pointed out that the basic military concept of the IDF was to move over to a counter-attack within two days. He ordered the GOCs to fly back to their commands, issue instructions and return at midday so he could review their preparations for war. He advised the conference that he had asked for a general mobilization of reserves, but because the minister of defence opposed it, the matter was to be decided by the prime minister.

Gonen telephoned Albert and his chief of operations in Southern Command from Tel Aviv, issuing rapid instructions: no moves were to be made which might arouse the suspicions of the Egyptians and lead to an escalation. War was expected at 6 o'clock in the evening and he suggested that Albert's forces be moved so that by 5.00 in the evening they would be in position according to the 'Shovach Yonim' plan for defence. When Albert suggested that this was cutting it too fine, they agreed for the forces to be in position by 4 o'clock. Albert returned to the orders group, over which he was presiding with the brigade commanders, and repeated the orders he had received.

The meeting in the prime minister's office took place at 8.00 in the morning. Present were Mrs Meir, Dayan, Galili, Elazar, Zeira, Gen. Zvi Zur (assistant to the minister of defence) and the various *chefs de bureaux* (Deputy Prime Minister Allon arrived in the middle of the meeting). Elazar and Dayan presented their respective stands, the latter continuing to oppose the general mobilization. 'If you want to accept his proposal I will not prostrate myself on the road and I will not resign; but you might as well know that it is superfluous,' he said to Mrs Meir. The meeting concluded with a compromise in which Elazar was authorized to mobilize 100,000 men. (He took advantage of this authorization to issue mobilization orders for a much larger number of troops.) The prime minister accepted Dayan's stand on a pre-emptive attack and turned down Elazar's request.

After approval had been given for mobilization, Gen. Tal issued special orders, feeling that those present were not taking seriously the danger of war and that they were unaware of the urgency of the situation. He emphasized that Israel was facing a surprise attack, that the forward-line troops would be subject to a massive artillery bombardment and to heavy tank and infantry attacks; they would call for help, while the main strength of the Israel Defence Forces would not yet be ready. It was therefore essential, in his view, that the army revolutionize its thinking immediately: it would not be possible to carry out conventional mobilization by divisions and brigades; the problem now would be to send isolated platoons and companies of tanks and other units as rapidly as possible to the two fronts, directly to the firing line. Improvisation would be essential in order to deal with local conflagrations.

At midday the members of the Cabinet were assembled from synagogues and from their homes. In the Cabinet room, attended by the chief of staff and the director of intelligence, Mrs Meir detailed the information which had been received about the probability of war breaking out that afternoon. She recounted her undertaking to Ambassador Kenneth Keating of the United States earlier that morning – that there would be no pre-emptive strike on the part of Israel – and advised the Cabinet that mobilization of the reserves had commenced at 10.00 that morning. According to one report, Minister of Justice J. Shapira asked, 'What will happen if the enemy attacks before 6.00 in the evening?' To this Minister of Defence Dayan is reputed to have replied: 'This is the most relevant question to be asked at this meeting.' To Minister of Trade and Industry Chaim Bar-Lev, H hour at 6 o'clock made no sense: this could be a mistake, for, after all, the information also referred to an air attack. But the reply he received was, 'No, it will definitely be at 6 o'clock.'

A discussion developed during which the Cabinet was assured that the steps taken to deal with the attack would be adequate in order to hold it before developing the counter-attack. In the midst of the discussion, at 1.55, Brig.-Gen. Israel Leor, Mrs Meir's military secretary, opened the door suddenly and announced, 'The news is that war has begun.' The wailing of the air raid sirens suddenly brought home to all that Israel was once again fighting for its existence.

That evening Mrs Meir broadcast to the nation: 'For a number of days our intelligence services have known that the armies of Egypt and Syria were deployed for a co-ordinated attack on Israel.... Our forces were deployed according to plan to meet the impending danger....'

5

Like a Wolf on the Fold

THE GOLAN HEIGHTS were occupied by Israeli forces in the last two days of fighting in the Six Day War, on 9 and 10 June 1967, when, in a battle that was soon to be acknowledged as a classic in warfare, the Israel Defence Forces launched a head-on attack against the Syrian-held positions on the plateau which menaced Israeli settlements in the valley below. The entire area of the Golan Heights had been converted by the Syrians in the 1950s and 60s into one large network of military positions and from their seemingly impenetrable fortifications the Syrian forces over the years mounted harassing operations against Jewish settlements in northern Israel. In the 1960s by use of the Golan terrain the Syrians attempted to divert the headwaters of the Jordan River from Israel and thus deprive Israeli agriculture of its main source of water. During the ensuing fighting almost the entire local population took to flight (together with the Syrian Army after it broke ranks and retreated in the face of the Israeli onslaught), with the exception of some 7,000 Druse inhabitants who remained and continued to live under Israeli administration.

The Golan Heights border on the upper Jordan Rift Valley of the Sea of Galilee in the west, on the Yarmouk Valley in the south, on the Ruqqad stream in the east and on the Hermon massif in the north. The total area is 480 square miles. The Golan plateau rises gently from south to north from 600 feet to 3,000 feet, its abrupt escarpments dominating the Rift Valley to the west and to the south. The chief characteristics of its topography were created through volcanic activity with lava pouring out from fissures and craters and covering the plateau with a continuous layer of basalt. Volcanic cones, or *tels*, which stand out like so many giant ant hills, dominate the lava-covered plateau.

A limited number of routes lead up from the Jordan Valley in Israel to the escarpment of the Golan Heights. The main approach is that rising from Zemach to El Al on two roads, one via El Hamma and the second via Ein Gev–Givat Yoav known as the Gamla Rise, which continues north-east through Ramat Magshimim and Juhader to the Rafid crossroads, thence north to Kuneitra where it joins the Kuneitra–Damascus road. A second route is that leading from the so-called Arik Bridge, which crosses the Jordan River near the confluence of the river with the Sea of Galilee in the Buteiha Valley. This road rises through Yehudia and Kuzabia, at which point it diverges, leading northwards to the Nafekh crossroads on the main Kuneitra–Damascus road or by a second-class road to the area of Hushniyah. The main historic route connecting the northern Galilee with Damascus crosses the River Jordan at the Bnot Ya'akov Bridge, whence the road rises steeply up the escarpment to the upper Syrian customs house and then via the Nafekh crossroads to Kuneitra on the main road to Damascus. To the north a road from Kibbutz Gonen climbs the escarpment to the Wasset crossroads, passing Kuneitra to the north and proceeding along the main road to Damascus, or turning left north of Kuneitra and leading to the Druse village of Masadah on the road to Mount Hermon. The northernmost route rises through the foothills of the Hermon from the source of the Dan River, a tributary of the Jordan, to Masadah and thence north to the heights of the Hermon or south to Kuneitra.

Two main routes running from south to north in a north-westerly direction cross all the east–west routes. The most easterly leads from the Rafid crossroads in the south, northwards through Kuneitra to Masadah and the Hermon heights. West of this route is the Tapline route, which accompanies TAP, the world's longest oil pipeline (which starts its journey in Bahrein in the Persian Gulf and crosses a distance of nearly 1,200 miles from Saudi Arabia through Jordan and Syria to the Lebanon) for 20 miles across the Golan Heights from the area of Juhader past the Nafekh crossroads and thence north to the Lebanese border.

The Israeli front line was divided from the Syrian front line by an area of no-man's land (some $\frac{1}{2}$–1 mile in width along most of its length) in which United Nations observers manned observation points along the main routes. The 'Purple Line' – the cease-fire line established between Syria and Israel on 10 June 1967 – held by Israel is a good military line, sited as it is for some considerable distance along a watershed. To the east the terrain falls away to the Syrian valley, affording good command over it for observation and fire, while in the south it is bordered by the Ruqqad escarpment falling down to the

Yarmouk River valley. Many of the volcanic hills dotted about the flat, basalt-black plateau, such as Mount Avital (3,970 feet), Hermonit (3,996 feet) or Tel Faris (3,989 feet), comprised an integral part of Israel's defence system along the 'Purple Line'. The position on Mount Hermon in the north afforded a good measure of observation, but above all it was of particular importance as an electronic observation post. And indeed, after the so-called 'Israeli' Hermon position was taken by the Israelis in 1967, the Syrians established a new position on a peak overlooking that held by the Israelis.

In 1972 Maj.-Gen. Yitzhak Hofi was appointed general officer commanding Northern Command in succession to Maj.-Gen. Mordechai Gur who was appointed Israeli defence attaché in Washington. Hofi, a squat, quietly spoken almost dour man, with a quiet authority born of years of leadership by example, was not a man given to many words. He had gained his laurels in the border fighting over the years and was one of the group of leaders who became household words to generations of young Israelis, known affectionately by his nickname 'Hacka'. In analysing the military problem posed to him by his new command, Hofi realized that the main difficulty, not present on any other Israeli border, was that the Israeli and Syrian armies were facing each other on an open plain eyeball to eyeball without any physical obstacle between them to delay the advance of an invading army. This was a situation considered desirable in terms of Soviet doctrine, which the Syrian Army had espoused, where an army is contemplating mounting an attack.

During the greater part of the year the Syrians maintained a fully mobilized army on an emergency footing – alerted, ready to go to war and concentrated in the area stretching from the cease-fire line back to Damascus. The main bulk of their forces was constantly in alert positions, and a cutting down of forces or a thinning out of the line was the exception to the rule, although the Syrians did thin it out during the winter when the heavy snows and rains turned the soil into a morass of mud, rendering it impassable at times even for armoured vehicles. On such occasions part of the Syrian forces would move to the area east of Damascus to train.

The Syrian Air Force, unlike its Egyptian counterpart, was not obliged to alter any of its bases after the Six Day War. Accordingly, the warning period available to Israel in the event of a Syrian air attack had not changed since then, nor had the potential danger to the civilian population. In addition the FROG (Free Rocket Over Ground) Battlefield Support Missiles (with a range of up to 55 miles) supplied by the Soviets to Syria were near enough to engage urban centres of population in Israel. A further consideration was that the Golan Heights had been settled by some fifteen Israeli civilian settlements; furthermore the Huleh Valley settlements in Israel remained within range of Syrian artillery, a situation that had been eliminated on most of Israel's other borders by the Six Day War. Above all, the defensive system of the Syrians was constructed in such a manner that they could at any time deploy for attack without much moving of forces and, indeed, without much warning.

The basic Israeli concept was to hold the line with the comparatively small forces of the standing army, basing defensive operations on massive support from the Air Force while giving time for the reserves to mobilize. The system of fortifications constructed along the line was backed by a mobile armoured force. These positions were solidly built and constructed to be able to withstand considerable punishment. There were seventeen such fortified positions south from the Hermon, manned by an average of fifteen soldiers each. They were well protected by mines and wire obstacles and were organized as fighting hedgehogs with their own infantry support weapons. Behind each a platoon of tanks was sited. The entire system was designed to deal with major outbreaks of artillery and tank fire and to act as a warning and blocking force in the event of an attack. A brigade district was responsible for the line, and with the commencement of hostilities Brig.-Gen. 'Raful' Eytan was put in charge of all forces on the Golan. As has been stated, the overall Israeli defence system was based on an assumption of advance intelligence warning, which would allow for mobilization of reserves in time and enable the forces assigned to the Golan to be in a position to meet any attack. This would have created the traditional ratio between Israeli and Arab forces over the years, roughly $2\frac{1}{2}$–3 : 1 in favour of the Arabs, a ratio with which the Israeli Command believed it could live.

In the winter of 1972–3, following activities by Palestinian terrorists on Israeli territory and in Europe, terrorist camps were attacked by the Israel Defence Forces, and particularly by the Air Force which was in constant action during the major outbreaks of fighting that winter. It inflicted such heavy casualties and such damage that soon the Syrians began to construct a missile system for surface-to-air defence. True, it was but a beginning, but the appreciation that the construction of such a missile system might limit the effectiveness of the Air Force on which the defence concept of Israel was based began to concern Gen. Hofi. The troops on the Golan were involved in a series of bitter fire fights – these 'battle days' continuing from October 1972 to January 1973, when they abruptly came to an end. The Israeli Command confidently believed that the punishment inflicted on the Syrians had had its effect, although in fact the real reason for the subsequent curbing of activities by the Syrians along their border was the visit of Gen. Ahmed Ismail, the Egyptian minister of war, to Damascus and the decision taken at the talks there in favour of war in principle.

During the years 1972–3 Northern Command undertook a major infrastructure development; new roads were built, hundreds of miles of unpaved tracks were constructed in order to facilitate the deployment of artillery and the movement of tanks. On Gen. Raful Eytan's suggestion the mobilization centres of the tank brigades designed to defend the Golan Heights were advanced from removed areas and brought near the Heights. (Exercises revealed that the mobilization period required had been halved as a result of these preparations.) Hofi put all the brigades in the command through exercises in order to gauge the exact periods of time required to move along the various axes which had been built to the front line. The improvements undertaken by the command, particularly those following the major incidents in the winter of 1972–3, included the improvement and lengthening of an anti-tank ditch along the 'Purple Line' designed to slow down any enemy advance and to channel such advances as might be made into armoured killing-grounds planned beforehand. A series of tank positions and ramps, which were to prove their value during the fighting, were built to enable the tanks to cover the anti-tank obstacle by fire.

The fighting along the border in the winter gave Northern Command an opportunity to learn certain lessons and to draw conclusions. In all the pitched tank battles which took place, practically all the Syrian tanks which were deployed were hit by Israeli tanks. In the second major flare-up which took place the Syrians introduced the use of Sagger anti-tank missiles and succeeded in putting a number of Israeli tanks out of action. The lessons were quickly learnt. Mortars were allocated to the armoured forces to deal with the Syrian infantry operating these missiles. This and other steps proved to be successful: in fact there were practically no missile hits in the third and final flare-up in the winter, despire the fact that large quantities were fired (thick bunches of missile guiding wires were found clustered around the Israeli positions).

Thus, with the line quiet after the winter fighting, the Golan was held by the Brigade District, with two infantry battalions in the line supported by four artillery batteries and backed by the Barak Tank Brigade with one battalion in the line and one battalion behind the line in training.

After the 1967 war the Syrian Army had also drawn conclusions and had begun to apply the lessons they had learnt in the war, developing a highly concentrated system of anti-tank defence from the 'Purple Line' right back to Damascus. They carried out a series of large-scale exercises, which culminated in a major exercise that was an exact replica of the Yom Kippur War attack. Israeli observation noted that Syrian training concentrated on the subjects of bridging anti-tank ditches, breaching obstacles and minefields, and making a major breakthrough. It became quite clear that the entire infantry force of the Syrian Army in fact constituted one large anti-tank obstacle. Much information was available on the missile systems in use, and Syrian positions designed to block penetration by the Israelis hinged all along the front line on static T34 tanks in built-in positions. All this, in addition to heavy concentrations of 57mm and 85 mm anti-tank guns, dual-purpose 100mm guns deployed all along the line in massive fortifications and anti-tank weapons in all the units from the RPG bazooka-type anti-tank weapon at platoon level to the Sagger anti-tank missiles at brigade level.

Early in the summer of 1973, the Syrians began to thin out their forces in the line – a reversal of the normal practice which called for a thickening of the line in the summer months. The 800 tanks facing approximately 60 Israeli tanks in the line were reduced to 400, and the 80 artillery batteries, facing some 4 Israeli ones, dropped to 40. On 11 September however air photographs revealed a thickening up of the line, bringing the force up to 550 tanks (an additional 150 tanks) and 69 batteries of artillery.

On 13 September an Israeli air patrol flying over the eastern Mediterranean in the area of the Syrian port of Latakia tangled with Syrian fighters which attempted an ambush. In the ensuing dog fights thirteen Syrian MIG fighter planes were shot down for the loss of one Israeli plane whose pilot was saved. Conscious of the fact, from long experience, that such action could not go unanswered by the Syrians, Northern Command took emergency precautions.

On 24 September Gen. Hofi attended a meeting of the General Staff at which an evaluation of the situation along the borders was being presented by the chief of intelligence and his aides. When he left the command to go to Tel Aviv he had with him the results of that morning's air reconnaissance. This time the air photographs revealed that the Syrians were already deployed in emergency dispositions with three infantry divisions in the line, each with two infantry brigades forward, together with the organic tank brigade and the mechanized brigade of the division. The force had risen to 670 tanks and 100 batteries of artillery – roughly the maximum force the Syrians had reached in previous emergencies. At the General Staff meeting Hofi raised the question of the situation along the northern front and pointed out that there seemed to be no chance that he would receive a warning in the event of an attack. Minister of Defence Dayan, who was present at this meeting, was clearly disturbed by Hofi's remarks and asked the chief of staff for information as to what was being done in this respect. He talked about the importance of constructing an artificial obstacle and was told about the minefields which were being laid along the anti-tank ditch.

On the eve of Rosh Hashanah, the Jewish New Year, 26 September, Dayan and Elazar visited the front line in the Golan Heights. The accompanying officers, including Hofi, noted that in the area of Kudne, only 2 miles' distance from the border and within range of the Israeli 81 mm mortars, there was a concentration of medium artillery – a clear indication to any military observer of an intention to attack. It gave rise to grave concern. The General Staff ordered elements of the 7th Armoured Brigade to move up to the Golan Heights where they were placed in reserve. Dayan, who was accompanied by representatives of the press and by television crews, gave an interview in which he issued a warning to the Syrians. That same day an emergency stand-to was declared in the Brigade District: leaves were cancelled and on its own accord brigade headquarters manned the mobilization centres despite the fact that orders to do so were received only on the eve of Yom Kippur, some ten days later. The mobilization system was checked and work to complete the anti-tank ditches under construction was stepped up. Thousands of mines were laid. The entire system, which had proved so effective in the past in the flare-ups along the border, moved smoothly into action.

On Tuesday, 2 October, air reconnaissance revealed that the Syrian force had grown to 800 tanks and 108 batteries of artillery. On Friday further reconnaissance revealed an increase to over 900 tanks and 140 batteries of artillery, and also that artillery groups with 130mm and 152mm guns were well forward in the line. An additional armoured brigade was identified in the southern sector. These were ominous signs. In all phases of this build-up Northern Command intelligence noted that the Syrian second line of defence was not occupied. This could lead to only one conclusion: the intention to attack. The two Syrian armoured divisions were in their permanent camps at Katana and Kiswe. On 2 October all the Syrian infantry brigades along the line were for the first time in their emergency positions in full force. The entire Syrian surface-to-air missile system was now manned, stretching roughly parallel to the Damascus–Sheikh Meskin road.

On Friday the highest state of alert for the Israeli standing army was declared by GHQ: the Israeli force on the Golan had increased to a total of 177 tanks and 11 batteries of artillery; Northern Command advanced headquarters moved up to the Golan Heights; all reserve units received advance warning to be prepared for mobilization and all regular mobilization staffs were confined to camp ready to mobilize; key personnel were returned from leave. All mobilized women and civilians in the army were removed by the Brigade District from the Golan, as was invariably the case when heavy exchanges of artillery were to take place. The military government staff in Kuneitra was cut down and a reinforcement of doctors and medical personnel was moved up into the area. Plans for the evacuation of civilian settlements were readied, although the plan itself was not put into operation until Yom Kippur. On Yom Kippur eve, 5 October, Brigade District reported the movement of giant convoys towards the border, but they received no clear indication from intelligence as to the picture.

Shortly after dawn on the morning of 6 October, Gen. Hofi was summoned from Northern Command to GHQ in Tel Aviv, where the GOCs of the commands were informed that war would break out that day and that orders for mobilization were pending a meeting with the prime minister. In the meantime, all steps were to be taken to ensure a maximum degree of preparedness and alertness to deal with the threat. The Air Force was in the final stages of readiness and the chief of staff had asked for permission to carry out a pre-emptive strike against Syria. After the meeting the GOCs of the commands called their headquarters urgently and issued preliminary orders. Hofi drove rapidly through the quiet streets of Tel Aviv to the airfield and flew north.

The entire Golan front was placed on a high state of alert; the fortifications were strengthened by an increase of manpower bringing them up to an average of twenty men per fortification. The 7th Brigade, which had moved up to the Golan Heights, was concentrated in the general area of Nafekh. Orders were issued for the evacuation of civilian villages, many of whom refused to move. And so with the Syrian Army poised to attack, the general officer commanding the Northern Command became involved in an acrimonious debate with representatives of the villages who did not want to be evacuated. By midday they began to leave and by the evening all women and children had left the area.

At midday Gen. Hofi was called again to GHQ; entering as Gen. Gonen, GOC Southern Command, was leaving the chief of staff. He reported on the preparations in his command and the progress in mobilization, presenting his plans to hold the Syrian attack. When he took his leave to co-ordinate several points with the staff, word arrived that the war had begun. Hurrying back to his command, the good wishes of his colleagues rang in his ears. He took Gen. Mordechai Hod, the former commander of the Israeli Air Force, with him as his air adviser and asked for Gen. Raful Eytan to be instructed to meet him.

It was roughly a year before that Eytan had received command of the division on the Golan Heights. He and Hofi had fought together in many battles in the ranks of the parachutists and he was by now a legend in Israel. Small, wiry, determined, with sharp square features, every inch a soldier. At the head of his battalion in the 1956 campaign he had parachuted to the Mitla Pass in the middle of the Sinai, and in the 1967 war had led his brigade in the Northern Divisional Group in Sinai to the Suez. He knew no fear and inspired confidence in the men he led. Appropriately enough this intrepid fighter had trained with the United States Marine Corps in Quantico, Virginia.

The Syrian Army was deployed on 6 October with three infantry divisions in the line. Each of these divisions was composed of two infantry brigades, a tank brigade and a mechanized brigade. The 7th Division with the 68th and 85th

Infantry Brigades held the northern sector from Kuneitra northwards; the 9th
Division with the 52nd and 33rd Infantry Brigades held the central sector from
Tel Hara to Kuneitra; and the 5th Division, including the 112th and 61st
Infantry Brigades, held the line from Rafid to the Yarmouk. In each infantry
brigade there was a battalion of approximately thirty tanks, while the mechanized brigade had a battalion of tanks and two armoured infantry battalions.
These three divisions in the line totalled 540 tanks; the two armoured divisions
behind them disposed of 460. The Republican Guard, a brigade in strength,
was designed to protect the regime in Damascus and was equipped with the
most modern T62 Soviet tanks. In addition there were two tank brigades and
some 200 static tanks in the line, making a total of approximately 1,500 tanks
directly involved.

The Israeli Army had always believed that the main effort of the Syrians
would be directed toward Kuneitra because the capture of this town would
give them a major prestige gain and would also open up the main route to the
Bnot Ya'akov Bridge and to Israel. The Rafid opening, east of the Rafid crossroads with its wide, open plain, afforded a natural tank approach and was
estimated to be the secondary effort of the Syrians in their planning. This view
was strengthened by the fact that the Syrian concentrations of medium and
heavy artillery were directed primarily at the area of the main bridge at Bnot
Ya'akov; 60% of the Syrian batteries counted were concentrated facing the
northern sector of the Heights. These were the main reasons for Hofi's estimate
that the most likely break-in point would be the area of Kuneitra, hence his
decision to deploy the 7th Brigade in the northern sector northwards from
Kuneitra, leaving the southern sector in control of the Barak Brigade.

At a conference held on Wednesday, 3 October, the various ways open to
the enemy had been discussed. Raful Eytan asked what would happen if the
enemy attacked with a force of two divisions through the Rafid opening. He
received no reply. As he left the room at the end of the conference, one brigade
commander smiled pityingly in his direction and remarked to a colleague that
he had never really grown above the level of a battalion commander. History
was to vindicate Raful.

The 4th Battalion, one of the two regular battalions of the Barak Brigade, had
been months in the line when war broke out. Their tanks were distributed by
platoons of three tanks each along the line and were sited in close support to
the fortifications to deal with any possible breakthrough between them.

On 13 September, after the shooting down of thirteen Syrian planes, the
entire battalion was alerted. Its forward units and the fortifications to which
they were linked daily reported the strengthening of the forward Syrian line

and increasing concentrations of artillery. They observed the Syrian anti-aircraft system creeping forward to cover gradually the entire area from Damascus to the southern Golan. From their past experience they anticipated trouble: the number of reconnaissances was increased, and plans were prepared for the usual day's artillery and tank battle. As the High Holy Days approached, it became clear that they were destined to spend them all in a high degree of preparedness. On Rosh Hashanah – 27 September, as the Golan Heights were thronged with tourist traffic and thousands of picnickers with hundreds of vehicles crowded the roads – they spent the day laying mines. During the ten days between Rosh Hashanah and Yom Kippur, the battalion and other forces in the line improved their positions, laid mines, extended the anti-tank ditch and observed and reported the massing of Syrian forces.

On the eve of Yom Kippur, 5 October, Lieut-Col. Yair, the battalion commander, received orders cancelling all leaves; artillery reinforcements arrived bringing the Israeli artillery presence on the Golan Heights to a total of eleven batteries. The northern sector to Tel Hazeika, some 4 miles south of Kuneitra on the frontier road, was held by the 4th Battalion plus a company of the 5th Battalion with a total of thirty-two tanks; the southern sector from Tel Hazeika southwards was held by two companies of Yair's battalion and one company of the 5th Battalion for a total of forty tanks. Yair's battalion headquarters was in Kuneitra, while the 5th Battalion's was in Juhader, 4 miles south-west of the Rafid opening; the Barak Brigade headquarters was in Nafekh. During the day volunteers from the Habad movement, an orthodox Hassidic sect known for its cheerfully religious and optimistic outlook on life and devoted to a zealous form of missionary activity among their fellow Jews, joined all the fortifications in order to organize prayers and the fast on the holiest day of the Jewish year, the Day of Atonement.

Sensing that 'something big was about to happen', Yair, a tall, regular armoured officer, dedicated and attached to his troops, visited the fortifications and the units attached to them early on Yom Kippur, only too mindful of the problems which would be posed by the ratio of forces in the event of an outbreak of war. The Habad visitors had been successful in their mission and to his amazement Yair found all the troops, including the non-religious boys, fasting and absorbed in prayer: 'On Rosh Hashanah it is inscribed and on the Fast Day of Atonement it is sealed and determined how many shall pass away and how many be born; who shall live, and who shall die, whose appointed time is finished, and whose is not. . . .' He listened and wondered too. He then called them together to explain the developments and appeal to them all to stop fasting, reminding them that the Syrians invariably began a day of battle at 2 o'clock in the afternoon because that gave them adequate time to make the initial strike while minimizing the prospects of a major Israeli counter-strike. Should fighting break out at 2 pm they would have in fact almost completed their fast, and if they were to insist on continuing it the only result would be to endanger their comrades. Emphasizing that he could not tell when their next meal would be, he cajoled them into eating and ordered them to pack their equipment ready for battle.

On arrival at Kuneitra he received a telephone call from the brigade commander telling him to prepare for very heavy artillery concentrations – the Syrians were removing the camouflage nets from their guns. Yair ordered the tanks in Kuneitra to disperse; it was clear that the inevitable day of fighting had commenced. Judging by the preparations on the other side, they were in for several days of artillery concentrations and tank battles. He issued the code word to all units to authorize them to move up to prepared positions and fire at the advancing enemy, directing his tank to the ridge known as the 'Booster', north of Kuneitra and south of the dominating Hermonit hill. As he drove up the slope 'all hell was let loose': as planes zoomed in on his forces, bombing and strafing, and the front as far as he could see became one line of fire, smoke and dust rose as the heaviest artillery concentrations he had ever seen tore into the Israeli positions along the entire front. Low-flying planes spraying machine-gun fire were swooping in to attack, dropping bombs as they pulled away. Across the open plain he could see in the distance a wave of Syrian tanks advancing like a horde of ants. Hurriedly he shouted orders to his supporting artillery to move into position and open fire against the Syrian concentrations. Speaking in his usual rapid manner, but attempting to subdue his voice, he ordered his tanks to open fire and wished all the boys good luck. Shells began to explode around his tank. It dawned on him that they were in for a very heavy day's fighting.

The 7th Brigade is one of the most distinguished formations in the Israel Defence Forces. Born in the field of battle in Latrun in 1948, fighting the Arab Legion in the desperate Israeli attempts to open the road to besieged Jerusalem, it later fought in the successful battles in which the embryonic Israeli Army cleared the Galilee of regular and irregular Arab armies. In the Sinai Campaign in 1956, under Col. Uri Ben-Ari, the 7th broke through the Egyptian lines in the central sector opposite Abu Agheila and fought its way across Sinai to the Suez Canal; in the 1967 war, under Col. Shmuel Gonen, it stormed the Egyptian lines at Rafiah, fought the major action at the Jiradi on the approaches to El Arish, and smashed its way again across the Sinai to the Suez Canal. It was the elite of the armoured forces.

Five weeks before the war all the generations of this brigade had been assembled at Latrun to recall its history on the twenty-fifth anniversary of Israel and of the brigade. Little did Col. Avigdor, its tall, spare, aristocratic-looking commander realize, as he faced the prime minister and the thousands of former brigade personnel in the amphitheatre that night in Latrun, that within a matter of weeks his brigade would be engaged in a life-and-death struggle to preserve the country whose anniversary was being celebrated.

The brigade had been involved in many of the incidents on the Golan Heights and on the Lebanese border and most of its officers were very familiar with the terrain. As tension rose on Rosh Hashanah eve, the 7th Brigade was ordered to move one battalion to the Golan Heights in order to strengthen the Barak Brigade. As he learnt of the developments, Avigdor made his own personal estimate of the situation, and reviewing the same period in years past he came to the conclusion that something must happen by Yom Kippur. His experience had been that whenever any hostile activity had occurred over the past few years which required an immediate reaction, little time was ever available for preparations. He resolved that his brigade would not be taken by surprise.

He ordered his artillery men to reconnoitre the Golan Heights to study the terrain and to prepare their targets and firing tables and convened his battalion commanders to recapitulate all the operational planning which they had at one time or another carried out in Northern Command. On his own initiative and without notifying his superiors, he took his battalion commanders and members of his orders group for a day's outing along the front line; they carried out observation, studied the terrain and reconsidered their plans. Ten days later one of the operational plans which they had studied on that day was to be put into operation as the brigade led the counter-attack into Syria.

At noon on Friday, 5 October, orders that they were to be in the highest state of preparedness to move were received. Avigdor was relieved, because in intelligent anticipation he had already moved up part of his advanced headquarters to the Golan. By now he realized his intuition was being vindicated: something very serious was about to happen and he felt that the brigade was in a race against time. A tremendous amount of traffic began blocking the roads as personnel, vehicles and ammunition moved up to the mobilization centres. All that night the battalions that had moved north prepared the tanks they had received from the reserve forces, arming and equipping them; the 2nd Battalion moved up that night to Sindiana on the Golan Heights, about 1 mile east of the Nafekh–Tapline crossroads; while the 7th Battalion took up its position on the Nafekh–Wasset road. The 1st Battalion moved on Saturday morning and by 12 o'clock was in position on the Wasset crossroads. The 7th Brigade was concentrated in the area of Nafekh.

On Saturday morning at 10 o'clock, Avigdor joined the brigade commanders in Nafekh at a conference with Gen. Hofi, who informed them that according to intelligence received the Syrians intended to launch a war on that day; it was estimated that the attack would commence some time around 6 o'clock in the evening. The 7th Brigade was assigned the task of reserve force for the Golan Heights in the area of Nafekh; it was to be prepared for a counter-attack either in the northern or the southern sector or to split into two and support both. Avigdor drove to meet the 2nd Battalion in Sindiana and there addressed the officers, company commanders and above, of the brigade. He advised them that war was imminent and went into great detail as to the tasks of the various forces. Fortunately they had been planning for this since Rosh Hashanah, ten days earlier. The brigade was ready for war.

He called an orders group at Nafekh for 2 o'clock in the afternoon, assuming that this would give time for the 1st Battalion, which had by now arrived, to organize itself. As the officers gathered to await Avigdor, the ominous sound of planes was heard. Before they realized what was happening, a deafening crash shook the camp as planes zoomed down strafing and bombing, and an intense artillery bombardment opened up on the camp. No operations group meeting took place – the battalion commanders streaked back to their battalions, while Avigdor moved brigade advanced headquarters out of the camp under air bombardment and heavy artillery shelling, waiting to get a feel of the battle before giving orders. An hour later he was ordered to move to the northern sector in the area of Kuneitra and to transfer the 2nd battalion to the southern sector under command of the Barak Brigade. The 7th Brigade was now responsible for the northern sector from the general area of Kuneitra northwards with two battalions of tanks.

Avigdor lived with an obsession about maintaining reserves, however small, and accordingly he proceeded to build a third battalion of tanks. He transferred one company from one of the battalions, placed it under command of his armoured infantry battalion and thus created a third battalion framework with tanks. As more tanks were moved up to him, the new battalion gradually became a proper tank battalion: for the purpose of manœuvre he now had available three pawns. He received under command Lieut-Col. Yair's 4th Battalion, which was in the line with the fortifications in the northern sector of the Golan Heights. Including the tanks of Yair's battalion, the brigade entered battle with approximately 100 tanks. Avigdor deployed as follows: the 1st Battalion was stationed from the fortification A1 on the 'Purple Line' directly east of Masadah on the foothills of Mount Hermon south for 4 miles to the Hermonit hill; the area from Hermonit south to the 'Booster' ridge overlooking Kuneitra from the north was assigned to the 5th Battalion.

· · · · ·

The Barak Brigade was a regular armoured brigade in Northern Command. It had been honed to a fine instrument of war as a result of years of current security operations along the border and major operations including the advance into Lebanon that penetrated up to the Litani River in September 1972 in retaliation for terrorist activities, an action which brought temporary quiet to the Lebanese border. The brigade had also been active in the fire fights which flared up along the Syrian front in December 1972 and January 1973. Indeed, it had seen action constantly since the Six Day War, including a major action mounted against the Syrians in June 1970. It was a highly professional and competent force, completely familiar with the terrain over which it was about to fight. Its forces held the line with the 4th Battalion in the northern sector under Lieut-Col. Yair and the 3rd Battalion under Lieut-Col. Oded in the southern sector. As tension grew on Rosh Hashanah the 7th Battalion of the 7th Brigade was moved up to the Golan Heights as a reserve for the Barak Brigade.

Maj. Dov, the brigade intelligence officer, was busy during the period of tension after Rosh Hashanah spotting, observing and reporting the increase in Syrian forces and the growing concentrations, and constantly reconnoitring the front line. On Friday evening the staff of the Barak Brigade met with the brigade commander, Col. Yitzhak Ben Shoham. Would they get warning of an impending Syrian attack or would it take them by surprise? Dov maintained that the Syrians could move and take the entire command by surprise. The deputy brigade commander, Lieut.-Col. David Yisraeli, disagreed, being of the opinion that some warning would be available.

On the morning of the 6th the brigade staff visited the front line and at 1 o'clock in the afternoon they met the brigade commander at Nafekh. Orders were given to mobilize reserves, since it was understood that that evening 'something would happen'. Although they were still not thinking in terms of all-out war, orders were given for the wartime operating procedures of the brigade to be applied. Gen. Hofi was called to the chief of staff, and Col. Ben Shoham as the senior officer present was left in charge of the area.

At 1.50 an air and artillery attack descended on the brigade headquarters The brigade commander issued orders for all forces to take up firing positions but to hold their fire. At 2.00 twelve Syrian tanks were reported to be crossing the line in the direction of Masadah between the two northerly Israeli fortifications A1 and A2. A platoon of tanks of Yair's 4th Battalion blocked these tanks as they attempted to cross the anti-tank ditch. At the same time tanks and infantry attacked the Israeli position A3 on the main Damscus road, while from the area of Kudne an attack by a battalion of some forty tanks was reported. Ben Shoham sent into action the reserves of the 4th Battalion, which destroyed the Syrian force in the north between A1 and A2. He then ordered this same company to move southwards and attack a force of twenty tanks which was engaging A3. The advance of the forty tanks approaching from Kudne was being held.

At 2.45 in the afternoon the Israeli position on Mount Hermon reported heavy shelling. There had been many hits and an enemy helicopter had been sighted *en route* to the position.

When the Israeli forces first established themselves on one of the peaks of Mount Hermon at a height of some 6,600 feet in June 1967, the importance of this foothold, from which the adjacent territories of Syria, Israel and Lebanon were so clearly visible, was readily apparent. Israeli resort enthusiasts set about developing skiing facilities in the area, thus making available at a distance of an hour's drive one from the other; mountain skiing on the Hermon and water skiing below sea level in the Sea of Galilee. An approach road was constructed, as was a ski lift to satisfy the thousands of skiing enthusiasts who flocked to this new area. But this was not what interested the Israel Defence Forces. From this position on a clear day one could see Haifa to the west and the Syrian capital of Damascus to the east. Not only did it afford excellent observation, its obvious advantages as a radar outpost and a site for sensitive electronic equipment were only too evident.

Accordingly a major position, a camp in itself, was erected to house some of the most sensitive and secret electronic equipment in the IDF. The entire Syrian plain bordering on the 'Purple Line' was in full view of the troops manning the position. There were observation posts on the position itself and at the upper level of the ski lift. Daily the artillery forward observation officer in the position reported on the growth in the number of artillery batteries and other targets dotting the plain below – the entire concentration of Syrian forces was there for the Israeli look-outs on Mount Hermon to see. The fortification jutted out like a squat tower on the peak. It was well built, but the upper system of fortifications on the lower building had not yet been completed. There were signs of negligence: the main gate of the position had been damaged and swung open on its hinges unrepaired; no communication trenches had been dug around the main fortification. A section of troops, an officer and thirteen men, were assigned to defend it.

On Yom Kippur day fifty-five troops were in the position, including the defence section from the Golani Brigade. They included Air Force and intelligence personnel to man the electronic equipment in addition to the normal service personnel required to maintain the position. Northern Command had never estimated that this position would be the object of a major Syrian assault

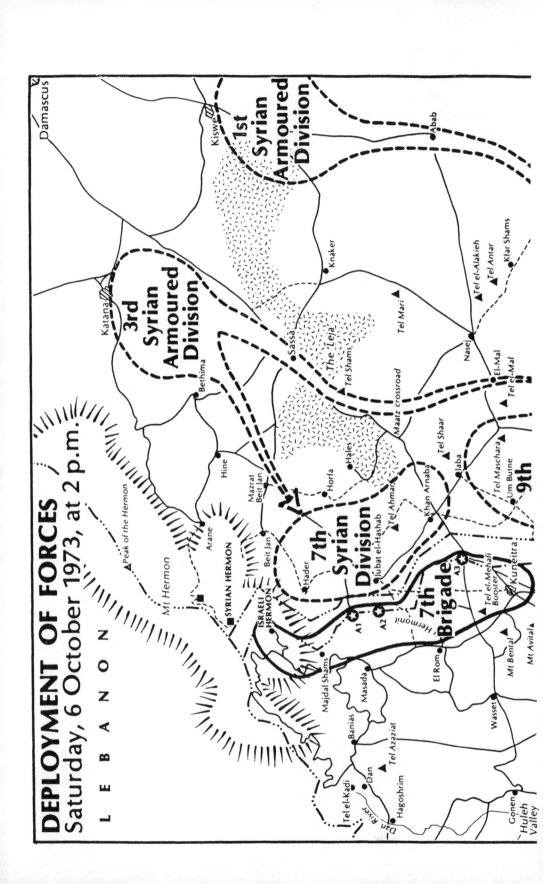

DEPLOYMENT OF FORCES
Saturday, 6 October 1973, at 2 p.m.

L E B A N O N

Damascus

Kiswe

1st Syrian Armoured Division

Abab

Katana

3rd Syrian Armoured Division

Knaker

Bethima

Sassa

Tel Mari

The 'Leja'

Tel Shams

Nasej

El-Mal

Tel el-Alakieh

Tel Antar

Kfar Shams

Tel el-Mal

Hine

Maatz crossroad

Hales

Tel Shaar

9th

Peak of the Hermon

Mazrat
Beit Jan

Horfa

Jaba

Tel Maschara

Mt Hermon

Arane

Beit Jan

Hader

Jubat el-Hashab

Tel Ahmar

Khan Arnaba

Um Bune

SYRIAN HERMON

7th Syrian Division

Tel el-Mehafi
Booster

ISRAELI HERMON

A1

A2

Hermonit

7th Brigade

A3

Kuneitra

Majdal Shams

Masada

El Rom

Mt Bental

Mt Avital

Banias

Tel Azaziat

Wasset

Tel el-Kadi

Dan

Hagoshrim

Gonen

Huleh Valley

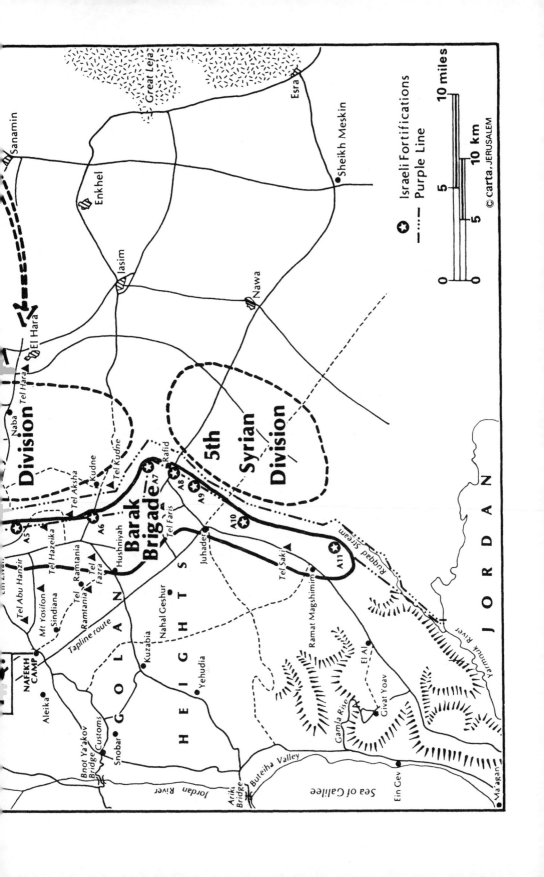

Israeli Fortifications
····· Purple Line

10 miles
10 km
© carta, JERUSALEM

Sanamin

Great Leja

Esra

Enkhel

Sheikh Meskin

Jasim

Nawa

El Hara
Tel Hara
El Hara

Naba
Tel Hara

Division

5th
Syrian
Division

Kudne
Tel Aksha
Tel Kudne

Rafid

Ein Zivan
A5
Tel Hazeika
Ramtania
Tel Ramtania

A6
Hushniyah
Tel Fazra

Barak
Brigade
A7
A8
Tel Faris
A9

A10

Tel Saki

A11

Rugged Stream

Tel Abu Hanzir
Mt Yosifon
Sindiana
Tel Ramtania

Tapline route

G O L A N

Nahal Geshur

Kuzabia

Juhader

Ramat Magshimim

NAFEKH
CAMP

Aleika

Bnot Ya'akov
Bridge Customs
Snobar

Yehudia

H E I G H T S

Gamla Rise

El Al

Givat Yoav

J O R D A N

Yarmouk River

Jordan River

Ariku
Bridge

Buteiha Valley

Sea of Galilee

Ein Gev

Ma'agan

because it was not on a major axis of advance. It could only be an object for routine raids. The fortifications were built to withstand artillery fire and Air Force bombing, but the trench system which would enable the infantry to fight effectively had not yet been completed.

On the morning of Friday, 5 October, the troops in the position woke up to see beneath them spread across the plain a vast concentration of Syrian armour and artillery. They reported and went about their normal routine duties. Receiving instructions to be on the alert, after the Kol Nidrei prayers in the small synagogue in the evening, they entered the main bunker and the heavy steel doors were closed. On the morning of Yom Kippur the observation posts were as usual manned: routine reconnaissance along the approaching routes took place; but many of the soldiers remained in the synagogue to pray.

At 1.45 in the afternoon several officers including the officer commanding the position and an artillery officer 'Bambi', looked down on the mass of Syrian forces in the plain below. 'Look,' shouted Bambi, 'they are removing the camouflage nets from the guns! At that very moment the first shells hit the position and the group in the observation post was blown back by the blast. All the troops on the position concentrated in the central hall of the bunker, listening as hundreds of shells exploded all around them. The platoon officer and the mortar sergeant climbed into the observation point, but the shell fire made it impossible to remain in the open and they were obliged to withdraw.

At 2.55 a report arrived that four Syrian helicopters loaded with troops of a Syrian commando battalion were approaching the upper level of the ski lift, a mile from the Hermon position. One helicopter exploded. The three others landed, discharged their troops and exchanged fire with the troops in the observation posts at the upper end of the ski lift (these troops escaped down the ski path to the lower level of the ski lift). Suddenly the look-out in the Hermon position reported Syrian troops advancing in two columns inside the compound of the Israeli position. Two heavy machine guns had already been damaged in the shelling and were out of action: there was one heavy machine gun left and an automatic rifle, but all personnel were armed with Uzi submachine guns. The Israelis started to fire and some Syrian troops fell. Some of the service personnel, for whom this was a first exposure to fire, clustered in the rooms of the bunker frozen by fear, and the pleas of those fighting to come and give a hand remained unanswered.

One after another those fighting fell, dead or wounded. At one point six Israeli soldiers were engaging at least a hundred attacking Syrian commandos. Anybody who raised his head for more than a split second was hit by snipers. The battle continued for forty-five minutes and under murderous fire the six fighters withdrew into the hall of the bunker. They blocked all entrances and concentrated in the air filter room. It was full of dust and it was almost impossible to see one another. The only way they could breathe was by covering their noses with flannelite which had been soaked in urine. They heard the Syrians exploding grenades in position after position as they broke in. Smoke from smoke bombs swirled through the room and the occupants began to choke. David Nachliel recalls that they decided to crawl into one of the internal connecting trenches in the large bunker in the hope that they would be able to break out (at that moment twenty of the fifty-five men in the position were in the connecting trench). The commander of the position, Bambi, the artillery officer, and Nachliel waited tensely for the Syrians. Three Syrians approached; the waiting Israelis threw a grenade, making them step back hurriedly. At that point they realized that the situation looked hopeless: some of them had only one loaded magazine in their Uzi; the generator had been hit and they sat there in the dark without any form of communication with the outside world, cut off from the other troops in the position, hoping that reinforcements would arrive.

The hours passed as the group sat in darkness and utter silence, straining their ears to listen to the sounds on the other side of the door. It was already 9.00 in the evening and it was clear to the officers that the only way to save the troops would be to move out of the communication trench and break out of the position, which was by now surrounded by Syrian commando troops. Slowly they moved through the trench to the destroyed radar equipment at the head of the position and then gradually lowered themselves out of the fortification. Trying not to breathe they slipped out of the darkness past the Syrian positions. Nachliel remembered a break in the fence around the position and led the others towards it. Twenty yards away they could distinguish three Syrian soldiers, but luckily they did not notice them slipping by. They passed through the fence and moved rapidly towards the Syrian area. For an hour and a half they moved silently, glancing back as explosions rent the position they had left behind. As they passed the upper area of the ski lift in the darkness, murderous fire was suddenly opened up on them from a range of 200 yards (the Syrians had positioned three ambushes along the road leading up to the ski lift in anticipation of vehicles arriving with reinforcements). The Israeli column lay flat – to meet this attack they had each a Uzi with one magazine.

Nachliel understood that the prospect would be very grim if he stayed in this position. Firing his Uzi from the hip, he ran as if amok straight towards the ambush; he continued running and some 100 yards later he met two more of the group. They were subsequently joined by the commander of the position and they carried on, only to run into another ambush. Grenades were thrown at them. They rushed on, rolling down the hill into dead ground. As they ran down the road, they recognized three Israeli tanks moving towards them; one of the tanks fired on them before they could identify themselves. In the morning an additional number of the group arrived, some seriously wounded. In all, eleven of the fifty-five who had manned the Hermon position on Yom Kippur reached safety. The remainder were either killed (Bambi was one of those killed in the ambush) or were taken prisoner by the Syrians.

The next day Gen. Hofi gave instructions for a counter-attack to be mounted, but because of the very heavy fighting along the front he postponed it. On Monday one of the escapees reported that there were people still alive in the Hermon position and that fighting was continuing. Hofi accordingly ordered units of the Golani Brigade to recapture it, but the Syrians were waiting all along the route leading up to the fortification: the units attacked and were driven back; with a loss of twenty-two killed and fifty wounded.

The Syrians proceeded to dismantle the equipment in the position and a few days later Soviet advisers arrived by helicopter. They examined the equipment meticulously and when they realized what a valuable catch this was, they gleefully embraced the Syrian soldiers.

For years the Syrian Army had prepared for this moment. They had trained meticulously on terrain similar to that which they were about to cross, repeatedly carrying out exercises that were all or in part replicas of the various elements of the attack which was carried out on Yom Kippur day. They trained in bridging the anti-tank ditches; time and again in their exercises they captured volcanic hills. They breached minefields and broke through obstacles, continuing to absorb the large quantities of Soviet equipment that were pouring into Syria from the Soviet Union. They observed the sparsely held Israeli line and learnt their lessons from the various fire fights along the line in which they had been engaged over the years. The fact did not go unnoticed that Israeli dispositions were designed to deal with sporadic outbursts of fighting, which had characterized the situation along the border over the years. Reconnaissance units crossed the lines regularly and noted the Israeli preparations: Israeli headquarters locations were mapped and pinpointed; the Israeli procedures that were repeated in times of tension and fighting were duly noted.

Like the Egyptians the Syrians were aware of the quality of the Israeli fighting forces and reached the conclusion very rapidly that this quality could be overcome only by quantity. Accordingly, in the six years following the Six Day War, the armoured forces of the Syrian Army increased five-fold as the number of tanks supplied to them by the Soviet Union reached some 2,000. This force was backed by an air force with some 350 first-line planes and by a

Soviet missile system (hastily supplied in the months preceding Yom Kippur) that was designed to neutralize the effect of Israeli air power. FROG missiles with a range of 55 miles were introduced, thus giving the Syrians the capability of engaging civilian targets in depth behind the lines without endangering the Syrian Air Force. All this was capped by a cruel hatred and extreme fanaticism that characterized the Syrian forces and created an air of intransigence which surpassed all extremism on other Arab fronts.

As the invasion force concentrated in the Syrian plain, every effort was made to hide the true purpose of the operation. Indeed, only on the morning of 6 October were orders issued advising battalion commanders that H hour for the attack would be at 3.00 pm on that day (2.00 pm Israeli time). Company commanders would be advised of the attack at 1.00 pm, while platoon commanders would be told at 2.00 pm – one hour before they were actually to move into action. Significantly enough, the orders captured later by the Israeli forces included instructions to remove all radio sets from the troops. The Syrian plan was a comparatively simple one. As their forces concentrated in the forward areas of the Golan Heights, orders were issued indicating that the Israeli forces were poised to attack the Syrian Army. The orders specified the defensive deployment of the Syrian forces and thereafter detailed plans for a counter-offensive in the event of an Israeli attack.

The Syrian forces moved into action in accordance with the Soviet doctrine which had been drilled into them over the years. The infantry brigades supported by their organic tank battalions and the armoured infantry broke through the front line in order to gain the first foothold, thus enabling the armoured brigades of the infantry divisions to pass through the infantry forces. The attack was mounted along the entire front. Contrary to Israeli estimates, but as Raful Eytan had suggested, the main breakthrough point was at the Rafid opening with the 5th Syrian Division leading. The Kuneitra opening was attacked with the 7th Syrian Division penetrating to the north of Kuneitra and the 9th punching to the south.

A detailed and elaborate procedure for the organization of observation along the line by the commanders of the various formations and units was established in such a manner as not to arouse suspicion: all senior officers were ordered to remove their badges of rank when near the front line; all documents relating to the attack were to be written in hand by the commanders themselves (brigade commanders, chiefs of staff of brigades, artillery support commanders and battalion commanders). The entire area was closed off to all unauthorized personnel. Camouflage orders were most stringent and all moves were to be carried out only at night, without lights and with a minimum of noise. During the day all units were to be dug in and hidden from view of the Israeli enemy;

they were required to be stocked up in advance with food supplies when they entered the area of the start line to eliminate unnecessary supply activity. The normal front-line routine was to continue in order to lull the Israelis into a feeling of security.

Ostensibly all this activity was to deal with an expected Israeli attack, but the routine plans (which it was made clear were being prepared for a counter-attack) in effect constituted the Syrian plan for attack. On 1 October the political guidance section of the army issued a circular announcing that Israel was spreading rumours about a Syrian intention to attack Israel. Political guidance officers were advised to be on guard in order to discount them and to point out that such rumours invariably preceded Israeli intentions to launch an attack on Syria. Should such an Israeli attack materialize the Syrian Army would be ready with all its forces to counter-attack – this was the reason for the stepped-up preparedness in the Syrian Army.

It is reasonable to assume that the Syrians had no illusions about the actual strength of the Israeli forces facing them, and it is of interest to note that they were aware of the fact that west of the 5-yard-wide tank ditch there was no further Israeli line of defence on the East Bank of the Jordan and that the villages established in the Golan Heights had not been organized for defence and were therefore of no military significance. They obviously appreciated that the next line of defence would be the old-established Israeli settlements on the West Bank of the Jordan.

As subsequently occurred in fact, the artillery softening up of the Israeli front line was to continue for fifty-five minutes, commencing exactly one hour before H hour and concluding five minutes before it. All watches were to be zeroed at 2.15 in the afternoon by Radio Damascus. H hour was to be at 3 o'clock and the artillery barrage was to open up at 2.00. The northern divisional attack was to be in two phases, moving in the general direction through Masadah to the area of Tel Azaziat on the Israeli border. The Syrians envisaged the total destruction of the Israel forces in the Golan Heights by the morning of Monday, 8 October.

The Moroccan Expeditionary Force received similar orders. Again the cover story was that an Israeli attack would take place, but that it would be held by the Syrian defences whereupon the Syrian Army would counter-attack. An entire detailed section of the order was devoted to the crossing of the anti-tank ditch, planned down to the minutest detail. A commando force was assigned to the slopes of Mount Hermon, from where it would launch an attack from the north in order to roll up the Israeli forces in the area of Masadah. An advance force composed of a company of tanks and a reinforced company of armoured infantry was to break out from the area of Masadah to Banias and to reach Tel el-Kadi or Tel Dan in Israel at the source of the Dan River, a tributary of the Jordan, overlooking Kibbutz Dan. This mission was to be accomplished by midnight on Saturday, 6 October.

The Syrian forces were ordered to ensure that the momentum of battle was maintained by night as well as by day, with detailed arrangements being made to ensure identification and control. Three bonfires were to be lit on Hermonit and Tel Ahmar in order to assist the units in identifying their location and as reference points for the artillery. By Sunday morning the forces were to be ready to engage Kibbutz Dan and to establish a defensive position ready to receive Israeli counter-attacks in the area of Kibbutz Hagoshrim–Kibbutz Dan–Banias. The forces were to be organized to be ready to develop the attack into Israel on receipt of instructions. The attack was to be in two phases. The objective of the main one was to reach a daily report line on the first day, with advanced elements reaching the Israeli border by midnight on the 6th; the completion of the capture of the Golan Heights was planned for the evening of Sunday, 7 October. At this stage the forces would be reorganized, strong anti-tank defensive localities would be created and the Syrian Army would be poised to develop the attack into Israel.

After the war President Sadat said in a newspaper interview that on the first day of the war the Soviet ambassador had come to him ostensibly with a message from President Assad that Assad was prepared for a cease-fire. On being contacted by Sadat, Assad however denied that he had made such an approach. The Soviets for their part are insistent in maintaining the accuracy of their version and indeed publicly rebutted Sadat's story. An analysis of the Syrian operation orders and their timetable tends to confirm the Soviet version: there is no doubt that the Syrians, seeing in the initial assault that their plan to take the Golan Heights within two days was about to materialize, decided to consolidate their gains immediately and to throw out feelers for a cease-fire. This would have achieved their immediate objectives, military and political, without running the risk of an Israeli counter-attack, which would doubtless be mounted as soon as Israel's reserves had been mobilized. At this stage Assad was thinking exclusively in terms of Syrian interests, but in retrospect it would appear that the Soviet-encouraged cease-fire moves early in the war would have served Arab interests both in Syria and on the Suez Canal far more effectively than did the continuation of the war.

6

The Onslaught (North)

THE ISRAELI FORTIFICATIONS holding the line reported that tank concentrations accompanied by armoured infantry and led by tank dozers and bridging tanks were advancing at all points. In the first hours the main thrust appeared to Gen. Hofi to be to the north of the so-called Kuneitra opening between positions A2 and A3, south of Jubat el-Hashab, and also on the route leading from Kudne in the area of position A6 with an additional attack being mounted along the Tapline route from the south in the area of position A11.

The Barak Brigade reported that it was fighting back and had knocked out a large number of tanks. In the first hour or so the situation looked good, but by 4.30 in the afternoon the picture had clarified itself enough to convince Gen. Hofi that a very serious situation was developing and that the enemy force deployed was out of all proportion to what the Israelis had known in the past. He ordered the 7th Brigade to move up to the line, giving them responsibility for the entire northern sector of the heights from A5 to Tel Hazeika northwards; south of that area the responsibility lay with the Barak Brigade.

From all sectors reports poured in describing the success of the Israeli tanks manning the pre-prepared ramps: enemy tanks were being destroyed, but alarming reports described the expanding flood of Syrian armour flowing in. The initial Syrian success in the area of Tel Aksha, between A5 and A6 on the Kudne route in the general direction of Hushniyah, against the very light forces holding it (at this stage it was not clearly appreciated that approximately 60 tanks of the Barak Brigade were facing a massed force of some 600 tanks) confirmed them in their decision to mount an additional effort here with the 9th Division and turn it into the main breakthrough.

Col. Yair stood up in his tank from the commanding position on the 'Booster' and observed the advancing columns of Syrian armour. An inferno of artillery fire covered his troops' position. Through the dust he noted the tell-tale outlines of tank dozers and bridging tanks rumbling slowly along at the head of the Syrian columns. He ordered his tanks to concentrate on destroying the bridging tanks, and during that afternoon all those in sight were put out of action at ranges of 2,000 yards, apart from two which managed to reach the anti-tank ditch north of A3 opposite the Hermonit hill. The Syrians threw across two bridges at this point and one company of ten tanks crossed the ditch.

Yair's battalion continued to fight, firing at every tank within range. The superb training which his men had received began to tell as one Syrian tank after another burst into flames and the plain below the 'Booster' became dotted with burning tanks and armoured infantry carriers. Yair saw Israeli planes coming in to stem the advancing masses, but one after the other they were shot down before his eyes.

As darkness fell he ordered a company commander, Avner, to move forward to where the Syrians had thrown bridges across the anti-tank ditch and to destroy them and the tanks which had crossed. Within a short while Avner reported that the mission had been accomplished.

As night fell Yair was placed under command of the 7th Brigade. The Syrians continued to advance across the plain in columns, using coloured lights and flags to distinguish their various units. The Israelis watched as under cover of darkness the Syrians moved to cross the anti-tank ditch, the hundreds of 'cats'-eyes' created by the infra-red lights on the sides of their tanks providing an eerie spectacle. Several of them blew up on the Israeli minefields, but still they came.

The Israeli forces did not have the advantage of adequate optical equipment for night fighting, and accordingly they gauged the position of the Syrian forces by the noise of the tanks and by the artillery flares that lit up the area and enabled the Israelis to engage them. Units in Yair's battalion were holding on desperately, moving from position to position to avoid the Syrian special infantry anti-tank units equipped with RPG anti-tank weapons. The fortifications were all under heavy attack by infantry and tanks and appealing for help. Yair ordered them all underground and plastered them with supporting artillery fire, while the tank platoons covering the positions dealt with the Syrian tanks that were supporting the attacking infantry.

.　.　.　.

In the area of Kudne, in which the major Syrian thrust was developing, A6 position reported that it was cut off. Northern Command authorized it to withdraw on Saturday evening. In the midst of all the confusion, by-passing large Syrian concentrations, a platoon of Israeli tanks broke through and evacuated all the men safely in the direction of Tel Zohar.

The troops manning positions A8, A9 and A10 were also authorized that night to withdraw. On Sunday morning the men from A8 and A9 were evacuated to the area of Rafid, where they were completely surrounded, but the relieving forces of A10 failed to break through. The position remained besieged, with its commander, a young lieutenant, lying wounded on a stretcher. For four days the platoon sergeant acting under his wounded lieutenant's instructions commanded the defence of the position, surrounded as it was by overwhelming Syrian forces. There was no doctor and the medical orderly kept one wounded soldier alive by administering an infusion. An Israeli battery of 175 mm guns was the only support that the position had from outside as artillery fire was brought down constantly on them. When the position was finally relieved four days later the relieving troops found the entire surrounding area strewn with dozens of dead Syrian soldiers, many of them on the fences. Seven tanks lay destroyed, mute testimony to the incredible bravery and determination of a handful of boys. One wrecked Syrian tank was actually blocking the main door of the fortification with its gun pointed at the door.

Col. Avigdor satisfied himself that the 7th Brigade was well in position. He received Yair's 4th Battalion under command and followed the successful battle that Yair was conducting against the Syrian advance – approximately sixty burning Syrian tanks in the field on the first day of battle was by any standard a very satisfactory result for a force like his. He noted with satisfaction that he had received a good battalion.

At 10.00 on Saturday evening the brigade first established contact with the enemy, who made the first of many attempts to break through the central sector of the brigade between the 'Booster' and Hermonit held by the 5th Battalion. The brigade deployed, and the tank crews watched unbelievingly as thousands of 'cats'-eyes' created by the infra-red lights moved slowly forward in bright moonlight. A heavy artillery barrage preceded the Syrian tanks. Avigdor ordered his forces to hold fire until the enemy approached, thus reducing the advantage afforded them by their infra-red equipment.

The Syrian 78th Tank Brigade of the 7th Division attacked in force, while the Syrian infantry bridged the anti-tank ditch. Their tanks crossed and moving slowly deployed across a wide front towards the waiting tanks of the 7th Brigade. Avigdor ordered his forces to fire when they reached a range of 800 yards. The Syrians attacked in waves and the night was lit up as one Syrian tank after another and many armoured personnel carriers caught fire and blew up. For five hours the battle raged along the front while the Syrian artillery covered the area held by the Israeli forces in heavy concentrations. At 3 o'clock on the morning of 7 October, the Syrians withdrew.

In the area south of A1 over forty knocked-out Syrian tanks were counted, while between Kuneitra and A4 over thirty lay strewn where they had attempted to break in.

At 2.00 on Sunday morning a Syrian column was observed moving northwards on the Rafid–Kuneitra road. The significance of this move was not lost on Col. Avigdor: were this Syrian advance to succeed he would be outflanked and his supply trains would be endangered. He therefore decided to send into action a force under command of Capt. Meir, a company commander popularly known as 'Tiger'. Aged twenty-six, Tiger was known for his buoyant nature and penchant for practical jokes, which ran foul of his battalion commander. As the prospects of receiving a company command receded, he had decided he would return to civilian life when his tour of duty ended. The war intervened.

Tiger moved his force in the direction of the fortification south of Kuneitra. He ordered two of the tanks protecting it to move back to the road and lie in wait for a possible Syrian force moving northwards. He moved his force southwards, placing his tanks at spaced intervals along the main road and ordering the second-in-command of his company, Mayer, to continue ahead for 1 mile, parallel to the Syrian column, in order to act as a look-out and as an ambush when the Syrians finally withdrew. 'They're coming,' reported Mayer, 'from the south. About forty of them.' They had by now passed Mayer's force and left it in their rear, advancing in perfect column formation. When the force was 1,300 yards away from him he ordered, 'All stations Tiger, fire!' A projector lit up the Syrian column, and Mayer's force, firing from the rear, set five tanks alight. Panic seized the entire Syrian column: tanks crashed into each other and pandemonium broke loose as one tank after another was set alight by Tiger's force, methodically and quietly picking off target after target. The Syrians were caught. They tried to reorganize, but were unable to identify the source of the fire. After forty-five minutes of battle Tiger counted twenty abandoned Syrian tanks.

As dawn approached Tiger moved southwards to Tel el-Hariyen, overlooking the road, and took cover between the trees and the undergrowth. Remnants of the Syrian force gathered at dawn and searched for them. Finally, assuming that their quarry had departed, they continued to move down to the main road straight into the ideal killing-ground Tiger had prepared for them.

Five Syrian tanks were destroyed in the first salvo. Tiger now moved down to the road and proceeded to roll up towards Kuneitra, seeking out the remnants of the enemy force: another ten T55 tanks which had taken refuge in abandoned artillery positions were knocked out, and a Syrian supply column approaching unsuspectingly was attacked. Reporting to the brigade commander that he had destroyed forty tanks, he asked for permission to follow the column. Avigdor refused and ordered him back. 'Tiger,' said Avigdor, 'I love you.' 'I love you, too, sir,' came the reply.

At Barak Brigade headquarters the picture for the first few hours was an encouraging one, with reports of Syrian tanks picked off 'just like on the firing range'. But by 4 o'clock things were beginning to look serious as, in the area of Kudne, a Syrian force numbering some 100 tanks succeeded in by-passing A6 position from the south. The brigade had no reserves: all forces were committed and Ben Shoham asked for the 2nd Battalion of the 7th Brigade as a reinforcement. Pressure was growing at all points and ammunition was beginning to run short because in the initial heat of battle many of the crews had been rather wasteful.

The 2nd Battalion reached A7 position and destroyed twenty tanks and accompanying infantry. At 5.00 in the afternoon Oded, the 3rd Battalion commander, reported that a large Syrian force had by-passed position A9 and was moving along the Tapline towards Juhader. Another breakthrough was reported in the area of A10 and the second-in-command of the 2nd Battalion took a company of tanks southwards towards Tel Saki in order to help relieve the pressure. He encountered a Syrian ambush, overcame it and moved south to Ramat Magshimim to attempt to block a Syrian advance in the area of Tel Saki. By 6 o'clock that evening three major Syrian efforts became evident. In the southern sector over 100 tanks had crossed the line, while on the Kudne road over 100 had penetrated along the Tapline route (in each case this meant that approximately a brigade had broken through). In the area of A10 an undetermined force of tanks and infantry was breaking through.

As evening wore on, the advanced headquarters of the Barak Brigade moved out from Nafekh in a half-track under the brigade commander, Col. Ben Shoham, who had decided that they must reach Juhader from where he would control the battle. The signals officer, Maj. Hanan, and the intelligence officer, Maj. Dov, accompanied him. Lieut.-Col. Yisraeli, the deputy brigade commander, and Maj. Katzin, the operations officer, remained in Nafekh.

Turkish-born Ben Shoham, aged thirty-eight, had an attractive personality which drew men to him. He was a born leader and a good administrator, quietly firm, personally brave and very much a self-made man. He always managed to create a pleasant atmosphere about him. When he joined the Barak Brigade, he gathered the officers together and told them that if there was one thing he would succeed in doing it would be to make them smile in all circumstances.

Slowly Ben Shoham's advanced headquarters moved southwards in the darkness along the Tapline route. They reached Juhader and searched for Oded's 3rd Battalion headquarters under an intense artillery barrage that followed them constantly. Wherever the headquarters moved and activated its communication sets, it was heavily engaged by artillery; they tried to read the battle but it was difficult. The forces they met *en route* were already running out of ammunition, while Syrian forces were continuing to cross the front line. Ben Shoham repeatedly asked the artillery to fire flares so that his tanks could identify the enemy, but fewer and fewer flares were fired. He tried to improvise, suggesting to Oded that he join him, but Oded reported from his positions near Juhader that he was surrounded and could not reach him.

As Ben Shoham grasped the seriousness of the situation, he called for his personal tank to move from Hushniyah and join him. The Brigade District was endeavouring to bring up supplies and ammunition to the line, and Capt. Giora, the operations officer of the district, now arrived on the Tapline route leading an ammunition column. Ben Shoham stopped him and advised him not to continue. Then he radioed Oded, suggesting that individual tanks of the 3rd Battalion infiltrate to the Tapline route, take on ammunition and return to him. Oded answered that he would see if this was feasible. Suddenly, out of the darkness, a tank emerged, moving along the Tapline route. They were surprised and thought that this was perhaps a retreating tank, but Oded reported that not one of his tanks had left the area. Ben Shoham ordered Giora to go forward personally, check the tank and order its commander to return immediately to the line. The officer ran towards the tank, which had meantime come to within 10 yards of Ben Shoham's half-track, shouting instructions at it. The crew in the tank panicked and slamming down the flaps they fled. Giora came rushing back with a look of horror on his face, shouting, 'A Syrian tank!' It was a close shave, for the brigade advanced headquarters with an ammunition convoy, without adequate protection, had been at the mercy of that tank. Ben Shoham ordered Capt. Giora to return immediately to Nafekh with the ammunition convoy.

Soon after, Giora came on the air to say that driving past the Hushniyah crossroads on the Tapline he had sighted some fifty tanks in the area with many vehicles. He had driven past them in the darkness but was convinced that they were not Israelis. The force that Capt. Giora saw at Hushniyah was in fact a Syrian brigade that had changed course and broken through to the south of A6 to avoid a platoon of three tanks that were fighting desperately to defend their position. The second-in-command of the 3rd Battalion having been wounded and evacuated, and his company commander killed, a platoon of three tanks was all that remained of the company. The tank crews had collected ammunition from those that were knocked out and had fought on.

The Barak Brigade, which had been reduced by the vast onslaught along its front to fighting by platoons, numbered 15 tanks by the late hours of Saturday night; it was engaging some 450 tanks.

Before Ben Shoham had left Nafekh, a cheeky-looking young boy with blond hair and freckles sauntered up. He was Lieut. Zvi ('Zwicka') Greengold of Kibbutz Lochamei Hagetaot. He had been assigned to a Company Commanders' Course and in preparation for it had been sent on two weeks' leave, but on hearing the news of the war, he had donned his uniform and hitch-hiked to Nafekh. Realizing that things were serious when he entered the headquarters, he asked the operations officer if there was any chance of his getting a command. While he was helping out with the wounded in the camp, he was informed that four tanks, three of which had been damaged in battle, were about to arrive; they would be repaired and he would be given command. In a few words the second-in-command of the Barak Brigade, Lieut.-Col. Yisraeli, said to him, Take them. You will be known as Force Zwicka. Get moving along the Tapline route.'

Zwicka helped remove two dead bodies from one of the tanks and readied the tanks for action. Having been ordered by the brigade commander to move towards him on the Tapline route and join him, Zwicka came into contact with a Syrian force while he was moving along the road. He advised the brigade commander that he was opening fire and entering the battle.

When Ben Shoham heard from Zwicka that he was being fired on by forces west of the Tapline, he realized that he was surrounded. Dov, his intelligence officer, suggested that it would now be impossible to return to Nafekh along the Tapline. Accordingly, Ben Shoham cut across country westwards, reaching the escarpment of the Golan Heights in the area of Ramat Magshimim. His tank and his half-track sited themselves in the area of the Gamla Rise on the road leading up from Ein Gev. Not far away, already in full view of the Sea of Galilee, they identified Syrian tanks. Moving in between the boulders on the slope to take cover, they tried to obtain a coherent picture. It was now 1 o'clock on the morning of the 7th. From what they could gather, there was one platoon of tanks at A6 without ammunition; Syrian forces were flowing in and by-passing it without hindrance. The 3rd Battalion commander, Oded, with a force of two platoons of tanks (six tanks), was in the area between the Tapline and A9, blocking a major Syrian advance. Here and there, individual tanks or small groupings of tanks reported in. The company of tanks that had been patrolling in the area north of A6 to Hushniyah had run out of ammunition and was endeavouring to head off any Syrian forces which tried to advance northwards to Kuneitra.

Cut off from his troops and isolated, Ben Shoham spoke to all the forces in a quiet and encouraging manner, urging them to hold on and promising them that help would soon be arriving. But the situation was clear to the remnants of the brigade. An hour later reports came in from Zwicka that he was fighting on the Tapline route, but that he was holding on and that his situation was good. However, from hints it was clear that he had lost his accompanying tanks and was on his own.

Zwicka had by now been in action most of the night. Listening to the radio communications, the whole command was aware of the existence of Force Zwicka. But little did they realize that this youngster was waging an incredible battle on his own against one of the main thrusts of the Syrian Army into the Golan Heights, with the ratio of roughly 50:1. He had set out on his historic battle at 9.00 pm and moved south along the Tapline route, a narrow road on the western side of which runs the Tapline flanked by two tall wire fences. Rather than advance as ordered to do, he chose to site his tanks in good hull-down positions and wait for the enemy.

Under command of Giora, Brigade District operations officer, the ammunition column moved toward Nafekh, having been turned back by Ben Shoham as already described. At that moment Zwicka was advised by his accompanying tanks that a column of Syrian tanks with small side lights was approaching. At 9.20 he sighted the first Syrian tank on the road. The first shot at short range set the Syrian alight – the shock putting the communications system in the tank out of order. Zwicka signalled to his nearest tank to come alongside; he changed places with its commander, ordering him to follow and imitate everything he did. After driving a few hundred yards, he found he had lost his accompanying tank; and as he came up over a hill he saw on the road three Syrian tanks with side lights on. Three rapid shots and the three tanks went up in flames and continued to burn all night. Zwicka was now on his own. He took up a position and waited. Half an hour later he observed a column of thirty Syrian tanks accompanied by trucks driving along in perfect formation 'as if on a parade ground'. Allowing them to draw close, he fired, hitting the first when it was 20 yards away from him. He then proceeded to play hide and seek with the Syrian force along the route, popping up from behind a hill, firing, scoring a hit, and then disappearing. So he fought, eluding the Syrian tanks – who imagined they had come up against a sizeable force – and knocking out in the process ten of them. At this point the Syrian convoy withdrew.

The second-in-command of the Barak Brigade in the meantime had been authorized by GOC Northern Command to leave Nafekh and command the force holding up the Syrian advance on the Tapline route, which now consisted of Zwicka and seven recently arrived tanks of Ran's 17th Reserve Brigade. This force, under command of Lieut.-Col. Uzi, a battalion commander, constituted the first reserve unit to engage the Syrian enemy – the fact that they were in action already at 10 o'clock on Saturday night indicates the incredible speed with which the mobilization had been undertaken.

Ben Shoham ordered Uzi, who had taken Zwicka under command, to endeavour to push the Syrians back. Basing himself on the report given to him by Zwicka, Uzi advanced southwards along the Tapline route, while Zwicka – with a platoon of three tanks – drove parallel to him between the wire fences protecting the Tapline. It suddenly dawned on Uzi when fire was opened from two directions against his small force, that Zwicka had not been aware of the exact situation as far as the enemy forces were concerned and had driven into a trap. For some three hours Uzi's small force waged a hopeless battle against forces which outnumbered them from two directions. By 1 o'clock on the morning of the 7th, having made a major contribution towards holding up the Syrian advance during the critical hours of that Saturday night, his unit had been wiped out. Uzi's tank was hit (apparently by an infantry bazooka shell) and blew up in flames. He was blown clear of the tank, but lost the sight of his eyes and his left arm.

Zwicka in the meantime had pulled back his force. Two of his tanks moved up slowly to the road, while he waited by the fence hoping to ambush the Syrian force. Before they knew what was happening, all three tanks were in flames. In a flash Zwicka and his crew scambled out of the tank. His shirt and trousers were in flames and he rolled himself over to the ditch at the side of the road. Fearful that his tank would blow up, he ran to the wire fence, scrambled over and fell on the other side. Running towards an Israeli tank, he yelled out some garbled instructions and before the commander of that tank knew what was happening, he was bundled out and ordered by Zwicka to join a second tank nearby that was evacuating wounded. He donned a helmet and called the brigade commander, announcing 'Force Zwicka.' The brigade commander's reaction of relief made him feel that it was all worthwhile.

Suddenly he realized that he was wounded and he began to feel the burns on his hands and on his face. He felt dizzy and thought that this was the end of his war; he began to dream of lying between clean new sheets. Everything was in a haze when suddenly Ben Shoham's voice over the earphones brought him back to reality. There in front of him were two Syrian tanks. He fired. And ordering his driver to reverse, he continued to fire.

·   ·   ·   ·   ·

Ben Shoham decided to wait until first light before attempting to rejoin his brigade. He asked Gen. Hofi for permission to take command of all the forces in the area of southern Golan; it was clear to him that by now the Syrians were swarming all over the southern Golan Heights, and remnants of the Israeli force were cut off. Permission was granted.

In the area of Juhader, Oded, commander of the 3rd Battalion, asked for air support with first light. As the sun rose, four Israeli Skyhawks swooped in to bomb the Syrians, but as they approached their target the tell-tale signs of surface-to-air missiles were seen. All four planes exploded in the air in full view of the hard-pressed troops of the battalion. Undeterred, a second flight of four planes flew in. Two exploded. Ben Shoham ordered his forces to concentrate on him, but by 8.00 in the morning an additional Syrian breakthrough northwards along the Tapline route finally cut off his troops from his command post. Oded advised him of this situation and obtained permission to withdraw from Juhader and to concentrate all his force, twelve tanks in all (all that was left of the Barak Brigade), and move up to Tel Faris.

That night the 46th Tank Brigade of the 5th Syrian Infantry Division had broken through in the Rafid area. The 132nd Brigade of this division exploited the breakthrough and fanned out along the Rafid–El Al road parallel to the Ruqqad escarpment. By first light on Sunday, 7 October, elements of the 5th Division reached Ramat Magshimim and linked up with the 132nd Mechanized Brigade. As success became apparent to the Syrian command, the 47th Tank Brigade advanced parallel to and north of the Rafid–El Al route. In the light of the coming dawn, the Syrians looked down in amazement on the breathtaking view of the Sea of Galilee. There across the sheen of the water lay the first large Israeli town they had sighted: Tiberias. Excitement rose. Here they were advancing against a defeated enemy. Victory was almost within their grasp.

Realizing that they were facing very formidable resistance in the northern sector and that a complete breakthrough had been achieved in the southern sector that night, the Syrian Command decided to exploit success and in addition to the 1st Armoured Division, which was now directed to enter through the Rafid opening, the mechanized brigade of the 3rd Armoured Division was also directed to the Kudne–Rafid opening. A total force of 600 tanks was now engaged in the southern Golan. Against this force stood the twelve tanks that Oded was concentrating in the area of Tel Faris, isolated units that had been cut off near the various fortifications along the line and the first trickle of reservists.

The reinforced breakthrough of the Syrians northwards along the Tapline route and westwards towards Ramat Magshimim was reported by the forces besieged in A10. And in the approaching columns of dust Ben Shoham was soon able to make out the advancing Syrian tanks. There was no point in waiting. He was cut off from the remnants of the forces of the southern Golan and there was no purpose in engaging this concentrated Syrian advance with only one tank and one half-track. Pulling out of the boulders where they had spent the night, they headed rapidly for the Gamla Rise, racing for the only route left open for them to descend from the Golan Heights. The Syrian tanks fired. Ben Shoham's tank answered in order to deter them, and they drove down the rise, taking with them straggling settlers on their way down to the Buteiha Valley. As Ben Shoham drove through the valley, he found the second-in-command of the 2nd Battalion, which had been seconded to him from the 7th Brigade, in a disabled tank. Taking this officer with him, the sole survivor of all the force which had fought in the area of El Al, he carried on northwards past the Arik Bridge on a secondary road on the east bank of the Jordan up to the upper customs house and thence to Nafekh, arriving there at 9.00 am.

Ben Shoham summed up the situation: most of his brigade had been destroyed; all that he had left was the small force operating on the Tapline route (blocking what was obviously a major effort on the part of the Syrians) and Oded's force cut off and isolated in Tel Faris. This he decided was no time for him to be sitting in headquarters. There was nothing for it but to go out and fight on the Tapline. He ordered Dov to join him in the tank. Dov clambered up, but just at that moment a dust-covered jeep drove up: it was Maj. Benny Katzin, the brigade operations officer, reporting that there was nobody left in Nafekh. 'Where are you going?' he asked. 'I'm joining the brigade commander's tank,' said Dov. 'What the hell, you're not an armoured corps officer! And in any case it is my turn to be with the brigade commander.' 'All right, I won't quarrel with you,' replied Dov.

The brigade commander, with his operations officer on board, moved towards the Tapline route to join the force commanded by Col. Yisraeli, the second-in-command of the brigade, who was fighting on the Tapline route with Zwicka. At this point the first elements of Ori's 79th Reserve Brigade began to arrive. They had been rushed piecemeal up to the Golan Heights, and Dov, together with the signals officer, began to organize a force to support the brigade commander on the Tapline route. They stood with the half-track on the road by Nafekh and every three tanks that arrived were organized by them into a platoon, netted into a communications network and directed in the tracks of the brigade commander. At the same time an additional force (under command of the second-in-command of the 2nd Battalion, who had been picked up in the valley that morning by the brigade commander) was ordered to advance along a parallel track to the Tapline route leading in the direction of

Hushniyah. The two officers managed to organize a company of tanks for each of these two routes and re-established Barak Brigade's headquarters at Nafekh. Soon reports began to come in from Ben Shoham that things were looking up 'I must have knocked out eight tanks so far. It looks good,' he reported. Dov found Gen. Raful Eytan in the headquarters at Nafekh. This usually calm and unemotional man greeted these comparatively junior officers affectionately. They told him the whole story of their odyssey and what they had done now in order to send forces to the brigade commander. Raful approved their action.

Maj. Dov was feeling happy with himself. After the incredible nightmare of the night he had spent with Col. Ben Shoham, his brigade commander, here he was again in the headquarters of the brigade. Assisting him in running the headquarters was the signals officer, Hanan, whose devotion was equalled only by the incredible manner in which he could juggle with communication networks and improvise. True, there was not much left of the brigade, but its forces, however small, with the brigade commander and his second-in-command, were fighting what was obviously the main thrust of the Syrian Army on the Tapline and defending this vital route. The situation was grim, but at least there was hope now that the reservists were arriving.

At approximately midday the second-in-command of 2nd Battalion, who had been sent along the track parallel to the Tapline route, reported that he was being attacked by a force of some eighty tanks (these were the advanced elements of the 1st Syrian Armoured Division, which had come through Rafid and Hushniyah) and that it was more than his six tanks could do to withstand the attack. Ben Shoham came on the air and urged him to hold on at all costs, otherwise they would by-pass the Israeli forces on the Tapline route and reach the headquarters at Nafekh. There was an ominous silence and no further reports were heard. At 12.30 reports came in that Syrian tanks had been sighted in the area of Tel Abu Hanzir, which meant that the Syrians had broken through the 2nd Battalion holding force on the parallel road and were behind Nafekh. At this point Raful came on the air and ordered Ben Shoham to withdraw to Nafekh along the Tapline in order to prepare the area for defence. Ben Shoham ordered David Yisraeli, his deputy brigade commander, to cover their small force as it withdrew to Nafekh.

Moving at the head of the column, followed by Yisraeli and three other tanks that were covering his withdrawal, Ben Shoham's tank knocked out more than five Syrian tanks and numerous trucks and armoured personnel carriers. In contact with brigade and division, Ben Shoham radioed instructions to Yisraeli, who transmitted them to the other tanks. As Yisraeli continued to battle and hold off the approaching Syrian tanks, he heard the blood-chilling report from the loader! 'Sir, no ammunition.' The Syrian tanks approached, aiming their muzzles at his tank; he was defenceless. Instinctively ordering the driver to charge, with the co-axial machine gun blazing away, Yisraeli's tank charged desperately at the advancing Syrians. Bewildered, the Syrians stopped in their tracks and their leader fired. Tell-tale smoke shot out of Yisraeli's turret. He had died trying to save his brigade commander.

Unaware of what had happened to Yisraeli, however, Ben Shoham continued to transmit orders to his faithful deputy; his tank continued towards Nafekh without the other tanks in the network being aware of what was going on. The Syrian tanks began to withdraw and Ben Shoham asked for an air attack to be mounted on them. Upright in the turret, he fired his machine gun at the Syrian troops who were abandoning their tanks. Moving on, some 300 yards before reaching Nafekh, Ben Shoham came across a disabled Syrian tank lying in the ditch with smoke drifting out of its turret. He and Katzin barely glanced at this familiar sight as they searched the hills for enemy tanks. The machine gun in the smoking Syrian tank came suddenly to life. A short burst and Ben Shoham and Katzin slid slowly to the floor of the tank.

Within minutes the three senior officers of HQ Barak Brigade had met the fate of so many of their comrades in arms. All Sunday night these three officers lay in the battlefield as the battle raged. The next day Dov organized a brigade detachment to bring back the bodies of the brave commander and his aides.

Lieut-Col. Pinie, deputy commander of the Brigade District, felt somewhat relieved. The district had succeeded in evacuating all the civilians from the settlements by that Sunday morning. Believing that their forces were more advanced than in fact they were, the Syrians had shifted their artillery fire forward. Thus, from approximately 11 o'clock, Nafekh was comparatively quiet. He was busy supervising the organization of the evacuation of the wounded when Raful ordered him to prepare the anti-tank defence of the camp. At midday he was moving around the camp collecting bazookas and organizing the headquarters troops for defence.

A squat, heavily build man with a gruff, no-nonsense manner of speaking, earthy and outspoken, Pinie had worked his way up through the infantry, spending most of his army life in the renowned Golani Brigade, and in which he ultimately commanded a battalion. When he reached the southern perimeter fence of the camp and sited the weapons, he froze. There, across the hilly terrain southwards only 2,000 yards away, virtually within small-arms range of advanced divisional headquarters, Syrian tanks were manoeuvring as they advanced. He rushed to Raful and informed him. Cool and collected as ever, Raful surveyed the scene through his binoculars. At 1.15 pm he gave orders for his advanced headquarters group to move out of the camp. Shells exploded around him as tank fire began setting targets ablaze in the camp. The first Syrian tanks were already flattening the southern perimeter fence, where but minutes before Pinie had sited his weapons, when Raful's half-track moved out of the northern gate, past a burning half-track that had been set alight at the entrance. He moved his headquarters north along the Tapline route and established himself in the open some 3 miles north of Nafekh. After the war Gen. Elazar asked him, 'Raful, when did you decide to leave Nafekh?' 'When it was no longer a disgrace to clear out; when Syrian tanks had by-passed the camp on both sides,' he replied.

Pinie thought rapidly as he surveyed the nightmare scene in the compound and dodged the machine-gun fire with which the Syrian tanks raked the camp. The troops he had placed in position had disappeared as the Syrian tanks lurched forward, flattening the fence. He beckoned two infantry soldiers who were at the gate of the camp with a bazooka and six shells to accompany him, shouting above the din to his operations officer and to the district assistant intelligence officer (who was armed with a machine gun) to follow him. They lay behind a rise in the ground near the fence and the operations officer – for the first time in his life under fire – sited the bazooka. Pinie acted as his number two. The Syrian tanks were firing systematically pointblank at one building after another; the nearest tank was by now 200 yards away from them. The operations officer fired one shell and missed. When the second shell missed, Pinie screamed at him, 'If you don't hit the bastard with the next shell, you lose your job as number one on the bazooka.' As they held their breath, the operations officer aimed and pulled the trigger. The third shell hit the driver's aperture. A sharp explosion and the entire crew abandoned the tank, running for their lives with Pinie's team firing at them. For two days that tank remained on the flattened fence with its engine continuing to tick over.

Two more Syrian tanks moved forward. Muttering 'This is it,' Pinie thought his fate had finally caught up with him. A deafening roar and the two tanks blew up. From behind them on the road outside the camp, the tanks of Ori's 79th Reserve Brigade arriving on the battlefield had fired. Pinie and his men then ran to the south-east corner of the camp, where in the area of the workshops they saw Syrian tanks engaged in battle with Israeli tanks. They took up their position and this time the assistant intelligence officer fired and hit a tank. A second tank appeared. It was their last shell – they fired and missed. As they looked in horror at the Syrian tank swivelling its turret towards them, it suddenly burst into flames under a striking tank shell. A lone Israeli tank approached from the workshops. It was Zwicka.

・　・　・　・　・

As dawn had approached on that Sunday morning, Zwicka, fighting along the Tapline route, joined up with Col. Yisraeli's force. Leading a main Syrian effort, the 51st Syrian Tank Brigade was being blocked by a company of tanks. Ten of the Syrian tanks and armoured personnel carriers were knocked out and Yisraeli's force advanced 100 yards. 'Finally,' thought Zwicka, 'we have come into our own after ten hours of fighting. We are advancing.'

The enemy force halted to redeploy, giving time for Zwicka and his colleagues to refuel and take on ammunition. By now they were doing well, improving positions as they fought and seemingly gaining the upper hand. Suddenly Yisraeli screamed at Zwicka that they must withdraw rapidly; the enemy had outflanked them and was about $2\frac{1}{2}$ miles behind them at Nafekh. During the withdrawal, as has already been described, Yisraeli's tank was hit and the small group with Ben Shoham at the head fought its way back, knocking out the Syrian tanks and armoured personnel carriers that were emerging over the crests on the flanks as they moved along. They were a total of three tanks by now. As they moved Zwicka discovered that the brigade commander's tank had moved ahead without them and that Shoham himself had been killed by small-arms fire.

Instinctively Zwicka decided not to continue along the road and thus avoided a Syrian ambush. He cut across country in the direction of the workshops in the Nafekh camp where he found another tank commanded by a reserve lieutenant. They began to operate together. Zwicka fired wildly at everything in sight – at the hills and the fences and at the Syrian tanks that had already flattened the perimeter fence. His tank driver was by now in a complete state of shock and incapable of reacting to orders. In the midst of all the pandemonium a new tank driver materialized and Zwicka followed the reserve forces of Col. Ori's 79th Brigade, who were now fighting around Nafekh, back on to the Tapline route.

Twenty hours after he had set out along the Tapline route, Force Zwicka drove back across the flattened fences of Nafekh camp. All around – on the fence, in the camp, on the hills – Syrian tanks and armoured vehicles lay blackened, burning and smoking. Slowly, painfully, wounded and bloody with clothes burnt, and blond hair blackened, Zwicka lowered himself from his tank. Apologetically he looked at Dov, 'I can't any more,' he whispered. Dov did not utter a word. He clasped Zwicka in his arms and hugged him, and then rushed him to the medical evacuation centre.

Like all the reserve commanders in the Israel Defence Forces, Col. Ori drove his men desperately on Yom Kippur to get them as rapidly as possible into the line. It was a new brigade, equipped with Centurion tanks with petrol engines that had not yet been converted to diesel. Ori was only too aware of the fact that these engines would cause much trouble. One hour after midnight on Sunday morning, he ordered four tanks to move up the Yehudia road under command of the deputy brigade commander; by 2.00 that morning his reservists were in action against the Syrian forces.

Early in the morning of the 7th he moved up with twenty tanks and deployed in the general area of Kuneitra on the right flank of the 7th Brigade. He ordered all his tanks to move up and join him, but when one of his battalions arrived at Nafekh, Raful stopped it and then broadcast an SOS ordering the entire brigade to concentrate around Nafekh. Ori moved back from the area of Kuneitra towards Nafekh, leaving a covering force near Kuneitra, and as he did so he observed a battalion of T62 tanks arriving on the Sindiana–Hushniyah route parallel to the north of the Tapline. This was the force that had destroyed the Israeli tanks covering Ben Shoham's desperate attempt to hold the Tapline route.

Hofi spoke to Ori and impressed on him that in his hands lay the fate of the whole area of Nafekh. As his force moved towards Nafekh from the east, his men reported that the Syrian tanks had broken the wire of the camp. All the defending forces appeared to have been destroyed; there seemed to be a complete loss of control. Ori was facing a serious psychological problem: it was now the supreme task of leadership to counteract the shock of the reservists who just a few hours earlier had been at home pursuing the normal routine of daily life. Here, they suddenly found themselves battling to save the Heights and Israel, fighting Syrians at the nerve centre of the area, seeing the dead and wounded on all sides and observing the terrifying evidence of the fierce and cruel battles that had already been waged, as dozens of smoking hulks, burnt-out tanks and exploding ammunition and vehicles covered the landscape in every direction.

Although a ceaseless artillery barrage made it impossible to get a clear picture of the fighting, Ori's tanks opened fire at pointblank range at the Syrian tanks in the Nafekh camp and gradually pressed forward. Waging an armoured battle of a most difficult nature, they exerted pressure relentlessly against the Syrians and gradually, by nightfall, the 79th Brigade had cleared the area around Nafekh and Nafekh camp itself. Meanwhile the only surviving tank in the covering force on the route from Kuneitra announced that it was under heavy pressure; Ori despatched a force to attack the Syrian armour. Eight Syrian tanks were destroyed and the pressure on the Kuneitra road westwards was eased.

Following the relief of the Nafekh camp on Sunday afternoon, heavy fighting continued in the general area of the crossroads as Col. Ori's brigade stepped up the pressure against the advancing Syrian forces. Pinie drove to rejoin his district commander, who was organizing the Jordan bridges for destruction and defence. On the road he saw sights that horrified him and aroused the nightmare memories of his childhood in war-torn Europe. Could this be the IDF? Here before him straggled units of a defeated army. He stopped one unit fleeing by standing in the middle of the road and pointedly reminding the officer in charge what the penalty for cowardice in the face of the enemy was even in the IDF. It was clear to him that the Israeli Army was at a loss when withdrawing.

Dov and Hanan, the last two remnants of Ben Shoham's advanced head-quarters, started up their half-track and drove along the Nafekh–Bnot Ya'akov Bridge road to Aleika. The scene on the road shocked them. All the signs pointed to a withdrawal motivated by panic: interspersed among the with-drawing administrative vehicles were artillery and tanks. Dov saw red as this sight, which the Israel Defence Forces had never yet experienced, unfolded before his unbelieving eyes. Conscious of the fact that he was as this moment the senior officer of the Barak Brigade, he swung his half-track diagonally across the road blocking it. 'Now,' he said, 'this is where we stop running. Nobody is going to pass us here.' As each unit or group approached him along the road, he stopped them and ordered the senior officer or NCO to turn about. Decisively and unequivocally he issued orders to create a defence locality straddling the road. Many of the units were only too happy finally to receive orders, cut off as they had been as a result of the fighting from their chain of command.

Col. Men, Raful's second-in-command, had been organizing the division from its main headquarters in the Jordan Valley. Upon hearing on the network that Raful was trapped in Nafekh camp, he dropped everything and decided to move to the rescue of his commander. He gathered together five tanks, which were in various states of repair, and moved up the road. Coming upon Dov's defence locality he added his authority in order to consolidate what Dov had commenced.

Dov strengthened the defence line he had established and sited some twenty damaged tanks (which he had gathered as they moved back) on both sides of the road near Aleika camp. Addressing the officers in this improvised force, he gave them a vivid description of the bitter situation. He emphasized that no armour remained between them and the Jordan: were the Syrians to pass the roadblock they had created, nothing remained to stop them crossing into the Galilee.

Radioing the Barak Brigade support units in the Jordan Valley to move up to him, bringing ammunition, fuel and technical units to repair the tanks on the spot, Dov created *ad hoc* platoons and companies, while Hanan gave them the necessary communications instructions and netted them into the general network. They drove into Aleika camp where they discovered an undamaged telephone. When they lifted up the receiver they actually heard a dial tone! Dov phoned the operations officer at command headquarters and gave him full details of the true composition of the force and what he had done. The second phone call was to an unbelieving and grateful wife to announce that he was still alive.

On Sunday evening Ori's 79th Brigade, now in the area of Nafekh, took command of Dov's force. Only then did Dov and Hanan, still moving in the half-track that constituted Barak Brigade headquarters, move down to their rear headquarters in the Jordan Valley.

7

The Holding Action

DURING THE NIGHT of 6 October Gen. Hofi returned to his advanced headquarters and transferred responsibility for the Golan front to Raful Eytan. The
picture was a desperate one: the southern sector was wide open; platoons were
pitched against whole battalions and sometimes brigades, the Syrian forces
pouring through the breaches in the line by sheer force of numbers. The
fortifications were under heavy attack but their reports continued to give an
accurate picture. A number were authorized by him to withdraw; the remainder
held on and fought with incredible tenacity and bravery. Not one was taken
by the Syrians during the fighting. All night Hofi urged the reservists on. The
suddenness of the mobilization had affected the smoothness of the machinery.
There were frustrating delays. Tanks were ready but ammunition was not
arriving. Ordering them not to pay any attention to organizational frameworks,
Hofi pressed the reserve commanders to rush the forces as they were ready up
to the line in platoons and companies.

As this nightmare of a night drew to an end, the picture was a dismal one.
The major battle seemed to be in the area of Nafekh, with the Syrians developing
a major thrust towards these vital crossroads in their new T62 tanks. On the
southern road the Syrian forces had taken Ramat Magshimim and were within
800 yards of El al. On the Gamla Rise they had reached the abandoned Syrian
works that marked their attempt to divert the Jordan River before the 1967 war.
On the Yehudia road leading to the Arik Bridge and the confluence of the
Jordan and the Sea of Galilee, their forward elements were 6 miles from the

Jordan River. In the centre they were operating in the general area of Nafekh camp.

Minister of Defence Dayan visited the command and realized that a battle critical to the very existence of Israel was being waged here. He called Gen. Peled, the commander of the Air Force, and told him that the situation on the Golan Heights was grave and the fate of 'the third Temple' was at stake. He urged him to concentrate all the air support at dawn to block the Syrian advance. Returning to Tel Aviv, he suggested in his report to Mrs Golda Meir that the army cut its losses in the Golan Heights and establish a line just forward of the upper lip of the escarpment overlooking the Jordan Valley, while preparing for a major stand if necessary along the bridges spanning the Jordan, which would be prepared for destruction. Mrs Meir lowered her gaze, inhaled deeply as she smoked, pursed her lips and was quiet. She was later to describe these hours as the blackest in her life.

Brig.-Gen. Moshe ('Musa') Peled, a hard-bitten and outspoken armoured officer, a farmer by birth, from the village of Nahalal in the Valley of Jezreel, took leave of the 14th Division, which he had received after concluding as commandant of the Command and General Staff School of the IDF. He had led this reserve division through its full cycle of training, and it was now a highly trained and effective force. He took leave of his command with mixed feelings, because deep down he could not escape the feeling that all was not well and that his going to university for a year's study (in accordance with the procedure adopted for senior army officers) seemed to be out of place. A few weeks earlier a conference of the divisional officers had been addressed by a senior officer from GHQ who had explained why it was the opinion of GHQ intelligence that the prospect of war was far removed. Gen. Peled, ever outspoken, was not impressed and reminded all assembled, including the lecturer, of a similar evaluation that had been given by GHQ intelligence in the spring of 1967, some months before the June war.

Nonetheless, he did not change his plans. A deputy commander arrived to look after the division in his absence, and on 3 October he took leave of the division, went home to Nahalal and began to make the necessary preparations for his year of study. Early on Saturday, 6 October his command chief of staff phoned him and said, 'We are all here. Why don't you join us?' The tone in his voice left no doubts. Peled donned his uniform, packed his kit and drove furiously to his superior headquarters. As he passed the Netanya crossroads, orthodox children standing by the roadside stoned his car, seeing the unusual sight of a car travelling on Yom Kippur. He stopped, got out, walked over to them and explained that there was tension and that soldiers have to report to duty. The children withdrew quietly. He continued his dash to his headquarters, arriving at 9.00 am to give orders to prepare for mobilization. Confirmation to mobilize arrived shortly thereafter.

The mobilization moved rapidly and smoothly; indeed far more effectively than had ever been achieved in the various exercises. But there were problems in equipping the forces. The equipment in his division was out of date, and much of it was out with units engaged in current security duties or in training. All the ingenuity and improvisation that characterizes Israel's reserve forces went into retrieving the division's tanks, optical equipment and vehicles from the various camps to which they had been dispersed. War caught the 14th Division in the midst of all this activity.

The General Staff was preparing plans to move Peled's division (which had not yet completed its mobilization) to the Suez front in the evening, but realizing that the division would not be ready to move so soon, the decision was postponed till the following morning. As reports from the Golan poured in, deployment of Peled's division was discussed early on Sunday morning. Members of the General Staff recommended delaying a decision until the situation clarified still further. Elazar did not accept the recommendation and issued orders for the division to move to the Golan Heights.

On Friday, 5 October, Maj.-Gen. Dan Laner, a reserve officer, was preparing for the holiday in his kibbutz, Neot Mordechai close to the Golan Heights, when the telephone rang. It was Gen. Hofi, who said that he was in Nafekh and that it looked as if something might be brewing up. Laner thanked Hofi for the information, telling him that he would be in the kibbutz all during the holiday. He put down the phone and then began to wonder what the general was doing in Nafekh. Lifting the phone, he dialled his number, suggesting that since he could not apparently reach home, he might like to come to the kibbutz for a meal. When Hofi declined his invitation, Laner realized that something untoward was happening. Again he lifted up the phone and called his divisional operations officer, ordering him to report on Saturday morning.

Dan Laner is one of the old 'war horses' of the Israel Defence Forces, having commenced his war service in World War Two. In the Six Day War he was chief of staff Northern Command. For a number of years he commanded the armoured forces in Sinai and was responsible for the Suez Canal front. In February 1973 he was released from active service, but in May he received an urgent call to report to Gen. Elazar, who told him that although intelligence estimated the contrary, he believed that war would break out in that year. Accordingly, he had decided to appoint Laner to form and command a new division and to activate it as rapidly as possible.

Laner was on duty at the kibbutz swimming pool on Saturday morning, 6 October, when the phone rang at 9.30. It was Gen. Hofi again, to tell him that things looked serious and that he should proceed immediately to his divisional headquarters. Laner drove to see Hofi in Nafekh and learnt for the first time about the concentration of Syrian forces facing the Israeli line. Hofi felt that there might be a chance that the Israeli Air Force would be authorized to make a pre-emptive attack. Their discussions were cut short when Hofi received a message ordering him to GHQ for a meeting at 1.00 pm.

That morning Laner had already activated the mobilization system in the division, and as he drove back to his headquarters the thought occurred to him that this might be yet another of those mobilizations that he had experienced over the years. After all, when he commanded in the Sinai, his forces must have been alerted at least thirty times. On the spur of the moment he stopped at his kibbutz to collect his bathing suit: there was a good chance there would be little to do during the mobilization period, so why not take advantage of the swimming pool at the regular military base next to his headquarters?

He was inspecting the progress in mobilization when an officer rushed in to notify him that fire had been opened all along the front – there were no details. He thought quickly: here he was with the divisional headquarters staff lacking most of the basic logistic elements and above all lacking the communications required to control the formations that would soon be placed under his command. His first step was to lay his hands 'illegally' on seven half-tracks, which he dispatched immediately to a nearby camp in order to effect communications co-ordination and tie the division into the various operational networks.

One by one the reserve officers arrived bewildered and curious. Laner ordered his advanced headquarters to concentrate at command advanced headquarters at 10 o'clock that night. All night he listened to the reports coming in, and when Hofi returned to command advanced headquarters from Nafekh, the picture was a dismal and desperate one. For the first time Laner realized what was happening. Dayan, who was present at the meeting, ordered that every method possible be used to block all routes leading to the Jordan River. Laner's proposal that they divide up the area of responsibility in the Golan was accepted and the area was accordingly divided between him and Raful with the dividing line half a mile south of the Bnot Ya'akov–Kuneitra road: Raful was responsible for everything north of that line including the road; Laner for all operations south. He had no idea what was going on on the battlefield.

Laner received four brigades under command: Ben Shoham's Barak Brigade, the 17th Reserve Tank Brigade, commanded by Lieut.-Col. Ran, the 14th Reserve Brigade and the 19th Reserve Brigade. He travelled to Almagor near the Arik Bridge and surveyed the situation of his embryonic division that Sunday morning. Ran, the 17th Brigade commander, had just been wounded in the fighting on the Yehudia road and his deputy had taken command. They were running short of ammunition. Ben Shoham, the Barak Brigade commander, reported that he was left with one tank and one half-track and obtained permission to withdraw down the Gamla Rise in order to return to Nafekh and organize some forces. The 14th Reserve Brigade commander reported that he was crossing the Galilee on tracks with two companies of tanks leading, some of which were falling, for technical reasons, by the roadside. The 19th Brigade commander reported that he was moving with approximately a battalion of tanks towards the southern end of the Sea of Galilee. As Laner stood on the bridge, a battalion commander of Barak Brigade arrived with two reserve companies of tanks. Laner directed him up the Gamla Rise, ordering the 14th Brigade commander to move his force up the Gamla Rise as soon as the tanks arrived. The 19th Brigade commander reported and Laner directed him to move with whatever force was available up to El Al and take up positions at the narrow pass on the El Al road. A third company of reserves of Barak Brigade arrived and he directed them up the El Al route.

And so they arrived. Units from different formations rushed to the front without any organization. As the first tanks of the reconnaissance unit of Raful's division arrived, the deputy commander of the 17th Brigade holding the attacking Syrian forces at the Kuzabia crossroads on the Yehudia road reported that the situation was becoming desperate, that the Syrian forces had already bypassed him and were within 6 miles of the Jordan River. Laner simply put his hand on the reconnaissance unit of his northern neighbour and ordered him to reinforce the elements of the 17th Brigade.

Standing at the bridge under intense shell fire, with all the approaching routes under heavy fire, Laner directed tanks by individual platoons and companies, without regard to their organic formation, up the two routes in his divisional area. On both routes the Syrian attack was within a ten-minute drive of the Jordan River and the Sea of Galilee. The reserve forces of the Barak Brigade had moved $2\frac{1}{2}$ miles up the Gamla Rise when the battalion commander in charge reported that he was being attacked by infanty. By some curious instinct Laner ordered them to hold their fire. The attacking forces were in fact infantry units of the Golani Brigade retreating before the massed Syrian armoured attack. The force advanced another 2 miles and was engaged $4\frac{1}{2}$ miles from the bridge by the advanced elements of the 1st Syrian Armoured Division. Eleven Syrian tanks were set alight and Laner ordered his troops to remain in position.

By Sunday evening four Syrian brigades were threatening the routes that

Laner was desperately trying to save. The 48th and 51st Syrian tank brigades crossed the Tapline route in the area of Hushniyah and advanced along the Yehudia route and parallel to it in order to reach the Gamla Rise and the area of the Arik Bridge on the Jordan. They had penetrated some 12 miles and were within 6 miles of the bridge when they were engaged by the advanced elements of the 17th Reserve Brigade, which had moved up on Sunday morning under command of Col. Ran. Had Ran's force been delayed by half an hour the Syrians would have reached the Jordan.

As the Syrian brigades approached, Col. Ran deployed his forces and in the battle that ensued destroyed fifteen tanks. The 132nd Syrian Mechanized Brigade had stopped before El Al while the 42nd Syrian Brigade fanned out to the north. The 47th Syrian Tank Brigade divided into two, with one half under the command of the brigade commander moving north from Ramat Magshimim towards the Yehudia road; the other half remained with the 132nd Syrian Brigade on the El Al route. Thus, half of the 47th moved against half of the 17th on the Yehudia road, while the other half of the 47th faced the remaining part of the 17th on the El Al route.

Having dealt with the Syrian force on the crossroads, Col. Ran with a battalion of tanks and a reconnaissance company saw half of the 47th Syrian Tank Brigade moving northwards towards his flank. He placed himself in position, opened fire and engaged the enemy. A heavy tank battle developed. In the course of the fighting, in which the Israeli force lost three tanks and the Syrians some thirty-five, Ran was wounded and evacuated, as was the commander of the one tank battalion he had under command in the battle. The senior company commander took command of the brigade and from that point on conducted a constant battle along the Yehudia–Hushniyah route west of the Tapline.

Noting that the situation on the Yehudia road was desperate, Laner's deputy, Brig.-Gen. Moshe, moved forward with the divisional advanced headquarters and took charge of the sector in which Ran's brigade was operating. Remaining well forward with the leading troops, he conducted the battle with a minimum force with courage and tenacity. On Monday morning he moved right forward to the front line where he discovered a very difficult situation: most of the units had lost their officers and he sensed an air of demoralization among the troops. His appearance on the scene and his talk to the troops changed the situation dramatically. He set eyes on a young ordnance lieutenant, the only officer he could find, and placed him in command of the force holding the Syrians, giving him exact instructions what to do. He helped him to organize the forward remnants in all-round defence; gathering the wounded he placed them in disabled tanks to protect the advance of the 17th Brigade on its rear

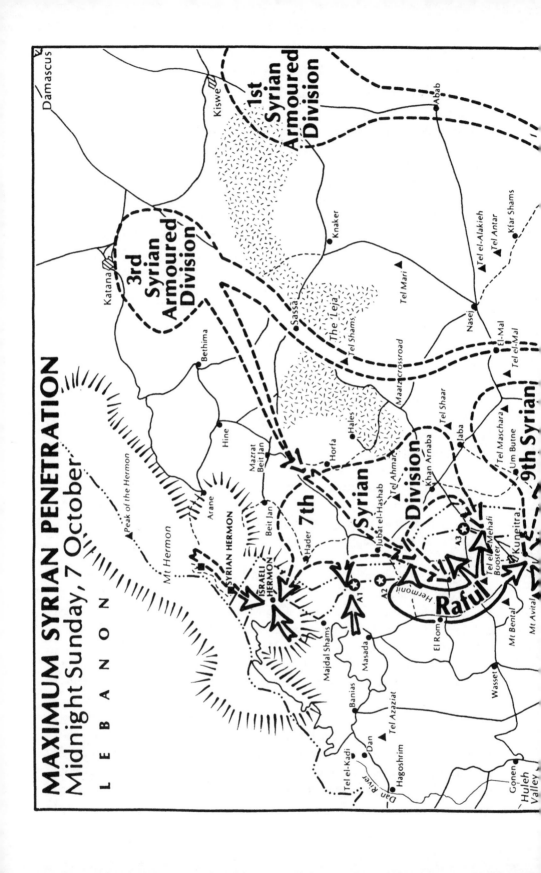

MAXIMUM SYRIAN PENETRATION
Midnight Sunday, 7 October

L E B A N O N

Damascus

Kiswe

1st Syrian Armoured Division

Abab

Knaker

Katana

3rd Syrian Armoured Division

Tel el-Alakieh

Tel el Antar

Kfar Shams

Bethima

Sassa

Tel Mari

Nasej

The 'Leja

Hine

Tel Shams,

Maatz crossroad

El-Mal

Tel el-Mal

Peak of the Hermon

Mazrat Beit Jan

Horfa

Hales

Tel Shaar

9th Syrian

Arane

Mt Hermon

SYRIAN HERMON

Beit Jan

Hader

Jubat el-Hashab

Tel Ahmad

Khan Arnaba

Jaba

Tel Maschara

Um Butne

ISRAELI HERMON

A4

A2

Tel el-Mehafi

Tel el Mehafi

Booster

Kuneitra

7th Syrian Division

Hermonit

A3

Raful

Majdal Shams

Masada

El Rom

Mt Bental

Mt Avital

Banias

Tel Azaziat

Wasset

Dan

Hagoshrim

Tel el-Kadi

Dan River

Gonen

Huleh Valley

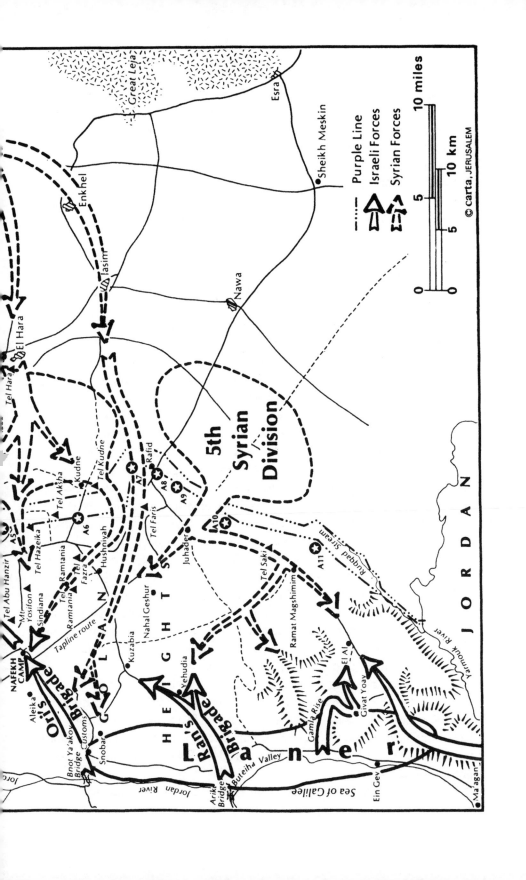

flank against the forces of the 47th Syrian Tank Brigade moving across country north from the El Al route. Brig. Moshe's handling of a very delicate situation on the Yehudia route and his personal example was a major factor in stabilizing the situation on this front.

On the El Al route, Lieut.-Col. Mir, who had rushed to the bottleneck between the Ruqqad canyon and the El Al area, was ordered to remain in a defensive position and not advance to Ramat Magshimim where he could see the Syrian tanks moving around. Contact was established at 11.45 and all day with a force of eight tanks he conducted a tank battle against the 132nd Mechanized Syrian Brigade and half of the 47th Syrian Tank Brigade. In the fighting the deputy brigade commander of the 47th, Maj. Kultum, was taken prisoner. He had moved his forces on the assumption that the El Al bottleneck was blocked and that there were no forces on the flanks. The Syrians had apparently been unable in their wildest dreams to imagine that this vital route would be left wide open.

Both the 47th Syrian Brigade and the 132nd Syrian Brigade of the 5th Division had stopped in their tracks for no apparent reason. It could be that Maj. Kultum's expectations that they must come up against a well-prepared defensive position at the most obvious place that military logic and advance planning would have dictated, was the reason for this surprising lack of initiative on their part. It could be that they were fighting 'according to the book', that is, having reached a given line as instructed and regardless of the absence of Israeli forces before them, they waited according to plan for the next wave to move through them. Perhaps the Syrian Command, observing their lack of success in the northern sector and the comparative ease with which their forces had broken through the southern sector, suspected a trap and feared for the flanks of the 5th Infantry and the 1st Armoured Division in that area.

The 1st Armoured Division had in the meantime thrust into the Golan Heights on the Kudne and Rafid routes and had halted in the area of Hushniyah for reorganization, prior to advancing in a main effort northwards along the Tapline route to break through to Nafekh and outflank Raful Eytan's division, which had so far blocked every Syrian advance.

At 2.30 in the morning of the 7th, the 19th Brigade arrived at El Al with its leading battalion of converted Sherman tanks. Col. Mir's force of the 17th Brigade came under the 19th Brigade's command. The Syrians attacked and the battle continued all day. By Sunday evening twenty-five burnt-out Syrian tanks littered the fields of Ramat Magshimim and El Al. Two Israeli tanks had been put out of action.

The reserves, which but the morning before had been at home with their families or in solemn prayer in synagogues, less than twenty-four hours later found themselves in an inferno of battle, fighting against odds they had never dreamt of. Israel's secret weapon, a genius for improvisation, was beginning to have its effect. The Syrian advance was being held.

8

The Epic of the 7th Brigade

As SUNDAY MORNING, 7 October, dawned on the 7th Brigade, the sight of
devastation and war unfolded itself before the weary eyes of the troops.
An armada of burning tanks and destroyed vehicles lay strewn across the
valley between Hermonit and the 'Booster', the killing-ground chosen by
Avigdor, which was to become known in the brigade and the Israel Defence
Forces as the Valley of Tears. Crew members were rushing around between the
flames; turrets blown off their chassis lay near the decapitated tanks; red and
purple flames licked around the ammunition trucks and armoured personnel
carriers, as from time to time one of the vehicles exploded and disintegrated.
Mushrooms of white smoke gathered over the tanks. 'Just like in the battlefield
in *Gone with the Wind*,' thought a young company commander in the 5th
Battalion, 'but this time in a modern electronic version.' The accurate Syrian
artillery fire had forced the tank commanders to take cover and close down the
hatches in the turrets. As they emerged again and surveyed the scene, a fresh
Syrian column advanced under cover of the heavy artillery fire, ready to do
battle a second time for the Valley of Tears.

The 78th Tank Brigade of the 7th Syrian Division launched a second attack
at 8.00 in the morning. It advanced along a front of some 2½ miles wide between
the 'Booster' and the Hermonit, endeavouring to insinuate a force up the *wadi*
running along the base of Hermonit in the direction of Wasset. The battle raged
elentlessly, with the 5th Battalion fighting against an entire Syrian brigade.
Coolly Avigdor directed the fighting, conserving his forces, always holding a

reserve in hand whatever the odds, endeavouring to think two steps ahead of the enemy, and always preparing solutions for the unexpected. His divisional commander, Raful, and he were in close contact as the brigade fought at ranges that varied from 10 to 2,300 yards. At the same time the 1st Battalion in the northern sector was attacked by two battalions of Syrian tanks accompanied by a force of armoured infantry in armoured personnel carriers. Most of the carriers in this attack were destroyed. At 1 o'clock the battle was over and the Syrian force withdrew, leaving dozens of tanks and vehicles burning along the 7th Brigade front.

The 7th Battalion, under command of Lieut.-Col. Avi, which had been south of Kuneitra, was now moved to the central sector overlooking the Valley of Tears at Hermonit. Avi was ordered to leave a small force to the south in order to protect the brigade flank. The 1st Battalion remained in the northern sector, licking its wounds after losing some ten tanks. That afternoon the Syrians mounted an attack in the area south of Kuneitra against the company that Avi had left behind when he moved to Hermonit. The total attacking force of some twenty tanks was destroyed.

Once again the Syrians returned to attack the central sector at 10.00 at night, with the inevitable mass artillery bombardment. But now the 7th Syrian Division was joined by the 3rd Syrian Armoured Division with elements of the 81st Brigade, equipped with the up-to-date T62 Soviet tanks, leading. Avigdor's brigade, which at no time after the first day of battle exceeded a force of 40 tanks, was holding a total force of approximately 500 Syrian tanks. Because of the absence of Israeli night-fighting equipment, the Syrian force was able to reach within close range of the Israeli tanks, and battle under a massive Syrian artillery bombardment was joined at ranges of 30–60 yards. The Syrian tanks, accompanied by infantry carrying RPG anti-tank bazookas, by-passed the Israelis, many Israeli tanks being destroyed by these RPG-carrying forces. The battle was desperate and was at its height when at 1.00 on the morning of Monday, 8 October, it died down as suddenly as it had commenced. The Syrians had experienced very heavy losses and in the darkness they were busy moving around on the battlefield, attempting to evacuate their damaged tanks and their wounded. Avigdor covered the battlefield with artillery fire, while using the respite to refuel and load his tanks.

At 4.00 am the Syrians began to harass the brigade anew, while a concentrated effort was made to repair the damaged Israeli tanks. As dawn approached first light revealed the terrifying picture to the exhausted Israeli tank crews: 130 Syrian tanks, knocked out, abandoned and smoking, and large numbers of armoured personnel carriers lay strewn around the Valley of Tears. Many of the abandoned tanks were behind the Israeli positions or between them. For the first time the 7th Brigade realized what had hit them: they had blocked an advance of over 100 tanks. Avigdor ordered the brigade to fire at every moving target at ranges of up to 3,000 yards. That night the Syrians had launched two battalions of infantry against the position on Hermonit. A small force of Golani Brigade, numbering less than twenty soldiers, had fought off the attack and to the picture of chaos and burnt-out armour on this bloody battlefield were added the bodies of dozens of Syrian infantry.

All day on Monday Avigdor's 7th Brigade fought against the concentrated attacks of elements of the 7th Infantry Division, the 3rd Armoured Division and independent units, such as the Assad Republican Guard equipped with T62 tanks. On the southern flank of the brigade south of Kuneitra, Tiger's company was attacked by an armoured force that had penetrated the area under cover of darkness. With a force of seven tanks Tiger held the attack throughout the day, thwarting all Syrian attempts to break through – some thirty Syrian tanks and two companies of armoured infantry carriers, some twenty vehicles, lay burning and smoking in the plain dominated by his tanks. In the afternoon three individual Syrian tank battalion concentrations accompanied by armoured infantry attacked and attempted to break through in the area of Hermonit. Casualties mounted as the enemy artillery identified the Israeli positions; indeed, most of the brigade's casualties were caused by artillery fire.

Avigdor and his forces were by now completely exhausted. They had been fighting without let-up for three days and two nights and the physical effect was beginning to tell. There was no time to sleep, there was no time to eat, there was no time to do anything but to dodge artillery shells and fight. Their senses were numbed by the constant pounding of artillery shots and katyusha rockets. Avigdor realized that the effectiveness of the tanks was dropping; every day their number was less. The brigade had already lost some fifty dead and a large number of wounded and he had at no time more than forty to forty-five tanks in fighting condition – and this thanks only to the incredible bravery and ingenuity of his ordnance unit. There was a sense of hopelessness as, despite the enormous casualties that the enemy were sustaining, each Syrian attack surpassed the strength and scope of the previous one. Sooner or later a weak point might give in his defences. He accordingly created a reserve of five tanks commanded by his brigade operations officer and ordered him to move back half a mile to the rear and be ready to block any possible Syrian breakthrough. Behind him, quietly controlling the battle in his composed, firm manner, was Raful, who was vindicating his reputation in these hours of test.

Taking advantage of their highly sophisticated night-fighting equipment, the Syrians had managed to turn night into day for their armoured forces and were aware of the advantage which this afforded them over the Israelis. On Monday night they attacked the central sector towards the 'Booster' in an action that lasted for three hours. Avigdor ordered his southern company (under command of Tiger) to counter-attack from the flank and the rear of the enemy that night. As Tiger advanced with his seven tanks, he came face to face with a company of Syrian tanks and armoured infantry moving on its way to the top of the 'Booster'. Battle was joined and the Syrian attack was broken.

Tuesday dawned with the tank force in the brigade sorely depleted. As the morning mist lifted, a concentrated artillery barrage, which dwarfed all that the brigade had known until then, descended on them. Katyusha rockets whooshed in, kicking up rocks and dust and covering the area with lead fragments. Syrian MIG 17s zoomed in low over the battlefield and discharged their bombs. Seven Syrian helicopters flew in over the Israeli positions to Bukata and four of them discharged their commando forces there. By 8 o'clock in the morning the barrage had reached a deafening intensity as thousands of shells and hundreds of katyusha rockets landed on the positions and forced the tank commanders to close their hatches and take cover in the tanks. The persistent intensity of the attack was obviously the curtain-raiser of a concentrated and determined Syrian effort to break the stubborn defence which had prevented them from penetrating the Israeli line in this sector. As he observed the vast force advancing and saw the entire front covered by a close pattern of bomb bursts and shell explosions, Avigdor sensed in the air a determination by the Syrians to break through this time whatever the cost. Emerging on a narrow front in the central sector from the screen of dust and smoke thrown up by the intense bombardment, a Syrian force led by 100 tanks, accompanied by armoured infantry in large numbers of armoured personnel carriers, advanced slowly in the direction of Avigdor's battleworn, exhausted forces.

The 7th Brigade opened fire at maximum range, but as fast as they were hit other Syrians came in their place, continuing in their inexorable advance towards the Israeli positions. They moved in and shortened the range. The Israeli commanders were fully exposed in their turrets and as the artillery concentration descended on the small Israeli force, the number of casualties among tank commanders grew to alarming proportions. Avigdor realized that to be more effective he must move his force out of the inferno created by the non-stop artillery barrage. Accordingly he ordered his force – now under very heavy pressure of the Syrian advanced units – to leave the high ground ramps from which they had been fighting and to withdraw some 400 yards to escape the artillery concentrations.

As Yair observed the continuous waves of Syrian reinforcements from his position covering A3 on the main Damascus road, he was ordered by Avigdor to concentrate his forces in the area and join the fighting in the 7th Brigade area. He moved back with six tanks and entered the battle. As he fought from the rear slope of one of the hills, his tank was hit and he was wounded. He joined another tank, his third. Leaving the vicinity of A3, he ordered all personnel inside under cover and requested Israeli artillery to shell the position for protection. From the high ground overlooking the Valley of Tears, his tanks picked off one Syrian target after another. Later in the day, with five tanks and armoured personnel carriers, and with the battle raging all along the front, Yair organized a supply convoy to the A3 position. His tank was hit by a bazooka fired by Syrian commandos in the outskirts of Kuneitra and the tank behind him reported that he had been killed. But Yair was alive, and continuing with the three armoured personnel carriers, drove past the 'Booster' and with the battle raging all around made a dash for the A3 fortification. As he entered with the supplies, the troops who had heard of his death but a short while before embraced him.

Suddenly, as the 7th Brigade withdrew from its hill – a form of ramp about 1 mile long – the artillery ceased and there were Syrian tanks on the hill firing at them. Avigdor surveyed the desperate scene: his 7th Battalion was now left with six tanks and was acting as a brigade reserve; Yair had moved back from the fortification and had concentrated six tanks; his operations officer was patrolling the area of Bukata and seeking out the Syrian commandos who had landed by helicopter that morning. Tiger, who was fighting on Tel Git on the main Damascus road north of the 'Booster' and was low in ammunition, asked permission to withdraw in order to reload. Avigdor refused telling him to use small arms if necessary, adding, 'Maybe the sight of Jewish tanks will frighten them off.' Shortly after however Avigdor relented when he heard that there was only one shell per tank. The situation now looked desperate. But after consultation with Raful, Avigdor rallied his forces, and the 7th Brigade counterattacked.

Avi arrived with his 7th Battalion; the battlefield was covered in smoke and dust which made it impossible to navigate. As he moved up the hill, there before him were Syrian tanks in the Israeli positions. The first tank did not notice him in the smoke; a rapid command to the gunner and the Syrian tank was in flames. Just as he was about to report to the brigade commander, three Syrian tanks advanced towards the burning tank. 'Rapid fire,' he ordered. The first Syrian tank slowly swivelled its gun towards his tank. 'Fire, fire!' he screamed at his gunner, who could not see the target enveloped in the dust. As it emerged from the cloud of dust, the gunner fired and instinctively swivelled. In one and a half minutes four tanks had been destroyed at pointblank range. Part of the Syrian force withdrew and the brigade retook the hill. Still the Syrians advanced, leaving behind burning tanks and capturing yard after yard of territory; long convoys behind them waited to enter the battle, while dozens of tank crews were rushing around the battlefield looking for new tanks to join or trying to escape down the valley.

In the northern sector the 1st Battalion, under command of Bats, was fighting with less than half of its tanks. Avigdor began to feel that he might not be able to hold this Syrian breakthrough, so he ordered Bats to leave three tanks holding his sector and to move to the northern flank of the battle in order to meet the threat of the Syrian force of T62 tanks of the Assad Republican Guard, which using the dead ground was trying to move up the *wadi* in the direction of El Rom. As battle was joined with this force, Bats was killed. Avigdor ordered Avi, commanding the 7th Battalion, to take under command all that was left of Bats' force. Together with this force, Avi engaged two battalions of T62 tanks, which had by now by-passed the 7th Brigade and were some 500 yards behind it in the *wadi*. Manoeuvring on the high ground around the valley, Avi's battalion destroyed the Assad force, which proved to be very mediocre on the field of battle. Avigdor now placed all the forces in the central sector under Avi. 'Don't worry, sir,' said Avi, reminding him proudly of his Yemenite origin, 'I'm a Black Panther. They won't get past me.' The Syrians continued desperately and with great determination to push on, fighting against some fifteen Israeli tanks holding on grimly at ranges of 250–500 yards, but now fighting from their original positions on the ramps which gave them considerable tactical advantage. The Syrians passed them and were now firing on them from behind. The heat of the flames from the burning tanks could be felt on all sides; the smell of gunpowder and burning cordite pervaded the atmosphere.

The 7th Brigade, attacked on all sides, was now fighting on a radius of 360 degrees. At this point in the battle, control and identification became impossible. Every tank and every small unit fought its own private war: Israeli tanks became mixed up and found themselves in the midst of a bunch of Syrian tanks; Syrian tanks lost their way in Israeli positions. The artillery of both sides pounded this nightmare of a battlefield as the Syrians fought desperately to achieve the breakthrough. The Israelis were by now fighting instinctively and barely consciously, realizing only in their subconscious the significance of what they were doing.

Avigdor could not escape the impression that this was the last battle. For some reason that he could not fathom afterwards, it did not dawn on him to withdraw to the rear, despite the fact that the brigade had reached the end of its tether as far as the physical strength and mental ability of the men were concerned. Their logistic capability and power of control were almost non-existent. They had been fighting for four days and three nights, without a moment's rest or respite, under constant fire. On average each tank was left with three to four shells. At the height of battle Avigdor turned and spoke to his operations officer. The officer began to reply but suddenly in the middle of his sentence slid to the floor of the armoured carrier, fast asleep. Avigdor spoke to Raful and told him that he did not know if he could hold on. Already in a daze, he described the condition of his brigade. Raful, as ever quiet, calm and encouraging, pleaded with him, 'For God's sake, Avigdor, hold on! Give me another half an hour. You will soon be receiving reinforcements. Try, please, hold on!'

At this critical moment, Lieut.-Col. Yossi, leading remnants of the Barak Brigade with a force of eleven tanks, entered the divisional area and was directed by Raful to Avigdor. Yossi had handed over command of his battalion in the Barak Brigade on 4 September and decided that his honeymoon would be a non-conventional one. So with his newly wed wife, Naty, he flew to the Himalayas. On Yom Kippur eve they rode by motorbike to the Chinese frontier. Back in Katmandu for Yom Kippur, the receptionist in the hotel said to him, 'You're from Israel, aren't you? Something is happening in your area. You ought to listen to the news.' Racing against time Yossi and Naty, using every form of subterfuge, managed to fly back to Israel via Teheran and Athens. From Athens Yossi phoned his family to bring his uniform and equipment to the airport. As he rushed northwards, little did he realize that he would receive command of the remnants of his former brigade. He hurried to Hofi's advanced headquarters and heard what had happened to the Barak Brigade. It was Tuesday morning.

When Dov had reached the Barak Brigade centre, remnants of the brigade began to arrive in dribs and drabs. Oded had in the meantime evacuated from the area of Tel Faris, taking with him some 140 infantry men who arrived on foot down the Gamla Rise. Dov and the other officers organized technical teams and began to recover abandoned tanks in the field, while ordnance units began to repair them. At noon on Tuesday a psychiatrist arrived from the medical centre of Tel Hashomer to take care of the soldiers of the Barak Brigade. He stood and looked at the dishevelled, unshaven, gaunt-eyed soldiers, some of them burnt and most of them blackened by the smoke and flames, working silently on the damaged tanks and putting them in shape. It was a moving and sobering sight. He asked them what they were doing and they explained that they were preparing the tanks to take them back into battle again. 'If they are going into battle again, I had better forget everything I ever learnt,' he remarked.

Dov notified command headquarters that he already had thirteen tanks ready for battle. He organized crews, brought in ammunition, begged some mortars and then he heard from command headquarters that Yossi was arriving to take command. The news of Yossi's arrival spread and Shmulick, who had been Yossi's second-in-command and who had been wounded in the first day of battle, escaped from the hospital in Safed and came to rejoin him and go back into battle. Conscious of the fact that they were to avenge the comrades of their brigade, Dov led Yossi's force to the front in a jeep. As they approached and received orders to join the 7th Brigade, Yossi heard on the radio that Tiger on the southern sector of the brigade front was out of ammunition and unable to hold out on the slopes of the 'Booster' against the Syrian advance.

Tiger's force was by now left with two shells per tank. 'Sir,' he radioed in a tone of desperation to the brigade commander, 'I can't hold on.' 'For heaven's sake hold on for only ten minutes,' implored Avigdor. 'Help is on the way.' When Tiger ran out of shells completely, he began to fill his pockets with hand grenades and withdraw. At this moment Yossi moved up to the 'Booster', opened fire and in the initial clash destroyed some thirty Syrian tanks. He had arrived just as the 7th Brigade, left with 7 running tanks out of an original total of approximately 100, was on the verge of collapse. Both sides had fought to a standstill. Avigdor had told Raful that he could not hold the Syrian attack, but suddenly a report came in from the A3 fortification (surrounded by Syrians and well behind the Syrian advance forces), that the Syrian supply trains were turning round and withdrawing. The Syrian attack had been broken; their forces broke and began to withdraw in panic.

The remnants of the 7th Brigade, including Yossi's reinforcements, totalled some twenty tanks. Exhausted, depleted to a minimum, many wounded, with their tanks bearing the scars of war, they now began to pursue the Syrians, knocking out tanks and armoured personnel carriers as they fled. On the edge of the anti-tank ditch, they stopped: the brigade had reached the limits of human exhaustion.

Avigdor stood in a daze looking down on the Valley of the Tears. Some 260 Syrian tanks and hundreds of armoured personnel carriers and vehicles lay scattered and abandoned across this narrow battlefield between the Hermonit and the 'Booster'. In the distance he could see the Syrians withdrawing in a haze of smoke and dust, the Israeli artillery following them. Raful's quiet voice came through on the earphones as he addressed them on the network of the 7th Brigade: 'You have saved the people of Israel.'

The Israeli Army can pride itself on many great battles, but few were as out-standing and as fateful as that of the 7th Brigade. Backed and strengthened by Raful's inflexible determination, Avigdor had fought a defensive and holding battle that was a classic in itself. A major element in his success was his intimate familiarity with the terrain over which he was to fight and the fact that his subordinate commanders were also at home there. The advantages and disadvantages of every piece of high ground were instinctive knowledge to the various commanders. The area had been prepared for battle: all the necessary range tables and the various ramps and alternative positions on all the hills had been prepared to give maximum advantage to an outnumbered force in fighting a defensive battle. Avigdor's highly trained brigade took full advantage of the preparations that had been made.

He had faced many problems. Above all, nobody had appreciated in advance the intensity of the fighting that would take place without let-up by day and by night, thus forcing the Israelis to fight without rest for days on end and to strain human will and endurance to the extreme. The Syrians took advantage of their superior equipment in night fighting and pressed home attacks every night. Having ruled the fields of battle at night in the past, the Israeli forces were now at a disadvantage. The ratio of forces was out of all proportion to what had ever been planned; the scope and strength of the Syrian attacks coming one after the other were of a nature and size for which the Israelis were not mentally prepared. Avigdor's brigade suffered from the limitations created by the static nature of the battle, which meant that the heavy, concentrated Syrian artillery took its toll of casualties and this toll proved to be a very heavy one, particularly among the Israeli commanders. On many occasions their vulnerability as they directed the fighting from open tank hatches under withering shell fire affected their ability to control the battle.

From the outset Avigdor realized that at all costs he had to prevent the Syrians from reaching the lateral Kuneitra–Masadah road. In order to effect this objective, he fought a defensive, static and holding battle, utilizing at all times mobile reserves to protect his flanks and to block any possible breakthrough in the brigade line. Yair's battalion was highly effective in supporting the fortifications in the line, which were important both because they diverted the Syrian forces and because their reporting from behind the Syrian lines was superb. At all times Avigdor maintained his three battalions sited on the high, controlling ground and deployed to the rear. By this method he invariably retained mastery over the killing areas. To offset the advantages the Syrians had by night, he was supported by flares from his artillery. The brigade fought in an area that was some 12 miles wide and 1–2 miles deep, while most of the Syrian forces attacking him concentrated in an area some 6 miles wide. Few commanders could credit the magnitude of the 7th Brigade victory until they saw with their own eyes the incredible scene of destruction and devastation with well over 500 armoured vehicles of all types strewn across the valley.

The experience of the 7th Brigade confirmed more than anything what a fatal error had been made by the Israeli Command and Government in not mobilizing in time – the 7th Brigade was initially the only concentrated armoured Israeli brigade against which the Syrian Army had to fight. Had the Syrian Army from the outset been obliged to attack *all* the brigades that were ultimately involved in the fighting in the Golan Heights, there would have been a different story. Instead they were thrown into battle haphazardly and piece-meal, at times inadequately equipped – not because the equipment was not available but because there was no time to collect or mount it. Had the Syrian Army come up against the entire Israeli force, there can be little doubt but that the entire 'Purple Line' would have been a series of 'Valleys of Tears'. Within two days of battle, having smashed itself against the Israeli armoured force, the remnants of the Syrian Army would have been desperately trying to hold back an advancing Israeli force into Syria with the supporting Iraqi and Jordanian forces still many days away. Had the Israeli Army in the north mobilized but twenty-four hours earlier and been ready for battle, as was the 7th Brigade, the Syrian Army would have been doomed.

9

The Counter-Attack

BACK IN TEL AVIV, Chaim Bar-Lev, former chief of staff, silver-haired, quiet, slow-speaking and calm, was visiting the supermarkets and stores in his capacity as minister of trade and industry. He had just arrived at the offices of the emergency organization charged with co-ordinating the civilian life of the country, when an urgent message came instructing him to come to the prime minister. It was 5.00 on Sunday afternoon when he was ushered into her office: she was sitting with her head between her hands, a depressed look on her face. She recounted to him how the minister of defence had come to her that day, after visiting the northern and southern fronts, and said, 'Golda, I was wrong in everything. We are heading towards a catastrophe. We shall have to withdraw on the Golan Heights to the edge of the escarpment overlooking the valley and in the south in Sinai to the passes and hold on to the last bullet.' She asked Bar-Lev to leave what he was doing, go up to the north and advise her what to do. He gladly agreed, but pointed out that it would be only proper for Dayan and Elazar to be consulted. She contacted them and they both readily consented, authorizing him to give orders on the spot should he think this necessary. Dayan asked him to see him before he left and he gave him a military shirt to wear.

Bar-Lev reached Northern Command headquarters at 8.00 that evening and saw on the maps in the war room how deeply the Syrians had penetrated into the Golan Heights. He realized that the situation was very serious indeed. The atmosphere was depressing. Bar-Lev began to talk in the quiet, slow, singsong that had made him a legend in the armed forces.

Looking tired and short of sleep, Hofi briefed him on the orders he had already issued early that morning for the organization for defence of all the approach roads descending from the Golan Heights, including the establishment of a series of anti-tank strongpoints. These orders, including the details of the defence organization of the area along the Jordan River, had been approved early in the morning by the minister of defence when he had visited the command (Laner had been designated as responsible for the defence positions before the bridges). Bar-Lev reviewed the report he had received and re-emphasized the importance of strengthening to the greatest possible degree the anti-tank obstacles along the main routes.

In the ensuing discussion with Hofi and members of his staff, the deployment of Gen. Musa Peled's division, which was now moving into the area, was considered. Proposals were made for the division either to concentrate in the area of the Bnot Ya'akov Bridge or to mount an attack along the southern route in the Golan Heights, the El Al route. Peled spoke against the moving of his division to the bridge: it had travelled many miles northwards on tracks, and to reach this bridge would have to continue for a considerable distance more. He urged that he be allowed to mount the attack on the first route he would reach, namely the El Al. Hofi had in fact already given orders for Peled's attack to take place along the southern routes, and Bar-Lev confirmed this.

Bar-Lev's calming presence – arriving as he did during the very difficult hours following the news of the destruction of the Barak Brigade and the death of Ben Shoham and his officers – contributed towards the improvement of the atmosphere in the command. Barely thirty-six hours after the Syrians had launched their attack, smashed the Israeli forces in the southern sector and pushed to within ten minutes of the Sea of Galilee, orders were being given here in Northern Command for a major counter-attack to be mounted on the next morning.

Next, Bar-Lev drove to Dan Laner's advanced headquarters across the Arik Bridge and up the Yehudia road. As he heard Laner's cautiously confident report and surveyed the incredible results which the hastily thrown-in forces had achieved on the Yehudia and El Al routes, he realized that the situation, while very serious, was by now manageable. The ratio of forces was dangerous but not hopeless. He explained to the officers at Laner's headquarters the critical nature of the battle on the Golan Heights; and describing the condition of the Barak and 7th brigades, said that it was now the duty of the Israel Defence Forces to upset the balance of the Syrian Command. When Peled was later describing Bar-Lev's visit, he said, 'On that evening Bar-Lev became one of the real heroes of the war.'

Returning to Tel Aviv, Bar-Lev reached Mrs Meir's office through the blacked-out streets of the city. He reported that the counter-attack would begin with a fresh division on the next morning. With luck he believed they could turn the tables; the situation was serious, but not hopeless. Mrs Meir thanked him and a look of relief came across her face. Standing her right arm on its elbow, she moved it demonstratively from side to side saying, 'The great Moshe Dayan! One day like this. One day like that!'

On Sunday evening Musa Peled received his orders from Hofi to launch a counter-attack in the southern sector on the following day. In addition to his division, all forces fighting on the El Al–Rafid route would now come under Peled's command. The chief of staff had decided to hold and consolidate in the south and to launch a counter-attack in the north. The situation on the Golan Heights was a dangerous one: no strategic depth was available; there was little room for manœuvre. The Syrians *must* be seen off the area. The mission of Peled's division was to push towards the Rafid junction, but he was worried: his tanks were arriving slowly – they were travelling on their tracks – and there were many technical failures *en route*.

At 10.00 that night Peled conducted an orders group at Tzemach at the southern end of the Sea of Galilee. His plan was to attack along two routes. The main effort was to be along the El Al–Rafid route, with the 19th Reserve Brigade (which had been in battle since Sunday afternoon and had already sustained losses) leading and the 20th Brigade ready to follow through. The 70th Reserve Brigade was to follow, mopping up and protecting the right flank above the Ruqqad escarpment. To the left of the main effort, the 14th Reserve Brigade was to advance along a line leading from the Gamla Rise at Givat Yoav through Mazrat Kuneitra via Nahal Geshur to Hushniyah.

At 8.30 on Monday morning the counter-attack began. In the area of El Al the 19th Brigade came up against heavy opposition, in the initial attack seven of its tanks going up in flames. Peled saw that the flat, open terrain allowed for the employment of more forces, and he immediately threw the 20th Brigade into the battle. The 20th provided a base of fire while one of its battalions attempted to outflank the enemy from the right. The battle was a slow and grinding process, with Peled's forces engaging the enemy on both his flanks. The Syrians retaliated with very heavy artillery concentrations, but the Israeli forces persevered and soon Peled felt that they were gaining the upper hand. The 14th Brigade attack went well – over fifteen Syrian tanks were destroyed and the brigade reached the first lateral road opposite Ramat Magshimim. He ordered them to direct a battalion against the enemy's right flank, but the battalion commander erred in navigation and moved in the wrong direction. When he realized what was happening, Peled ordered the 19th and the 20th

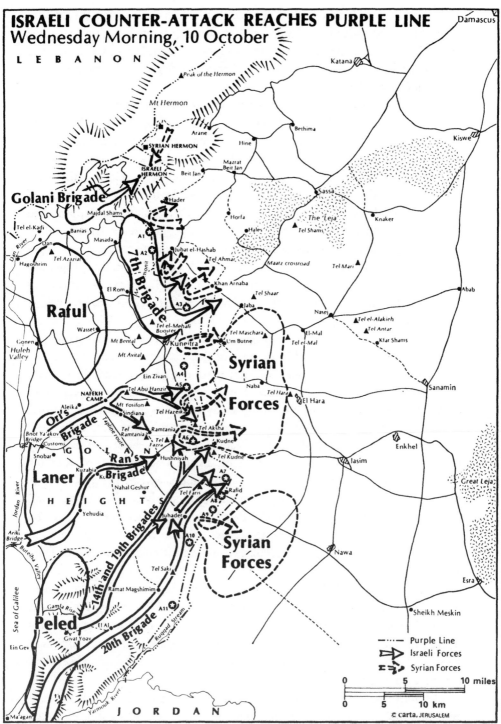

ISRAELI COUNTER-ATTACK REACHES PURPLE LINE
Wednesday Morning, 10 October

L E B A N O N

Damascus

Katana

Peak of the Hermon

Mt Hermon

Arane

Bethima

Kiswe

SYRIAN HERMON

Hine

ISRAELI HERMON

Beit Jan

Mazrat Beit Jan

Sassa

Golani Brigade

Hader

Majdal Shams

Horfa

The Leja

Knaker

Tel-el-Kadi

Banias

Masada

A1

Jubat el-Hashab

Hales

Tel Shams

River

Dan

Hagoshrim

Tel Azaziat

A2

Tel Ahmar

Maatz crossroad

Tel Mari

7th Brigade

Khan Arnaba

Tel Shaar

Abab

El Rom

A3

Jaba

Nasej

Tel el-Alakich

Tel Antar

Raful

Tel el-Mehati Booster

Kfar Shams

Wasset

Mt Bental

Kuneitra

Tel Maschara

Um Butne

El-Mal

Tel el-Mal

Gonen

Huleh Valley

Mt Avital

A4

Syrian

Naba

Tel Hara

El Hara

Sanamin

Ein Zivan

A5

Tel Abu Hanzir

Forces

NAFEKH CAMP

Mt Yosifon

Tel Hazeika

Aleika

Sindiana

Enkhel

Orr's

Bnot Ya'akov Bridge

Customs

Tel Ramtania

Ramtania

Tel Aksha

Kudne

Iasim

Brigade

Snobar

G O L A N

Tel Fazra

A6

Tel Kudne

Great Leja

Kuzabia

Kfar

Hushniyah

Ran's

Brigade

Nahal Geshur

Tel Faris

A7

Rafid

Laner

H E I G H T S

A8

Yehudia

Juhader

A9

Syrian

Ariki Bridge

Buteiha Valley

A10

Forces

Nawa

Tel Saki

14th and 19th Brigades

Ramat Magshimim

Esra

Sea of Galilee

Gamla Rise

Sheikh Meskin

Peled

El Al

Givat Yoav

A11

20th Brigade

Ein Gev

Ruqqad Stream

- - - - Purple Line
Israeli Forces
Syrian Forces

J O R D A N

Yarmouk River

0   5   10 miles
0   5   10 km

© carta, JERUSALEM

Ma'agan

WA—E

brigades to attack head on. With a force that included converted World War Two vintage Sherman tanks equipped with British 105 mm guns, they smashed through a Syrian force equipped with the most modern Soviet tanks. Most of the Syrian force was destroyed (sixty abandoned Syrian tanks were counted between Ramat Magshimim and El Al).

The 20th Brigade then advanced northwards, with the 19th Brigade refuelling and protecting the left flank of the advance. Peled ordered the 19th Brigade to utilize the lateral road running north from Ramat Magshimim and to broaden the divisional front by moving on the left flank of the 14th Brigade. Fighting a mobile armoured battle, the division advanced and by 1 o'clock in the afternoon, reached the Tapline crossroads at Juhader. As the advance elements of the 19th Brigade reached the Israeli village of Nahal Geshur, they approached carefully, expecting to find Syrians there. To their surprise an Israeli soldier, who belonged to a unit which was stationed in the village emerged carrying a rifle and a grenade. His orders on Saturday had been to defend the village, but since he had lost contact with his comrades and had received no countermanding orders this boy had remained alone to defend it (the Syrian Army had by-passed the village on Yom Kippur).

While the division was advancing, reports were received that an enemy tank company was moving around in the rear of the 20th Brigade and threatening the supply columns. The second-in-command of one of the brigade's battalions travelling with two half-tracks of battalion headquarters had driven over a fold in the ground and had suddenly come on six Syrian tanks concentrated together. As he saw them this officer – who but for the war would have been at his desk this Monday morning as Mr Caspi, headmaster of a school – instinctively ordered the two half-tracks to charge with all the weapons aboard, machine guns and submachine guns, firing. Bewildered and surprised the Syrian crews jumped out of their tanks and began to defend themselves with grenades and machine guns. They were wiped out. Peled had in the meantime ordered the 19th Brigade to detach a battalion to seek out this force, but when it arrived its mission had already been accomplished by the intrepid schoolmaster from Ramla.

Meanwhile, the lead Battalion of the 20th Brigade had reached the area of Tel Saki, a hill 110 yards to the east of the main road. Here they ran into an anti-tank defence locality (based on both sides of the road leading from Tel Saki to Juhader), coming under heavy fire from anti-tank missiles and anti-tank guns and suffering losses. They were pinned down and the brigade had to launch a major attack to relieve them.

The 20th Brigade had been mauled by the first impact. To its left the 14th Brigade nibbled away at the Syrian defences, the extent and depth of which

Peled and his brigade commanders did not appreciate. Towards evening the 19th Brigade, advancing on the left flank of the 14th, came up against the same anti-tank defensive position. At this point the position was still being organized and manned by the Syrian forces. The 19th Brigade commander did not hesitate: with all weapons blazing, the brigade force charged the Syrian position (part of which had not yet been manned) and overcame part of the defence locality.

The division was now nibbling into this position on all three axes of advance. They realized how formidable it was. What they had come up against was in fact a major defensive anti-tank position, with an imposing mixture of tanks, infantry, anti-tank missiles and anti-tank guns, all covered by heavy concentrations of artillery. The 132nd Mechanized Syrian Brigade had pulled back in the face of Peled's onslaught in this area, but a composite Syrian anti-tank battalion, composed of three companies of BMD 2 Sagger armoured vehicles firing anti-tank missiles and two companies of 106mm recoilless anti-tank guns, was ordered to join the 132nd Brigade on the morning of 8 October. One Syrian officer taken prisoner described how they awaited the Israeli counter-attack that morning at 10 o'clock. Observing the Israeli armoured advance from the south, every company in the line fired some thirty missiles against their tanks.

All day long on Monday Dan Laner's division waged a bitter battle against the Syrian forces on the Yehudia road. Ran's 17th Brigade was under considerable pressure and was down to half its strength. The deputy brigade commander, who had taken command after Col. Ran was wounded and evacuated the day before, was killed in the afternoon (Laner sent in his divisional deputy to replace him). As the brigade advanced, it ran into an ambush. Two companies of the brigade (under command of the brigade operations officer) moved back, effected a wide, flanking movement, and coming up behind the Syrian force engaging the main force of the brigade, they destroyed all thirteen Syrian tanks in the ambush. The brigade itself now comprised one tank battalion and a reconnaissance unit which had been placed under command.

Throughout the day Ori's 79th Brigade was also battling with the Syrian forces which continued to press relentlessly along the Tapline route in an endeavour to reach Nafekh and by-pass it. He was under command of Laner's 21st Division and the main Syrian effort concentrated in the direction of Sindiana towards Nafekh on the Tapline route.

Manœuvring the 17th Brigade advancing up the Yehudia road from the west in the direction of the Tapline and Hushniyah and the 79th Brigade advancing from the north in the general direction of Sindiana–Hushniyah, Laner increased pressure on the forces of the 1st Syrian Armoured Division that were pushing northwards along the Tapline route and westwards towards the Jordan. This Syrian division, under Col. Tewfiq Jehani, was proving to be a very formidable opponent, with Jehani urging his troops forward relentlessly and at all stages in the fighting insisting on maintaining momentum and on seeking out ways to by-pass the enemy. The very high standard of this division was reflected also in the behaviour of the 91st Brigade commander, Col. Shafiq Fiyad, whose forces led the division. This brigade, when it became obvious that Nafekh was being stubbornly defended, by-passed the crossroads and dashed westwards across country. Its forward elements reached the area of the main Israeli supply concentrations at Snobar some 12 miles inside the Golan Heights, an advance that proved to be the deepest penetration achieved by the Syrians in the war, reaching almost the upper customs house some 4½ miles from the Jordan River (their tanks were but a ten-minute tank drive from the Jordan River at the Bnot Ya'akov Bridge).

Ori, commanding the 79th Brigade, called in his reserve force (which he had placed in the area of Ein Zivan, south of Kuneitra), and ordered it to move from the rear in a wide, flanking movement and push southwards towards Sindiana, thus endangering the flank of the advancing Syrian forces. Stretched to the utmost, he contacted Raful Eytan and asked for a company from the 7th Brigade lying to the north. His request was granted and he moved the six tanks he received southwards along the Tapline route. As the situation tidied itself up, Ori concentrated his force moving southwards. Towards evening he led his brigade in storming Sindiana, inflicting very heavy casualties. By evening his forces were in full control of the Tapline route in the area of Nafekh, and were deployed along the Sindiana–Ramtania–Hushniyah route and the east–west route immediately north of Sindiana. Hingeing on Sindiana, his brigade was poised southwards ready to continue.

But it was now that the shock of the battle, the violent transposition from the holiday atmosphere before Yom Kippur to the horrors of these two days, suddenly hit Ori. His officers were being killed one by one – he had just now lost two more of his company commanders – and his reservists were bewildered and shocked. The experience they had been through had been traumatic, and he found that he had to make a superhuman effort to summon up all his physical reserves in order to exercise the leadership which was absolutely vital in this bitter, harsh and cruel battle. But for the success at Sindiana, he wondered what would have happened to the brigade; for overcoming the tremendous force in the area had instilled a new feeling of confidence in the men. He spoke to them and saw that Sindiana had convinced them that given a reasonable ratio on the field of battle, they could give as good as they got.

Both from the military point of view and for his troops' morale, Sindiana was the turning point.

On Tuesday morning the Syrians counter-attacked Sindiana and Ori's forces came under very heavy katyusha and artillery fire. He waited for the Syrian attack and destroyed their tanks at extreme ranges. In the afternoon, as the 17th Brigade approached the Tapline route from the west, Ori led his brigade against Ramtania and Tel Ramtania overlooking Hushniyah. (Hushniyah had become the focal and administrative centre for the Syrian forces in the southern Golan Heights. The area was held by the 1st Armoured Division and had been converted into an anti-tank defence locality of major and formidable proportions by the units of the 5th Division, which had achieved the original breakthrough in this sector.)

Ramtania was a heavily fortified position, a prolongation of the main anti-tank defensive locality based on Hushniyah. The terraces on the line of hills parallel to the Tapline route, were seething with tanks, anti-tank guns, Sagger missile positions and RPG positions. Potentially it was a most dangerous situation and the flank of any force moving along the road would be exposed to a fatal concentration of anti-tank fire.

Ori placed a force of ten tanks to engage the position and neutralize his eastern flank. The remainder of the force moved on the Sindiana–Ramtania and Sindiana–Tapline routes. The commander of the force on the Tapline route was hit and his force joined Ori. Heavy artillery concentrations were descending on the brigade incessantly. Half an hour before darkness, however, with Ori's advanced headquarters in the centre, the brigade stormed Ramtania. The battle was literally fought yard by yard until finally the position was overcome.

That night Ori again surveyed his brigade: they had sustained very heavy losses. All day long they had been fighting, not stopping for a moment's rest, not even for food. But as the brigade moved into night laager in the area of Ramtania, he noted that the force was becoming more integrated and that the greatest asset of all in fighting – an *esprit de corps* born of partnership in war and danger in common – was emerging. The brigade reorganized, reaching over a battalion in strength.

By the evening of Tuesday Laner had closed the northern and western pincers on the main Syrian concentration at Hushniyah. Ori's 79th Brigade was at Tel Ramtania overlooking Hushniyah and the 17th Brigade was deployed on the Tapline route facing eastwards and refuelling. From the south-east Peled's division was closing the trap.

At 3 o'clock on Tuesday morning, 9 October, Peled issued orders to his orders group giving the general line of advance the division was to maintain. The

20th Brigade would advance towards the border, keeping the Rafid–Tel Faris road on its left flank; the 14th Brigade would continue to the left of the main El Al–Rafid road, while the 19th Brigade would maintain the impetus towards Hushniyah. His intention was that the shock of the division's attack would take it across the 'Purple Line' and that Tel Kudne, which was the dominating position in the enemy's hands in this area, would be taken by the division in its stride.

The disorganized and haphazard manner in which the forces had been thrown into battle at the outset was highlighted by the fact that this was the first time since the division had entered battle that Peled found himself together with all his subordinate commanders. They had been through the nightmare of the mobilization and the mad rush across Israel on tracks to reach the battle front. Outnumbered and in some cases with inferior equipment, they had reached the line only just in time to stop the Syrian advance to the Sea of Galilee. Their division had launched the first major counter-attack of the IDF against the attacking Arab forces. Fighting for every yard, they had gradually pushed them back. As Peled contemplated his reservists, red-eyed, weary, blackened by smoke and covered in dust, and recalled what they had been through in the past two days, he felt that he was in the presence of a very heroic group. They had long since passed the barrier of fear.

The attack developed with first light. Instead of the defensive infantry anti-tank locality, which they had encountered the day before, they came up against masses of armour. The 132nd Syrian Brigade had withdrawn, while the 46th Syrian Tank Brigade covered the southern flank of the 1st Division which was now fighting desperately in the area of Hushniyah.

In the meantime Peled's forces in the right flank had been linking up with the Israeli fortifications, until then cut off by the Syrians. For Peled and his commanders the meetings with these unassuming boys, who had held on against the Syrians under the most severe odds, was an experience they would never forget. The confidence and quiet heroism of these youngsters – bloody, dust-covered, wounded, dazed – made them all very humble and turned those encounters into moments that would never be forgotten.

The armoured battle continued unabated with the 19th Brigade being ordered to attack Hushniyah. Co-ordination with Laner's 21st Division moving from the west and the east of Hushniyah was established, and they reached the high ground south-east of Hushniyah by 11.00 that morning. Peled ordered the brigade to storm a hill because the forces there were causing serious losses to the left flank of the 14th Brigade.

Col. Mir, commander of the 19th Brigade, moved at 11 o'clock in order to co-ordinate his attack with that of a battalion of the 17th Brigade, which would attack along the Yehudia route. As they approached, Mir observed masses of Syrians in the position, which was some 2 miles wide and 1 mile deep. About fifty tanks and a large number of anti-tank weapons, missiles and anti-tank guns were concentrated there. The force under Mir's command now numbered less than half a battalion of tanks. Within ten minutes most of his tanks were hit; a battalion commander was wounded, and the attack became disorganized and failed.

Meanwhile the 20th Brigade on the right flank of the attack was wearing down the 46th Syrian Tank Brigade and by noon had reached the vicinity of Tel Faris. Enemy opposition was fierce, while Syrian armoured forces continued to move in from Syria across the 'Purple Line'. (Peled's division was in fact straddling two of the 1st Syrian Armoured Division's three axes of advance, and the 20th Brigade had by now become a wedge penetrating the mass of enemy armour.) By noon on Tuesday, the 20th Brigade's situation was precarious.

Col. Jehani, commander of the 1st Syrian Division, was facing a serious dilemma: Ori's repeated attacks had decimated the 91st Syrian Brigade under Col. Fiyad; the Israeli forces under Raful, north of Kuneitra, were holding the line which his northern neighbours had failed to penetrate. He had concentrated his divisional supply system in the area of Hushniyah prior to developing his attack towards Israel, but the entire area was now threatened by the pincers of Laner's forces from the west and the north and of Peled's forces from the south. If the armoured forces, which he was throwing in desperately against Peled's right-hand sweep, would not arrest it, his entire division would be doomed. In addition, the Israeli Air Force was now in battle, having dealt with many of the threatening surface-to-air missile sites, and the area of the Hushniyah camps was under effective air bombardment. Determined as he was, the situation was beginning to look very serious to Col. Jehani. He ordered his forces in the Hushniyah pocket to exert pressure eastwards against Peled's encircling force, with the result that part of Peled's division found itself under pressure from two opposing directions.

Unaware of Jehani's predicament, Peled ordered the 14th Brigade in the centre to attack with all its strength and to penetrate to the greatest possible depth. The 14th Brigade's attack succeeded in gaining control of the Hushniyah–Rafid road, thus relieving the left flank of the 20th Brigade and reducing the pressure on that force. The 20th Brigade sent a reconnaissance force to capture Tel Faris, but as it came up the hill, Syrian tanks destroyed part of it, whereupon a group of Israeli volunteers climbed the heights of Tel Faris from the rear. As they scaled the ridge, a PT76 amphibious tank fired on them. An NCO ran forward, climbed the tank and dropped grenades inside. The excellent observation post afforded by this hill was in Israeli hands. Unknown to the Israelis, however, a small Syrian unit remained hidden on the slopes of the hill and continued to direct Syrian fire until it was discovered on Thursday, 11 October. The 19th Brigade was ordered to attack the area of Hushniyah once more with artillery support and for the first time with close air support. This time the brigade outflanked the Syrian positions and came in from the rear. The attack began at 4 o'clock, with two battalions leading, and battle was engaged with the 40th Mechanized Brigade of the 1st Syrian Armoured Division. With all the artillery support available and with air support, the 19th Brigade captured the hill and continued along the Syrian defence position from Hushniyah, passing through the village and taking up positions on its northern side. When the brigade stormed Tel Fazra, its tanks were down to two-thirds.

After the tanks of the 19th Brigade had broken through the positions, Syrian forces moved back into them under cover of darkness and the brigade found itself again in the midst of a Syrian force. Throughout the night the 15th Syrian Mechanized Brigade of the 3rd Syrian Armoured Division (which had been attached to the main effort) tried to break through to reinforce the 1st Armoured Division in Hushniyah, but it was held by units of the 20th Brigade before Tel Faris.

At 3 o'clock on Wednesday morning, Peled held an orders group emphasizing the general intention to take Tel Kudne. By now the 20th Brigade held the Rafid crossroads and Tel Faris and Peled's forces had closed up to the 'Purple Line', apart from the area of Hushniyah, where the 19th Brigade – with a total force of half a battalion of tanks – was still engaging Syrian forces. The orders were for the right-hand 70th Brigade, which had been protecting the right flank of the division along the Ruqqad escarpment, to cross the 'Purple Line' at El Hanut and roll up the Syrian positions along the Ruqqad to Buka'a; the 20th Brigade was to move along the Tapline route and capture the Syrian positions on the west bank of the Ruqqad; the 14th Brigade was to move to the Israeli fortification on the Kudne road at A6, while the 19th Brigade was to pass through the 14th Brigade along the Tel Fazra–Kudne route.

Attacking individually all the brigades came up against well-established Syrian anti-tank defences. Losses in tanks were heavy. The 19th Brigade passed through Tel Fazra and moved up on the hilly ground leading to Tel Kudne. The brigade was already across the 'Purple Line' when its commander informed Peled that if he continued the attack against the heavily fortified position at Tel Kudne, nothing would be left of his force. As he spoke two of his tanks blew up on the Syrian minefield. Realizing that he had dissipated his strength too much, Peled decided that the only solution would be to concentrate the division in an attack on Tel Kudne. This he proposed to Gen. Hofi. Aware of what had happened to Peled's division in these isolated attacks and about to issue orders to Raful Eytan to attack into Syria, Hofi ordered Peled to remain in position. By Wednesday, 3.00 pm, the remnants of Peled's division were drawn up along the 'Purple Line'.

As the attack was mounted against Tel Kudne, Col. Jehani moved his forward headquarters from the Tel eastwards. While Peled's division was moving out on Wednesday morning to the 'Purple Line', Laner launched his forces in co-ordination. Ran's 17th Brigade attacked Hushniyah from the north from the area of Ramtania. The area between the Hushniyah crossroads and Tel Fazra was the killing-ground. Peled's forces had moved up with tanks on Tel Fazra. The 17th Brigade was moving south from Ramtania while Ori's 79th Brigade was directed to attack the ridge of terracing on the southward side of the Kuneitra route and to support the 17th Brigade. Ori's forces advanced, believing that the Syrians had in the meantime withdrawn, but they were suddenly subjected to a hail of RPG and Sagger anti-tank fire. Seeing this Ori stormed the terraces with the tank reserve under his command, losing five tanks in the first wave. A covering force reported that the Syrians were fleeing eastwards. By ten in the morning, the 79th Brigade mission had been accomplished and the 17th Brigade was being covered.

By midday on Wednesday, almost exactly four days after some 1,400 Syrian tanks had stormed across the 'Purple Line' in a massive attack against Israel, not a single Syrian tank in fighting condition remained within the 'Purple Line'. The Hushniyah pocket, in which two Syrian brigades had been destroyed, was one large graveyard of Syrian vehicles and equipment; hundreds of guns, supply vehicles, armoured personnel carriers, fuel vehicles, BRD Sagger armoured missile carriers, tanks and tons of ammunition were dotted about the hills and slopes surrounding Hushniyah.

Along all the routes of the Syrian advance, the pride of the Syrian Army lay smoking and burnt out. Each individual Israeli force had gained a great victory in itself. Some 200 tanks had been destroyed along the Yehudia road by Ran's 17th Brigade, of some 40–50 tanks.

The Syrians had left behind in the Golan Heights 867 tanks, some of which were of the most modern T62 type, in addition to thousands of vehicles, anti-tank vehicles, guns and sundry equipment. The most modern arms and equipment which the Soviet Union had supplied to any foreign armies dotted the undulating hills of the Golan Heights, testimony to one of the great tank victories in history against the most incredible odds and to the indomitable spirit of the Israeli forces, which within four days had suffered a crushing disaster, had recovered and had in one of the most heroic battles in modern military history turned the tables and driven the invading force back to its starting line.

10

The Break-in

THE STRATEGIC DECISION of the Israeli General Staff had been in favour of priority for the Golan Heights. In this area there was no depth, such as in Sinai, and any local Syrian breakthrough could well endanger the Israeli centres of population in the northern Galilee. The Syrians therefore had to be seen off the area as rapidly as possible; after which the Syrian Army had to be broken, thus removing the military threat poised against the country's northern frontier. Only then could the weight of Israel's military force be turned against the Egyptian forces.

An additional consideration was the fact that help in the form of reinforcements – above all from Iraq, but also from Saudi Arabia and Kuwait – was on the way. It was obvious to the Israeli General Staff that King Hussein of Jordan, until now sitting awkwardly on the fence of non-intervention, would be influenced in his future decisions by the fate of the Syrian Army. Time was of the essence, as reports of the Iraqi troop movements towards Syria were received. Furthermore, the withdrawing Syrian Army could not be given a chance to recover and to absorb the equipment beginning to flow in from the Soviet Union.

At 10 o'clock on Wednesday night, 10 October, the General Staff held a conference to decide whether to consolidate positions along the 'Purple Line' or to continue the attack into Syria. Minister of Defence Dayan entered during the conference and Elazar outlined the pros and cons of the problem to him. Dayan was hesitant about an advance into Syria, mindful as he was of the

Soviet problem posed by such an advance. Elazar however was of the view that the Israelis had to achieve a penetration some 12 miles in depth; this, he believed, would neutralize Syria as an element in the war and bring pressure to bear on Egypt.

Dayan took Elazar and a number of officers to see Mrs Meir. There followed a discussion in which Dayan tended in favour of the attack. In the end the prime minister decided in favour of the continuing the push into Syria. Gen. Elazar issued orders to Northern Command accordingly. The counter-attack would commence on Thursday, 11 October.

Hofi decided to launch the attack in the northernmost sector of the Golan, choosing this area because the left flank of the attacking forces would rest on the slopes of Mount Hermon, which would be impassable to Syrian armoured forces. The axis of advance constituted the shortest route to Damascus, and the resultant threat to their capital city could influence the Syrian deployment. The terrain was rolling ground, affording good observation on the main Kuneitra–Damascus highway, along which Laner's forces were due to advance.

Raful Eytan, with the 7th Brigade in the lead, was to command the break-in. Laner's 21st Division, with Ori's 79th Brigade and Ran's 17th Brigade under command, was to attack two hours after Raful's division along the heavily fortified main Damascus road. Should Laner's division be blocked, it would follow Raful's. If, however, Laner were to succeed along the Damascus road, Raful would cover him and support him from the high ground to the north as he advanced. H hour was 11 o'clock on Thursday (it was difficult for the Israeli forces to attack earlier in the morning because the sun would be in their eyes). Laner would move at 1.00 pm.

When the Syrians had withdrawn two days earlier, they left Avigdor with some twenty tanks, of which eleven were Lieut.-Col. Yossi's last-minute reinforcements. Day and night his ordnance personnel worked themselves to a standstill repairing the damaged tanks of the brigade. Maj. Sam, Avigdor's ordnance officer, performed miracles. In the meantime, Lieut.-Col. Amos, who had been abroad and had abandoned everything in a wild rush to fly back to Israel, joined the brigade with a battalion of fresh tanks. Two days after he was down to his last reserves, Avigdor was ready to move into battle with newly arrived reinforcements.

The brigade mission was to take Tel Shams and Mazrat Beit Jan. Its southern boundary was to be the main Kuneitra–Damascus route passing through Khan Arnaba, Tel Shams and Sassa. The break-in point was chosen on what proved to be the correct assumption that the area was less strongly defended in the north. As Avigdor saw it, one of his main problems was to get through the Syrian minefields, because success or failure would be dictated by the rapidity with which he managed to deploy all his forces in battle. The break-in area was rocky, hilly and well wooded.

Avigdor divided his brigade into two forces. The northern force was composed of Avi's 7th Battalion and Amos's newly arrived reserve battalion – its mission was to capture Hader and Mazrat Beit Jan. The southern force, led by the remnants of the Barak Brigade commanded by Lieut.-Col. Yossi, consisted of two battalions of tanks with additional forces: the 5th Battalion under Lieut.-Col. Josh, a battalion under Yossi and Yair with the remnants of his 4th Battalion. Their mission was to capture Jubata, the high ground north of Khan Arnaba, the Hales camps and Tel Shams.

On Wednesday evening, after the command orders group, Avigdor assembled all his commanders. Looking at them and recalling what they had been through in the past four days, many with difficulty managing to keep their eyes open, men to whom he knew the country owed so much, a strange emotion moved him. He launched into a touching address. In their logical sequence, the dry recital of the elements of an operation order, instinctive to every officer in every army, became a moving pronouncement. He was inspired as he faced the red-eyed, weary officers who had led their men so valiantly in so fateful a battle. He outlined the plan for the break-in to Syria and the exploitation of success against the Syrians. In leading their men to victory, they would be avenging the comrades who had fallen at their side.

Dov joined Avigdor's advanced headquarters, and at 11 o'clock on 11 October units of what had been the Barak Brigade crossed the 'Purple Line' and led the 7th Brigade forces into Syria. The remnants of a brigade that had literally fought to the last had risen again and were leading the Israeli Army. As Dov observed Yossi's battalion attacking, covered by Yair's tanks, he found that he was crying. Barak was a brigade in which 90% of the commanders had died or had been wounded: only one original company second-in-command and two platoon commanders remained; not one company commander had survived the first battles. And yet here again the brigade was in action.

Facing Avigdor's forces was the Moroccan Expeditionary Force in brigade strength backed by some forty tanks and covering the approaches to Mazrat Beit Jan. Facing Yossi's southern effort was a Syrian infantry brigade, reinforced with anti-tank weapons and some thirty-five tanks. The advance forces found the breaches through the Syrian minefields and, backed by artillery and air support, broke through them. The fighting was at short ranges through heavily-wooded areas covered with thick undergrowth.

The northern effort under Avi broke through the wooded area and in bitter fighting gradually gained control of the high ground and captured the Hader crossroads, forcing the 68th Syrian Brigade of the 7th Armoured Division to

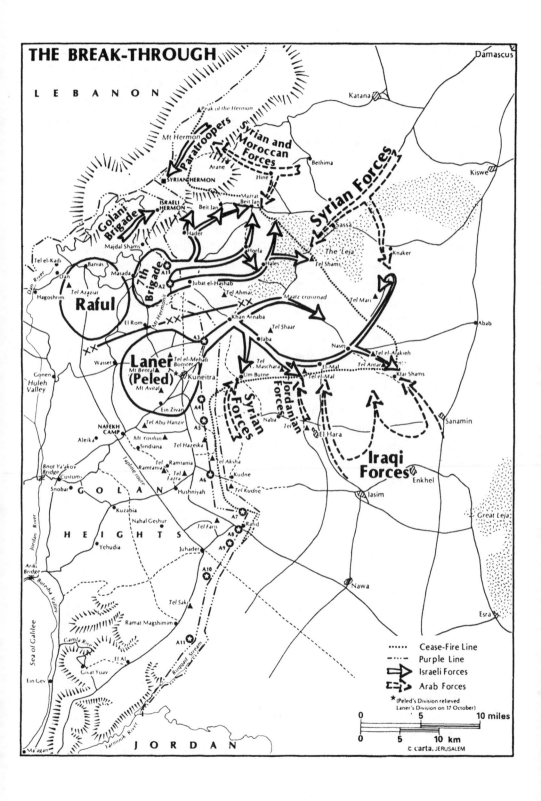

THE BREAK-THROUGH

LEBANON

Damascus

Katana

Peak of the Hermon

Mt Hermon

Paratroopers

Syrian and Moroccan Forces

Bethima

Kiswe

Arane

SYRIAN HERMON

Hine

Mazrat Beit Jan

Syrian Forces

Golani Brigade

ISRAELI HERMON

Beit Jan

Beit Jan

Hader

Sassa

7th Brigade

Majdal Shams

Horfa

The 'Leja

Knaker

Tel el-Kadi

Banias

A11

Hales

Tel Shams

Masada

A2

Jubat el-Hashab

Dan River

Dan

Tel Aziziat

Tel Ahmar

Maatz crossroad

Tel Mari

Hagoshrim

Raful

El Rom

Mt Hermon

Khan Arnaba

Abab

Wasset

A3

Tel Shaar

Jaba

Nasej

Tel el-Alakieh

Gonen

Huleh Valley

Laner (Peled)

Tel el-Mehali Booster

Mt Bental

Tel Maschara

Um Butne

El-Mal

Tel Antar

Kfar Shams

Mt Avital

Kuneitra

Syrian Forces

Naba

Tel el-Mal

Jordanian Forces

Ein Zivan

A4

Tel

Sanamin

NAFEKH CAMP

Tel Abu Hanzir

A5

El Hara

Iraqi Forces

Aleika

Mt Yosifon

Sindiana

Tel Hazeika

Enkhel

Bnot Ya'akov Bridge

Customs

Tel Ramtania

Ramtania

Tel Aksha

Kudne

Iasim

Snobar

G O L A N

Tel Fazra

Hushniyah

Tel Kudne

Jordan River

Kuzabia

Nahal Geshur

A7

Great Leja

H E I G H T S

Yehudia

Tel Faras

Rafid

Juhader

A8

A9

Ariki Bridge

Buteiha Valley

A10

Nawa

Tel Saki

Ramat Magshimim

Esra

Gamla River

A11

Sea of Galilee

El Al

Givat Yoav

Ein Gev

Rukkad Stream

Ma'agan

Yarmuk River

J O R D A N

```
·········  Cease-Fire Line
─·─·─·─   Purple Line
⟦⟧        Israeli Forces
⟦⟧        Arab Forces
```

★ (Peled's Division relieved Laner's Division on 17 October)

0   5   10 miles

0   5   10 km

© carta, JERUSALEM

withdraw. Several days later the commander of this brigade, a Druse, Col. Rafiq Hilawi, stood in a camp on the outskirts of Damascus. His badges of rank were torn off him, as with his eyes blindfolded he faced a firing squad. He had been court martialled and sentenced to death for withdrawing, his guilt having been compounded by the intense suspicion with which the Syrian regime tends to regard the Druse people.

Avi and Amos's forces advanced on Mazrat Beit Jan, but were held up by a counter-attack of some forty Syrian tanks supported by the Syrian Air Force. On Friday their forces broke into the village and heavy fighting continued for some six hours, with battle being joined at short ranges and with the Syrian forces counter-attacking along the routes from the north and from the east. The Syrian Air Force and artillery attacked indiscriminately. Avigdor sent a covering force from the south to beat off the Syrian counter-attacks and by 5 o'clock in the afternoon Mazrat Beit Jan and the hills surrounding it were in Israeli hands. Golani infantry with armoured elements moved in to hold them.

In the southern sector of the brigade, Yossi's first major battle was on the high ground of Tel Ahmar overlooking Khan Arnaba from the north. The Syrians fought obstinately with missiles until the Israeli forces overcame them. This brought the right flank of Raful's division and the left flank of Laner's division in sight of one another. By Thursday evening the 5th Battalion had captured the Druse village of Horfa, while on Friday morning Yossi's battalion occupied the Maatz crossroads, where they came under heavy Syrian air attack. Yossi himself was wounded but continued to command the battalion. He was ordered to attack the dominating feature of Tel Shams along the main Damascus road. Three times his battalion attempted to move forward, but each time it was held up by heavy anti-tank missile fire from Sagger anti-tank units hidden among the rocks and boulders of the volcanic 'Leja' plain on both sides of the road, which rendered the area almost impassable to armour. Avigdor attempted to mount an attack with the 4th and 5th battalions by developing a wide sweep through the 'Leja'. They leapfrogged across this difficult terrain, destroying some twenty Syrian tanks at ranges up to 2 miles; but the terrain proved to be impassable, and the attack was held up by the Syrians.

Avigdor moved his advanced headquarters to Hales and decided that he would attempt again to take Tel Shams by means of a deep, flanking movement to the left of the main road over a passable route that would be covered by fire from the 4th and 5th battalions on the main road. The Syrian Air Force was mounting desperate attacks and heavy artillery concentrations were descending on the advancing Israeli force. Avigdor ordered Yossi to join him at Hales, and there, seated on the balcony of an Arab house, they observed the terrain and planned the line of approach of Yossi's forces, hoping to take Tel Shams by surprise from the rear. As they surveyed the scene through binoculars and pored over air photographs, incongruously one of the Syrian Druse villagers fed them and plied them with superb Turkish coffee. Seeing the complexity of the terrain and the dominant position of Tel Shams, Avigdor concluded that there was a fifty-fifty chance of success. He therefore decided not to issue an order to attack, whereupon Yossi volunteered to attack and to lead his battalion.

By now Yossi had two companies totalling twenty tanks in his battalion. One was ready to move and the other was loading. Avigdor decided not to wait for the second company, assuming that when ready it would move into battle in Yossi's wake, probably after half an hour. From the balcony vantage point in Hales, he surveyed the scene as Yossi's force made its way cautiously through the boulders and rocks of the 'Leja', along the path they had discovered. Soon Yossi reported that eight tanks had reached the slopes of Tel Shams from the rear – some 500 yards from the position – taking ten tanks by surprise from the rear and destroying them at close range. He informed Avigdor that he was leaving two tanks to cover him and was about to storm the position from the rear. Israeli artillery support opened up and the attack went in at 4.30 in the afternoon. The tanks began to climb Tel Shams and all were convinced that the attack was successful, but at the last minute four out of the six attacking tanks were knocked out by anti-tank missiles. Among the casualties was Yossi himself, whose long odyssey from the Himalayas came to an end in Rambam Hospital in Haifa. Avigdor tried to relieve them with the help of the force on the main Damascus road, but this, too, was covered by Syrian anti-tank missiles. A special patrol had to be sent in by foot to evacuate the wounded.

Avigdor later admitted that this attack had been a mistake. Only when Yossi's force had moved out did Avigdor remember to ask for and receive belated permission from Raful, who was left with little option with Yossi's tanks well under way. The fact that this attack had been a case of misuse of armour was to be emphasized when on Saturday night, 13 October, Raful ordered units of the 31st Parachute Brigade to take Tel Shams. Storming the dominating height at night, these crack units of the Israeli Army, once again in their element, captured the position for a total loss of four wounded.

Dan Laner's division broke into the Syrian positions along the main Damascus road two hours after Raful's forces penetrated to the north. A battalion of Ori's 79th Brigade deployed to give covering fire while Ran's 17th Brigade charged along the main road. Col. Ran, who had been wounded in his brigade's first encounter with the Syrian forces on the Yehudia route on the Sunday, returned heavily bandaged to take command of his brigade again.

Ran was a typical example of the Israeli youth who had grown up in the kibbutz. In the War of Independence his father had commanded one of the renowned Palmach formations. Shortly before the war Ran's younger brother was seriously injured in a road accident while serving in the army, and he was lying unconscious in hospital when Ran was wounded in battle. Not far from him in the southern Golan, their third brother, an officer in the Barak Brigade, had been killed while stemming the tide of the Syrian onslaught. His death had deprived Israel of one of its most promising young musical composers.

Aware of what had happened to the family, when the chief of staff heard that Ran had been wounded, he gave orders to relieve him of his combat command. The next that Elazar heard of Ran however was that he had refused to obey the order and had returned to battle. Hearing of this decision, Ran had reacted violently: 'I am not a child. This is the war of the people of Israel, and nobody is going to make my decisions for me.'

With his reconnaissance unit leading, Ran moved forward under a murderous concentration of artillery. Seventeen tanks of the reconnaissance unit were knocked out and it was clear that the brigade was in very serious trouble, having run up against a major concentration of Syrian anti-tank defences. Laner saw Ran's situation and decided to extricate his brigade from the battle. He ordered the 2nd Battalion of Ori's 79th Brigade to move in and help relieve his forces. As the situation looked its most desperate, Ran's remaining battalion mounted a second charge and two tanks of the leading platoon reached Khan Arnaba crossroads. When Laner heard this on the radio, he ordered the 79th brigade to cancel its plan to extricate the 17th and to exploit the breakthrough that had taken place. Ori's 79th Brigade passed Khan Arnaba and was followed by the 19th, which had been transferred to Laner from Peled's division. The 19th Brigade by-passed to the right, moved south to Jaba and attacked Tel Shaar. In the attack Ori's half-track was hit and caught fire, and he joined a tank. The Syrians fought desperately and attempted to counter-attack from the east but were repulsed. Ran however was now left with five running tanks in his brigade. The Syrian force which had been by-passed in the attack closed in on the main road and cut it in the area of Khan Arnaba. Part of Laner's force was now cut off, unable to evacuate its wounded or to receive supplies. All night long the area was a virtual death trap for Israeli tanks, swarming as it was with Syrian infantry with bazookas. The forces Ori had left behind to cover his advance began to move in. The commander of the first group was killed; the commander of the second wounded.

At this point the division sent in a parachute battalion, which was heavily engaged all night mopping up the Syrian forces and evacuating the Israeli wounded. When the paratroopers saw the condition of the tank crews they were horrified. They begged them to rest and without a word began to load the tanks with fuel and ammunition, to prepare tea and food for the crews and to do everything they could to relieve them.

The Syrian Command was by now showing signs of desperation. A note of hysteria was replacing the tone of confident victory which had for the past five days characterized the Arab broadcasts. The Israeli forces were advancing into Syria against a very depleted Syrian Army. The Israeli Air Force had come into its own, having destroyed part of the surface-to-air missile system: its planes were ranging far and wide into Syria to bomb strategic targets, such as the country's oil stores and power stations. At one stage Syrian planes returning from missions could not find an undamaged airfield in which to land (some however landed on motor routes specifically constructed for the purpose). Israeli planes were continually rendering Syrian airfields unusable, thus hindering the massive Soviet airlift that was daily flying in dozens of heavy transports, while Israeli naval attacks on Syrian ports were endangering the sea supply line from the Soviet Union. The bulk of the Syrian Army was being concentrated along the approaches to Damascus, and the Arab Foreign Legion, comprising units from Morocco, Saudi Arabia, Iraq and later Jordan, was assigned the task of delaying the Israeli advance. Announcements were made to the effect that even if Damascus were to fall, Syria would continue to fight.

The Syrian Government issued desperate pleas for help. President Assad, who but a few days ago had tried to use Soviet good offices with President Sadat of Egypt to agree to a cease-fire when it seemed as if the Golan would fall to the Syrian attack, was only too aware of the seriousness of the error in not pressing for a cease-fire at the outset. And while Syria was bleeding and fighting on the approaches to its capital city, its ally, the Egyptian Army, was sitting placidly on the east bank of the Suez Canal content to consolidate its gains and hesitant to endanger its success by advancing. Assad pleaded with the Egyptians to apply pressure on the Israeli forces and thus relieve his front. Gen. Ismail, the Egyptian minister of war, promised action. And indeed he later explained that the armoured battle of 14 October had been motivated by a desire to relieve the pressure on Syria.

The Syrians turned to their Soviet allies, who stepped up the airlift and increased supplies to their sorely pressed army. Aware of the fact that the Syrian front was in danger of collapsing, Moscow issued veiled threats, such as an announcement on the Soviet media that 'the Soviet Union cannot remain indifferent to the criminal acts of the Israeli Army'. The Soviet ambassador to the United States, Anatoly Dobrynin, presented the Soviet threat to Kissinger, indicating to him that Soviet airborne forces were now on the alert to move to the defence of Damascus.

Additional units of the US Navy moved to join the Sixth Fleet in the Mediterranean, while the Soviet fleet moved to protect the ports of Latakia and Tartus in Syria. The Soviet Union began to urge Arab countries to join their fellow Arabs in battle. Leonid Brezhnev sent a message to Houari Boumedienne, the Algerian ruler, urging him to do his Arab duty; and Soviet tanks were shipped via Yugoslavia to the Algerian units assigned to the Egyptian front.

Independent of these developments, in Israel a decision had been taken not to become involved in the capture of Damascus. The effect of such a move on the Arab world could be a very serious one, and its military value would at best be dubious. Furthermore, involvement in the conquest of a city of a million hostile inhabitants could be a very costly proposition indeed; the Israeli Command was only too aware of the danger of being drawn with its limited forces into the wide open spaces of Syria. When to these considerations were added the Soviet interest in the security of Damascus and the Soviet threats, it was obviously not in Israel's interest to advance beyond a point from which Damascus could be threatened by Israeli artillery fire.

Consequently only a few pinpoint air attacks against specific military targets in Damascus were approved by the Israeli Government, including a very successful one against the Syrian General Staff building. Indeed these attacks were approved only after the Syrians had launched surface-to-surface FROG missiles at civilian targets in the Galilee. The immigrant town of Migdal Haemek near Nazareth and Kibbutz Geva were among the civilian areas attacked by these missiles. Little damage was caused, but the significance of such indiscriminate attacks against civilian targets was not lost on the government. Nevertheless at no stage was advantage taken of Israel's capability to shell Damascus. Merely the threat remained.

On the morning of Friday, 12 October, Laner advanced his division. The 19th Brigade moved south and captured the village of Nasej. Ran's 17th Brigade came under fire from Tel Maschara, by-passed it and reached Nasej. Ori's 79th Brigade followed the two leading brigades and stopped in the area of Nasej to refuel its tanks.

Ordering the 17th and 19th brigades to advance towards Knaker, a move designed to outflank Sassa and to place both his own and Raful's division well forward on the main road to Damascus, Laner set up his advanced headquarters on Tel Shaar. A battalion of the 19th Brigade reached Tel el-Mal, thus reinforcing Laner's southern flank as his forces moved in a north-easterly sweep towards Knaker. Despite the heavy losses they had sustained, the 17th and 19th brigades were advancing northwards from Nasej towards Knaker and had already reached Hill 127, 2½ miles south of Knaker, where there were signs that the Syrian forces were breaking. The enemy was for the first time on the run, and Laner's forces pressed on with renewed vigour.

Standing on the dominating height of Tel Shaar, Laner through binoculars followed the clearly visible advance of his forces along the Nasej–Knaker road. During a lull in the advance, he began to survey the entire scope of the Syrian plain. As he looked southwards he suddenly froze. Some 6 miles away a force of approximately 100–150 tanks in two major groupings was deploying and moving northwards towards his open flank. For a moment he thought that this might be Peled's division moving after it had broken into Syria, but Northern Command assured him that this division was stuck at Rafid and that these were not Israeli forces. Realizing that he was about to be attacked on his wide-open flank while his forces were pursuing the rapidly withdrawing Syrians to the north-east, he immediately ordered Ori's 79th Brigade to stop refuelling and to deploy to the south of Nasej as rapidly as possible. Ran's force and the 19th Brigade were ordered to stop in their tracks on the road to Knaker and pull back to cover his southern flank. The order flabbergasted them and the brigade commanders pleaded with him: here, after all they had been through, they had the Syrians on the run, and now the fruits of victory were to be snatched from their grasp. But he refused to entertain their pleas and ordered them to turn southwards immediately.

In the meantime, without reference to the developments of Laner's southern flank, Hofi had decided to strengthen his efforts and ordered Peled to transfer the 20th Brigade to Laner. And a few moments after Laner had sighted the enemy force advancing across the plain towards his southern flank, the 20th Brigade commander reported for duty in his advanced headquarters. He was ordered to deploy his brigade in the area of Tel Maschara and Tel el-Mal.

In accordance with the undertakings it had given to Gen. Ismail, the Egyptian minister of war, with the outbreak of war the Iraqi Government had dispatched its 3rd Armoured Division to Syria. Two brigades arrived in the first week ending 11 October – an armoured brigade with 130 tanks and a mechanized brigade with 50 tanks. These were to be joined by another armoured brigade with 130 tanks some days later. Reaching the Great Leja on Friday, 12 October, before dawn the Iraqi tanks were taken off the transporters and advanced across the plain towards the southern flank of the Israeli forces, which were moving towards Knaker and were endangering the Kiswe military camps west of Damascus. An armoured brigade moved in a northerly direction while a mechanized brigade moved in a north-westerly direction towards Tel Maschara. The first Iraqi tanks came up against Ori's 79th Brigade, which engaged them at 300 yards' distance; he knocked out seventeen tanks and the Iraqi force stopped in its tracks.

Night came on and it was clear to Laner that the force which he now knew to be Iraqi would launch a major concentrated attack. The 20th Brigade commander was disturbed because one of his battalions was late in arriving and he sent out a brigade headquarters officer in a jeep to look for it. Driving in the darkness the jeep collided with a tank. The officer stood up to advise the tank that it was off course, discovering to his horror that he had bumped into an Iraqi vehicle. (The Israeli battalion was finally extricated with artillery support from amid the newly arrived Iraqis.)

As darkness fell Laner prepared for battle. The 19th Brigade was deployed along the road at the foot of Tel Shaar; Ori's 79th Brigade was deployed from the 19th Brigade northwards to the crossroads and then southwards towards Nasej; Ran's 17th Brigade was spread south along the road from Ori's to Nasej, while the 20th Brigade was sited along the Maschara–Jaba road. Thus Laner created a box from Maschara to Jaba to Maatz to Nasej, leaving an opening of some $4\frac{1}{2}$ miles between Maschara and Nasej. The situation was one armoured commanders dream about.

It was a bright moonlit night when Laner's deputy, Brig.-Gen. Moshe, and his intelligence officer informed him that the Iraqis were advancing into the opening between Nasej and Maschara. Laner could hardly believe them and went to the observation point to ascertain for himself. All divisional guns and tanks were turned inwards to the centre of the box with orders to fire at any moving target. Suddenly the Iraqis stopped and by 9.00 pm there was complete quiet. Laner's reports had created an atmosphere of tension and expectancy, and as the hours passed without developments, snide comments began to be made by the staff officers of Northern Command. Laner was feeling uncomfortable.

The 3rd Iraqi Armoured Division had in the meantime been reinforced by its 6th Armoured Brigade and at 3 o'clock on the morning of Saturday, 13 October, they launched a divisional attack, moving right into Laner's box. Laner's forces held their fire as the Iraqi division moved into their trap. The first streaks of light were appearing in the east when the Sherman tanks of the 19th Brigade opened fire. Their range was 200 yards.

Battle was joined and the Iraqis withdrew in disorder, leaving behind some eighty destroyed tanks. Not one Israeli tank was hit. The 8th Iraqi Mechanized Brigade suffered the brunt of the casualties in the first major armoured battle in which the Iraqi Army had ever engaged, and it lost almost a complete brigade in a matter of minutes. Laner's forces moved on to capture Tel Maschara and Tel Nasej, while paratroopers mopped up on the hills.

With the advent of the Iraqi armoured force in the field of battle, the 3rd Armoured Division was later followed by another armoured division. Hofi decided to cover his flanks, while at the same time developing local efforts to improve the Israeli positions. The 7th Brigade took the hills south and north of Nasej and fought back counter-attacks by day and by night at Mazrat Beit Jan, Tel Shams and Tel el-Mal until the cease-fire. The discovery that arms taken in one battle, including AML armoured cars, were Western revealed that Saudi Arabian troops had entered the line and were fighting.

All during this period Raful initiated very successful night raids with paratroopers and units of the Golani Brigade against tanks, positions and supply routes behind the enemy lines. The Golani Brigade alone accounted for the destruction of at least twenty enemy tanks in these raids and, indeed, in this respect Raful was the one outstanding Israeli commander who maintained the traditions that had been established over the years in the Israeli forces.

Laner's forces were by now utterly exhausted and at the end of their tether, yet the 19th Brigade captured two heights of great tactical and strategic importance – Tel Antar and Tel el-Alakieh – which were to prove vital later in holding the Israeli line. By this time a shortage of 155 mm artillery ammunition was being felt, and the forces were advised that tank ammunition was in short supply. The order was to hold.

On Tuesday, 16 October, Laner's division was again under attack. His forces reported that Centurion tanks were advancing and when they saw the red pennants on the antennae, they realized that these were tanks of the 40th Jordanian Armoured Brigade, which had entered Syria on the 13th. It was one of the quirks of history that Jordan's crack 40th Armoured Brigade was rushed to save Syria from the threat posed to its army and capital city by the Israeli forces, for in September 1970 during the civil war in Jordan (when King Hussein was fighting for his existence against the Palestinian terrorist organizations in the streets of his capital city) the Syrians had attempted to stab him in the back and had launched an armoured force of divisional strength against Jordan in the area of Irbid–Ramthia. The Jordanian 40th Armoured Brigade fought bravely against the invasion and held the superior Syrian forces until the Syrians were urged by their Soviet advisers to withdraw when various moves in the area indicated the possibility of American and Israeli involvement.

War caught King Hussein by surprise – according to his own admission. He was soon under pressure to enter the war, but he realized that while he was pinning down Israeli forces along his border, an attack against Israel itself would bring the full force of the Israeli Air Force against his armoured forces.

His experience in 1967 in this respect was sufficient. Furthermore, he owed little to his northern Arab neighbour and recalled only too well how he had borne the brunt of the Israeli counter-attack in 1967 while the Syrians looked on and did not intervene to help him. As pressure grew among his officers, Hussein mobilized his reserves and on 13 October the 40th Armoured Brigade crossed into Syria at Dera'a, entering the line between Syrian and Iraqi forces on the south of the Israeli enclave pushing into Syria.

The Jordanians moved towards Tel Maschara and suddenly broke to the west before Tel el-Mal. Ran moved his brigade up to the slopes of the Tel and waited until the Jordanian tanks drew near before opening fire. He hit twenty-eight and the Jordanian brigade withdrew. At this point, in an unco-ordinated manner, the Iraqis began to move from Kfar Shams in the east towards Tel Antar and Tel el-Alakieh. The 20th and 19th brigades held the attack while Laner ordered Ran's 17th Brigade to move in a wide, outflanking movement to the south. Battle was joined and after a number of hours the Iraqis withdrew, leaving some sixty tanks burning on the battlefield.

Inter-Arab co-ordination proved to be very faulty on the battlefield. Every morning between 10 and 11 o'clock a counter-attack was mounted against the southern flank of the Israeli enclave by the Iraqis and Jordanians, supported by the Syrian and Iraqi air forces. Rarely did they succeed in co-ordinating and establishing a common language: on two occasions the Jordanians attacked while the Iraqis failed to join in; frequently Iraqi artillery support fell on the advancing or withdrawing Jordanians; and on a number of occasions Syrian planes attacked and shot down Iraqi planes.

On 17 October Peled's division relieved Laner and took over responsibility for the southern sector of the Israeli enclave. Hofi ordered him to capture Um Butne, a village with dominating high ground around it, some 4 miles due east of Kuneitra and controlling the Kuneitra opening. It was essential to widen the Israeli opening into the enclave now held within Syria, and the capture of Um Butne would give more depth to the southern flank of the enclave. Further-more, by taking Um Butne the Israeli forces would add an additional element of security to the Kuneitra opening and obtain control of an additional lateral north–south road within the enclave.

A parachute battalion commanded by Lieut.-Col. Elisha of the 31st Para-chute Brigade, which had captured Tel Shams so successfully but a few nights before, advanced under cover of an artillery barrage and captured the village, including six Syrian tanks, practically without loss. Because the village itself could become an artillery trap, at 3.00 in the morning orders were given to continue the attack. The battalion advanced accordingly and captured the high

Maj.-Gen. Dan Laner greeting an officer.

Brig.-Gen. Moshe (Mussa) Peled issuing orders during the counter-attack in the Golan Heights.

Generals Dayan and Hofi with the troops.

Maj.-Gen. Hofi in conference with Lieut.-Gen. Bar Lev during tense hours at Northern Command headquarters. Maj.-Gen. Mordechai Hod is leaning over between them.

Maj.-Gen. Benjamin Peled, GOC Israeli Air Force.

Maj.-Gen. (Raful) Eytan.

Rear Admiral Benjamin Telem.

Israeli armour advancing in the Golan Heights.

Syrian tanks knocked out while attempting to cross the anti-tank ditch (in the background, a destroyed bridging tank).

left to right General Adan (Bren), General Elazar and General Magen.

General Adan (Bren) holding a quick consultation in the field with one of his brigade commanders.

A briefing for Generals Gonen (left) and Elazar, who is flanked on the right by General Ezer Weizman.

Maj.-Gen. (Albert) Mandler, standing by map, briefs the chief-of-staff on Sunday, 7 October. Seated (left to right) are Generals Gonen, Elazar, Adan (Bren), Ben-Ari and Rabin.

Colonel (now Brigadier) Danny Matt.

Maj.-Gen. Arieh Sharon.

Israeli troops by the sweet-water canal near Ismailia.

A breach in the Israeli rampart on the Suez Canal viewed from the Egyptian side.

Israeli tanks crossing the pontoon bridge to the west bank of the Canal.

ground to the south of the village. First light was approaching when Northern Command ordered the paratroopers to be relieved by armoured infantry. The paratroopers withdrew and the hand-over took place at the southern end of the village. Suddenly eight Syrian tanks equipped with optical equipment for night-fighting approached and fired at a range of 800 yards into the relieving battalion. Battalion headquarters was hit and control was lost. The Syrians brought down heavy concentrations of fire on the armoured infantry, and it looked as if Um Butne would be lost.

Peled ordered the 14th Brigade to advance a battalion of tanks and help to extricate the armoured infantry. Unequipped with infra-red equipment, 14th Brigade moved in. The first four tanks, including that of the battalion commander, Lieut.-Col. Moshe Meler (who was later to become one of the leaders of the protest movements after the war), were hit. Meler was wounded, and his replacement as well as a company commander were killed. An additional force of a reconnaissance unit now entered battle under command of the 14th Brigade, destroying the attacking Syrian force and consolidating on the hills south of the village. Relieving the forces during an attack, before the inevitable counterattack would be mounted, proved to be a costly error.

As this battle was being fought throughout Thursday night and well into Friday morning, Peled's division was engaged in a second heavy battle on its eastern flank. The 20th Brigade was deployed in the area of Tel Antar and Tel el-Alakieh. As dawn approached the tanks moved up to the high ground on the two hills. As they drove up, anti-tank fire was opened on them from a range of 200–300 yards. It was a battalion of Iraqi commandos which under cover of darkness had crawled up the hills and had taken up positions in the Syrian trenches. The commander of the 20th Brigade did not hesitate and at first light the brigade stormed the summit of the hills, crushing many of the Iraqi soldiers under their tank tracks. Thirty-five Iraqi bodies were found on the spot and many others were killed as they fled down the hills.

The rising sun revealed before them on the plain a large enemy force concentrating and deploying in an area centring on Kfar Shams to the south-east. An Iraqi attack in divisional strength was being mounted. Heavy artillery was directed on the 20th Brigade, as a force outnumbering it by 3 : 1 moved across the plain to attack. Some 130 tanks and over 100 armoured personnel carriers supported by heavy artillery concentrations advanced towards them.

Peled deployed the 19th Brigade on the western flank of the 20th. All morning long the fierce battle raged as the Iraqis tried desperately to retake these two strategic hills dominating the Great Leja. Three major attacks were mounted: in the first the tanks advanced in the first wave, followed by armoured personnel carriers; in the second attack armoured personnel carriers, with tanks moving in close support, led the attack with their infantry dismounting 3,000 yards from the Israeli positions and leading an infantry assault; in the third attack the Iraqi tanks led with the infantry following behind. For some seven hours the battle raged as time and again the Iraqis, this time fighting determinedly, continued their assaults. It was a day in which Northern Command could not hope for air support (the Israeli Air Force was entirely preoccupied on the Suez front with the Egyptian Third Army, which was about to be cut off by the Israeli sweep towards the city of Suez on the west bank of the Canal). It succeeded in making up for the lack of air power however by very effective use of concentrated artillery support.

During the first Iraqi attack against the 20th Brigade, the 19th Brigade came under heavy fire and was pinned down. By dint of armoured manœuvre it managed to extricate itself from this situation and made a broad sweep towards the southern flank of the Iraqi attack. This move broke their first attack in the early morning.

At 10 o'clock, as the Iraqis mounted their second attack, the 40th Jordanian Armoured Brigade moved out of the area of Tel Hara towards the western flank of Peled's division at Tel el-Mal and Tel Maschara. The Jordanians advanced – in a formation much wider than the Iraqi formation – against Tel Maschara, which was held by a small Israeli force of a company of tanks with supporting infantry. It was obvious that something had gone wrong on the Arab side because the Jordanian and Iraqi attacks were unco-ordinated while the Israeli forces were only too well prepared to take advantage of this. The Jordanian attack this time was late.

Peled's orders were that the force on Tel Maschara, which would not be reinforced, should hold the Jordanian attacking force by allowing it to advance to within short range. The reconnaissance unit on the Um Butne hills to the west would attack the left flank of the Jordanians as soon as they had become involved with the Israeli force at Tel Maschara.

The Jordanians advanced slowly, taking over an hour to move towards their objective. This enabled the Israeli artillery to concentrate entirely on the attack of the Iraqi force that had come to grips with the 20th Brigade. (In the meantime the sun had risen and was no longer blinding the Israeli forces.) By noon the Jordanian forces had reached Tel Maschara and began to climb up the hill. The Israeli force holding the hill engaged them and destroyed the advanced elements. At this point the reconnaissance unit launched its attack on the Jordanian flank. The Jordanians left some twelve tanks burning on the hill and began to withdraw, with the Israeli forces harrying them in their flight until 3 o'clock in the afternoon. The total Jordanian armoured loss that day was some twenty tanks.

Meanwhile the third and final Iraqi attack was being mounted with determination as wave after wave of armour moved up to attack the 20th Brigade. The Israelis had suffered heavily during the day and the brigade commander felt that it was touch and go. In the middle of the battle, he created a reserve of three tanks and placed it in the rear. The Iraqis advanced up the hill against the heavily depleted Israeli forces with tanks sometimes firing at ranges of 5 yards. Iraqi tanks became interspersed among the defending Israeli tanks: the situation was critical as the battle swayed to and fro on the two hills. At this point the 20th brigade commander ordered his reserve of three tanks to move out across the plain in a wide, flanking movement to the north and attack the Iraqi forces from their northern flank. They moved in a wide sweep and came in from the north – which the Iraqis believed to be protected by Syrian forces – taking the Iraqi forces by surprise. The sudden appearance of a force on their northern flank knocked the Iraqis off balance and at the last and most critical moment they turned and withdrew. Some sixty Iraqi burning tanks dotted the plain and the slopes of Tel Antar and Tel el-Alakieh, and about the same number of armoured personnel carriers; columns of dead Iraqi infantry clearly marked the line of approach in the three major attacks. Although Arab counter-attacks continued daily against the Israeli enclave until the cease-fire, this was the last major armoured battle to be fought on the northern front.

On the night of 20 October Hofi ordered units of one of Israel's leading parachute brigades and those of the Golani Brigade to recapture the Israeli position on Mount Hermon. The paratroopers, who were to attack from the heights of the Hermon downwards, were ordered to capture the Syrian positions while the Golani units, who were ordered to move up from below, were directed towards the Israeli position that had fallen with the outbreak of war. At 2 o'clock on 21 October the parachute forces were lifted by helicopter with fighter planes covering them. A battalion under Lieut.-Col. Hezi secured the helicopter landing areas and its mission was to clear the area up to half a mile from the Syrian position, the taking of which would be the responsibility of Lieut.-Col. Elisha's battalion.

Taking the Syrians by surprise with an unexpected attack at 2.00 in the afternoon, and supported by the Air Force and by Israeli artillery, the leading force under Hezi had to advance about 5 miles along the crest of Mount Hermon (8,200 feet high) with Syrian artillery endeavouring to intervene. Three Syrian helicopters approached, but all crashed on the hillside, apparently hit by artillery. The Syrians threw in their Air Force and Hezi's advancing forces looked down on the dog fights taking place below them. As darkness came on, his battalion stormed the so-called Serpentine Syrian position: the officer leading the attack was killed; the Syrian commandos in the position broke and fled, leaving seven dead. Hezi continued to mop up until they reached another Syrian position. On their way they reached a rocky formation, which they mopped up without loss. Later they were to discover that this position, which was the Syrian command post on the Hermon, had received a direct hit from Israeli artillery. There were twelve Syrian dead and this fact could account for the comparatively poor showing of the Syrian commandos in defence of the Hermon. Elisha's battalion now moved through with artillery support and stormed the Syrian position, which was found to be empty. By 3.30 in the morning of 22 October the Syrian part of Mount Hermon was in the hands of the paratroopers for the loss of one killed. Elisha prepared his forces to move towards the Israeli position on Hermon in case they should be ordered to do so by the Northern Command.

Meanwhile the Golani forces moved up along three routes, advancing as they had in the fruitless counter-attack early in the war. They were led on the main road by five tanks. When they reached the area where their attack had been broken on 7 October, they were engaged by covering Syrian forces, which lay in readiness observing their advance. A comparatively large enemy force of commandos, over a battalion in strength, was scattered over the rocky hillside in holes and behind rocks. Each soldier was equipped with telescopic sights for day and night firing. Anti-tank missiles were deployed to prevent the advance of the supporting Israeli tanks. The Syrians, difficult to identify in the darkness and equipped with night-vision telescopic lenses, picked off the Israeli soldiers one by one. The brigade commander and a battalion commander who were with the leading group were wounded. Two companies of Golani reinforcements were flown up and the paratroopers were ordered to begin to move down, but the Golani forces fighting desperately without their command, and in a situation that had now become critical, achieved their mission without outside help. As things looked their blackest and the situation seemed hopeless, the brigade operations officer took command, gathered his broken forces under heavy fire and personally led the last desperate assault. The Syrians broke as one by one they were winkled out of their holes and from behind the boulders. By 10 o'clock on 22 October Mount Hermon was again in Israeli hands. This attack alone cost the Golani Brigade 51 killed and 100 wounded. Some days later a young sergeant of Golani, speaking in a heavy oriental accent, told the story of the battle on Israeli television in a matter-of-fact manner. 'We were told that Mount Hermon is the eyes of the State of Israel, and we knew we had to take it, whatever the cost.'

.   .   .   .   .

On the evening of 22 October the Syrians accepted a cease-fire proposed by the United Nations Security Council. They had lost some 1,150 tanks in the battle, in addition to well over 100 Iraqi tanks and some 50 Jordanian tanks. In the Golan Heights alone, 867 Syrian tanks were recovered (perhaps of the greatest significance was the fact that many of them were in good running order); 370 Syrian prisoners fell into Israeli hands and it was estimated that they had lost some 3,500 troops killed.

On the Israeli side every single Israeli tank in battle was hit at one stage or another, but the men of the ordnance corps proved to be some of the great heroes of the war, moving around in battle and repairing the tanks under fire. Some 250 Israeli tanks were knocked out, of which almost 100 were a total loss; the remainder were repaired. Israeli casualties were some 772 killed, 2,453 wounded and 65 prisoners, including pilots.

In his characteristically quiet and unassuming manner, Gen. Hofi had led the forces of Northern Command to a brilliant victory in a battle waged initially under the most adverse circumstances. He commanded his team of outstanding divisional commanders in a resolute and effective manner. The absence of controversy and recrimination about the Golan campaign reflects in no small measure the success of his leadership.

The Israel Defence Forces had fought a battle which, perhaps more than any other, revealed the true quality of the Israeli troops and of the Israeli people.

11

The Onslaught (South)

On 15 July 1973 Maj.-Gen. Shmuel Gonen was appointed GOC Southern Command, replacing Maj.-Gen. Ariel Sharon who had retired from the army to go into farming and politics. A tough, abrasive sabra, born in Jerusalem, he had spent the early years of his life in an ultra-orthodox theological seminary, a yeshiva. In the Six Day War he commanded the 7th Brigade in a series of battles across the Sinai Desert, which marked him out as one of the outstanding commanders in the Israeli forces. Wounded several times, an avid marksman with a large collection of weapons of war, he was known as a strict disciplinarian who could behave at times in an impossible manner towards his officers and yet who inspired in his men a confidence which led them to follow him in battle. 'Gorodisch', as he continued to be known in the army by his original name, was regarded with a mixture of respect and dislike. He was a stickler for the little matters that make up discipline and went out of his way to combat the negligence that had begun to affect the Israel Defence Forces. He had had many close brushes with death and was known to be fearless under fire.

Southern Command was responsible for the whole of the southern part of Israel – the Negev and Sinai. The Negev is in the main a sandy desert with a number of areas of settlement, particularly around Beersheba and at the port of Eilat on the Red Sea. The Sinai Peninsula – some 37,200 square miles in extent – is a large triangular wedge between the Gulf of Akaba in the east and the Gulf of Suez in the west, bridging the continents of Africa and Asia on the one hand and the Mediterranean and the Red Sea on the other. It is divided into three distinct regions: in the north the sandy coastal Mediterranean plateau with its low hills and deep not always passable sand dunes (some of them 75–100 feet high) dotted here and there with brackish wells and oases; the centre – a gaunt and formidable largely limestone escarpment known as the E-Tih Desert, and finally the spectacular southern Sinai with its deep *wadis* and high pinnacles.

The north-western side of the triangle is bordered by the Suez Canal for a distance of 110 miles. The Canal itself (180–240 yards wide, 50–60 feet deep) constitutes what Gen. Dayan described as 'one of the best anti-tank ditches available'. The east bank is a wind-swept desert, while the west bank, along which a sweet-water canal runs, has a cultivated belt running parallel to it. The banks are steep and concrete-reinforced, the highest level of the water being 6 feet below the bank. Earth and soil (removed both by the digging of the Canal and by dredging operations) was concentrated along the east bank in the form of a dyke some 18–30 feet high (Israeli engineers had raised this rampart at the critical areas to a height of 75 feet.) The tides change frequently, the difference in the water level varying between 1–6 feet in various parts of the Canal, a fact of great importance in carrying out crossing operations.

From the Canal the desert rises in an undulating manner for some 5 miles to a line of sandy hills and thence stretches back to a mountainous and hilly ridge, through which a number of passes such as the Mitla Pass and the Gidi Pass in the south lead. The northern area from roughly Kantara to Port Said is a salty marsh area criss-crossed by a number of routes which the Israeli Army had constructed. Parallel to the Suez Canal along the entire route runs a road bearing the code name of 'Lexicon' on the Israeli maps; parallel to it some 5 miles to the east runs a road known as the artillery road. (The various outstanding features in the desert had been given code names, as had the various fortifications along the Canal, and they will be referred to by these in this account.) The area is criss-crossed by a vast network of roads, both lateral and perpendicular.

The Suez Canal line was held by a division under command of Maj.-Gen. Avraham (Albert) Mandler. A very fine and sensitive personality, he was known as one of the most disciplined and considerate officers in the IDF. On the eve of war the forces at his disposal totalled some 280 tanks in three brigades, with a special command including an infantry brigade holding the northern area of marsh land. Albert – a tall, taciturn, ruddy-faced officer, aged forty-five, with piercing blue eyes – had commanded the armoured brigade that had performed the almost impossible in breaking the Syrian line holding the Golan Heights in 1967.

With his appointment as GOC Southern Command, Maj.-Gen. Gonen handed over command of his reserve division to his predecessor in the command, Gen. Sharon. Gonen was unhappy with the staff work and level of discipline he found in Southern Command and began to introduce a number of changes. He also approached the General Staff with a proposal that the fourteen fortifications along the Canal which had been blocked up should be opened. Approval was given to open a number of them, including one – on the east bank of the Great Bitter Lake – that had been so hermetically sealed that it took three weeks to reactivate.

During the first months of his appointment, Gonen set priorities in the construction budget in the command, allowing first of all for the construction of tank ramps along the second line of defence, thus enabling tanks to engage in depth from a second line an enemy which had crossed the Canal. For over a year Mandler had been pressing for this but approval had been delayed in the Ministry of Defence. A second priority was given to preparation of the infrastructure necessary for an Israeli crossing of the Suez.

In his visits along the Canal, Gonen noted that the Egyptians had elevated the ramp on their side to a height of some 130 feet, from which they could look straight over the Israeli rampart and down on to the Israeli fortifications and the tank ramps protecting them, out of sight when they had been first built; the raised rampart also gave them observation to the second line of defence along the so-called artillery road 5–8 miles back. Gonen's answer to this was to order the building of earthworks which would hide activity in the second line of defence from the eyes of the Egyptians; he also ordered the construction of long-range observation towers 230 feet high to enable the Israeli forces to look over into the Egyptian front-line area. But it was too late.

During this period inspections by Gonen revealed that the standard of maintenance of the optical equipment in the tanks and in the fortifications was inadequate. He went over all the operational planning with his staff, reminding the General Staff that in the event of an emergency the reservists in the line should be replaced by highly trained infantry.

When Gen. Gavish had been in command, construction of a system to be introduced in the Bar-Lev line and to be operated from the various fortifications had been undertaken. Underground oil storage tanks were to be constructed, under the strongpoints, with pipes leading from them so that the Canal could be sprayed with a film of oil that could then be ignited electrically from inside the fortification and turn parts of the Canal into a moat of fire. In 1971 however, when only two such installations had been built, it was decided that because of the speed of the current in the Canal, this device would not be very effective. Accordingly the construction of additional facilities was discontinued.

Nevertheless when the General Staff decided to abandon the project early in 1971, Southern Command was authorized to test one installation in the Canal in order to create an appropriate psychological effect on the Egyptians. They indeed were impressed and devoted much thought and planning over the years to overcome this 'obstacle'.

For years the Egyptians kept a close observation of this system, which gradually silted up and became clogged with sand. On 11 July 1973 the 8th Egyptian Infantry Brigade Intelligence issued a circular on the subject. According to the document (which fell into Israeli hands during the war), since the end of 1971 the Israelis had neglected the equipment and all maintenance activities had ceased. The Egyptians had noted the construction of twenty such facilities along the Canal, but patrols sent over to investigate had discovered them all to be dummy installations. The pipes in the equipment which had been identified had been cut or bent under the weight of the earth piled on top so that no liquid could flow through them; they were covered in rust and clogged with sand, while construction work on the fortifications had closed up whole parts of the system. The summary concluded, correctly as it happened, that the Israelis had abandoned the idea of using the equipment and were leaving it in the area for psychological warfare purposes.

Nevertheless, much was subsequently made by Ahmed Ismail, the Egyptian minister of war, and by Gen. Shazli, the Egyptian chief of staff, of the ingenuity with which they had neutralized this equipment all along the Canal. Indeed the story of how Egypt planned to deal with this problem and how 'in fact' it was overcome was the subject of long and detailed descriptions by Ismail and Shazli after the war and of admiring descriptions by many war reporters.

When he came to the command in July, Gen. Gonen decided to try to revive the system. He gave orders to his chief of engineers to check the two existing installations, to clean them out, check the tanks and to find cheaper alternatives in order to achieve the same purpose. A simpler and more effective method was devised and tested in September, but there was no time in which to apply it to the Canal.

In the course of the preparations on the eve of war on 5 October Gonen gave instructions for these two systems to be set into operation. An engineering team headed by 2nd Lieut. Shimon Tal reached the Hizayon strongpoint at Firdan on the morning of Saturday, 6 October, and explained to the men in the position how to operate the system. Since the controls were in the fortification that had been blocked up and inactivated, the Hizayon troops were told that they would have to run along the Canal several hundred yards, open the pipe manually and throw a phosphorescent grenade into the oil on the water. Having explained the system at Hizayon, Lieut. Tal continued southwards to

Matzmed at Deversoir. But while he was demonstrating to them how to operate the installation, the opening barrage of artillery fell on them.

At midday on Saturday, 6 October, warning was flashed to Maj.-Gen. Albert Mandler's divisional headquarters in Sinai advising of an imminent artillery bombardment and instructing all forces to be on the alert. Brig.-Gen. Pino, Albert's deputy, again pressed his commander to instruct all forces to activate the 'Shovach Yonim' plan and move forward to the Canal. At midday Albert agreed and the instructions were issued.

At 1.45 Gonen arrived back at his headquarters from the General Staff meeting in Tel Aviv. He called Albert and reviewed the various orders that had been issued. In closing he told him that he felt the time had come for him to begin moving his armoured brigades down to the front. Albert replied laconically, 'Yes, I suppose we had. We are being bombed at this moment.'

Reports describing massive artillery bombardment, air attacks, crossings of the Canal and fighting began to pour in from the strongpoints along the Canal. Some fortifications (particularly where the officers were in charge) reported in a matter-of-fact manner; others, whose officers had been killed at the outset, were in some cases hysterical. In some, NCOs, and in one case a private soldier, took command and led the men in battle. All pleaded for air and artillery support and for armoured reinforcements. All were promised that these were on the way.

By 3 o'clock it was clear to Albert that the Egyptians were staging a major attack all along the front. And by 4 o'clock it was evident that the crossing of the Canal was a major amphibious operation taking place along its full length. Gonen tried to read the battle in his headquarters as the reports flowed in and the highly developed communication system in the command provided a clear picture of what was going on in every strongpoint along the Canal. For two hours he tried to identify the enemy's main effort (the Egyptians had in fact estimated that the absence of such a main effort would delay the Israeli counter-attack). By 4 o'clock it was clear to Gonen that there was no main effort, but that the crossing was more successful in the northern sector of the Canal than in the southern sector.

The total strength of the Egyptian Army (which is one of the largest standing armies in the world) included some 800,000 troops, 2,200 tanks, 2,300 artillery pieces, 150 anti-aircraft missile batteries and 550 first-line aircraft. Deployed along the Canal were five infantry divisions and a number of independent brigades – infantry and armour – backed by three mechanized divisions and two armoured divisions. Each infantry division included a battalion of tanks for every one of the three brigades, for a total of 120 tanks in every infantry division. The three mechanized divisions included two mechanized brigades and one armoured brigade, for a total of 160 tanks per division. The two armoured divisions were composed of two armoured brigades and one mechanized brigade, for a total of about 250 tanks per division. In addition there were independent tank brigades, two parachute brigades, some twenty-eight battalions of commandos and a marine brigade.

The Second Army was responsible for the northern half of the Canal and the Third Army for the southern, the Second Army front being held by the 18th Infantry Division from Port Said to Kantara and the Firdan Bridge, by the 2nd Infantry Division from the Firdan Bridge to north of Lake Timsah, and by the 16th Infantry Division from Lake Timsah to Deversoir at the northern end of the Great Bitter Lake. The dividing line between the two armies ran through the centre of the Great Bitter Lake. The Third Army had under command the 7th Infantry Division, responsible for the sector of the Bitter Lakes to half-way down the southernmost section of the Suez Canal, and the 19th infantry Division south to and including the city of Suez. Each of the assaulting infantry divisions was reinforced for the crossing by an armoured brigade drawn in part from the armoured and mechanized divisions.

Facing this force in Sinai along the 110 miles of the Suez Canal were a total of 436 Israeli soldiers in a series of fortifications 7–8 miles apart and three tanks actually on the water front. Seven artillery batteries were in the line at 2 o'clock and the remainder, for a total of some seventy guns, followed on later. Of the tanks planned to be holding the line, 277 were forward in Sinai at that hour.

At H hour 240 Egyptian planes crossed the Canal. Their mission was to strike three airfields in Sinai, to hit the Israeli Hawk surface-to-air missile batteries, to bomb three Israeli command posts, radar stations, medium artillery positions, the administration centres and the Israeli strongpoint known as Budapest on the sand bank east of Port Fuad. Simultaneously 2,000 guns opened up along the entire front: field artillery, medium and heavy artillery and medium and heavy mortars. A brigade of FROG surface-to-surface missiles launched its weapons. Tanks moved up to the ramps prepared on the sand ramparts, depressed their guns and fired pointblank at the Israeli strongpoints. Over 3,000 concentrated tons of destruction were launched against a handful of Israeli fortifications in a barrage that turned the entire east bank of the Suez Canal into an inferno for fifty-three minutes. At the same time commando and infantry tank-destroyer units crossed the Canal, mined the approaches to the ramps, prepared anti-tank ambushes and lay in wait for the advancing Israeli armour.

At 2.15, when the planes had returned from their bombing mission, the first wave of 8,000 assault infantry crossed the Canal. Along most of the Canal they

WA—F

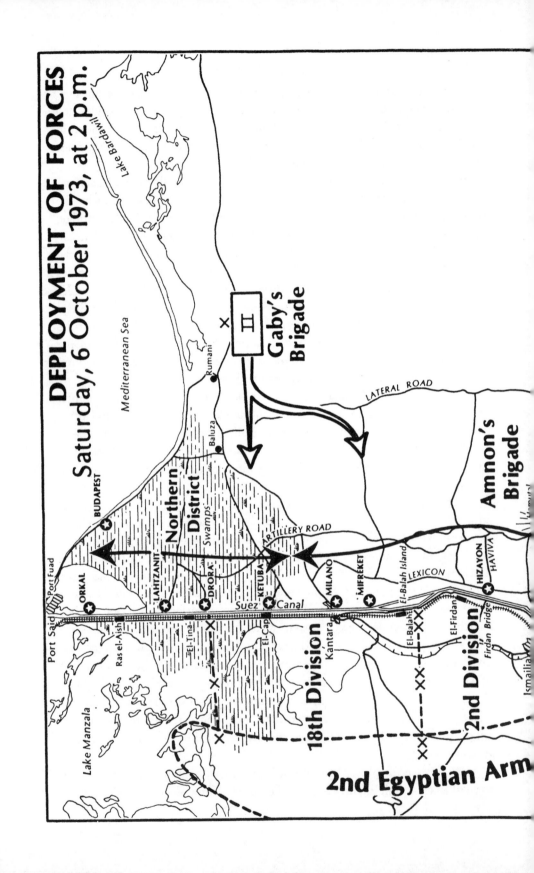

DEPLOYMENT OF FORCES
Saturday, 6 October 1973, at 2 p.m.

Lake Bardawil

Mediterranean Sea

Rumani

Gaby's Brigade

LATERAL ROAD

Baluza

Northern District

Swamps

BUDAPEST

Amnon's Brigade

ARTILLERY ROAD

Port Said
Port Fuad

ORKAL

Ras el-Aish

LAHTZANIT

DRORA

KETUBA

Suez Canal

MILANO

MIFREKET

El-Balah Island

LEXICON

HIZAYON

HAVIVA

El-Tina

El-Cap

Kantara

18th Division

El-Balah

El-Firdan

Firdan Bridge

2nd Division

Ismailia

Lake Manzala

2nd Egyptian Army

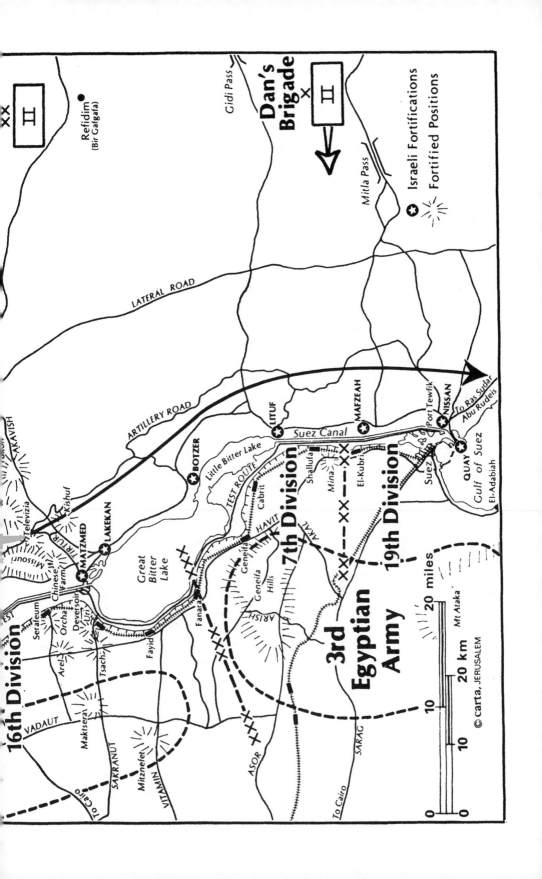

II
XX

Refidim
(Bir Gafgafa)

Gidi Pass

Dan's Brigade
X
II

Mitla Pass

● Israeli Fortifications
☆ Fortified Positions

LATERAL ROAD

ARTILLERY ROAD

AKAVISH

Kishuf

Televizia

Missouri

TIRTUR

Chinese Farm

MATZMED

LAKEKAN

BOTZER

Little Bitter Lake

LITUF

Suez Canal

TEST ROUTE

Great Bitter Lake

Cabrit

Shallufa

MAFZEAH

Mina

El-Kubri

Port Tewfik

NISSAN

To Ras Sudar
Abu Rudeis

Gulf of Suez

El-Adabiah

QUAY

Suez

19th Division

7th Division

HAVIT

Geneifa

Geneifa Hills

AKAL

ARISH

SARAG

3rd Egyptian Army

To Cairo

Fanara

Fayid

Tsach

Uri

Deversoir

Orcha

Arel

Serafeum

WEST

16th Division

VADAUT

Maktser

SAKRANUT

Mitznefet

VITAMIN

To Cairo

ASOR

Mt Ataka

© carta, JERUSALEM

20 miles

20 km

0   10   20

0   10   20

crossed in areas not covered by fire from the Israeli strongpoints and organized for action; in most places they avoided the Israeli strongpoints, by-passing them and pushing eastwards.

An analysis of the operations carried out by the Egyptians, coupled with the detailed reports that have been published in Egypt by the various commanders involved, enables us to reconstruct the entire operation. The crossing took place with the first wave on the afternoon of 6 October, landing between the strongpoints while the strongpoints themselves were pinned down by concentrated artillery fire. The first waves of the attacking infantry divisions were ordered to establish themselves 1–2 miles in depth. This phase was completed by sundown on 6 October. Following this, special infantry units trained for the purpose were to attack and capture the strongpoints. Parallel to this, commando units were introduced in depth behind the enemy lines for harassment purposes and tank-hunting units were ordered into position to prevent the Israeli tanks from deploying according to plan on the ramps between the strongpoints. A special operation in this phase was the crossing of the Great Bitter Lake by the 130th Marine Brigade. Its amphibious vehicles attempted to by-pass Israeli forces and link up with commando forces in the area of the Mitla and Gidi passes.

Until sundown 7 October the forces were organized for defence against counter-attacks, further advance into Sinai and deepening of bridgeheads to a depth of 4–5 miles. During this period all units of the infantry division crossed and on the night of 7 October the armoured brigades attached to the infantry divisions crossed too.

All forces west of the line Ras Sudar–Tasa–Baluza were under command of the two Egyptian armies, while all commando forces east of it (which included the commando forces, each of a battalion strength, that were landed at Sudar and the Mitla and Gidi passes) were under command of GHQ.

By the evening of Monday, 8 October, the infantry divisions (with an addition of a tank brigade to each division) were in position in full strength on the east bank of the Canal. After fending off the anticipated Israeli counter-attacks, the forces attempted to widen each bridgehead, having been ordered to fan out and meet each other, to a depth of 6–8 miles. Following this a mechanized brigade of the 6th Mechanized Division crossed on the southern flank of the 19th Infantry Division (the southernmost division) in readiness to move down Wadi Sudar, when the attack eastwards would be developed.

The next phase, ending by Thursday morning, 11 October, was to be devoted entirely to waging a defensive war and causing the enemy maximum possible losses in his counter-attacks. At the same time the Egyptians planned to push down the coast of Sinai towards Ras Sudar and Sharm el-Sheikh.

From Thursday until Tuesday, 15 October, the 4th and 21st Armoured Divisions crossed the bridgehead to mount a major attack. The main effort of the attack was to be directed towards the capture of the nerve centre of Refidim (Bir Gafgafa). The 4th Armoured Division with the 25th Armoured Brigade was to advance from the area of the Gidi Pass through Um Mahza to Refidim. The second arm of the pincer towards Refidim was to be mounted by the 21st Armoured Division from the area of Ismailia and Deversoir through Tasa to Refidim. Secondary efforts were also to be developed.

Every move in the first phase had obviously been planned and prepared to the minutest detail. A division crossed in a sector some 4–5 miles wide, the first wave being entrusted with seizing and holding the earth ramparts. When the second wave reached the earth ramparts, forces of the first phase were to advance 200 yards and remain in their positions. Within an hour of the attack, third and fourth waves moved to join the first and second waves. As soon as the support units of the attacking battalion had crossed, the entire force would advance.

Each bridgehead was to be 5 miles wide and $3\frac{1}{2}$ miles deep and remain so until the arrival of the tanks and the artillery, when it was to be enlarged to a base of 10 miles wide and 5 miles deep.

And so, moving exactly as they had been trained, dozens and in many cases hundreds of times, the Egyptian forces stormed across the Canal. In some areas there was heavy Israeli resistance; in other areas it was comparatively light. The major crossing of the Egyptian Army however took place as planned in the open, unoccupied areas between the fortifications. Thus while the initial Egyptian estimates had been that the crossing would cost some 25,000–30,000 casualties, including some 10,000 dead, their casualties in the initial crossing, which totalled only 208 killed, were lower than any Egyptian planner had imagined. In the Second Army area the crossing went according to plan with few hitches. But in the area of the Third Army there were problems, because the Israeli rampart proved to be wider than the Egyptians had estimated and also because the nature of the soil at the southern end of the Suez Canal prevented it from disintegrating under the high-pressure water hoses, tending instead to become a morass of mud.

The commander of one of the two infantry divisions in the Third Army who encountered strong Israeli reaction later recounted that he lost 10% of his men in the initial assault, although he had estimated that he would lose 30%. He related the story of a lone Israeli tank that fought off the attacking forces for over half an hour, causing very heavy casualties to his men when they tried to storm it. When they finally overcame it, the Egyptian general recounted how, to his utter amazement, he found that all the crew had been killed with the exception of one wounded soldier, who had continued to fight. He described how impressed he and his men were by this lone soldier, who told them he had been born in Germany and who saluted the Egyptian general as he was carried away on a stretcher to a waiting ambulance.

All through the night of the 6th–7th, the Egyptian bridging units worked feverishly at establishing some ten bridges across the Canal. The next day these bridges were to come under heavy and persistent attack by the Israeli Air Force and many of them were to be seriously damaged. However, their sectional construction and the ease with which they could be handled allowed, as Gen. Shazli was later to point out, for a very rapid replacement of damaged sections, and also enabled the Egyptians, when any area came under heavy attack, to float the bridge down the Canal to an alternative site or to lash it to one of the banks during daylight hours. Thus the Israeli claims that nearly all the bridges had been hit on the first day were correct, as indeed were the Egyptian claims that forces were crossing on their bridges without let-up. By midday, 7 October, the 7th Infantry Division had crossed with all its forces south of the Bitter Lakes, as had the 25th Armoured Brigade.

Phase One of the crossing was carried out between 6 October and 9 October. Ten bridges were thrown across the Canal, three in the area of Kantara, three in the area of Ismailia–Deversoir and four in the area of Genefa–Suez.

Parallel to the attack, commando battalions and units were landed in depth along the entire length of the front from the area of Port Fuad in the north down to Sharm el-Sheikh at the southern tip of the Sinai Peninsula. This phase of the Egyptian plan was not particularly successful. Fourteen helicopters loaded with Egyptian commando forces were shot down by the Israeli Air Force, while Israeli forces throughout the Sinai were rapidly organized to deal with them. In the second part of the first phase, namely on the night of 6 October, Egyptian forces mounted their attack as planned against the Israeli strongpoints along the Canal.

At Albert's headquarters the picture of the situation along the Canal was confused. His armoured forces were moving towards the Canal but there was no clear indication of their situation. The general estimate had been that the main brunt of the attack would fall on the northern sector. Accordingly, the armoured brigade under Col. Gaby was directed to the northern sector. Col. Amnon's brigade moved westwards in the centre while in the southern sector Col. Dan's brigade was ordered through the Gidi Pass to a position south of the Bitter Lakes.

The approximately 300 tanks at Albert's disposal during Saturday afternoon were divided almost equally between the three brigades under his command. The impression at divisional headquarters that evening was that the armoured forces had reached all the fortifications, apart from those located on the narrow dyke north of Kantara, at Firdan Bridge and on the quayside at Port Tewfik. There were five tanks in the latter position, but the position itself was by then cut off.

In the first few hours of the fighting, Pino, who had become Albert's second-in-command two months earlier, tried to piece together a coherent picture. Unable to do so from the reports, he took a helicopter and flew along the artillery road as far south as the Gidi and Mitla passes. On numerous occasions the helicopter had to avoid Egyptian MIGs and MI8 helicopters. He succeeded in bringing back what he believed to be the first comparatively clear picture of the situation to his divisional commander. By 1 o'clock on the morning of the 7th the picture that Gonen received in his headquarters was that the Israeli forces had returned to the water line – apart from the area north of Kantara, two fortifications in the central sector and the quayside position at Port Tewfik. Neither Gonen nor Albert felt any urgency about evacuating the strongpoints along the Canal at this time.

The problem of inaccurate front-line reporting was highlighted by the fact that on Saturday evening the situation on the ground, as reflected in the picture received at command headquarters and GHQ, was a satisfactory one. Hence there was no point in giving orders to the fortifications to evacuate because the reports indicated that the tanks had reached the water line on Saturday evening and had linked up with them. At 6 o'clock on Saturday evening Gen. Elazar spoke to Gonen, advising him that if there were fortifications which did not obstruct the main effort of the enemy and only endangered the men, he was authorized to evacuate them. He emphasized that he did not want to defend the whole Canal by means of these fortifications but rather to hold strongpoints that would hinder the development of the enemy's major efforts.

At this point Elazar was thinking two days ahead. Realizing that he could influence little of what was happening on the ground at any given moment – except in special circumstances – he understood that the holding battle would be a very difficult one and that the Egyptians would be bound to penetrate in some places. On Sunday the holding battle would continue, but he was already thinking in terms of a series of counter-attacks on Monday. At midnight, as soon as he was satisfied that the communications system from the forward headquarters in Sinai was effective, Gonen moved forward into Sinai. All night he received reports that tanks were patrolling between the fortifications and were linking up with them. In the northern sector near the Mifreket strongpoint, Gaby's forces reported that they had knocked out a bridge.

On Sunday morning the Egyptians renewed their attack. Now the very alarming results of the night's fighting were dawning on the Israeli Command: by morning Gaby's forces were left with 10 tanks; Albert reported that out of the 290 tanks with which he had started fighting, he was left with one-third along the entire length of the Suez Canal. Egyptian pressure was growing as, foiled in their attempt to hose open the Israeli rampart by water jet in the southern sector, they began to bulldoze it. The reserves were far away while the regular holding forces were being worn down. Without air support Gonen saw no solution until the reserves arrived. Albert repeatedly requested air support, and Gonen advised him that help would arrive within twenty minutes. 'I don't have twenty minutes,' came Albert's tired reply. At 6.45 am the Air Force made a number of preparatory strikes against the missile system before coming in for close support, and then suddenly Peled, the commander of the Air Force, notified Gonen that there would be no more air support because of the situation in the north. During the morning he urged Peled, 'Unless you deploy your force here I have nothing with which to hold the attack.' At 9.30 that morning, following the approval of the chief of staff, he authorized Albert to evacuate the fortifications where feasible.

At 8 o'clock Maj.-Gen. Avraham (Bren) Adan arrived in advance of his division and was given command of the northern sector. At 1 o'clock the central sector was placed under command of Maj.-Gen. Ariel Sharon. Thus, by Sunday afternoon, the northern sector was held by Bren, the central sector by Sharon and the southern sector by Albert.

Amnon's armoured brigade had been in the forward areas of Sinai for some time and was due to be relieved on 8 October. It was a highly trained brigade, which had not left Sinai since the Six Day War, a high percentage of the officers having served during the War of Attrition. The battalions of the brigade rotated between service in the front line and periods of training behind the line. Amnon, tall, fair, with an owlish look behind his spectacles and distinguished by his neatly kept, large handlebar moustache, had commanded his brigade for over a year. It was responsible for an area stretching from El-Balah Island down to Ras Sudar in the south. A battalion in the north was under Lieut.-Col. Yomtov; another battalion under Lieut.-Col. Shaul Shalev held the central sector and the 3rd Battalion under Lieut.-Col. Emmanuel held the southern sector.

On Thursday, 4 October, the brigade company commanders and above took leave of Albert who was due to leave the division on Sunday morning. In his farewell speech after lunch Albert, while expressing doubt that he would in fact be relieved because of the state of tension along the Canal, stressed the problems of operational alertness and discussed the coming war. On Friday evening he invited Amnon to a personal meeting. He talked about the various indications

showing that war was imminent and checked with him the situation in his
brigade, inviting him again for an orders group on Saturday morning. At this
orders group all operational plans including 'Shovach Yonim' were recapitulated. In the middle of the conference Albert was called to the phone by the GOC
Command, Gen. Gonen. On his return he advised the brigade commanders that
6 o'clock was the possible enemy H hour.

The forces were to deploy in accordance with the 'Shovach Yonim' plan
not later than 5 o'clock in the afternoon but on no account before 4 o'clock, in
case the move forward of Israeli forces should lead to a deterioration in the
situation and an escalation that could bring the Egyptians to open fire. Amnon
rushed back to his brigade and issued the orders for 'Shovach Yonim'. At 1.30
information was received that the command must be on artillery alert as indications were that the enemy was about to open fire. Amnon added a few words
of encouragement to the battalion commanders and sent them post haste
back to their units.

At 2.00 on 6 October Egyptian air bombardment began and a massive
artillery barrage opened up on the Israeli front-line positions in a scope and
intensity they had never known. In the first minute of the attack, 10,500 shells
fell on the Israeli positions at the rate of 175 shells per second. Reports began
to flow in of enemy crossings in assault boats. When the shelling began, Amnon's
units were either on the move forward or the men were in the process of mounting the tanks. The tanks rushed forward to their pre-planned positions only to
find that Egyptian tank-hunting units had occupied them and were launching
against the advancing Israeli tanks a hail of RPG bazooka shells. At the same
time from the top of the rampart on the Egyptian side overlooking the Israeli
approaches they were engaged by tanks and Sagger anti-tank missiles. As
Amnon was to recall, 'The whole of Sinai was on fire.' The Israeli tank units
fought and suffered their first casualties. The Egyptian infantry fought stubbornly. Hundreds were killed by the advancing tanks, but the wave of Egyptian
infantry continued to advance.

Amnon, whose area of responsibility was narrowed to the central sector,
identified two major crossing areas opposite Ismailia and Firdan. He sent one
company of tanks against the effort opposite Ismailia and a second company
to Firdan. The situation in the Firdan fortification was becoming desperate
because of the number of casualties it had suffered. Amnon's force tried desperately to link up with this fortification, Hizayon, but in vain. He sent a patrol
northwards and lost contact with it when it ran into a force of infantry north
of the so-called Chinese Farm. The second-in-command of the battalion, Maj.
Yaacov Javits, was seriously wounded and died shortly after; the company
commander was wounded and the patrol was disrupted. Near Ismailia four

tanks were knocked out, and opposite Firdan most of the tank company was hit.

At 8 o'clock in the evening Lieut. Zeev Pearl's tank leading his company in the attack towards Firdan was hit. His gunner and his loader were killed and Pearl was wounded and blinded. The driver continued to move forward, but when they reached the vicinity of the Hizayon fortification at Firdan the tank was hit again. Reversing they reached the road parallel to the Canal, where they turned northwards and drove unmolested for 9 miles. Near El-Balah Island the tank ran off the road and stuck in the marshland. The driver helped his company commander out and, holding him by the hand, led him first in the wrong direction – towards the Canal. Soon realizing his mistake, he corrected himself and led his commander for miles across the desert in the midst of the inferno of war towards the Israeli forces. As dawn broke they approached an Israeli artillery battery, but for some time they were pinned down by fire from the Israeli forces, before they were finally identified and evacuated. The force fighting opposite the Firdan had disintegrated. The battalion second-in-command evacuated the damaged tanks.

Of two companies in the area of Ismailia and Firdan, two tanks under command of Maj. Eliezer continued to fight. They held the crossroads opposite Firdan all night and held off fifty enemy tanks. In the Ismailia sector Amnon deployed units along the Canal road, sending a battalion under command of Lieut.-Col. Amram to Hizayon. As he approached the Canal, Amram's force ran into a large infantry ambush firing RPG bazookas. He rushed the ambush, broke through it and reached the Canal in the area of Ismailia, but was then obliged to withdraw to the area of the Firdan crossroads.

All day long on 7 October the fighting continued and Amnon saw his brigade being gradually worn down. At the Firdan crossroads Eliezer with his two tanks was conducting his incredible battle. The battalion commander, Lieut.-Col. Shaul, was fighting at the Chinese Farm with two tanks and three armoured personnel carriers. Opposite Ismailia were remnants of two battalions. One battalion commander was wounded and the remaining battalion commander joined the two remnants together for a total of half a battalion of tanks. Amnon's brigade was down to twenty tanks.

Suddenly reservists began to arrive. Amnon had forgotten completely about them until he received instructions to report to Gen. Sharon, who had assumed command of this sector. He hurried to Sharon's headquarters.

Col. Dan's brigade had been in the rear. It had just completed its training cycle and was due to move forward into the line and relieve Amnon's brigade on 8 October. Dan was a well-built, determined-looking sabra, born in a kibbutz thirty-six years ago, who had commanded one of the crack parachute battalions in the army. He attended the operations group given by Albert on the morning 6 October where it was planned that his brigade would take part in a counter-attack in the event of the Egyptians getting a foothold on the east bank of the Canal. At the conclusion of the conference on Yom Kippur morning he asked, 'Why not move immediately into position according to "Shovach Yonim"?' The reply was, 'It is not certain that the Egyptians will attack and the movement of Israeli forces by day could lead to escalation.'

As they were preparing to move, however, Egyptian planes attacked his forces in camp at 2 o'clock. Dan divided them, sending one battalion through the Mitla Pass, one battalion through the Gidi and a third battalion along a route between the two in case one of them had been blocked by the enemy. As he set out to mount a counter-attack against the southern sector, Albert ordered him to move northwards opposite the central sector. Dan however was of the opinion that it looked as if a major crossing would take place in the south and proposed that he continue in that direction. Albert compromised and agreed for two battalions to remain opposite the Gidi Pass while one battalion moved north in accordance with the divisional instructions.

At 4.15 Dan's forces were through the passes and were informed by Albert that the situation was a very serious one – the Egyptians were crossing along the entire length of the Canal. Dan was ordered to take command of the southern sector and do his best. This meant that Dan's brigade was responsible for a front some 35 miles wide, stretching from the junction of the two Bitter Lakes south to Ras Masala, some 12 miles south of Suez. Facing his sector were the 19th Egyptian Infantry Division, the 7th Egyptian Infantry Division, the 6th Mechanized Division and behind it the 4th Armoured Division. These forces totalled some 650 tanks, in addition to the 130th Independent Marine Brigade, which was due to cross the Bitter Lakes in amphibious vehicles and block the Mitla and Gidi passes.

The 19th Infantry Division, the 7th Infantry Division and the 130th Marine Brigade crossed to the east bank that day (the 6th Mechanized Division followed later, on 9 October). Dan sent one battalion along the Gidi Pass road with orders to link up with the Lituf fortification at the southern end of the Little Bitter Lake and with Botzer, the fortification at the junction of the Bitter Lakes, and to block all attempts to cross in the sector. With his headquarters and one battalion under Lieut.-Col. Uzi, Dan himself moved along the Mitla route southwards to link up with the fortifications on the quay at Port Tewfik and opposite Suez. The third battalion was to operate in the area of Mafzeah fortification and the Mitla route and to hold the area.

The northern battalion advancing along the Gidi route met the 130th

Egyptian Marine Brigade some 10 miles east of the Canal moving towards the Gidi and Mitla passes. They engaged the advancing force which, with its thin-skinned PT76 amphibious tanks and BTR amphibious armoured personnel carriers, was no match for the Israeli tanks, however much they outnumbered them. Dozens of Egyptian tanks and vehicles were destroyed and the 130th Marine Brigade withdrew in disarray.

Sgt Mohammed Mahmoud Nada recorded his first hours in Sinai in his diary. He was a naval frogman and was attached to a unit of the 130th Marine Brigade which crossed the Bitter Lakes on 6 October.

> ... we crossed at 2.30 [on Saturday]. ... We await the order to advance and attack. There are losses, tanks have blown up. The first tank which blew up is mine. ... On Saturday our advance was blocked and some ten amphibious tanks went up in flames. Enemy tanks were advancing and shelling us. We took up positions in order to block them ... dug slit trenches for protection. We are concerned about the Israeli Air Force which could surprise us tomorrow morning. We are being shelled. ... This is the cruellest night which we have ever known in which we faced death, hunger, thirst, fear and cold. ...

On the next day, 7 October he records:

> Last night was the longest, the most difficult and the most horrible night in my life. War is filthy and terrifying and I hate it, but at the same time I am prepared to sacrifice my life. There is nothing for us but to wait for the death which the Phantom planes or the tanks will bring us in the morning. Most of the companies took a heavy beating. ... In the morning I found my company ... we don't know where we are or what we are supposed to do. We have not fired a single bullet but our losses are heavy. ... My slit trench is but a few centimetres removed from the shores of the Bitter Lake. Some of the news broadcast over the radio causes us to roar with laughter. ...

Having disrupted the Egyptian marine brigade's advance, the Israeli battalion reached the water front and the fortifications.

By 8.00 on the evening of 6 October Dan's forces had reached all the fortifications in his sector, apart from the one on the quay at Port Tewfik, whose approaches had been mined and were swarming with Egyptian anti-tank ambushes. Along this entire sector of the Egyptian Third Army front, Dan's forces continued to block all Egyptian attempts to cross. They picked off the pontoons loaded with tractors which the Egyptians tried to move across the Canal and evacuated the dead and wounded from the fortifications.

By 2 o'clock on Sunday morning it was clear to Dan that this was real war and not merely a war of attrition. It was also clear to him that the fortifications were not contributing materially to blocking the crossings and were pinning down the Israeli armoured and counter-attack forces, including all the artillery support necessary for the protection of the strongpoints. He contacted Albert and asked for permission to evacuate all the fortifications so that he would be free to fight with armoured vehicles against the crossing Egyptian forces. The reply he received was negative. When he then asked for fresh infantry forces to reinforce the fortifications and leave him free to deal with the advancing Egyptian armour, he was informed that there were no forces for reinforcements. On more than one occasion Dan spoke to Albert and implored him to make up his mind: 'Either we defend the fortifications or we block the Egyptian attack. We can't do both.' Albert replied that there was no alternative but to do both and that he had no authority to order the evacuation of the fortifications.

All night long Dan's forces rushed from disrupting Egyptian attempts to cross the Canal to the fortifications, whose appeals for help were frequent and insistent. Each move to the fortifications meant a battle with anti-tank ambushes, then back to the crossing points, again through ambushes, and so to and fro throughout the night. When Dan had crossed through the passes at 4.00 on Saturday afternoon he had had a total force of approximately 100 tanks; by 8 o'clock on the morning of the 7th he was left with 23. Two-thirds of all the losses in men and vehicles incurred by the brigade during the war were lost on that first night.

At 9 o'clock on Sunday morning the first Egyptian armoured units crossed the Canal. Using a reconnaissance unit, Dan created a series of long-range observation points and set up his own intelligence network. As armoured forces were reported on the east bank of the Canal, he moved his small concentrated force and engaged them, destroying large numbers of Egyptian tanks at long ranges.

Meantime the requests and appeals from the fortifications were pouring in as their situation became desperate. At 11 o'clock he contacted Albert and said that he insisted on a decision. Either the tanks remain with the fortifications to the end or he would cut himself off from the fortifications and concentrate on mobile defence against the Egyptian armoured forces. He was authorized to break contact with the fortifications and to concentrate on holding the Egyptian advance, but was told that he could not hope for any reservists and that the Air Force was busy in the Golan.

Dan withdrew his tanks from the fortifications and concentrated on the crossings through the sand dunes, 2–3 miles east of the lateral artillery road. He had under command three batteries of artillery; facing him were seventy-five.

At 1 o'clock Lituf fortification to the south of the Little Bitter Lake reported that the Egyptians had succeeded in penetrating and had given them an ultimatum to surrender or be killed. Dan contacted the second-in-command of the division, asking for permission for the troops of Lituf to surrender. Although he pointed out that they were of little value in the defence of the line, his request was turned down. As the company commander in charge of the strongpoint had been killed, and a private soldier was leading a determined fight, Dan organized the break-out of the garrison with his tanks and his artillery. But the escaping troops moved in the wrong direction – and instead of reaching the Israeli tanks reached an Egyptian tank unit. The entire force was taken prisoner.

All during 7 October Dan faced most of the Egyptian Third Army with a battalion on the Gidi road drawn up west of the artillery road, a battalion on the Mitla road (also drawn up west of the artillery road) and a battalion, which was being reorganized and re-equipped after the punishment it had taken in the previous day's fighting, to the rear of the Mitla Pass. Each battalion numbered some ten tanks, but his armoured infantry had been taken from him. The fortifications were fighting and continued to report, and he estimated that he was facing a possible massive attack forward by the Egyptians. He accordingly decided to concentrate his brigade into one armoured fist and to launch a pre-emptive attack on the Egyptian concentrations.

While one battalion feinted an attack westwards towards Lituf at the southern end of the Little Bitter Lake, Dan developed a two-battalion attack in the direction of Mafzeah on the Suez Canal. His force reached the Lexicon canal road, fighting all the way, setting tanks on fire and blowing up dozens of vehicles (many of them with ammunition). Carefully husbanding his forces, firing at long ranges and continuing a classic armoured battle of fire and movement, he did not give the Egyptians a chance to develop any effort against him. On Monday evening he received approval to evacuate Botzer, where he had a platoon of tanks. All the men mounted the tanks and withdrew safely.

On Tuesday the Egyptians mounted a first concentrated attack of two mechanized brigades across the artillery lateral road in the direction of the Mitla Pass. Dan placed one battalion in the sand dunes covering the approaches and another battalion to the north of the crossroads of the Mitla road and the lateral road; a third battalion waited to the south of the crossroads. The Egyptians mounted a frontal attack on the battalion in the sands and on the battalion north of the crossroads moving northwards in order to by-pass Dan's northernmost battalion. Dan moved his easternmost battalion from the sands to the northern flank of his northern battalion and the Egyptian forces engaged these two battalions in a frontal attack in a tank fire fight. Then his southern battalion attacked the southern flank of the attacking enemy force, which was now committed and engaging two battalions along the lateral road. Twenty Egyptian tanks and many armoured personnel vehicles were set alight by this force. The Egyptians withdrew in disarray from what was a classic armoured battle in which Dan as brigade commander concentrated his brigade and moved his battalions effectively in a battle of manœuvre. This was the type of battle that Dan continued to wage for days on end in the southern sector of the Canal, carefully employing his depleted brigade as a concentrated armoured fist.

During most of the first week in October Gaby's brigade, of which he had received command six months earlier, had been on alert. On Thursday evening the stand-to had been cancelled and early on Friday morning preparations were being made to go on holiday leave. Then, at 10 o'clock, mobilization orders were received. As the forces in his brigade were moved to Sinai, Gaby detailed troops to remain behind in order to look after the brigade's organic vehicles and much of its equipment. He was convinced that in a day or two they would be back in camp after the Egyptian exercise was over. Nevertheless he moved with his advanced headquarters and reported to Albert's headquarters at 5.30 on Friday afternoon. He was instructed to be ready to operate according to the 'Shovach Yonim' plan. The battalion commanders moved out at first light on Saturday, October 6, to reconnoitre the approaches to the Canal.

When the Egyptian bombing attack began at 2 o'clock, part of his forces were on the move. Part of his brigade was detached from him and his instructions from Albert were to move with the remainder to Tasa and then north along the main north–south road towards Baluza. Listening to the networks, Gaby got a fair idea as to what was happening along the Canal. Half-way towards Baluza he was ordered to establish contact with the brigade in the northern sector. He had communications problems and the first operational order he received was to link up with the Mifreket fortification at the northern end of El-Balah Island. He spoke to the armoured battalion fighting in the northern sector and the picture that emerged was a very sombre one indeed. In brief he understood from the battalion commander, Lieut.-Col. Yomtov, that his battalion had been practically wiped out and there was nothing to do but come and rescue the remnants.

At his request the battalion commander in the line came back to meet him as he moved towards Mifreket and gave him a picture of the situation. At the same time Brig.-Gen. Kalman Magen (who had been scheduled to replace Albert on the next day) came on the air advising him that he was now commanding the sector north of Kantara and ordering him to split the battalion-size force moving with him into two: two companies of the force were to continue to Mifreket, while the other half was to move east of Kantara to link up with the fortification known as Milano. Gaby placed the Mifreket force under command of the battalion commander, Lieut.-Col. Amir, while he himself decided to lead the force to Milano, estimating that this would be the more difficult of the missions. Lieut.-Col. Yomtov, whose battalion had been decimated along the Canal, joined him with the remnants of his force.

When Amir reached the Mifreket stronghold, he divided his force into three, sending part of it half a mile south of the fortification, another part 1 mile north and retaining a force within the area of the fortification. Three times during Saturday night Amir's force linked up with Mifreket. Moving to and fro along the Canal, it was engaged constantly by RPG-firing Egyptian infantry and by anti-tank missile fire from the Egyptian rampart on the opposite side of the Canal. His tanks blew up on mines laid by the Egyptians who had crossed in the assault; Egyptian infantry swarmed all over the area. Within Mifreket he found seven scared soldiers, commanded by a signal man because their officer had been killed. Amir contacted Gaby and suggested to him and Magen that the force in Mifreket be withdrawn, as it was of no fighting value, but permission to evacuate it was withheld until dawn on Sunday.

The force north of the fortification reached the Egyptian crossing point and damaged the bridge there, but it reported that the Egyptians had succeeded in repairing the damage with amazing rapidity. This force continued to fire at everything crossing the bridge and to hit targets that included tanks, which were already crossing at midnight on Saturday. They reported that they had destroyed three tanks, a concentration of trucks and a concentration of anti-tank weapons.

One of the soldiers in Amir's battalion was Yadin Tanenbaum, a quiet, modest boy who was trained as a tank commander. As his battalion began to move towards the Canal along the Refidim–Tasa road, tanks began to fall out during the journey for technical reasons, and Yadin's tank was one of the five tanks in his company which finally reached the Canal. Commanding the tank was Ovida, a very promising young artist, while Yadin, who was the gunner, was an outstanding flautist who had already travelled abroad to give concerts. No one in the tank really knew what was happening. Although they all estimated that an incident of considerable proportions was taking place, nobody thought of war.

Ovida's tank was one of the first two to reach the Canal. The company commander told his troops that apparently an infantry force had crossed the Canal; it was not too serious, but they had to deal with it. He urged them not to be nervous, to behave like men and to be ready to fight. They did not know the area into which they were moving and had no maps. Haim, the communications man, remembers that they were directed by moonlight to turn right and then left. Encountering Egyptian infantry they wiped them out without any losses, but still they did not realize – although they were already fighting along the banks of the Canal – that this was war. Artillery fire harassed them from the other side of the Canal, but as they moved against the Egyptian infantry, the Egyptians fled.

At about 11 o'clock at night Ovida's tank, now near the Mifreket fortification, got stuck in the marshy soil, but as they tried to turn they ploughed deeper into the sand. Other tanks tried to pull them out by cable but in vain. The crew stayed with the tank. After an hour's wait they identified a bulldozer moving slowly up an opening in the rampart. Yadin aimed, fired, and the bulldozer blew up. A few minutes later a tank appeared behind it and Yadin aimed and fired at a range of 55 yards, setting it on fire. This was their undoing – because the fire lit up the surroundings and made their own tank into a target. Suddenly there were two sharp reports and the tank was hit by anti-tank fire. The driver and the communications man managed to jump out of the burning vehicle, but in the tank a promising young flautist and a promising young artist lay dead. Later Leonard Bernstein was to compose a piece for the flute in memory of the young flautist who fell in one of the two first tanks to reach the Suez Canal on Yom Kippur day.

The force to the south of the fortification continued its desperate battle in an area of sand dunes and marsh swarming with infantry anti-tank ambushes. Early on Sunday morning Gen. Magen authorized Gaby to withdraw this force with its casualties and to evacuate the Mifreket fortification. Amir's forces now had to renew their efforts to reach the strongpoint. Three times they approached the position, and on each occasion they lost one tank. (This force had already been whittled down to one-third of its tanks; Gaby's entire brigade was down to a total of approximately twenty tanks.) Amir contacted Gaby to warn him that he could lose his entire force and still not stand a chance of relieving the fortification, whereupon Gaby authorized him to withdraw with the dead and wounded in the damaged tanks. The remnants of Amir's battalion worked for hours to tow out the damaged tanks and load the dead and wounded on them. As they were moving out with thirteen men clinging on to one tank, it received a direct hit and all on board were killed. The force stopped again under fire to collect all the dead, strapping them to the decks of the tanks. By 11 o'clock on Sunday morning the remnants of this force, less than ten tanks managed to withdraw and concentrate at crossroads 5 miles from the Canal.

Meanwhile, the northern force of the brigade under Gaby had hurried northwards towards Kantara. As they approached the ghost town, fire was opened and a number of tanks were hit. For the first time Gaby saw bright lights moving eerily through the darkness towards his force in the midst of a hail of automatic fire. Only later did he realize that these were anti-tank missiles being fired at night. The force was obviously in great danger, as it was entering a built-up area. In two columns they charged down the main road of the town while fire was poured on them from all the windows, but they managed to negotiate it and rushed on to link up with the Milano fortification. The mad rush through the streets of Kantara had completely disrupted Gaby's force: most of the tank commanders, who were exposed to fire from buildings in Kantara, had become casualties. However, the entire communication system was awry, and as they fought along the Canal rampart there was a complete lack of communication and co-ordination. Gaby, Yomtov and a company commander moved under fire from tank to tank, shouting instructions to each tank commander to watch the force commanders and imitate them. The force was by now down to approximately one-third of its strength, including a number of tanks that were being towed so that their guns could be used.

Gaby was also receiving reports from Amir, to his south, and he spoke to Gen. Magen: the condition of the unit holding the Milano fortification seemed to be reasonable and the commander seemed confident. Magen therefore ordered Gaby to move northwards in order to reorganize. The force moved as directed with sporadic fighting continuing all the time. Yomtov's tank was hit again and Yomtov and his crew climbed on to Gaby's tank (Gaby's operations officer had been killed before Kantara and Yomtov remained with him for the rest of the war as operations officer).

At 3.30 in the morning Amir had concentrated the remnants of his force some 4 miles along the southern road in the northern marshes. Many of his tank crews were lost in the darkness but here the Egyptians came to the rescue. Along the Canal a number of searchlights pointed skywards, obviously reference points for the Egyptian artillery. Using these Gaby was able to give instructions to the crews cut off or stuck in the marshes on how to reach him. Soon individual single tanks began to close on him. Two tanks reached Amir at Mifreket in this manner. Two other tanks sank in the marshland not far from Milano, but the crews remained in their tanks and throughout Saturday night, Sunday and part of Sunday night these two tanks continued to fight, directing Israeli artillery fire and holding the Egyptian infantry forces at bay until their ammunition had run out. One of the crews then abandoned tank and managed to make its way back on foot to the Israeli lines.

At 8 o'clock on Sunday morning Gaby heard the voice of Gen. Bren Adan on the radio. He had arrived and was taking control of the northern divisional sector. Gaby heaved a sigh of relief, realizing that Bren's arrival meant that the reserves were on the way and that behind them the whole Israel Defence Forces were moving. In the clear on the radio, and without thinking, Gaby asked, 'What have you arrived with?' Impatient of this question over the radio, and in no mood for small talk, Bren answered curtly, 'One hundred divisions.' In the course of the morning hours Bren ordered him to concentrate what was left of his brigade on the main road east of Mifreket, where Amir's forces had arrived.

Gaby had moved down into Sinai ready to deploy with a brigade of tanks. Half of his force had been taken from him as war broke out; he was now left with one-quarter of his original strength.

12

On the Bar-Lev Line

THE RESERVE TROOPS from the Jerusalem Reserve Brigade holding the
northern half of the Suez Canal were a typical cross-section of average Jeru-
salemites, a mixture that reflected perhaps more than anything else the widely
varied composition of Israel's population. There were shopkeepers, trades-
men from the old-established oriental community, new immigrants with little
knowledge of Hebrew, university professors, senior government officials,
farmers and kibbutzniks from the hill villages in the Jerusalem corridor.
Some of the troops were old-timers who had served in the brigade in the Six
Day War, but the vast expansion of the Jerusalem population after that war
led to an influx of newcomers who had never before served under conditions
of war. Many of them were immigrants, and a relatively high percentage of
them had not served the period of conscription in the regular army and had
merely undergone a period of basic training to enable them to do reserve duty.
Many were inexperienced soldiers with little or no battle experience.

Not once was Lieut.-Col. Reuven (a reserve officer who had once commanded
a battalion of the Golani Infantry Brigade) to wonder at the policy that had
placed troops of this standard on Israel's most vital front line. On Yom Kippur
day he was stationed with his battalion headquarters at the brigade headquarters
in the northern sector conmanded by Col. Pinhas. At midday he was called
to the brigade commander for an orders group and was advised that in all
probability war would commence at 6 o'clock; meanwhile all units were to be
placed on alert for an enemy artillery barrage. He realized that this situation

would come as an incredible psychological shock to his unseasoned troops, and his instinct was to travel to all the strongpoints and speak to his men, but as such a tour would have taken some seven hours, he telephoned every fortification instead and spoke to the officer in charge. Reuven later recounted that it took him at least five minutes, in every single case, to convince his officers that he was talking about real war. The fortifications had seen the Egyptian reinforcements and the suspicious movements of units for the past week, but as they looked out on this hot, quiet Saturday morning across the placid waters of the Suez Canal, the scene was a pastoral one: farmers were going about their daily chores; Egyptian troops were without headgear or equipment, and some were fishing peacefully in the waters of the Canal. Reuven had to convince his men to disbelieve their own eyes and prepare for an imminent war.

At 1.30 the brigade commander issued orders for immediate preparedness for 'Shovach Yonim' and at 2 o'clock reports came in that the fortifications were being shelled. Forty-five minutes later reports arrived that the Egyptians were crossing the Canal; the northern fortifications already reported that they were being attacked by infantry. As he followed the reports, it became clear to Reuven that those fortifications in which the firing points had been fully manned had beaten back the Egyptians, while those in which the men had been ordered to take shelter, on the assumption that this was only an artillery attack, leaving only observers outside were penetrated by Egyptian forces.

According to the 'Shovach Yonim' plan, the key to the defence of the front line lay with the armour, which was to close the open spaces between the fortifications. As Reuven listened to the reports of the various tank platoons, however, a harrowing pattern emerged. All along the line, Egyptian tanks sited on top of the western rampart of the Canal, together with anti-tank missile units, were picking off the approaching Israeli tanks one by one. In a number of areas Egyptian commando units had occupied the ramps prepared for the Israeli tanks and were engaging them with RPG bazookas. It soon became clear that most of the first-line tanks had been hit; indeed, of all the tanks that had rushed forward to reach the ramps in his battalion sector, only two reached the northernmost fortification of Budapest on the sand bank east of Port Fuad. The fortifications began reporting wave after wave of attacking Egyptian infantry and hundreds of assault boats and rafts crossing the Canal.

The reaction in each fortification reflected the determination of the commander on the spot; in many cases, however, the officers had died at the outset. Reuven spoke to the Ketuba fortification, the first fortification on the dyke north of Kantara, where the officer in charge had been wounded. Corp. Zevulun Orlev, the headmaster of a retarded girls' school, had taken command and was in full control of the situation. Calmly he directed artillery fire and reported that many Israeli planes were being shot down near by. Reuven asked the brigade for tank reinforcements, but when he realized that there were no such reinforcements, he told the fortifications that they had no choice but to hold on, because no armour, artillery or air support would yet be available.

As soon as fighting had commenced, Reuven had moved forward with his advanced headquarters to be as near as possible to the fortifications. All night he sat in the midst of the northern swamps speaking to the fortifications, encouraging them and pleading with the brigade headquarters for help. He heard Gaby's brigade arriving in the area, but as the hours went by he realized that it, too, was being decimated.

Dawn broke on the morning of the 7th with Budapest in the north cut off by the Egyptian commando forces. Reuven returned to Brigade District headquarters, where Gen. Magen had taken over, only to be told that there was not one tank available to relieve the fortifications. All those present felt they were facing a catastrophe: the positions along the Canal were cut off; there was no air, artillery or armoured support; part of the meagre artillery support in the area had been knocked out by enemy fire. Mifreket had fallen, and in Milano there were dead and wounded, including the company commander. All fortifications reported they were running out of ammunition. Lahtzanit, midway on the dyke between Kantara and Port Fuad, had already fallen. Then, at approximately 11 o'clock, the brigade commander announced that authority had been received to evacuate the fortifications. Soon after, the men of Drora, on the dyke south of Lahtzanit, broke out eastwards in their half-tracks and returned to the Israeli lines safely.

On Yom Kippur morning, while the unit holding Ketuba was being led in prayer by three boys from a religious seminary in Jerusalem, the officer in charge received orders for 'Shovach Yonim'. The worshippers moved from the hut outside the fortification into the bunker, and when war broke out the entire position was ready for battle – the only item lacking was the tanks, which they believed would arrive rapidly. When the intense shelling began, the troops, most of them in their middle and late thirties, took up positions. Lieut. Satan, commander of the fortification, received a severe wound in the chest and was moved into a bunker for a blood transfusion. Corp. Orlev, who now assumed command, looked out, raised his head in the fearful inferno of the attack and saw two arrow-like groups of assault boats crossing to the north and south of the fortification. In each boat were twenty Egyptian soldiers. From the ramparts across the Canal, murderous pointblank fire was being directed at the fortification in order to force its defenders to keep their heads down.

Orlev manned the heavy machine gun and opened fire. Following him all positions opened fire. A signal man and a rabbinical supervisor fired bazooka shells at the boats, sinking them one after the other; within a matter of minutes all the Egyptian boats had been sunk, and they estimated that over 100 dead Egyptians were floating in the Canal. Egyptian tanks now moved up to the ramparts and engaged the position pointblank with fire. By this time there were six wounded in Ketuba, two of them seriously; there was no doctor and blood plasma was running out. Orlev contacted the position to the north, Drora, and had its doctor instruct the medical orderly how to look after the wounded and how to give infusions. Their lives were saved. As night fell one of the soldiers translated simultaneously the orders they could hear from across the Canal as the Egyptians prepared for another attack. Orlev relayed the orders by radio to the bunker, where they were passed on to the artillery in the rear. Two guns supported the position, and with Orlev directing artillery fire for the first time in his life, they achieved superb results right in the centre of the Egyptian concentrations.

The stubborn reactions of Orlev and his troops were such that soon the Canal was filled with floating dead bodies of the Egyptians – and as the moon came up the men in the position could not stop imagining that these bodies were frogmen or commandos swimming under the water towards them. Some eleven boats were sunk or blown out of the water in the first day's fighting by the men of Ketuba.

At 3.00 on Sunday morning Egyptian infantry and commandos had moved in from the north and the south along the dyke and were preparing for attack. They employed four fire bases to pin down the troops in the fortifications. Orlev now had eleven men capable of fighting (three of these had been wounded but had returned to the positions). Sizing up the situation, he gambled and concentrated his entire small force facing the Egyptian troops, which he later estimated to be some 200, moving from the south. The Egyptians advanced close to each other along the dyke. The Israeli force opened concentrated fire and after forty-five minutes of battle the southern attacking force withdrew, leaving the area strewn with dead soldiers. The northern Egyptian advance stopped when it saw the fate of its comrades.

As the fighting continued, the number of casualties in the position rose. One of the wounded soldiers who had returned to battle covered in bandages was shot by an Egyptian sniper just as he sank an additional boat loaded with commandos. He was evacuated to the bunker, managed to utter the 'Shma Israel' prayer in his last breath and died. The fighting force was down to seven men; two were dead, eight were wounded and two were in shock. Suddenly Orlev identified what seemed like a large vessel in the Canal some 2 miles south of the fortification; it was a huge ferry with tanks on board. He asked for air support, and a Skyhawk plane swept down on the ferry and sank it. Nonetheless, Egyptian forces were concentrating on the east bank: Orlev could identify six tanks and over a battalion of infantry preparing to attack his position. He realized that there was little chance that seven soldiers, battle weary and exhausted, with ammunition running out, could hold out against this force.

At 1 o'clock on Sunday afternoon Orlev issued orders to his seven men for the defence of the position. An hour later orders were received to evacuate it, but by that time six Egyptian tanks had reached a point 1 mile away and, under cover of their fire, the Egyptian infantry had begun to advance slowly forward. One of the men who had been in a state of shock for twenty-six hours heard the orders for evacuation, ran to one of the two half-tracks left in the position and fled, together with the signal man. The remainder of the force, including the wounded, had to leave in the remaining half-track. They loaded four machine guns and as many weapons as possible on it to fight their way out. Before leaving, Orlev called the headquarters to ask in which direction to move. 'What the hell are you still doing there?' came the astonished reply. Under intense Egyptian fire, the men of Ketuba drove along the track that crossed the swamps and finally reached the Israeli lines.

The northernmost Israeli position along the dyke of the Canal was known as Orkal. It was a large defensive area composed of three fortifications: Orkal A, B and C. When the fighting broke out, Orkal A was manned by twenty men under Company Commander Gad Somekh, who was in command of the entire complex; Orkal B was held by six men under command of Lieut. David Abu Dirham; and Orkal C was held by eighteen men under command of Lieut. Desberg.

At 2 o'clock on Yom Kippur, when Egyptian planes bombed the position and an artillery barrage descended on it, Abu Dirham ordered his troops underground. He saw one of the five Egyptian tanks facing the position break down as it manœuvred to take position on the rampart; another tank hit a mine. Abu Dirham searched for additional anti-tank weapons and cursed when he recalled that only two days earlier an ordnance officer from brigade head-quarters had decided that a bazooka was superfluous in this fortification and had removed it with the shells. As the battle raged, he saw another tank disabled on the minefield protecting the fortification to the north.

The shelling slackened off and Abu Dirham called down to his troops in the shelter to come out. Some of the service personnel were terrified and he went down into the position in a rage and ordered them out. Only then did they take up their firing positions. By now Egyptian infantry had begun to advance along the dyke and had reached the concertina-wire fences. Abu Dirham manned the heavy machine gun, and as the Egyptians advanced in rows – 'just like Napoleon's troops' – he and his troops cut them down row by row. Still they came on. The attack continued for an hour and a half until the Egyptian infantry withdrew, dragging their wounded and weapons with them. A damaged Egyptian tank on the opposite rampart continued to fire pointblank at the position, and the only anti-tank ammunition Abu Dirham had was anti-tank rifle grenades. He fired fourteen such grenades from a distance of 250 yards in an eliptic trajectory. Three of them hit the tank, and the third hit (which was his fourteenth grenade) silenced it.

Night had fallen and Orkal A reported that its situation was serious. Leaving command of his position in the hands of Sgt Arieh Segev, an ex-paratrooper, Abu Dirham found his way to Orkal A by flashlight. When he entered the fortification, he found the firing positions empty. Down below, in the bunker, he found a unit in a state of depression. He ran round the firing positions and found the company commander, Gad Somekh, dead in one and Lieut. Ezra dead in another. In a third position he found a machine-gunner who was completely untrained and who in later fighting would repeatedly call Abu Dirham to help him adjust.

Abu Dirham surveyed the scene and decided to take things in hand. Men were milling around inside the position demoralized by the loss of their officers. There were two tanks in the position, but the commander of one was wounded and the gun of the second tank was out of commission. After organizing the force for defence and taking command, he contacted Orkal C and spoke to the officer there, Lieut. Desberg – who had been wounded in the head but was nonetheless fighting with his men. Desberg reported that the Egyptians had already penetrated the area of the fortification and there was hand-to-hand fighting in the trenches. Abu Dirham's first reaction was to organize a counter-attack on Orkal C. But when he considered the losses and the condition and training of his troops, he realized that this would be an impossibility.

It was at this point that the Egyptians mounted a heavy infantry attack from the north. All night long, and through the following day, the force of which Abu Dirham had assumed leadership – including a number of untrained personnel responsible for services – fought against repeated Egyptian attacks from the north and an Egyptian advance from the direction of Orkal C. By Sunday afternoon Egyptian tanks began to engage the positions at pointblank range and pick off one firing position after another. The ammunition supplies were low, and Abu Dirham asked for air support. A few planes came to the rescue, and he watched as an Israeli Mirage fell in the marshes near the position. At 2.00 pm he saw men carrying a white flag. Orkal C had fallen. Abu Dirham knew that had he but fifteen trained soldiers at his disposal, he could have retaken the position and continued to hold on.

As soon as permission was received from the battalion commander, Abu Dirham organized his force to break out. He laid all the men flat in the position's half-track and manned the vehicle's gun, firing as he went. Accompanied by the two tanks, the force charged its way out, under heavy fire, within yards of the Egyptian forces holding Orkal C. The men continued firing and fighting along the dyke for 4 miles trying to reach Lahtzanit and the first route eastwards across the marshes.

Two miles before Lahtzanit, one of the tanks received a direct hit, and Abu Dirham prepared to evacuate the eight soldiers from the tank onto the half-track. As they were transferring, the half-track's engine received a direct hit, and the occupants were thrown in all directions. The second tank continued towards Lahtzanit. Abu Dirham threw a grenade and charged while firing, only to find that he had been hit in the hand and had charged alone: his men were all lying scattered in the ditch by the side of the track. Blood was spattered all over the place, and he could not tell who was dead and who was alive. Running among them under fire, he hit them with the butt of his weapon shouting, 'All those alive, raise a hand!' Finally some began to crawl after him for some 60 yards to the north as the Egyptian forces were closing in and pouring fire on them. But suddenly, there in front of them, only 10 yards away, were Egyptians. There was no way out.

On Sunday night Abu Dirham and his men who had fought such a dramatic and determined battle were taken prisoner.

At the southern end of the Suez Canal, a battle of incredible bravery and stubbornness took place as the garrison in the 'Quay' fortification – built on the breakwater at Port Tewfik opposite Suez – withstood the attempts of forces of the Egyptian Third Army to overcome it. The heroism of these forty-two regular army soldiers under the command of Lieut. Shlomo Ardinest, including the tank crews which were cut off, became a legend not only in the Israeli army but among the Egyptian forces that faced it.

The opening hours at this fortification were similar to elsewhere along the line. A massive artillery bombardment and a direct assault by a force of inflatable boats, each carrying ten soldiers, was mounted across the Canal. For two and a half hours the garrison fought off the Egyptian attack and sank most of the boats in the water. During the afternoon four tanks broke through to the position, but they had been attacked on the way and arrived damaged and with six wounded. By evening Dr Nahum Verbin had fifteen wounded in his sick bay, one of whom died soon after. Early in the fighting one of the two officers in the position was wounded, and Shlomo Ardinest a yeshivah, or orthodox seminary, graduate, remained the sole officer.

On Sunday night the Egyptians mounted another attack, and many managed to cross the Canal and climb the rampart. The troops in the position rolled grenades down the rampart to break this frontal attack, but an Egyptian unit broke into the fortification from the south with the help of flame throwers and set the stronghold's fuel store alight. When Egyptian soldiers charged into the position, screaming and drunk with victory, the garrison wiped them out in fighting that was almost hand-to-hand.

The position was surrounded by water on three sides and was connected to the mainland by a single road on a breakwater some 7 yards wide. On the Canal side of the breakwater rose the sand rampart, along which lay hundreds of Egyptian soldiers who took up positions at night. The fortification was completely cut off. When dawn broke on Sunday morning, the troops in the fortification realized how serious their position was: the open, white, windswept and sand-covered areas were massed as far as the eye could see with vehicles and Egyptian troops; not far away large numbers of tanks, vehicles, guns and missiles were crossing the Canal. Ardinest called for artillery on these Egyptian concentrations, but little did he know that at that time all that stood between the Mitla and Gidi passes and the thrust of the Third Army were the twenty-three surviving tanks of Dan's brigade.

For three days an intense artillery barrage descended on the position and thousands of Egyptian soldiers attacked it; in many cases they reached the wire fences, near enough to throw grenades into the Israeli trenches. They were followed by Egyptian tanks, prepared to blast the fortification at pointblank range. From the damaged Israeli tanks in the position the crews ranged by trial and error, setting one Egyptian tank after another on fire. Dr Verbin had by this time run out of morphine and was going through agony watching the wounded trying to bear their pain silently. He had no infusions left, not a single syringe, and the bandages were running out.

On Tuesday morning Ardinest looked out in the direction of the neighbouring fortification and saw that an Egyptian flag had been raised over it. He knew that the Egyptians had penetrated to a depth of 6 miles from the Canal and that his position was the last one holding out. By this time the position had only ten men trained for combat plus an additional ten trained for support duties, including the doctor, the medical orderly, the cook – and two yeshivah students who had come to organize the prayers on Yom Kippur. One soldier was hit by a bazooka shell and Dr Verbin performed the first open tracheotomy of his life without any form of anaesthetic. He saved the boy's life.

Ardinest moved among his troops encouraging them and promising that help would arrive. On Thursday he was asked by headquarters whether he could hold out for another forty-eight hours. Saying he would try he told the troops that help was on the way. Dr Verbin knew that from a medical point of view the fortification did not have the means to withstand another attack – he could not handle another wounded man for he had nothing with which to treat him. Seeing that the wounded were going through agony, he suggested that the position surrender, using the good offices of the Red Cross. Ardinest and the garrison sergeant would not hear of it.

Friday passed and when Saturday morning arrived it was a week since war had broken out, and the unit was still holding out. GHQ promised that help would come in twenty-four hours. Two hours later the men of the 'Quay' fortification were informed that they were authorized to surrender via the Red Cross at 11 o'clock on Saturday morning. There was no alternative: Dr Verbin was conscious of the problem of the wounded while Ardinest discovered that his entire force was left with only twenty hand grenades and a few belts of ammunition for the light machine guns, no match for the concentration of Egyptian forces surrounding them on all sides. There was nothing for it but to surrender.

When Ardinest told the troops that they had to surrender, they washed themselves in the few drops of water left in the jerry cans, tidied themselves up, changed their battle-soiled clothes and prepared to surrender proudly. A member of the Red Cross crossed the Canal with two Egyptians. Lieut. Ardinest and Dr Verbin crossed back with them. They approached the Egyptian commander and saluted, Ardinest crossing back with the Egyptians, who wanted to check that the position had not been booby-trapped, while Dr Verbin remained on the west bank of the Canal as a hostage. Ardinest insisted that the Red Cross move out with his men and retrieve three of the Israeli bodies outside and place them with two other bodies for burial in the fortification. He paraded his men and prepared them to march into captivity with their heads held high. Before leaving the position the survivors debated whether to take the Torah, the holy scroll, with them or to bury it with their dead comrades. The majority decided in favour of taking it with them into captivity. Thus, with heads held high, led by a soldier carrying the Torah, this brave group emerged into the sunshine. The thousands of Egyptians surrounding the position watched the proceedings in awe.

Ardinest was transferred to the west bank, but after a few moments high-ranking Egyptian officers took him back to the position. 'Where are your heavy machine guns?' they asked him. 'Where have you hidden them?' 'We don't have any,' he answered. 'Liar,' they shouted at him, refusing to believe that this garrison had held out for a week with only four light machine guns and proceeding to search high and low for the non-existent weapons.

The Egyptians raised their flag ceremoniously over the position, while Ardinest folded the Israeli flag with shaking hands, one fold after the other. He handed it to the Egyptian commander, who received it with a salute, and looked back at the position he had defended so bravely. Forcing back the tears, the young commander crossed the waters of the Canal and joined his troops in captivity.

At the northern end of the Israeli line, on the sandbank some 7 miles east of Port Fuad, was the fortification known as Budapest. It was commanded by a reserve officer, Capt. Motti Ashkenazi (who after the war was to become one of the leaders of the protest movements that demanded the resignation of the minister of defence), and manned by eighteen men. The lack of discipline in the position when it was handed over to him by an armoured infantry unit and the condition of the position itself and its equipment horrified him.

Fire was opened on Budapest at 2 o'clock on Saturday and the barrage continued for two hours at an estimated density of thirty shells a minute. Three men were killed in the initial barrage; the 120mm mortar in the position yard was hit, and all the intercommunication systems were knocked out. The entire position was covered in one dense pall of smoke and it was impossible to see in any direction. Budapest was the only position along the line reached by a platoon of Israeli tanks in accordance with the orders of 'Shovach Yonim'. Instead of three tanks, however, only two arrived, and on one of these the gun was jammed. (It was later repaired during the battle by the technicians in the position.)

At 4 o'clock on Saturday the Egyptians mounted a mixed armoured and infantry attack on the position from the direction of Port Fuad. The Egyptian force included sixteen tanks, sixteen armoured personnel carriers and jeeps mounting recoilless anti-tank guns, followed by trucks loaded with infantry. The sole tank in order engaged the enemy at ranges of 800–1,300 yards, supported by the fire of the fortification: eight armoured personnel carriers and seven Egyptian tanks were set on fire. As the Egyptian force began to withdraw some of their vehicles sank in the sand. By the end of the battle, seventeen Egyptian vehicles had been abandoned, and Israeli Phantoms bombed and strafed the withdrawing forces. Two hours after the armoured advance had begun, some 200 Egyptian commandos established themselves on the sandbank 1 mile east of Budapest. The fortification was now completely cut off.

On Sunday the shelling continued, and the Israeli Air Force flew in from the sea over Port Said and Port Fuad to carry out what Ashkenazi saw as suicide missions. The air was filled with anti-aircraft fire and missiles being fired by the battery; planes blew up and crashed all around the stronghold; one Phantom that had succeeded in evading five missiles was hit by the sixth and blew up 100 yards in the air above Budapest. Every plane was fired at by a battery of at least six missiles simultaneously. Sick at the sight, Ashkenazi radioed that he would forgo air support – somehow his force would manage.

That day four Egyptian Sukhoi fighter bombers attacked the position, causing much damage, while heavy guns from Port Said and the field artillery at Port Fuad pounded them all day long. The Egyptian commando force that had cut off the fortification destroyed an Israeli force, supported by armour, on its way to relieve Budapest. On Monday the massive artillery attack continued to harass the position. However Israeli pressure against the Egyptian commandos was continuing and on Tuesday night the Egyptian force was evacuated by sea. On Wednesday the Israeli Air Force attacked in the area, but the troops in the area witnessed several Israeli planes being shot down. That day a convoy together with the commander of the northern sector of the Canal, Gen. Magen, broke through to Budapest with ammunition and food. The shelling continued intermittently, but the battle for Budapest was essentially over. On Thursday Ashkenazi's unit was relieved by fresh forces.

Later an Egyptian commando unit was again to cut off Budapest. Again the Israelis had to fight to break open the route to the fortress, for the lessons of previous mistakes had not been learnt. Nevertheless Budapest held out until the end of the war and achieved the distinction of being the only front-line position in the Bar-Lev line that did not fall to the enemy.

The stand put up by the fortifications against the attacking Egyptians varied according to the quality of command in the individual positions. In general, where the command was experienced and determined and had at its disposal at least a minimum of well-trained soldiers, the fortifications held out for days. Despite the massive attack that took place against the small numbers of Israeli troops in the positions and the comparatively low standard from a training point of view of many of the soldiers, most of the fortifications fought and accounted for themselves well. (It must be remembered that they were being systematically pounded to rubble by anti-tank missiles and tank guns firing from the Egyptian ramparts, sited so that they could fire straight down into the fortifications.)

Not a single position was abandoned without orders; some continued to fight literally to the end. Some, such as the group led out of Milano on Sunday night, left their fortification just before a major Egyptian armoured assault was about to be launched. In others great ingenuity and daring went into evacuating the units, in many cases carrying their wounded with them, through the dense concentrations of Egyptian infantry, artillery and armour that filled the bridgeheads; some passed through by answering challenges in Arabic; others failed. Some encountered problems identifying themselves when they reached the Israeli lines and came under heavy fire. The Milano garrison was saved by the ingenuity of a young officer who waved a *talith*, a prayer shawl, to and fro, whereupon the front line units held their fire. The entire saga of the Purkan fortification opposite Ismailia, which fought for sixty-eight hours, was recorded by a radio technician serving in the reserve unit who had taken along a tape recorder. It is an unusual document in the history of war and has been published.

The main problem of the fortifications along the Canal was the fact that over the years they had become a compromise between strongpoints designed to hold the Canal against an Egyptian attack and warning and observation outposts. As the former they were too weak and dispersed; as the latter they were too strongly manned. Had the line been manned in preparation for the attack in accordance with the 'Shovach Yonim' plan there is no doubt but that many of the fortifications would have given a far more effective account of themselves; the Egyptians would have incurred heavy losses and failed to gain a foothold at a number of points, and the Israeli reserves would have discovered a less difficult situation on their arrival than the one they encountered. Although the Egyptian attack would doubtless have established a foothold on the east bank of the Canal, because of the unrealistic ratio of forces and the fact that the main base of anti-tank missiles was the high rampart on the Egyptian bank, the bridgeheads thus established would doubtless have been more vulnerable to Israeli counter-attack than in fact proved.

But the principal error was in not deciding early on, as Col. Dan requested, whether or not the armoured reinforcements were to concentrate on linking up with the fortifications or on repelling the Egyptian crossings. The correct picture of events along the Canal was out of focus until the morning of Sunday, 7 October. But by that time the repeated armoured attempts to link up with the fortifications had cost some two-thirds of Albert's armoured force. This indecision proved to be costly.

13

An Opportunity Lost

BY 1 O'CLOCK in the afternoon of 7 October, Gonen had divided the front: Bren's division was responsible for the northern sector, Sharon's for the central and Albert's for the southern sector. What had in fact occurred was that on Saturday afternoon brigades had taken over responsibility of battalion sectors and now divisions were taking over responsibility for brigade sectors. Sharon proposed that a major counter-attack be launched by all the divisions on Sunday evening. Gonen refused because he wanted to consolidate and straighten his line; he had very few forces at his disposal and if he were to commit one or two divisions, the enemy would be free to launch a major attack in another sector. At 3.30 Gonen transferred an armoured brigade to Albert for the defence of the passes, and Amnon's brigade came under command of Sharon. At 10.00 that night paratroopers entered the area of Ras Sudar in the south. The area was then placed directly under command of Southern Command – all forces in which were still engaged in the holding battle – thus narrowing Albert's area of responsibility.

Gonen ordered Bren to evacuate the fortifications at approximately 11 o'clock on the morning of the 7th. At 11.40 the minister of defence arrived at Southern Command. Before his helicopter landed, Gonen advised him to turn back because there were Egyptian commando units in the hills overlooking the headquarters. Dayan landed, however, and asked for a report of the situation. His reaction to it was 'This is war. Withdraw to the high ground,' tracing on the map a line east of Refidim through the mountains Jebel Ma'ara and Jebel Yalek to Abu Rudeis on the Gulf of Suez. 'Leave the fortifications, let whoever can evacuate. The wounded will have to remain prisoners.' Gonen agreed about the fortifications but argued that there was no necessity to withdraw to the mountains. Dayan left the matter to the decision of the command, and Gonen decided to maintain advance forces on the lateral artillery road with the main force on the main lateral road. As he took leave of Gonen, Dayan remarked that everything he had said was to be taken as 'ministerial advice'.

Meanwhile reserves were arriving and by the evening of the 7th most of Southern Command was deployed along the artillery lateral road with reserves on the main lateral road. The Egyptian advance was now being held all along the line, although the pressure was considerable. This situation emphasized a basic fallacy in the 'Shovach Yonim' plan, which assumed that a force of 300 tanks could withstand the full striking force of the Egyptian Army, for here were three divisions fighting and hard-pressed to hold back the attack.

At 2.30 pm Dayan returned to general headquarters and suggested that the army withdraw to a more readily defensible line, namely the line of the passes. His tone was very pessimistic: the State of Israel must be defended, and therefore the lines must be shortened. He suggested abandoning the Gulf of Suez, leaving only a force at Sharm el-Sheikh. In the Golan Heights he proposed consolidating a line before the escarpment falling down to the Jordan Valley, and preparing a line along the Jordan River. Maintaining that it was essential to hold a line before Ras Sudar on the Gulf of Suez and not at Sharm el-Sheikh, Elazar issued orders accordingly, and this deployment was to be vindicated during the war. Dayan proceeded from GHQ to meet the prime minister and again put forward his proposal for a general withdrawal. He was convinced that it was essential to shorten the lines.

At 4 o'clock Elazar was summoned urgently to join the prime minister and the minister of defence. He expressed his view that it was essential to consolidate along a temporary line well to the west of the passes from where he would launch a counter-attack on the next day. In his view a withdrawal to the line of the passes would involve far too heavy a cost for the Israeli forces by giving up or endangering major headquarters and camps. He also vetoed the idea which Sharon had put forward in Southern Command (namely to attack immediately with a possibility of crossing the Canal), because of the high risk involved; although he was in favour of a counter-attack against the main concentrations of enemy forces that had already crossed. He asked for and received the prime minister's authority to proceed to Southern Command and decide on the spot.

Elazar arrived at Southern Command accompanied by Yitzhak Rabin, a reserve general, later to become prime minister of Israel, and met Gonen, Albert, Bren and Magen at 7 o'clock. (Sharon failed to arrive because of helicopter trouble, but he came in time to meet the chief of staff as he was leaving.) Elazar set out the plan for the counter-attack on 8 October: Bren's division would attack the Egyptian Second Army from the area of Kantara, while at the same time Sharon's division would be held in reserve in the area of Tasa; in the event of Bren succeeding, Sharon would then launch an attack against the Third Army, moving from the area of the Great Bitter Lake southwards, but should Bren's attack be unsuccessful, Sharon's forces could be thrown in to reinforce it. Elazar emphasized that Sharon's forces would be held as a reserve for Bren's northern attack and that their movement would be subject to the chief of staff's personal approval. Albert's forces were to hold in the south, ready to support Sharon should he attack the Third Army.

In his brief Elazar emphasized that he did not want the forces to reach the Canal and warned them to keep away from the rampart because of infantry anti-tank concentrations. Gonen asked for permission to cross to the west bank in the event of success and Elazar agreed, on condition that Egyptian bridges were taken. Then he added the further condition that the actual crossing would be subject to his approval, which would be forthcoming only if particularly propitious circumstances developed. When Sharon arrived, he raised with Gonen the question of the relief of the fortifications and showed him a plan he had prepared for this eventuality. Gonen was opposed to a night attack, especially after the unfortunate results of the fighting on Saturday night. But he ordered Sharon to prepare his plans for the morrow and said that he would decide on the attack in the morning after reviewing developments. Elazar then returned to GHQ and authorized Northern Command to launch its counter-attack on the Golan Heights on Monday morning.

The command order was to launch a concentrated divisional attack from north to south along the east bank of the Canal while maintaining a distance of some 2 miles from the Canal to avoid the anti-tank missiles employed on the Egyptian rampart. The purpose of the attack was to destroy the Egyptian forces on the east bank of the Canal and to effect a limited crossing to the west bank at the southern extremity of each sector. Bren's division was to attack in the sector held by the Second Egyptian Army.

Bren's division was deployed along the main lateral road – namely, the Baluza–Tasa road. Gaby's brigade was to move southwards between the Lexicon road (running along the Canal) and the artillery route to destroy the enemy in the area and reach the Hizayon and Purkan fortifications, opposite Firdan and Ismailia, respectively. On Gaby's left flank, but west of the artillery route, Natke's brigade was to advance southwards towards Purkan, facing Ismailia. Arieh's brigade was to move southwards east of the artillery road towards Matzmed, at the northern extremity of the Great Bitter Lake, where a limited crossing of the Canal would be attempted on Egyptian bridges. Thus far the orders issued by Bren accorded with the orders he had received from Gonen. After the destruction of the enemy forces by Bren's division, Magen's forces were to come in from the north and mop up along the east bank of the Canal.

The two leading brigades moved from north to south under intense Egyptian artillery fire. South of Kantara, Natke's forces were engaged by units of the 18th Egyptian Infantry Division. They dealt successfully with the Egyptian advances, wiped out the Egyptian infantry, destroyed a number of tanks and continued on their way with a minimum of losses. Gaby moved without encountering any enemy forces until he reached the area of Firdan at 9.30 am. The reports coming into Southern Command were good. There were signs of panic among the enemy, and a wave of optimism spread throughout command headquarters. Bren received orders to broaden his front and, if possible, to seize hold of three bridges north of the El-Balah Island, at Firdan and at Ismailia, with a minimum of force. Although Bren was taken aback by this change of plan in the course of the operation, he was convinced that it was based on good intelligence in the command. Accordingly, he ordered Gaby to attack the area of Firdan and asked for air support. In all, he was supported by two batteries of artillery from Sharon's division. His own artillery had not yet arrived in Sinai.

In the late morning, it suddenly became clear to Bren that his brigades were not moving in accordance with orders and were, in fact, moving too far to the east, along the artillery road, and away from the bulk of the enemy forces. Arieh's brigade was even further removed, actually some 20 miles from the Canal at one stage of the operation.

The result of this mistake, which was not corrected in time, was that instead of rolling down the north flank of the narrow Egyptian bridgehead, the massed forces of Bren's division were moving across the front of the Egyptian bridgehead. Accordingly when the attack was finally launched, it developed from east to west right into the deployed Egyptian positions – instead of from north to south, where the Egyptians least expected it.

Natke was advancing comfortably and had destroyed some twenty enemy tanks. Air support was very limited, and the air strikes were few and far between. Arieh's brigade advanced rapidly towards Ismailia and received orders *en route* to prepare to seize bridges. By midday Gaby's forces were approaching the Canal and were engaged by Egyptian tanks and infantry, which they could see clearly on the ramparts on the Egyptian side of Firdan. Gaby's left-flank battalion attacked along the Firdan route (Haviva) and almost reached the Israeli ramparts along the Canal. Suddenly hundreds of Egyptian infantry appeared out of the sand dunes around him, all firing anti-tank weapons at short

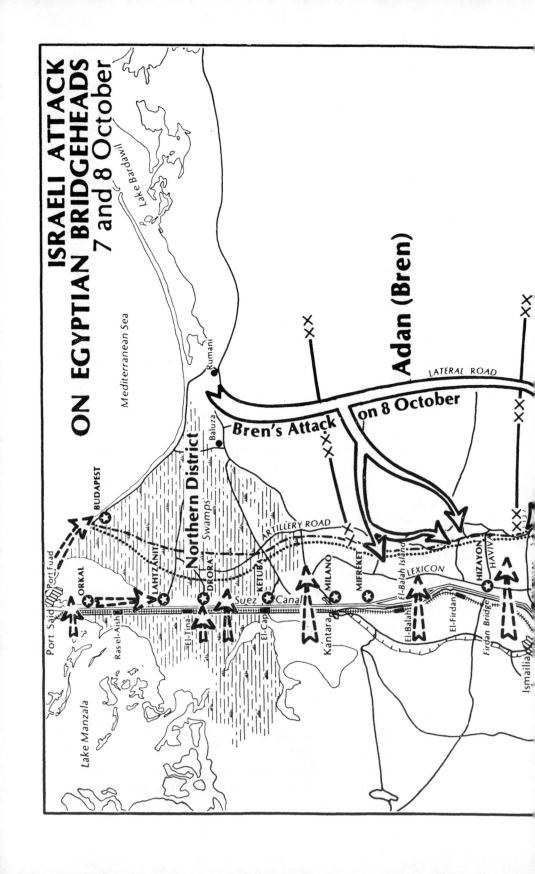

ISRAELI ATTACK ON EGYPTIAN BRIDGEHEADS 7 and 8 October

Adan (Bren)

LATERAL ROAD

Bren's Attack on 8 October

Mediterranean Sea

Lake Bardawil

Rumani

Baluza

BUDAPEST

Northern District

Swamps

ARTILLERY ROAD

ORKAL

LAHTZANIT

DRORA

KETUBA

MILANO

MIFREKET

El-Balah Island

LEXICON

HIZAYON

HAVIVA

Port Said

Port Fuad

Ras el-Aish

El-Tina

El-Cap

Kantara

El-Balah

El-Firdan

Firdan Bridge

Ismailia

Suez Canal

Lake Manzala

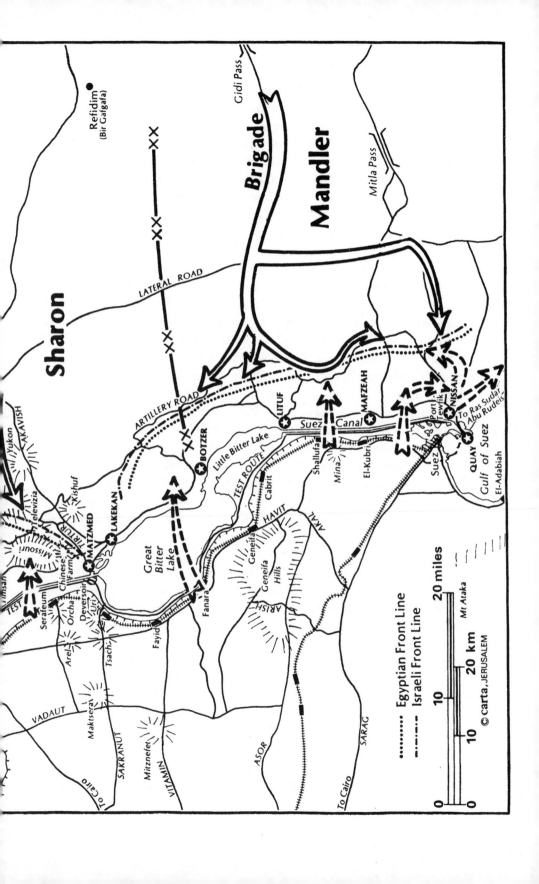

Sharon

Brigade

Mandler

Refidim
(Bir Gafgafa)

Gidi Pass

Mitla Pass

LATERAL ROAD

ARTILLERY ROAD

Yukon

AKAVISH

Kishuf

Televizia

TIRTUR

Missouri

Chinese Farm

MATZMED

LAKEKAN

BOTZER

LITUF

Little Bitter Lake

MAFZEAH

Suez Canal

Shallufa

Mina

El-Kubri

Serafeum

Orcha

Deversoir

Uri

Fayid

Tsach

Arel

Maktsera

Mitznefet

VITAMIN

Great Bitter Lake

Fanara

TEST ROUTE

Cabrit

HAVIT

Geneifa

Geneifa Hills

AKAL

ARISH

NISSAN

Port Tewfik

Suez

QUAY

Gulf of Suez

El-Adabiah

To Ras Sudar
Abu Rudeis

VADAUT

SAKRANUT

ASOR

SARAG

To Cairo

To Cairo

TEST

20 miles

20 km

Mt Ataka

© carta, JERUSALEM

Egyptian Front Line

Israeli Front Line

range. The battalion commander was wounded, and the battalion withdrew, eaving twelve tanks aflame in the area.

At about 11 o'clock, Gonen – who was under the impression that all was going well with Bren and mindful of the problem of time and distance involved in moving Sharon's division southwards to attack the Third Egyptian Army that afternoon – decided to move Sharon's division southwards to the area of the Gidi Pass in order to hold it in readiness. When Sharon reached the Gidi Pass, Gonen would advise him whether to attack from north to south towards Suez or from south to north, according to the developments on the front. He informed the chief of staff and received his approval for the move.

Meanwhile, reports from Bren indicated that six of his tanks had been hit, and he requested air support. Gonen did not consider the loss of six tanks to be a major command problem, and accordingly he ordered Sharon not to stop at the Gidi Pass but to continue southwards. When he failed to receive a reply from Sharon, Gonen dispatched his chief of staff by helicopter to locate Sharon's division. He found one brigade in Tasa, one brigade 6 miles south of Tasa and a third brigade with Sharon's advance headquarters in the area of the Gidi and Mitla passes.

In the meantime, Bren had ordered Natke, who had left one battalion facing Kantara, to move south to Firdan with two battalions in order to join up with Gaby and mount a two-brigade attack at that point. Bren was on a nearby hill observing battle. At 2.30 pm the two brigades – which were not really more than two battalions in strength between them – moved out. Gaby moved out along Haviva towards Firdan, and Natke moved along a parallel route 2 miles to the north. In the meantime, at approximately 2 pm, Arieh's brigade had established contact with the enemy opposite Ismailia, some 4 miles from the Canal, and was pressing westwards.

As the attack developed everything went wrong. Natke's forces – advancing on the road north of and parallel to the Firdan road – moved forward rapidly and found themselves 800 yards from the Canal surrounded by thousands of infantry. Eighteen of his tanks were set on fire and destroyed. The battalion commander leading the attack, Lieut.-Col. Asaf Yagouri, was blown out of his tank and taken prisoner. His capture was highlighted by the Egyptian media; and in their ecstasy and excitement at capturing a senior Israeli officer, the Egyptians turned Yagouri's battalion into a brigade and Yagouri into a brigade commander. In fact, what was to have been a two-brigade attack turned out to be no more than an ill-conceived battalion attack.

Natke is a short, plain-spoken, earthy type, unaffected by any form of sophistication. In the Six Day War he had served as a battalion commander and had been seriously wounded in his legs, undergoing over twenty operations (a great part of one of his legs is artificial), and yet this experience had not broken his spirit; on the contrary he had laid siege to his superiors until they had finally relented and given him a fighting command – a reserve tank brigade – despite his disability. He requires assistance in order to mount or dismount a tank, but his obstinacy is a password in the army, where he is known as a human bulldog.

He had received orders from Bren at 4.30 am on the 8th to advance carefully southwards and mop up from north to south while avoiding the Canal rampart. Overcoming light resistance and knocking out eight enemy tanks on the way, as has already been mentioned, he was continuing southwards when he heard that Gaby's brigade was in trouble attacking towards Hizayon on the Canal at the Firdan Bridge. Having received orders to join him and together mount an attack towards the Canal in the general area of Hizayon, he met Gaby under a very heavy artillery barrage and was briefed by him. The air support they were getting was ineffective and the artillery support – one battery of four pieces – was very weak.

They launched the attack at 2 o'clock, moving through the undulating sand dunes under very heavy artillery. (Natke had attached himself to a battalion with his advanced headquarters.) After fifteen minutes they were under anti-tank fire. The leading battalion reported that two tanks had been knocked out and that the second-in-command of the battalion had been killed. Concentrated katyusha fire blocked their advance and they could not see more than a distance of a yard ahead because of the black smoke and dust covering the area. When they were 800 yards from the Suez Canal, a hail of anti-tank fire descended on them. Natke looked around him as the smoke lifted and saw tanks exploding on his right and left. What he saw convinced him that they must pull out. Of the force he had attacked with, only four tanks (including the one he was in) were capable of withdrawing from the inferno into which they had charged. As he began to withdraw Bren came on the network and asked him: 'What happened, why are you withdrawing?' Natke replied, 'If you continue to ask me questions there will be nobody left to answer in a few minutes.' They pulled back.

Brig. Hasan Abu Saada, the commander of the Egyptian brigade facing Natke, described the attack as follows:

... The enemy opened his attack moving forward at a speed of 40 kilometres an hour. As soon as the Israeli tanks crossed the camouflaged infantry trenches the infantry jumped out of the trenches like devils and began to attack the 190th Brigade. Our tanks and all the anti-tank equipment concentrated in the area operated against the enemy and destroyed him. In three minutes the 190th Israeli Armoured Brigade was destroyed ... Asaf Yagouri, the commander, with another four soldiers, was taken prisoner ....

A second attack was again broken by Egyptian infantry. It must be remembered that Bren's forces were fighting without infantry or armoured infantry, without air support and without artillery, apart from two batteries. Against them were fighting the forces of the 2nd Egyptian Infantry Division, commanded by Brig. Hasan Abu Saada, in co-ordination with forces of the 18th Infantry Division reinforced by the anti-tank reserves of the Second Army.

The Egyptians launched an attack on Arieh's forces at about 3 pm, moving in a north-easterly direction from the area of Machsir and Televizia to the area of the crossroads at Hamutal. At 3.30 pm Hamutal fell to the Egyptian attack. An hour later, the Egyptians, developing their attack further, captured an adjacent position, Ziona. As Bren looked over the battlefield from his observation point, he was unhappy about the deployment of his forces. He called Gaby and Natke to him as the enemy shelling continued ceaselessly (Bren's advanced head-quarters was hit by artillery fire, killing some of his staff), but when he was receiving reports from the two brigade commanders, calls from their battalion commanders asking for help could be heard: a mechanized brigade and a tank brigade were attacking eastwards from the Firdan towards the artillery road, while a similar tank force was attacking from Missouri towards the Ismailia road. The description coming in was of a concentration of armour 1 mile wide, with tanks and armoured infantry personnel carriers advancing. The two brigade commanders rushed back to their formations, reporting within five minutes of their arrival that the situation was critical. Both asked permission to improve their positions to the rear and, although Ben knew this meant withdrawal under pressure, he agreed.

At 2 o'clock, when he realized what was happening on Bren's front and that it was too late for Sharon's forces to develop an attack against the Third Egyptian Army, Gonen ordered Sharon to reverse his southward move and return to the central sector. Bren heard Gonen describing his situation in his sector to Sharon and asking him to mount a counter-attack in order to relieve the pressure. Sharon replied he would give an answer in five minutes' time, whereupon Bren informed the two brigade commanders that they could hope for a counter-attack by Sharon within fifteen minutes and asked them if they could hold on. They answered in the affirmative and told him that although they were setting alight many Egyptian tanks, the heavy pressure was being maintained on them. Five minutes later Sharon replied that he would not mount the attack.

By 4 o'clock in the afternoon, when Natke had rushed back from Bren's advanced headquarters, he found that in addition to being heavily outnumbered, the Israeli forces were fighting with the sun in their eyes. Battle was joined at a range of 2,500 yards, but gradually the Egyptians advanced, shortening the range to 600 yards. At approximately 5 o'clock the sun set; visibility improved considerably and the defending force began to destroy large numbers of advancing Egyptian tanks and armoured personnel vehicles. To his right Natke saw one of the officers destroying twenty-five Egyptian tanks one after the other. All along the line the Israeli tanks were hitting back. A second wave of armoured personnel carriers and infantry-carrying trucks advanced to within 400 yards of the Israeli line. But by the time it was dark, their attack was broken and they began to withdraw, with the Israeli forces following them with fire.

Darkness fell and the reports were that the attack was being held. The burning tanks created a series of bonfires across the desert. Meanwhile, Sharon's division was returning from the south.

That evening the divisional commanders gathered at Southern Command headquarters to meet the minister of defence and the chief of staff. Bren reported that he had had heavy tank losses in the day's fighting, and it was clear that the command could not afford another similar day of fighting. Gonen proposed that the policy now be to conserve forces, hold the enemy and build up additional strength; only when the full strength of the force had been reconstituted would they move over and strike a decisive blow.

Many of the basic errors in the deployment of Israel's forces had been highlighted on this critical day. Many of the principles of war were ignored and the conviction of many in the Israeli Armoured Command that armoured forces could operate freely without close infantry support was proved to be one of the dangerous concepts that had entered Israeli military thinking since the Six Day War. The Israeli armour attacking with the *élan* of cavalry charges, without infantry support and with inadequate artillery support, made no sense whatsoever in face of the masses of anti-tank weapons which the Egyptians had concentrated and which were by now known to all the Israeli commanders. The initial error made by Bren's brigade commander – not rolling down the Egyptian bridgehead from north to south in an area 2 to 5 miles from the Canal, as planned – led to the attack developing from east to west into the Egyptian fortifications, instead of against the Egyptian northern flank. Furthermore, Bren's armoured force was not concentrated during the attack and was frittered away piecemeal. Had a two-divisional attack, with all the necessary support, been mounted in the Firdan area, there could well have been a reasonable chance for the Israeli forces to roll up the Egyptian bridgeheads from their flanks. Instead, the reporting from Bren's division created an erroneous impression at command headquarters, and Sharon's division spent its day moving to and fro with little fighting.

The 8th of October was a wasted day. The Israeli forces not only suffered heavy casualties but lost a number of important positions in the area of Hamutal. It may well have been possible to deal a crippling blow to the Second Egyptian Army by means of a well-co-ordinated attack, for the Egyptians were not yet fully organized on the ground. Indeed, there was a chance to create a two-divisional *schwerpunkt* against the Egyptians and then possibly exploit success across the Canal. But the opportunity was lost.

The failure of the Israeli attack added considerably to the self-confidence of the Egyptian forces. However it played a very important function in preventing them from developing offensive operations and in containing their bridgeheads. A major opportunity to change the direction of the war in the south was missed.

Maj.-Gen. Ariel Sharon, known throughout the Israeli Army as 'Arik', had retired from the army as GOC Southern Command in July but – rather characteristically – like all his other activities his retirement was accompanied by a considerable amount of public interest. He indicated that he had resigned from the army because it had been made clear to him that he would not be the next chief of staff. He threw himself into politics and joined the Liberal Party; in the course of a few months, by dint of the sheer determination and perseverance that characterizes all his activities, he had managed to create an alignment of centre and right-wing parties (to be known as the Likud), which would fight the coming election against the governing Labour Party.

Sharon is a strange mixture. He is a born leader of men in the field. As many have put it, he has natural instincts that enable him to size up any situation in the most difficult circumstances, not by any means of logical process of staff work but by a healthy intuition. By the same token he is considered to be a poor staff officer. His tour of duty as chief of staff to Gen. Elazar (when the latter was GOC Northern Command) led to a relationship that would reflect itself in the Yom Kippur War, and his period at GHQ as a staff officer is not re-called by many with enthusiasm. He proved himself to be a genius in improvisa-tion, but although this characteristic is vital on the field of battle, when applied to routine life it can be frustrating in the extreme to others. Once having seized hold of a problem, he is a bulldog and will not let go until he has solved it; but a problem can be his main centre of interest one day to the exclusion of all other matters, while the next day he can without warning ignore it. He is utterly un-predictable, egocentric and anything but an ideal member of a team. On the other hand he is possessed of a powerful personality and leadership and is the type of commander with whom the members of his command down to the last private soldier identify completely (all refer to him affectionately by his nick-name).

Arik is a swashbuckling, popular, back-slapping extrovert, always readily available to the press. Most important, he is the antithesis of the man who replaced him as GOC Southern Command, Maj.-Gen. Gonen, orderly, dour, a strict disciplinarian, a professional soldier within a military framework. The relations between them were further complicated by the fact that Gonen had commanded a reserve division under Sharon, and now suddenly the tables had turned and this 'junior officer' was in command of Gen. Sharon, who in turn had received command of Gonen's reserve division. Gonen now had under command an officer who not only had been his superior a few months earlier, but one whom very senior, tried and seasoned officers found extremely difficult to control. And now the control of Sharon was one of Gonen's problems – one of his main problems.

On assuming command of the central sector, Sharon decided to block the enemy advance along the artillery road with his main forces while holding the reserve along the main lateral road. At the same time he planned operations in order to save the garrisons in the fortifications along the Canal. He spoke to them several times, encouraging them to hold on and promising that every effort would be made to save them.

On the night of 8–9 October the garrison at Purkan had escaped, taking all night to make its way across the sands but becoming stranded in the desert in the midst of a tank battle. Sharon ordered Col. Tuvia to organize a force to retrieve the men, but then Amnon approached Sharon and asked for special permission to be allowed to pick them up; he had been in touch with them from the first moments of the war and felt a peculiar attachment to them. Sharon approved.

Amnon organized a task force composed of his tank, an armoured carrier with his brigade artillery commander in it, a tank with a battalion commander, Lieut.-Col. Shaul Shalev, a tank with an air-support officer and four armoured carriers lightly manned and including a doctor. This rescue force moved towards the forward Israeli line. On the high ground near Hamutal he saw Tuvia's tanks facing an Egyptian force somewhat larger than a brigade on a ridge in the distance: the forces were engaged in battle and the entire area of sand dunes in between the two crests was swarming with Egyptian infantry units; furthermore, the Israeli forces were under an intensive artillery barrage. Somewhere in the midst of all this pandemonium of a battlefield lay the men from Purkan waiting to be rescued.

Amnon decided that there was no time to be lost if the men were to be saved. He contacted the commander of the stranded group and told him to fire a green rocket to identify his position. When Shaul, the battalion commander, identified the rocket, they set out with the three tanks leading and the half-tracks behind,

Amnon to the left of the force. As he moved he saw thirty men standing on a dune 100 yards from him, but although this was not the direction of the rocket, he approached nevertheless. They were Egyptians. Charging them in his lone tank he was drawn into a private battle of his own. In the meantime the armoured carriers were engaged by Egyptian infantry firing anti-tank weapons and they were all hit, with all the officers wounded. One carrier was evacuating the wounded when it received a direct hit from an anti-tank missile; it was abandoned by all on board, but continued to move aimlessly across the desert. All but two of the force managed to return. By this time however Shaul had identified the Purkan men, had reached them and was loading them on the tank, and when Amnon (having succeeded in wiping out most of the Egyptian force) drove down the hill, he suddenly saw a monstrous-looking body moving slowly towards him – in the midst of an inferno of a tank battle – it was a tank carrying thirty-three men on it.

This operation – perhaps more than any other – emphasized one of the points which had invariably been a central theme in the Israel Defence Forces. From the divisional commander down, every rank was involved in saving the unit from Purkan. To save a handful of men, three senior officers (a brigade commander, a battalion commander and a brigade artillery commander) exposed themselves to great danger to lead the rescue group. It may be that this was a very expensive method but it is an indication of the quality of leadership in the Israeli Army and the self-sacrifice of the officers who would not ask others to enter an area of danger which they were not prepared to enter themselves.

On Tuesday afternoon Sharon attacked with Tuvia's brigade and Amnon's brigade in order to retake Machsir and Televizia, a second-line fortification which had fallen to the Egyptians. Sharon maintained that Gonen's orders were to attack the Egyptians as they were withdrawing but not to maintain the attack if the Egyptians stood their ground. Gonen maintained that he had not authorized this attack: he ordered Sharon to stop it, but later learned that it was continuing. Sharon for his part had seen that an Egyptian attack on Hamadia had been smashed by Tuvia that morning, but noted that a larger number of Egyptian troops were still in the area. He began to push them back in order to remove the danger of infantry-borne anti-tank missiles from his armoured forces. Gonen flew by helicopter to Sharon's advanced headquarters and ordered him personally to stop, but although he said he was stopping, again Gonen was later to learn that he had continued – losing in the course of the day many tanks. After this incident Gonen telephoned the chief of staff asking for Sharon to be relieved of his command.

Meanwhile a report was received that an Israeli tank with its crew had been cut off on Televizia. Amnon attacked the position and overcame it without much opposition, rescuing three soldiers. One man in the entire brigade, Shaul Shalev, the battalion commander who had rescued the men from Purkan, was killed (by artillery fire) during the operation.

Amnon's brigade was now facing the so-called Chinese Farm, so named because it was an experimental agricultural area in which Japanese instructors had been developing experiments before the 1967 war; seeing the Japanese inscriptions the Israeli troops, not particularly well versed in East Asian scripts, had named the place the Chinese Farm. Amnon's units probed gently in this area, and as they did the divisional reconnaissance unit attached to them moved first in a south-westerly direction, reaching the water's edge along the Great Bitter Lake, and then northwards towards the Chinese Farm, hugging the edge of the lake. That night the unit was in position in the general area of Lakekan on the lake, but on the next morning, 10 October, it was ordered to return. The probe had revealed the boundary between the Egyptian Second and Third armies and the soft underbelly of the Second.

At midday on 9 October Elazar reviewed matters at the chief of staff's conference. The news from the counter-attack in Syria was good and he felt that pressing forward in Syria with the purpose of taking it out of the war was the first priority. Accordingly the policy on the Egyptian front must be to endeavour to improve the ratio of forces by allowing the Egyptians to attack and incur casualties against the Israeli defence. After breaking the major Egyptian attack that had to come, the possibilities of counter-attacks, including the crossing of the Canal in the area of Deversoir, would become viable.

Addressing the editors of the Israeli press on Tuesday evening, 9 October, Gen. Dayan emphasized that the Israeli policy now was to give top priority to the Syrian front in order to neutralize the danger there. Every effort would be made to destroy the Syrian armed forces and to hit Syria strategically by bombing headquarters and economic targets, the only limitation arising out of a decision not to strike at the civilian population. Turning to the Egyptian front, he stated quite unequivocally that they did not have the strength to throw the Egyptians back across the Canal; it would not be possible to carry out both operations – taking the Syrians out of the war and throwing the Egyptians back across the Canal – at the same time. While discussing the problem of the line in the south, he indicated that it would be essential to decide on new and shorter lines. Referring to the southern Sinai, he hinted at the possibility of a defence line which would cover only Sharm el-Sheikh. He expressed the view that:

> We cannot throw them back now and defeat them. . . . What we should and can do is to deploy along new lines on this side and also in the southern part

of Sinai, and this we shall do. . . . I do not believe that under normal circumstances any decision of the Security Council will stop [the Arabs] if from a
physical, military point of view they will be able or believe they will be able
to continue the war. First of all there will not be such a decision, for the
Chinese and Soviets will apply a veto. Secondly they will ignore such a
decision to stop. One cannot rely on this. Israel can only rely on two elements: (1) The lines which her forces will hold and (2) The continued
growth of Israeli strength in the future.

Describing the Israeli losses and the line, he said:

Hundreds of our tanks have been knocked out in battle. Part we can retrieve
. . . part we cannot retrieve. . . . In three days we have lost fifty planes. . . .
My personal estimate is that somewhere in this third of Sinai between the
Canal and before the mountains we will have to establish a line which they
cannot pass, not because it is an obstacle line like the Andes Mountains, but
because it is a line which when manned by our forces, they will not be able
to cross. The same is true as far as the southern part of Sinai is concerned. . . .

Dayan announced at the meeting that he proposed to go on television that
evening in order to announce the truth to the public about the fall of the Bar-
Lev line and to give a clear picture of the sombre situation. One of the editors
said to him, 'If you tell the public today on television what you have told us,
this means an earthquake in the nation's consciousness and in that of the Jewish
people and of the Arab people.'

The atmosphere created by Dayan's press conference was such that there
were many who contemplated his appearance before the nation with great
trepidation. In view of this concern, Mrs Meir requested him not to appear on
television that night, and instead Gen. Aharon Yariv (the former chief of
intelligence, who was acting as assistant to the chief of staff) went on the air to
present a clear and balanced picture of the situation.

14

Decision in the Desert

AT THE CABINET meeting on Tuesday, 9 October, Gen. Chaim Bar-Lev, the minister of trade and industry, complained about the dismal atmosphere which he felt had been created in the GHQ command post by a variety of visitors and hangers-on who were filling the place and offering unsolicited advice. That day the chief of staff called him over to GHQ, explaining to him that he was not happy with the situation in the south: many of the fortifications were still cut off and a relationship which was prejudicial to an efficient conduct of the campaign had developed between Gonen and Sharon. He offered the ex-chief of staff the post of GOC Southern Command; Elazar did not think that Gonen had failed in his command, but that the situation that had developed was unhealthy. Bar-Lev accepted on condition that a satisfactory arrangement could be made with Gonen and on condition that the prime minister and the minister of defence agreed. He drove home to collect his uniform and personal equipment and was called from the shower by the prime minister, who thanked him for accepting the post and invited him to a meeting of the Cabinet. Immediately thereafter the minister of defence phoned him: 'Get down there and make decisions.'

When Bar-Lev arrived back at GHQ at 10 o'clock that night Elazar advised him that Gonen had reacted very strongly to his proposal, maintaining that what they were in fact doing was dismissing him and holding him personally responsible for what had happened. Bar-Lev countered that he was not prepared to become an adviser to Gonen and would not go to Southern Command unless his status was clearly defined. It was explained to Gonen that while it was felt that he did not deserve to be disgraced publicly, in view of the unfortunate circumstances it was essential that Bar-Lev be in command. At this point the idea of making Bar-Lev the personal representative of the chief of staff in Southern Command with full command authority was born. Bar-Lev agreed to accept this formula on condition that it was made perfectly clear that he was in command and not an adviser. He went to sleep on a couch in the chief of staff's office and a few hours later Elazar woke him to tell him that Gonen had accepted his proposal. That night, for the first time in the war, Elazar slept for three and a half hours.

Bar-Lev arrived at Southern Command headquarters on Wednesday morning, 10 October. He had a frank, open discussion with Gonen who expressed he fear that this meant his end as far as the army was concerned, but Bar-Lev disagreed and explained why. They agreed on a working arrangement which was later to prove to be highly successful. To his staff and to the divisional commanders who were present, Gonen announced that henceforth Bar-Lev would be number one on the scene, adding, 'In this war I will have a private chief of staff on my own.'

Having clarified the situation, Bar-Lev visited the divisions and watched the battles in progress: the Egyptians were pressing all along the line to take the artillery road with infantry and armoured attacks, but the Israeli armour was wreaking havoc among them. As he visited Sharon, the latter expressed his grave reservations about the new situation of *status quo* that had been created in the south while the major effort was concentrated on the Golan. He proposed that his division, in co-ordination with Albert's to the south, push with two armoured brigades along the east coast of the Bitter Lakes in order to roll up the infantry divisions of the Third Army. With two of his brigade commanders, Amnon and Haim, Sharon presented his plan on 11 October, but Gonen rejected it because in his view it would obviously be an expensive operation for very little gain; furthermore, the two as yet uncommitted armoured brigades would be badly mauled instead of being prepared for the major armoured battle that would follow an Egyptian armoured advance, which according to Soviet doctrine must take place on the sixth or seventh day of the war. Bar-Lev decided against Sharon's plan.

Finding relations between Gonen and Sharon to be very strained with mutual accusations flying around, Bar-Lev began to experience the problems of exercising command over Sharon; in every case he made a point of giving clear, specific orders to him. But on 12 October he proposed to the chief of staff that Sharon be relieved. Elazar said he would consult with the minister of defence, but when he did so Dayan said that such a move could create political problems. Nevertheless during the war Bar-Lev formally proposed relieving Sharon twice.

From 9 October Southern Command continued to fight a containing battle, recouping their strength while successfully holding Egyptian attempts to advance. Indeed, apart from the small area lost as a result of the Egyptian attacks on Arieh's brigade in the area of Hamutal on the 8th, the Egyptians did not advance one yard during the remainder of the war. An indication of the effects of resupply, continued mobilization and the outstanding efficiency and devotion of the ordnance corps in repairing the damaged tanks, could be gauged from the fact that by 15 October Bren's division, despite its losses since 9 October, disposed of twice the number of tanks it had had under command six days earlier.

The Israelis had the advantage of being very familiar with the terrain, but they had to deal with three to five Egyptian attacks daily. However, because the Egyptians fought in a very schematic way, the Israeli forces soon had the measure of their enemy and operated with an increasing degree of self-confidence. At night Egyptian infantry would crawl forward to the slopes of the line of high ground held by the Israelis some 5–6 miles from the Canal, coming to within 2,000 yards of the forward Israeli units (one morning they awoke to find Egyptian infantry among the sand dunes behind them). The attack would invariably begin with a concentrated artillery barrage lasting half an hour, which would be concluded with five minutes of rapid-fire concentrations fired by fifteen battalions of artillery and batteries of katyusha rockets; the barrage would conclude with a large quantity of phosphorescent ammunition. At this point the tanks would begin to advance with the infantry interspersed between them in armoured personnel carriers. When the attacking forces reached the line of infantry that had crawled forward at night and had dug itself into the sand, this line would now emerge from out of the ground and follow the tanks.

At a considerable distance to the flanks Sagger anti-tank missile units were deployed. Sometimes as the line of infantry approached – having sustained a large number of casualties from small-arms and artillery fire – it would stop and a fresh line which had dug itself into the sand overnight would emerge and continue with the attack. All these Egyptian attacks were broken with heavy losses, both in armour and in infantry, but nevertheless time and again the Egyptian infantry would surge forward in attack only to be mowed down by the waiting Israeli armour and artillery. Invariably the pattern of attack would renew itself. The Egyptian losses were heavy, and Israeli respect for the determination and daring of the Egyptian infantry grew.

An Egyptian divisional attack on Gaby's brigade on the 9th penetrated the Israeli lines, but Bren, concentrating his armour, smashed the Egyptians by drawing them on to Gaby's brigade and then unleashing Natke's brigade at their northern flank and Arieh's brigade at their southern flank. On the 10th the Egyptians mounted five separate attacks against Bren's division. This scene was re-enacted all along the line. Sharon's division was attacked by formations of the 21st Egyptian Armoured Division, but by handling his formations carefully and using his reserves, he smashed the Egyptian advance; the enemy forces withdrew, leaving fifty tanks on the field of battle.

In the south Albert's division, which had by now been reinforced, contained the enemy, with Dan's brigade acting as a concentrated armoured fist moving around harassing the Egyptian Third Army, exacting casualties and in many ways gaining control of the field of battle. On Wednesday, 10 October, an Egyptian mechanized brigade advanced southwards parallel to the Gulf of Suez, but it was held by an armoured force under Gen. Gavish, who was commanding southern Sinai. The attacking Egyptian force, which included some fifty tanks, joined battle with the Israeli tanks in the area of Ras Sudar. The leading Egyptian tanks were knocked out and the advance stopped in its tracks. Since the enemy force was now out of range of its missile umbrella, the Israeli Air Force destroyed the entire column.

Gradually the Israeli forces took control of the battlefield, allowing the Egyptian assaults to break up on the Israeli defensive anvil. Confidence was growing. Answers to the anti-tank weapons that had been encountered were being produced, and not one position held by the Israelis along the Egyptian bridgeheads was taken by enemy forces. That Wednesday morning Gonen reported to the chief of staff that he felt a marked change along the front line. The ratio of losses had changed radically: the graph of Israeli losses had dropped markedly while that of the Egyptians was rising. The reserves were arriving. Ordnance was preparing the tanks and the command was gathering strength.

At this stage discussion concerning the next Israeli step began. It was already clear by 10 October that the only move that could unbalance the Egyptians and allow the Israeli Army with its flair for speed and manœuvre to come into its own and to get away from the static war into which it had been drawn, was to cross the Canal into Egypt. This had always been a cardinal element in Israeli military doctrine, and indeed from 1968 planning for the defence of Sinai against an Egyptian attack took into consideration the necessity to prepare a counter-attack across the Canal. Over the years equipment had been planned and built (though it was inadequate) and various areas along the Canal had been organized as prospective crossing points. The sand ramparts were purposely thinner there and the exact points of openings had been marked.

The necessary infrastructure preparations had been made in the areas of Kantara, Deversoir (north of the Great Bitter Lake) and north of Suez, and, indeed, were still under way when war broke out. The prepared bridging equipment had been moved into Sinai and special ruler-straight roads had been laid for the specific purpose of towing pre-prepared bridges to the water. What was later known as the 'yard' – an area 150 yards by 700 yards with high sand walls around it – had been constructed for the purpose of launching a bridging operation.

As the Israeli strength increased – particularly in tanks – Southern Command began to plan the next move, preparing an outline for an attack across the Suez Canal at Deversoir (they had noted that this was the boundary between the Egyptian Second and Third armies and also that there was no heavy concentration of Egyptian forces in the area). The attack would be a two-divisional one. Bar-Lev accepted the concept. On the night of 9–10 October the preconstructed bridge that had been moved down on Gonen's instructions to Yukon west of Deversoir was finally assembled.

On the evening of the 11th Gonen presented his concept at a command conference, but Bren and Sharon had their reservations, proposing that the crossing should take place at one of the other points that had been prepared. But Gonen did not accept their view, maintaining that while at Deversoir there was a good possibility that the forces could reach the Canal without a heavy struggle, reaching it in the other areas suggested would require a major battle and breakthrough before the actual crossing could be undertaken. Bar-Lev decided in favour of Deversoir for the following reasons: firstly, one flank of the crossing would be protected by the Great Bitter Lake; furthermore the west bank at this point, where there was only one sweet-water canal and one strip of agricultural development to be crossed, was far more conducive to a battle of manœuvre than at Kantara, where the crossing forces would encounter numerous canals and ditches and many agriculturally developed areas; in addition this area constituted the border line between the two Egyptian armies.

The timing of the attack was dependent to a great degree on the anticipated moves of the Egyptian Army. The problem which faced the Israeli Command was that the Egyptians now had the option of sitting tight, with five infantry divisions on the east bank of the Canal with their armoured divisions concentrated and fresh on the west bank of the Canal or concentrated and ready for battle within the bridgeheads. The only move that could break this log jam was an Israeli crossing of the Canal, but a crossing to the west bank – with two armoured divisions, two mechanized divisions and two independent armoured brigades totalling some 900 Egyptian tanks all concentrated there and in themselves outnumbering the Israeli armoured forces – could be a very dangerous operation. Both Elazar and Bar-Lev felt that it was inadvisable to make the crossing until a serious dent had been made in the Egyptian armoured force.

On Friday, 12 October, Bar-Lev flew back to GHQ and presented the plan for the crossing of the Canal to Gen. Elazar. They presented it to the minister of defence. It is obvious from an examination of the tactical situation along the Canal at the time that three alternatives existed for the Israeli forces: (1) to launch a major attack against the existing two Egyptian bridgeheads in order to push back the Egyptian forces across the Canal; (2) to cross the Canal immediately; (3) to wait for the anticipated Egyptian attack (according to the Soviet doctrine, they should have mounted a major armoured attack on 11-12 October), smash it and then counter-attack across the Canal.

Elazar proposed waiting for the Egyptian attack and dealing with it before crossing the Canal. Dayan was sceptical and not very enthusiastic about the whole operation, adding that he was not prepared to 'wage a *jihad* against it'; the Israeli crossing of the Canal would not decide anything, nor would it bring the Egyptians to ask for a cease-fire. He was of the opinion that it was not for Elazar to make decisions on the basis of political considerations, pointing out that if from a military point of view Elazar thought that it was a desirable move then he had to make his decision and act accordingly. With that he left the meeting.

Thereupon Elazar contacted Dayan's personal assistant, Brig. Raviv, and told him that he insisted on a decision being given by the minister of defence. Dayan brought the matter to a meeting chaired by the prime minister and attended by the members of the *ad hoc* war Cabinet in addition to a number of generals.

Bar-Lev presented his plan. A discussion ensued in which conflicting views were presented. After all, they were discussing one of the most involved operations an army could undertake and to base such an operation on one supply route would be in defiance of accepted military doctrine. Furthermore in the present situation there would have to be a major effort to break through before reaching the Canal. As the discussion developed and the ministers began to pose questions, Bar-Lev felt that the operation might not be approved. During the meeting however intelligence was received that the long-awaited crossing of the Egyptian armoured forces to the east bank had commenced and that there were indications that this was in preparation for a major attack. Bar-Lev seized this opportunity to ask for a postponement of a decision about further moves, suggesting that first and foremost Southern Command prepare itself to break the Egyptian attack. He purposely did not ask for approval of his proposed crossing plan.

On Friday evening Bren's division was taken out of the line to prepare itself for the crossing of the Canal. Indications were in the meantime growing that with the crossing of the Egyptian armoured forces that day, the long-awaited Egyptian armoured attack was imminent. The chief of staff decided to postpone the crossing until after the main armoured battle, in which the Israeli forces would attempt to destroy the maximum number of Egyptian tanks and draw into the bridgeheads from the west bank as much Egyptian armour as possible.

On Saturday, 13 October, the Egyptians launched probing attacks all along the line. The Egyptian plan was, in fact, to make for the Refidim (Bir Gafgafa) nerve centre by means of a wide pincer movement, with an armoured division and an armoured brigade advancing from the Gidi crossroads through Um Mahza to Refidim and another armoured division advancing to Refidim from the area of Ismailia–Deversoir via Tasa. Gonen deployed the forces in the command with instructions that the efforts along the Mediterranean coast and the Gulf of Suez were to be blocked by armoured forces and that thereafter the Air Force – out of range of the surface-to-air missile system – would deal with the attacking forces. As for the central and southern sectors, should the attack be a frontal one, Albert and Sharon were to hold it; if the effort continued towards Refidim, Bren's division (in addition to part of Sharon's forces) was to be held in reserve for a counter-attack from the flank. One of Bren's brigades was moved down to the area of the Refidim opening.

In the morning the chief of staff went to Southern Command and flew on to Sharon's advanced headquarters to review the plans for the armoured battle, which seemed imminent, and for the projected crossing of the Canal. Sharon was against waiting for the Egyptian attack and proposed attacking the Egyptian forces on the east bank of the Canal and nibbling away at their bridgeheads. The chief of staff however chose to wait for the armoured battle, but gave orders to plan the crossing of the Canal for the night of 14 October whether the Egyptian attack took place or not.

Gonen flew to the meeting at Sharon's headquarters by helicopter. Seated beside him was Ezer Weizman, a reserve major-general and former commander of the Israeli Air Force and later chief of operations branch at the General Staff headquarters. Speaking to Albert, who reported that he was not too happy with the battle his forces had waged that morning in the area west of the Gidi Pass, Gonen told him that he would come and visit his headquarters after he had finished with Sharon, asking him where they were to meet. Albert gave a code point in the Gidi Pass and continued, 'I suggest we meet at the Gidi–lateral road crossroads.' Gonen asked him a further question but there was no reply. Gonen turned to Weizman, 'Ezer, Albert has been killed.' 'What nonsense, you ass,' retorted Weizman. But Gonen was certain: 'If Albert doesn't answer me on the radio he can only be dead.' The radio operator tried to raise a reply but in vain. The helicopter landed at Sharon's headquarters and there waiting for Gonen was a message from his deputy advising him that Albert had been killed by Egyptian fire. He entered the meeting and whispered the news to Gen. Elazar, who issued orders to summon Brig.-Gen. Kalman Magen from the northern sector to replace Albert.

At 11 o'clock that morning, *en route* from his headquarters to the conference at Sharon's headquarters, Albert had landed by helicopter in full view of the Egyptian positions. His advanced headquarters in two armoured personnel carriers was waiting for him, and he moved forward to an observation post in the front line. A brigade reconnaissance unit five hundred yards away covering the front radioed a warning that the observation point to which Albert's armoured personnel carriers were moving was accurately ranged by enemy artillery and missile fire. It is not known if the warning was received or not: no acknowledgement was received from Albert's advanced headquarters. As Albert surveyed the scene through binoculars, a missile hit the vehicle. Killed by his side was Rafi Unger, a correspondent of the Israeli Broadcasting Service who had been attached to his division.

With Mandler's death, an officer of unusual integrity was lost to the Israel Defence Forces. His sense of loyalty to his superiors and to those under his command was most marked. He was a very honest man who was meticulous in his ways, in many ways a model as far as his character was concerned. After the outbreak of war those near him could sense that he felt a degree of personal responsibility for not having acted according to his instincts, which had told him that war was imminent. He believed that the situation would have been radically different had his forces been in position according to 'Shovach Yonim' as planned. He was however one of the most disciplined officers in the army and not one person heard one word of reproach from him after the outbreak of war.

Numerous stories grew up around his death. One was that Gonen – stricken with remorse by the fact that he and Albert had discussed the latter's location in clear on the radio – went to a hilltop, announced his own location in the clear over the radio and waited for the inevitable Egyptian artillery barrage. The real fact of the matter is as follows. On the next day Gonen was travelling in a jeep after visiting the battlefield in Magen's area; behind him sat a young second lieutenant. As they travelled through the sand dunes, the young officer recounted that he had been with Albert when he was killed, mentioning the indiscretion of the commanders in discussing Albert's location over the radio. 'Near here, General, is where General Albert was killed,' he said. Gonen stopped on the road and asked him how soon after revealing his location had

Albert been killed. The answer was thirty seconds. Thereupon Gonen called his headquarters, announced in clear who was speaking and gave his exact location. 'Now we shall see,' he said to the second lieutenant. They sat in silence, and a cold sweat appeared on the young officer's brow as the minutes passed. After what seemed an eternity, but which was only ten minutes, Gonen turned to the officer, smiled and said, 'Have I proved my point?'

On Sunday morning, 14 October, the Egyptian armoured forces launched their attack between 6 and 8 o'clock. Dayan arrived at Southern Command head-quarters sceptical that this was the main attack, but Bar-Lev and Gonen were convinced that it was. In the northern sector the 18th Egyptian Infantry Division, strengthened by a tank brigade equipped with T62 tanks, attacked from the area of Kantara with the object of reaching Rumani. Commando units were heliported to points in the salt marshlands. In the central sector opposite Sharon, the 21st Armoured Egyptian Division, which had completed crossing into Sinai that morning together with a tank brigade from the 23rd Mechanized Division, broke out of the bridgehead along the central route leading from Ismailia. In the southern sector of Magen's division (formerly Albert's), two tank brigades attempted to break out eastwards towards the Gidi and Mitla passes, one brigade on each axis. Part of this force endeavoured to insinuate itself along the *wadis* towards the passes. To the south a special task force (comprising an infantry brigade from the 19th Infantry Division, a tank brigade and the 113th Mechanized Brigade from the 6th Mechanized Division) moved towards Ras Sudar in a southerly push along the coast of the Gulf of Suez.

Thus began one of the largest tank battles ever to take place in history – apart from the battle of Kursk in the Soviet Union in World War Two – with some 2,000 tanks locked in battle along the entire front. The Israeli forces had carefully prepared themselves for this battle and now looked forward to it. At 5 o'clock in the morning Amnon was waiting with his brigade in the central sector. It was a sultry, heavy morning. The Egyptians opened with a heavy artillery attack. Suddenly from the direction of the Chinese Farm he observed what appeared from a distance to be a vast river of tanks flowing towards him: it was the 1st Brigade of the 21st Egyptian Armoured Division. He engaged the advancing enemy, but some of the enemy tanks using the cover afforded by the folds in the desert infiltrated and reached the high ground held by the Israeli forces. They were destroyed at ranges of 100 yards. As Amnon, extremely well placed on the high ground, watched the Egyptians advancing in a schematic headlong attack against his fire base, he threw against their southern flank the divisional reconnaissance unit, reinforced by an additional company of tanks. When the battle concluded, the 1st Egyptian Tank Brigade had been destroyed. Ninety-three knocked-out enemy tanks were counted, while Amnon's brigade had suffered only three tanks hit, all by missiles; not one tank had been hit by Egyptian tank fire. Having clashed with Amnon's brigade to the south and Haim's to the north, the 21st Egyptian Division ranged against Sharon's forces had by the end of the day's battle incurred a total loss of 110 tanks.

The southern effort of the Egyptians, which endeavoured to make a deep, flanking movement to the south and turn northwards to reach the Mitla from the south, came up against Israeli parachute forces which were holding the pass at Ras Sudar. Magen's tanks were deployed in anticipation of such a possible flanking movement and Dan's brigade was waiting at the Mitla Pass. Within two hours of battle, most of the 3rd Armoured Brigade of the 4th Egyptian Armoured Division had been wiped out. As Israeli armour blocked the advances of the enemy, the Israeli Air Force entered the battle and within two hours some sixty Egyptian tanks and a large quantity of armoured personnel carriers and artillery were in flames. Southern Command waited in vain for the Egyptian attack to develop with increased strength and to penetrate deeper, but the Egyptian forces were poorly led; their tactics were unimaginative and schematic. The Israeli forces had a field day. Not a single advance was registered by the enemy. In the northern sector the Israelis counter-attacked and re-established contact with the Budapest fortification, which had been cut off.

The results of this major battle raised the morale in the Israeli forces: they felt finally that they were back to their usual form. While 264 knocked-out Egyptian tanks were counted on the battlefield (in addition to the losses inflicted by the Israeli Air Force) the Israeli tank losses on that day totalled only 6 (until this stage Egyptian reporting had been meticulously accurate, and this was the first day on which the Israelis felt that the Egyptians were reverting to their previous habit of false reporting). Bar-Lev phoned Mrs Meir and in his quiet and measured tone said, 'It has been a good day. Our forces are themselves again and so are the Egyptians.'

As the results of this major and in many ways fateful battle and their significance dawned on the Egyptian commander, Gen. Saad Mamoun, GOC Second Army, he suffered a heart attack. He was replaced by Gen. Abd el Munem Halil. The Egyptian command realized the seriousness of the defeat. According to Egyptian prisoners, Gen. Saad Al Shazli, chief of staff of the Egyptian armed forces, admitted in addressing his troops that the Egyptian attacking forces had been surprised on all axes of advance by Israeli tanks and anti-tank battalions equipped with anti-tank guided missiles of the SS11 type, which had succeeded in blocking their attacks and inflicting very heavy tank losses.

Analysing the losses sustained by the Israelis in their initial counter-attack to the Canal and against the Egyptian bridgeheads on 6 October and the heavy losses sustained by the Egyptians in their attack on the 14th, he reached the conclusion that it was impossible to ensure the success of any attack – whether of tanks or of armoured infantry – without destroying or silencing in advance the anti-tank missiles.

On the Israeli side the conclusion to be drawn from the battle was clear: Elazar issued orders for the Canal crossing to take place on the following night.

15

The Crossing

AT AN ORDERS group held at Southern Command on 12 October, Sharon's division was given the task of leading the Canal crossing with a brigade of paratroopers, reinforced by tanks. His mission was to cross in the area of Deversoir, with his left flank hinging on and protected by the Great Bitter Lake, and establish and hold a bridgehead 3 miles wide northwards from the Lake – thus putting Egyptian mortars and anti-tank missiles out of range of the preconstructed bridge which in the meantime would be towed to the Canal and laid across it. The tanks would pass through the agricultural strip running parallel to the Canal along the sweet-water canal and begin in the initial phase to knock out Egyptian surface-to-air missile sites, thus clearing the air above the bridgehead for the Israeli Air Force. Bren's division would be held in readiness to cross immediately after Sharon, while Magen's division was to be prepared to cross on a given order.

On Saturday, 13 October, orders were issued for the mobile pontoons located in Sinai to be concentrated to the east of the proposed crossing area; and on Saturday evening Haim was readied to detach a battalion from his brigade in order to train in the highly involved process of towing the pre-constructed bridge.

On the evening of 14 October Gen. Elazar described to the Cabinet the resounding defeat which the Egyptian armoured forces had sustained in the armoured battle that day and the plan for the crossing of the Canal. Being plied with many questions – many present took part in the discussion – he expressed the opinion that the crossing could definitely give the Israeli forces a limited advantage in improving their position along the Canal. Should it be *very* successful however it could improve their position considerably and could even result in a major collapse of the Egyptian Army, with thousands of Egyptian soldiers being taken prisoner and with the dispositions on the other side of the Canal completely undermined. The prospects of success were good; how good, one could not be sure, but there were chances of a major victory. Elazar admitted that the attack could also be a failure, but from his personal knowledge of the circumstances and the facts, he thought that prospects of this were minimal.

At 11 o'clock that night a second orders group was held at Southern Command: the plan was recapitulated and it was decided that on its way to effect the crossing Sharon's division would at the same time widen the corridor to the Canal on the east bank – capturing the Chinese Farm and the Missouri stronghold – up to a point 3 miles from the water line. That would open the two axes leading to the Canal – Akavish and Tirtur (the latter was a road that had been built for the specific purpose of towing the preconstructed bridge to the Canal). The crossing would be carried out by a brigade of paratroopers in inflatable boats, supported by ten tanks, which would cross on rafts. Two bridges would be established: a preconstructed bridge and a pontoon. The assault force would secure the bridgehead and, when additional forces crossed, would move southwards; should any difficulty be encountered in widening the corridor on the east bank, Bren's division would cross after the assault units and only thereafter would the remainder of Sharon's forces cross.

Bren was to cross the bridge on the morning after Sharon's crossing and to sweep southwards on the eastern flank of Sharon's southern sweep. His mission was to destroy the surface-to-air missile batteries in the area and thus enable the Israeli Air Force to establish supremacy in the air over the battlefield. The attack was to develop in order to cut off the Egyptian Third Army and destroy it. Simultaneously with the crossing, the northern force under Brig.-Gen. Sasoon (who had replaced Magen) and Magen's division in the south were to launch an attack along their fronts in order to pin down the enemy forces.

In the first days of the war, when every commander was busy fighting the holding battle, few bothered about the bridging equipment. Gonen had ordered forward a preconstructed bridge to Yukon a week before the war. Sharon had pressed for bridging equipment to be advanced; but the tendency was to try (as indeed they did on 8 October) to cross using existing Egyptian bridges. However 15 October found Southern Command facing serious bridging equipment problems.

An hour and a half before the planned crossing, Sharon and Brig. Tamir examined the situation and knew then that they could never meet the time-table according to the operation order. Sharon said that there were three possibilities: (1) to postpone the attack until the next night; (2) to clear the area to the Canal on the night of the 15th and to cross only on the 16th in the evening; or (3) to carry out the original plan without reference to the timetable which had been laid down. He spoke to Bar-Lev who was prepared to postpone the H hour of the crossing to midnight. Sharon felt that had he claimed he was incapable of working according to the planned timetable, Bar-Lev would have agreed to postpone the attack by one day. Instead Sharon decided to carry out the original plan without reference to the timetable and to deal with the situation as it developed.

Sharon's plan was for Tuvia's brigade to launch a holding attack at 5 o'clock in the evening in order to pin down the Egyptian forces in the area of Televizia and Hamutal, while Amnon's brigade made a wide southerly flanking movement through the sand dunes at 6 o'clock in the evening. One force of Amnon's brigade would capture the Israeli fortification of Matzmed, where the Suez Canal entered the Great Bitter Lake; a second force would clear Akavish road; while the third force would push northwards to widen the corridor in the direction of the Chinese Farm and would clear Tirtur road. The parachute brigade under Danny Matt would follow Amnon's brigade along Akavish; Haim's brigade would follow Matt's brigade, and the divisional crossing would be completed by Amnon's brigade. The basic assumption of the entire plan was that the bridge would be in the water by morning. While Tuvia was securing the corridor on the east bank, one force of Haim's brigade was to cross with Danny Matt, with another force of Haim's towing the preconstructed bridge.

At 5 o'clock in the afternoon of 15 October, Israel's bold and daringly conceived crossing of the Canal was launched. Israeli artillery opened up along the line. At the same time Tuvia's brigade attacked the area of Televizia and Hamutal to draw the main weight of the Egyptian 16th Infantry Division and the 21st Armoured Division north, in the direction of the Tasa–Ismailia road, and to focus the Egyptian Command's attention on the northern sector of the front. At 7 o'clock Amnon's brigade moved forward, By 9.30 Sharon estimated that the Egyptian forces were collapsing, and at 10.30 he reported that Akavish road was open. He had a force north of the Chinese Farm, but there was contact with enemy armour at the Tirtur–Lexicon crossroads and he had incurred casualties there. Bar-Lev asked, 'Have you got enough infantry to comb the area and for protection?' Sharon answered that there was infantry, but he did not know if it was sufficient.

At Southern Command headquarters, with both the minister of defence and the chief of staff present, an air of anxiety began to pervade the proceedings. Bren, concentrated and prepared for crossing, was ordered to be in readiness to attack Missouri in the morning and to reinforce Sharon's attack again in the corridor. It was clear that very serious problems were being encountered on the ground. The basis of Sharon's first optimistic communication to Southern Command had been Amnon's report that his brigade had advanced and occupied Matzmed, sweeping along Akavish and clearing it. In fact, as soon as the Egyptians had overcome the shock of Amnon's appearance on the scene with two armoured battalions, and after his armoured force had passed, they raised their heads, came out of their holes in the sand with their anti-tank weapons and – unknown to the advancing Israelis – closed Akavish again.

In the meantime reports were received at Sharon's headquarters that heavy anti-tank resistance was being encountered at Tirtur and the Chinese Farm, while the main Israeli move to the Canal was taking place some hundreds of yards to the south. Despite this very dangerous situation, Sharon ordered Danny Matt to follow Amnon's forces. Moving along the road under fire Matt reached the Canal and began the crossing; Sharon's advanced headquarters, following in Matt's wake, came under fire as well. Amnon, who had moved two hours later than planned and had carried out two of his missions, did not know that at Akavish the Egyptians had closed behind him. He had failed to clear Tirtur and was blocked opposite the Chinese Farm suffering very heavy casualties. The preconstructed bridge was stuck on Tirtur, a section had broken on it and the engineers maintained that the repair would take some hours.

When Amnon started out at 4 o'clock in the afternoon he had four tank battalions and three infantry battalions on half-tracks. At nightfall he moved down from the high ground in a south-westerly direction (along the route which the divisional reconnaissance unit had reconnoitred to the Great Bitter Lake on 9 October). His force reached Lexicon on the Great Bitter Lake without encountering any resistance and then turned northwards. The divisional reconnaissance unit divided into three sub-units: one unit skirted the north-east shore of the Great Bitter Lake and moved towards Matzmed; the second moved to the north of the first to reach the Canal; while the third moved to the north of the second and also reached the Canal. Thus this reconnaissance unit closed in on the Canal in a three-pronged attack with the southern prong taking Matzmed.

The 7th Battalion continued to the west of Lexicon, passing the Chinese Farm on its right, attacking northwards in an endeavour to reach an Egyptian bridge 6 miles north of Matzmed; the 18th Battalion followed the 7th on its east flank and attacked east of Lexicon in a north-easterly direction towards Missouri, while the 40th Battalion attacked in a north-easterly direction, with one company at Tirtur and one company at Akavish, taking the Egyptian forces deployed along these two routes from the rear. The 42nd Infantry Battalion – with half a company of tanks – followed the divisional reconnaissance unit to the west of Lexicon to mop up the Egyptian infantry. An additional infantry force ('Force Shmulik'), composed of two regular parachute companies and half a company of tanks, followed the 40th Infantry Battalion to clear up the Chinese Farm east of Lexicon; a third reserve infantry battalion under Maj. Nathan was held in reserve.

The divisional reconnaissance unit reached Matzmed and the points north of it along the Canal according to plan. After Amnon had passed the Lexicon–Tirtur crossroads heading northwards with the two battalions, fire was opened from the same area on the 18th Battalion as it moved forward east of Lexicon towards Missouri. But although tank, missile and bazooka fire hit the battalion, knocking out eleven tanks, the battalion commander continued on his mission with the remaining tanks.

Unknown to Amnon, his force had moved into the administrative centre of the 16th Egyptian Infantry Division, to which the 21st Armoured Division had also withdrawn after being so badly mauled on 14 October. His force found itself suddenly in the midst of a vast army with as far as they could see concentrations of hundreds of trucks, guns, tanks, missiles, radar units and thousands of troops milling around. The Israeli force had come up through the unprotected southern flank of the Egyptian Second Army at the junction of the Egyptian Second and Third armies, had entered by the back door, as it were, and had suddenly found itself plumb in the centre of the administrative areas of two Egyptian divisions and literally at the entrance to the 16th Infantry Division headquarters.

Pandemonium broke out in the Egyptian forces. Thousands of weapons of all types opened fire in all directions and the whole area as far as the eye could see seemed to go up in flames. The 40th Armoured Battalion reached the Tirtur–Lexicon crossroads and attacked, but the deputy battalion commander, Maj. Butel, was wounded and the attack was disrupted; a second company under Maj. Ehud moved up Akavish and cleared the route. The situation now was that the divisional reconnaissance unit had reached Matzmed and the Canal to the north of Matzmed; while Amnon with two battalions was north of the Chinese Farm attacking northwards; the Tirtur–Lexicon crossroads were closed and the remainder of the brigade with a large number of casualties was to the south of the crossroads. The infantry forces were suffering very heavily.

The 7th Battalion, between Lexicon and the Canal, continued northwards according to plan; but the 18th, half a mile north of the Chinese Farm, came up against an enemy force including dug-in tanks and entered a fire fight. Amnon

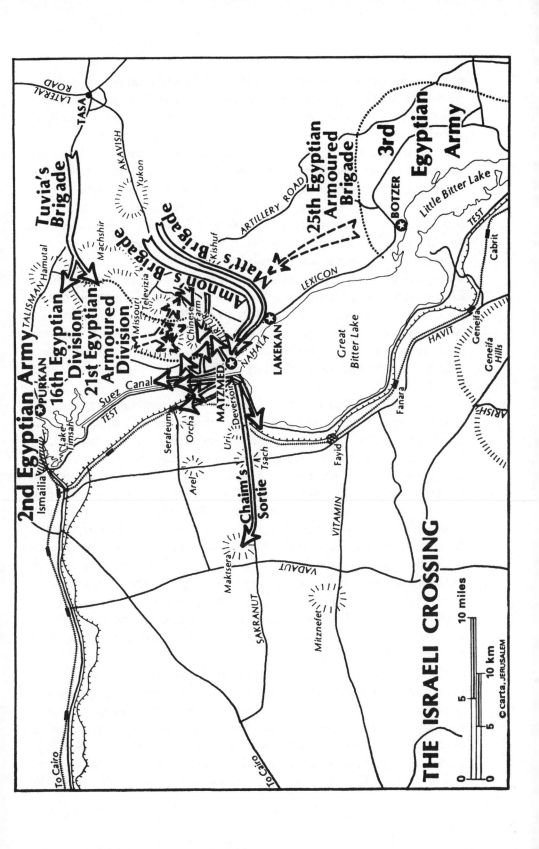

THE ISRAELI CROSSING

described the situation to Sharon and Matt, who was following him, and proposed that Matt's brigade move along the Nahala road hugging the Great Bitter Lake to the north-east with the crossroads 800 yards on his right flank closed.

It was by now 9.00 in the evening. There were indications that the enemy was preparing for a counter-attack from the north; the pressure on the 7th Battalion and the 18th Battalion increased. The numerous casualties could not be evacuated because the Tirtur–Lexicon crossroads were blocked, so a battalion evacuation centre formed itself with all wounded next to Amnon's tank. At 10 o'clock, the 7th Battalion commander, who was by now 6 miles north of Matzmed, reported that he was down to one-third of his strength. Realizing that the brigade was spread far too wide, Amnon ordered the 7th Battalion to withdraw some 2 miles and form a line with the 18th Battalion half a mile north of the Chinese Farm. As they were moving, the battalion commander, Lieut.-Col. Amram, was wounded in the leg and was evacuated in the tank that was picking up the wounded on the battlefield (this tank stood all night next to Amnon's with the wounded battalion commander acting as loader–communications man inside).

In the meantime, Gideon Giladi, a company commander in the 40th Battalion who had had to assume command, reported that most of the remaining tanks of the battalion had been hit but that he was organizing what was left. At 11 o'clock he reported that he had five tanks fit to move and he was prepared to move along Tirtur and clear it in order to open up the route for the pre-constructed bridge. Amnon ordered him to wait until the situation clarified. At 11.15 units of the 14th Egyptian Armoured Brigade attacked from the north while the 7th Battalion was pulling back. The second-in-command reported to Amnon that the battalion was now left with a bare minimum of tanks in running order. The remainder had either been hit or had broken down and they had suffered a large number of casualties. Amnon ordered him to move southwards to the 18th Battalion, which was fighting to the north of the Chinese Farm, and placed under his command a unit from the divisional reconnaissance unit under command of Lieut. Rafi Bar-Lev, Gen. Bar-Lev's nephew. That night Rafi Bar-Lev was killed.

The scene in the area was one of utter confusion: along the Lexicon road raced Egyptian ambulances; units of Egyptian infantry were rushing around in all directions, as were Egyptian tanks. The impression was that nobody knew what was happening or what to do. On all sides trucks, ammunition, tanks, surface-to-air missiles on trucks, radar stations were in flames in one huge conflagration which covered the desert. It was like Hades. Days later the entire area between the Canal and Missouri was to appear from the west bank of the

Canal as one vast, eerie, unbelievable graveyard. As a background to this scene the concentrated forces of artillery on both sides fired with everything they had.

Shortly after midnight Amnon ordered his reserve paratroop battalion commanded by Lieut.-Col. Nathan to take under command Gideon Giladi's tank company and to attack the blocked crossroads. Two hours later, while Danny Matt's forces to the west were crossing the Canal, Nathan reported that the tanks had been knocked out by the enemy, that his entire attack had been disrupted, and that he was moving in on foot with his men to recover the wounded. In this attack Gideon Giladi was killed. His brother Amnon (both of them were from Ashkelon) had fought as a company commander in the 7th Brigade in the Six Day War and had been killed in battle. Gideon, then a paratroop officer, had taken an oath that he would command his late brother's company. Going through a conversion course to armour, in due course he reached the battalion in which his brother had served and was finally posted to command his company. At the crossroads on the night of 15–16 October he followed in his footsteps.

As Nathan's forces advanced, it was not clear to him that he was leading his paratroopers against a major, concentrated Egyptian force of at least divisional strength. He had no clear intelligence picture of what was waiting for him. Gideon's company stormed the crossroads and after a few minutes reported to Nathan that they were open. Nathan ordered six half-tracks in his force to move in a flanking movement towards the enemy fire, and as he moved he heard a report from Gideon that he was being attacked by a large variety of weapons. Suddenly Gideon fell silent. Nathan's advanced half-tracks, under command of Gideon Halevi, stopped. Halevi reported that he could not move and had incurred severe casualties. As the remaining half-tracks in his force manœuvred to help Halevi, they too were hit. Intense fire covered the entire area. Anybody who lifted his head was hit, and all attempts to reach the stranded half-tracks were beaten back by the Egyptians. The unit was now caught in the open under murderous fire, unable to move in any direction and unable to relieve the forward elements which had been cut off. The men lay on the ground digging into the sand with their fingernails in an endeavour to find shelter. As soldiers were hit, others rushed forward to carry them out of danger and were mowed down themselves. By a miracle Nathan and some of his vehicles managed to withdraw from the fire-stricken area, but to his horror he saw that only remnants were left of his force.

A company of tanks joined Nathan and moved forward in an attempt to rescue the trapped force. In all the ditches criss-crossing the Chinese Farm, tank commanders could see hundreds of infantry with missiles and bazookas. They rushed forward in a suicidal effort to reach the paratroopers, firing everything they had into the ditches and at the Egyptian positions – but in vain; a hail of Sagger and Shmel missiles pursued the tanks wherever they moved. Nathan now begged Amnon for support in order to reach his trapped forces. Quietly Amnon promised to do his best, although Nathan did not realize at the time that Amnon himself was fighting desperately in the midst of the Egyptian positions and had sustained a large number of casualties. As time went on, it dawned on Nathan that hopes of rescuing the trapped men were dwindling. All attempts to reach the surrounded advance forces failed.

Halevi, it transpired, had sustained a number of casualties and he and his men had refused to abandon the wounded. He tried to leapfrog his unit out of the battle area with the wounded, covered by two sections of heavy machine guns, but as they moved slowly and painfully towards their own lines Egyptian armoured forces closed on them and blocked their route of withdrawal. In the battle which ensued, the entire Israeli force was wiped out. As Nathan reorganized his force (which had sustained twenty-four killed and eighteen wounded) his closest friend called him aside and revealed to him that one of the dead in the battle had been his brother.

The story of this paratroop battalion and the losses which were incurred revealed one of the weaknesses of the IDF and at the same time one of its main strengths. This battalion was a long-established one with a magnificent fighting tradition which had become a legend to many young people. Over the years it had become one large family and to a degree a club, membership of which was much sought after. Kibbutz Beit Hashita lost twelve sons in the war; five of them were killed that night in this one battalion. The battalion commander lost both his brother and some days later on the west bank his best friend, who had volunteered to serve as his driver. The very elements which gave such strength to this unit were to cause this degree of concentrated sorrow.

Along Tirtur efforts were still being made to extricate the remnants of the Israeli attacking forces. Amnon was with two battalions to the west of the Chinese Farm, while the remainder of the brigade was to the south of the crossroads evacuating the dead and wounded and reorganizing. Reviewing the situation Amnon decided that he would counter-attack the crossroads from the rear. He ordered the new commander of the divisional reconnaissance units, Lieut.-Col. Yoav Brom, to attack from Matzmed along Tirtur from west to east (he assumed that the enemy was deployed to meet an attack from the east and from the south and would therefore be taken by surprise). The force attacked but Brom was killed 30 yards from the crossroads, which disrupted the attempt. Amnon ordered the second-in-command of the unit to withdraw and reorganize, at the same time ordering his deputy brigade commander, Lieut.-Col. Eytan, to take the company of the 40th Battalion (which had opened the Akavish road) and attack the crossroads from the south. At 4 o'clock the attack took place. Three tanks including that of the second-in-command of the brigade were hit, and the attack failed.

Col. Danny Matt (now a brigadier-general) is a well-known figure in the Israel Defence Forces. A tall, distinguished-looking man with a neatly trimmed, square beard and well-kept moustache, he shows many signs of the wounds he received over the years. In the Six Day War he commanded a parachute brigade under Sharon in the Sinai and twice landed by helicopter during the fighting in Syria towards the end of the war. In 1968 he commanded the daring 120-mile raid into Egypt in the area of Najh Hamadi. From 1969 he held an appointment as commander of the reserve parachute brigade which under Gen. Motta Gur had captured the Old City of Jerusalem during the fighting in the Six Day War.

At 6.00 on the morning of the 15th Matt was called to an orders group at Sharon's headquarters. His brigade was then concentrated at the Mitla Pass with orders to cross the Canal that night; it began to move after he had given preliminary orders and rushed back to Sharon's headquarters with his planning group.

Matt's orders were that his brigade reconnaissance company and a company of engineers under his second-in-command, Lieut.-Col. Arik, would lead the crossing of the Canal and establish the first foothold on the west bank. The engineer company would cross at four points with demolition equipment. Everything had been prepared for the breakthrough. An alternative second-in-command of the brigade was placed in charge of the 'yard'. This area, measuring 700 yards by 150 yards, had been prepared by Sharon during his period as GOC Southern Command. Protective sand walls surrounded it and it marked the exact point for the crossing: there were positions in it for units, which would act as a fire base in order to engage enemy forces on the other side of the Canal, and the necessary arrangements for a troop movements headquarters. Following the initial foothold, a battalion commanded by Lieut.-Col. Dan would widen the bridgehead to the south, while a battalion under Lieut.-Col. Zvi would widen it northwards. This bridgehead was to be no less in width than 3 miles northwards, and the crossings of the sweet-water canal 1–1½ miles westwards were to be seized.

Matt was informed that he had sixty inflatable boats available and that they would be delivered to the brigade by 10 o'clock in the morning. At 1 o'clock he presented his plan to Sharon who approved it, but information from the brigade was that there was no sign of the boats. At 1.30 he returned to his brigade with orders to move out at 4.30 in the afternoon. The boats, however, had not yet arrived, and instead of the sixty half-tracks promised, he had only thirty-two. It was clear to Matt that reliance on normal procedures and channels would leave him without the means to cross the Canal. One of his battalion commanders took the initiative and sent his headquarters company commander with thirty drivers to head for the general area of Refidim and bring back as many half-tracks as he could find – by fair means or foul. This resourceful officer reached Refidim and found twenty-six half-tracks lined up in convoy outside the canteen, while the drivers were having refreshments inside. He looked for the officer in charge, who told him that he had to deliver the half-tracks to one of the divisions and was awaiting instructions. 'I'm the man you are waiting for,' the company commander announced confidently, 'and I don't need your drivers. They can stay in the canteen.' He took the half-tracks and drove off, bringing Matt's half-track force up to fifty-eight.

Still no sign of the boats. At 2 o'clock Matt was driving through the desert from divisional headquarters towards his brigade, pondering how on earth he would cross the Canal without boats, when he met a paratroop lieutenant-colonel looking for a job with one of the units. Matt gave him the job of finding the boats and notifying him by radio. Half an hour later the officer came on the air to advise him that he had found the boats 3 miles west of Tasa (because of similarity in code names, they had been sent to the wrong rendezvous).

Matt's orders group at 3.30 took exactly twenty-five minutes. He ordered the brigade to move by 4.30 and advised his commanders that whatever had not been organized should be put right as they moved forward towards the Canal. As the brigade came on the road leading to Tasa, it ran into the most impossible traffic jam; traffic control seemed to have broken down – they moved 15½ miles in two and a half hours, reaching the Tasa crossroads at 7 o'clock. Having still not been linked up with the assault boats, for they were 3 miles to the west on the route to the Canal, Matt's troops now moved into what was an even worse traffic jam and it took them two hours to negotiate the 3 miles. At 9 pm Matt finally reached the boats that were supposed to have been delivered to him at 10.00 that morning. Each half-track loaded one boat and the remainder of the brigade moved in soft vehicles, including buses. Matt knew that soft vehicles would not be able to move once they entered the range of the enemy artillery, so he loaded each half-track with twenty-five men, laying them flat in layers with a boat covering each half-track. In the traffic jam at Tasa, all the soft vehicles remained stuck in the sand and only the four-wheel-drive vehicles continued. But the slowness of the movement of the column and the frequent stops enabled the brigade to complete various arrangements for the crossing, including the issue of lifejackets and other equipment.

With fewer armoured half-tracks than originally planned, Matt was obliged to adapt his plans to the forces available as they moved towards the Canal. He placed the 'yard' – the embarkation area – under his second-in-command with forces to act as a fire base along the east bank in order to pin down enemy forces on the west bank; this included also the traffic control organization under command of a field officer and the assault engineers. Since the brigade reconnaissance company had had to remain behind because it was travelling in soft vehicles, the battalion of Lieut.-Col. Dan would be obliged to take the entire planned bridgehead on the west bank. The 'yard' was planned with two embarkation points: a green beach and a red beach to be illuminated by the respective colours. Each man in the force knew what his colour was and the same system applied to the west bank. The crossing plan called for Amnon's brigade to move from the south, clear the approach route of Matt's brigade and continue 3 miles north of the embarkation points to the west of the Chinese Farm.

When he was some 6 miles from the Canal, at approximately 10.30 in the evening, Matt received under command a company of tanks which moved at the head of his column, followed by the second-in-command of the brigade with the assault crossing force, the brigade advanced headquarters and Dan's battalion with the rest of the brigade following as best it could. From the Akavish–Tirtur crossroads – a distance of 750–1,000 yards – the column came under artillery, missile and heavy machine-gun fire; some of the vehicles and boats were hit. Each time they lit lights for identification purposes, a hail of artillery descended on them. The assault force turned off the main road shortly after midnight, westwards towards the location of the 'yard' some 2 miles away.

Amnon's brigade had passed before as planned and the area was reported to be free of enemy. But Matt wanted to be absolutely certain, so he instructed his second-in-command to move the tank company 800 yards northwards and establish itself on the crossroads to afford protection against any possible intervention from north or east. The company of tanks moved forward, ran into an ambush at the crossroads and was completely destroyed, without Matt receiving any report about its fate. At 12.20 am the traffic control points had been set up and by 12.30 the assault group, under the second-in-command of the brigade, had entered the 'yard'. When Amnon's brigade had passed earlier in the evening, he had ranged the target area on the other side of the Canal, and now Matt ordered the entire artillery support which was at his disposal to open up on an area on the west bank some 1,000 yards wide by 220 yards deep. Matt's headquarters was now located at the entrance to the 'yard' and as the Israeli forces poured fire on the west bank, all the necessary preparations including the traffic movement control were readied.

As they prepared to move into the water they discovered that the soil in the northern part of the 'yard' was softer and muddier than they had previously imagined. Accordingly they changed the plan, embarking at one embarkation point while continuing to disembark as planned at two disembarkation points on the west bank. Meanwhile Egyptian shelling continued to harass Matt's forces: the traffic control point on the road leading to the 'yard' sustained a direct hit, while at its entrance a half-track also received a hit; four boats were destroyed.

After they had unloaded the troops and the boats, the half-tracks were planned to continue northwards and eastwards along the road leading back to Tirtur. But after a short while the officer in charge of them came back and announced that he had run into Egyptian armour and infantry. At the same time a report was received that the company of tanks leading Matt's brigade, which had moved to protect his flanks at the crossroads, had been completely destroyed. The empty half-tracks had run into Egyptians some 700 yards from Matt's headquarters and had come back. Now -- instead of an orderly flow of one-way traffic – they were faced with the problem of two-way traffic on the narrow road under heavy fire as the column of empty half-tracks moved back along the road on which the remaining loaded half-tracks were advancing.

Despite the proximity of the Egyptians to the crossing point Sharon urged his division on. And at 1.35 am on 16 October the first wave of Israeli troops crossed the Canal and set foot on the west bank – ten days after the Egyptian onslaught on the east bank.

The engineers cleared the concertina wire and the trip-wire obstacles on the bank, but found no mines. Reporting by flashlight that all was well, they moved along the Canal to the second planned disembarkation point. When directional lights had been set up on both points, the forces began to cross. A sense of relief overcame the entire army which had tensely awaited the news. The Israeli artillery had plastered the narrow landing strip with tons of shells, but the area which they had shelled had been free of Egyptians. The troops moved on foot. The brigade advanced headquarters crossed at 2.40 in the morning and by 5 o'clock all infantry forces had crossed. At 6.43 am, the first tank of Haim's brigade crossed on a raft and by 8 o'clock in the morning Matt's forces held a bridgehead which ran 3 miles northwards from the Great Bitter Lake as had been planned.

Meanwhile, in an atmosphere of tenseness at Southern Command headquarters, the situation was under review. Seeing what was happening on the east bank and conscious of the bitter struggle which was going on in the corridor, the minister of defence proposed pulling back the paratroopers: 'We tried. It has been no go.' He suggested giving up the idea of the crossing because: 'In the morning they will slaughter them on the other side.' Gonen's reaction was: 'Had we known that this would happen in advance, we probably would not have initiated the crossing. But now that we are across, we shall carry through to the bitter end. If there is no bridgehead today there will be one tomorrow, and if there is no bridge tomorrow there will be one in two days' time.' Bar-Lev overheard the conversation and in his characteristically quiet voice, drawing out his words in an exaggeratedly slow manner, asked what they were talking about. When Gonen told him, he replied: 'There is nothing at all to discuss.'

At dawn, when Amnon moved to high ground to survey the scene, he saw a terrifying sight: in all directions the desert was covered with a vast fleet of burning and smoking tanks, vehicles, guns, transporters; dead infantry lay everywhere. It seemed as if there was not a single item of military equipment which had escaped destruction: there were command caravans, mobile work-shops, huge transporters carrying SAM 2 missiles, mobile kitchens. The rem-nants of the Israeli forces were there too, and frequently the distance between them and the Egyptian vehicles was no more than a few yards. The *New York Times* correspondent, Charles Mohr, described his visit immediately after the war to the scene of the battle: 'In a short stretch of a few thousand yards stood twenty-four totally burnt-out Israeli Patton tanks. Few of their crews could have survived . . . less seriously damaged tanks had already been removed for repairs. About a hundred Egyptian tanks littered the battle area. At one point a Patton tank and an Egyptian T55 stood about three yards apart.'

As Amnon looked at the scene, a company commander of the 40th Battalion who had supported the infantry attack at the crossroads during the night con-tacted him by radio and told him he was prepared to attack the crossroads. Amnon took three tanks, which had been repaired that night, with him, and joined in the attack, following the route from west to east taken at night by the divisional reconnaissance unit. While Amnon attacked from the direction of the Canal along Tirtur, the company commander, Capt. Gaby, attacked from the south. They captured the crossroads and found that the area had been com-pletely organized for anti-tank defence with tanks, anti-tank missiles and hundreds of infantry troops equipped with a large quantity of RPG bazookas. In addition the shoulders of the roads had been mined so that any Israeli tank attempting to by-pass knocked-out tanks on the road blew up on the mine-fields; hundreds of guiding wires of anti-tank missiles lay strewn across the road as if a giant spiderweb had collapsed. Egyptian tanks had been firing from behind the dykes in the Chinese Farm at ranges of 20–30 yards (this explained the difficulties which the night attacks had encountered). It was clear now that Amnon's brigade had been able to move past this crossroads on the evening before with battalions of armour, because the Egyptians had been taken by surprise; but they had recovered rapidly and had now organized themselves.

This time Amnon and Capt. Gaby's forces did not storm the crossroads, but with good daylight observation they were able to fire from a distance, gradually nibbling away at the Egyptian force and wearing it down. The Egyptians for their part had been under a concentrated Israeli attack all night long with repeated assaults on their position. Exhausted by the night's fighting and having sustained very severe casualties, the Egyptians were unable to sustain this slow battle of attrition; they suddenly broke and fled. At this point Amnon received two battalions of tanks from Sharon (one commanded by Lieut.-Col. Ami and one by Lieut.-Col. Uzi). With these forces he mounted another attack on Tirtur, attacking from north-east and from the west, while Ami attacked from north-east towards south-west, coming under a hail of anti-tank and tank fire that forced him to withdraw. The Egyptian forces had concentrated on the southern ridges of Missouri and dominated the area: it was from there that the fire was directed.

Amnon's brigade was now very severely mauled: he had lost over half his brigade; a very high percentage of the officers and tank commanders were casualties. Tirtur was still closed. Although the crossroads were now held by the Israelis, the Egyptians were pressing from the north against the forces holding the line to the west of the Chinese Farm. Leaving a battalion to hold this northern line, Amnon withdrew his brigade to Lakekan on the shores of the lake to reorganize.

Early in the morning of 16 October, Sharon notified Bar-Lev that the pre-constructed bridge had broken down and that it was estimated that it would take an entire day to repair it; furthermore, the Tirtur–Lexicon crossroads was a heavily fortified anti-tank locality and he required additional forces in order to open it up. Describing the pressure of the 14th Egyptian Armoured Brigade on Amnon's brigade from the north, Bar Lev gave advance warning to Bren's division, being held in readiness to cross the first bridge, that it might have to intervene in the battle to open the roads to the Canal.

Later in the morning Sharon reported that ten tanks of Haim's brigade were crossing on rafts to join Matt's forces on the west bank; some time later he reported that the whole of Matt's brigade, together with their half-tracks and thirty tanks of Haim's brigade under personal command of Haim, had crossed. Haim had already begun to fan out from the bridgehead in order to attack the surface-to-air missile positions. However the problem of the Chinese Farm had not yet been solved.

In the meantime a new debate was developing between Sharon and Southern

Command. Sharon was of the opinion that the success in establishing a bridge-head across the Canal must be exploited immediately. Irrespective of whether or not a bridge was erected, Bren's division should be transported on rafts to the other side and then the Israeli forces on the west bank should rush on. Bar-Lev turned this proposal down on the 16th and again on the 17th, when Sharon renewed it, pointing out that this was not a raid across the Canal; he considered it would be the height of irresponsibility to launch an attack in corps strength numbering hundreds of tanks across the Canal with a supply route which had not yet been secured and without a bridge. In his view the tanks would run to a standstill within twenty-four hours. Furthermore he did not wish to rely on vulnerable rafts. And since the Egyptians were fighting stubbornly against the Israeli corridor on the east bank, if they were to move Bren's division to the west bank there would not be sufficient forces left in this sector to deal with major enemy counter-attacks. Bren's division was to complete the clearing of the corridor on the east bank of the Canal.

Shortly after 6 o'clock on the morning of the 16th, Gonen flew by helicopter to Bren's advanced headquarters, which was on the high ground overlooking Akavish. Taking Bren's deputy, Brig. David, he drove back along Akavish to the bridges. Two miles east of the artillery road, they came on the pontoon bridge: half a dozen pontoons were on the road, and further back, parallel to and north of the road, was the preconstructed bridge, which had been broken while being towed. An ordnance officer was in charge of the repairs together with Lieut.-Col. Aharon ('Johnny') Tanne, the Southern Command chief of engineers. Gonen was told that the bridge would be repaired within half an hour. The pontoon bridge could not move further westward because Akavish was still held by Egyptians.

Gonen and David continued along Akavish by jeep until Gonen suggested that they leave the vehicle – a jeep was a moving target but nobody would fire on two isolated persons. They began to walk in the direction of the battlefield. From the top of a sand dune they observed the Chinese Farm below and saw a battle of Israeli tanks against Egyptian missiles. A lone Egyptian tank fired at them from a distance of 1,500 yards, but they remained and looked at the scene from their observation point – they could see that Akavish was physically blocked by the Egyptians and that the Chinese Farm was strongly held. Gonen returned to Bren's advanced headquarters at 10 o'clock and spoke to Sharon, who told him that he hoped to clear the route within an hour and a half. Sharon maintained that the bridge could not be moved forward, but Gonen advised him that he had just left the bridge and that it was now in a position to move. He assigned responsibility for getting the pontoon bridge to the Canal to Bren's division – with personal responsibility on Bren's deputy,

David – and gave orders to Sharon's deputy, Jackie Even, to be responsible
for the preconstructed bridge. Giving Bren a warning order to be ready
to move by noon to clear Akavish and Tirtur and to get the pontoon bridge
to the water, he reported by radio to Bar-Lev who in turn advised Sharon.

At approximately midday Gonen advised Sharon that he was ordering Bren
to clean up Akavish and Tirtur, while Sharon's mission would be to capture
the Chinese Farm and the southern half of Missouri westwards to the Canal.
But since Sharon's tanks were out of ammunition, it was decided that he would
wait until Bren had opened the two routes, before filling up with ammunition
and fuel and attacking the Chinese Farm. The situation in which Sharon's
tanks found themselves now – with empty 'bellies' – only served to emphasize
the very hazardous nature of the operation which had been mounted in the
circumstances. Gonen forbade the transfer of any further forces to the west
bank pending the opening of the supply route.

At 4.30 on the afternoon of the 16th, Dayan, Bar-Lev and Gonen met in
advanced headquarters of the Southern Command. Gonen said that if neither
bridge nor pontoons reached the Canal, they would have to withdraw from the
west bank. If there were pontoons but no bridge, the force could remain there
but Bren's division could not be transferred to join it; as soon as a bridge was
in position all the forces necessary could cross.

Bren was concentrated south of Tasa ready to exploit success and cross on
the bridge across the Canal. He moved forward with his advanced headquarters,
travelling on the sands parallel to the road because the road itself was blocked
with bumper-to-bumper traffic with giant pontoons stuck in a sea of vehicles.
Interspersed along the columns were fuel and ammunition supply trains. He
passed the damaged bridge with officers bunched around desperately trying to
repair it under concentrated Egyptian artillery fire. The morning of the 16th
was misty. As it cleared up, he looked down along Akavish and saw Israeli
tanks travelling along the road and then suddenly exploding in flames (he sent
down half-tracks to collect the crews as they crossed the sand dunes). Seeing
that the road was blocked, he sent his leading battalion under Lieut.-Col. Amir
in a broad, flanking movement to cross the Canal according to plan. Amir's
tanks were moving onto the rafts when Sharon contacted Bren, telling him
what Amnon had been through all night and that his tanks were now without
ammunition. Bren agreed to leave Amir with him for support and he was
sent to relieve Amnon's forces between the Chinese Farm and the Canal,
thus enabling him to withdraw and reorganize. Amir succeeded in holding
concentrated Egyptian armoured attacks during the 16th and 17th. Gonen in
the meantime arrived at Bren's advanced headquarters and Bren's deputy
David was assigned to concentrate the pontoons and get them to the Canal.

Gradually nine pontoons were concentrated, a sufficient number to build a bridge.

When Bren was ordered to open Akavish and Tirtur, he moved his tanks down from the hills to the road towards Televizia, which was held by Tuvia's forces in Sharon's division. Missiles were fired at them from the sand dunes; they had no infantry, and Bren understood that this was going to be a very costly operation. At 2 o'clock Southern Command informed him that he would receive a parachute force which would soon arrive by helicopter. All day they waited but there was no sign of the paratroopers. (They arrived at night with Col. Uzi in command.) The planning was done rapidly and at 11.30 at night they moved into action without adequate preparation.

The plan was for Itzik's battalion to move towards the Canal, combing an area about 1 mile wide linking Akavish and Tirtur. The problem as it had beed presented to them did not seem an involved one. For three hours the battalion moved in formation through the area: along the road moving towards the Canal were sections of bridges, tanks, pontoons; the troops on the road waved them on. Yaki's company was leading the battalion on its northern flank when it suddenly came under heavy fire from artillery and machine guns. The company stormed the source of fire and Yaki was wounded, a platoon commanded with him was killed and a large number of his unit were casualties. Yaki bandaged himself and again led a charge, but again it was broken. The second company under Margal moved forward to help them, but came under heavy fire from all sides too. One unit tried to outflank the enemy, but there was no end to the enemy position and it came under fire. Most of its officers and NCOs were wounded or killed. As Margal's company rushed to help them – artillery fire could not be employed because it was difficult to locate the Israeli forces – Margal himself was fatally wounded.

Bren ordered the force to leave Tirtur and concentrate only on Akavish, but the fire was so heavy that the paratroops could not disengage. There were large numbers of wounded and armoured personnel carriers were sent in to try to evacuate them. It was 3 o'clock in the morning; dawn would break within another hour and if he did not get the pontoons to the water, Bren realized that yet another vital day would pass without a bridge across the Canal. While the paratroopers were fighting desperately between the two roads, he decided to make one more attempt. He sent a force of armoured personnel carriers along Akavish to report on the situation: the road was clear. After overcoming the problem of removing the destroyed tanks from the road, David advanced with the convoy of pontoons along Akavish to the lake and thence northwards along its shore. As dawn approached and the sun rose, the convoy reached the 'yard'.

Meanwhile it became clear to the paratroopers that they could not capture the enemy position before them, but as they engaged the Egyptians the division began moving behind them with the bridging equipment towards the Canal. The battalion commander, Itzik, realized that he must now hold the line at all costs, engage the enemy and evacuate the wounded. He created a line some 75–100 yards from the Egyptian lines, with his paratroopers constantly risking their lives by rushing into no-man's land to evacuate the wounded. An armoured unit tried to reach his force but failed. Later, guided by smoke which brought down a hail of Egyptian fire on Yaki's forces, the tanks arrived. They advanced towards the Egyptian position and within two minutes three tanks were set on fire by missiles. Despite the intense and murderous Egyptian fire, the paratroopers held on grimly in a battle which lasted for fourteen hours, facing a divisional position, while to the rear movement towards the Canal continued. Finally armoured personnel carriers rushed in under fire and evacuated the wounded. As the battalion was finally pulled out of its position by Tuvia's relieving armoured forces, Itzik remained behind to cover them with his advanced headquarters firing at the Egyptians. His losses in that battle were 40 killed and 100 wounded.

While this battle was raging, Bren ordered two brigades to move and clear the area of Akavish and Tirtur: Natke's brigade deployed to the south of Akavish, moving northwards across Akavish and continuing in the direction of Tirtur; Gaby's pushed from east to west. Tuvia's brigade too having come under his command, Bren pressed on the Egyptian forces in the Israeli corridor from east to west with three concentrated armoured brigades. Bren's forces evacuated the paratroopers from the field at 11.00 in the morning, but as this battle was developing a report was received that an Egyptian armoured brigade was moving up from the south on Lexicon along the coast of the Bitter Lakes. Bren asked for Arieh's brigade and received it.

In the dark about the Israeli crossing and totally unaware of its implications the Egyptian Command did appreciate that a major effort was being made by the Israeli forces to open a corridor north of the Great Bitter Lake. But it never dawned on them that while fighting of such intensity was going on in the area of the corridor, the Israeli Command would nevertheless launch a major effort across the Canal without an assured supply route. On 17 October a determined effort was made by the Egyptian Second and Third armies to close the Israeli corridor and cut off all Israeli forces between Lexicon and the Canal: the 14th Egyptian Armoured Brigade had fought for two days against Amir's lone tank battalion to the west of the Chinese Farm and by the evening of the 17th had been largely destroyed, while the forces of the Egyptian 16th Infantry and 21st Armoured divisions launched two major attacks against Bren's forces at Tirtur and Akavish.

The counter-attack was mounted from Missouri and the Chinese Farm towards Akavish. The sand dunes were covered by Egyptian tanks as they moved forward. Natke and Gaby waited for them and engaged them in a major armoured battle. Amir, who was to the west of the Egyptian attack, harassed them from the rear. Twice the Egyptians mounted a major attack and finally withdrew, leaving a large number of tanks in the field. The Israeli forces suffered a loss of six tanks, of which three were from missiles. The losses sustained in this attack by the Egyptians were to seal the fate of the Chinese Farm. At this stage the Egyptian Third Army launched the 25th Armoured Brigade from the south in order to complete the joint operation undertaken by the two Egyptian armies. It advanced northwards along the Great Bitter Lake in the direction of the 16th Division bridgehead north of the Israeli corridor with the mission of cutting the corridor and destroying the Israeli forces which had penetrated the bridgehead.

At 10 o'clock Dayan arrived at Bren's advanced headquarters on the hills near Kishuf; shortly after, Bar-Lev arrived. Dayan asked to be taken over to Sharon, but Bren convinced him not to go forward and that instead he would bring him back. Meanwhile a helicopter arrived with Gen. Elazar and with Uri Ben Ari, Gonen's deputy, and soon Sharon himself had arrived in a half-track. They all sat down on the hill in a circle with maps to decide whether in the circumstances they should continue with the crossing, and who would cross and when. Sharon proposed that Bren's division should deal with the corridor on the east bank and he would cross with his division. Bren opposed this, suggesting that they stick to the original plan, namely that Sharon should hold the corridor and that his – Bren's – division should disengage from the enemy, refuel, fill up with ammunition and cross the Canal according to plan. Elazar decided in favour of Bren's proposal, ordering Sharon to clean up the corridor and widen it; only then was he to cross. Tuvia's brigade would revert to Sharon and would exert pressure against the enemy, enabling Gaby's brigade to disengage. As they were talking, Amnon (whose brigade was reorganizing in the area of Lakekan on the shores of the Great Bitter Lake) reported that the dust raised by the approaching Egyptian armoured brigade moving northwards was coming dangerously near.

Amnon had placed four tanks on Lexicon south of Lakekan to protect his brigade. When he received the first reports of the advance of the 25th Egyptian Armoured Brigade, he was sceptical. He went forward himself and looked down the coast of the Great Bitter Lake, and there 1 mile away stretched along the lake shore slowly moving towards him was an armoured brigade. It was moving bunched up, clearly visible – an ideal target. Battle was joined at midday, with Amnon's tanks opening fire at long range and knocking out the first two tanks in the Egyptian column.

Bren had in the meantime left the conference with his advanced headquarters and was rushing southwards, parallel to the lake, along the artillery road. During the conference, as Amnon's reports came in, he had already ordered Natke to leave one battalion in the area of Akavish and Tirtur and to place an armoured ambush to the east of Lexicon facing the Great Bitter Lake. At the same time he ordered Arieh, moving with his brigade along the lateral road, to sweep around and come across country on a secondary route, deploying to the east of Botzer at the southern end of the Great Bitter Lake, thus placing himself to the east and to the rear of the advancing Egyptian brigade. The 25th Egyptian Armoured Brigade comprising ninety-six tanks, large numbers of armoured personnel carriers, artillery, fuel and supply trucks moved slowly into the trap: to the north blocking the road at Lakekan was a small unit of Amnon's forces; to the west was the lake and between it and the road an Israeli minefield; to the east Natke was deployed and to the south-east Arieh's brigade closed the Egyptians off in the rear.

Natke's brigade opened fire first. Part of the Egyptian force turned to leave the road, moved towards the lake and tried to go back on its tracks. They ran into the Israeli minefield along the lake. The remainder charged towards Natke's forces – who were waiting for them in the sand dunes – and were destroyed by his tanks. When the Egyptians had been locked in battle with Natke's forces for half an hour, Arieh's brigade moved from the Gidi road in a wide, left-flanking movement towards Botzer. Bren sent a company of jeeps to delineate the area of responsibility between his two brigades. Arieh's force opened fire: the Egyptian brigade was completely boxed in and the shore of the lake became a line of fire and smoke as one by one the tanks and vehicles in the Egyptian force were picked off (Magen's division from the south lent artillery support to Arieh's attack). Some of the Egyptian tanks began to flee. Part of Arieh's force followed them and ran into an Israeli minefield near Botzer. By 5.30 in the evening the battle – a classic of its kind and the dream of any armoured commander – was over. Eighty-six T62 tanks out of a total of ninety-six had been destroyed; four of them, including the tank carrying the Egyptian brigade commander, escaped into the Botzer fortification. All the armoured personnel carriers were destroyed, as were all the supply trains. The Egyptian infantry troops fled back to Botzer. Israeli losses were the four tanks that had run into the minefield near Botzer when chasing the Egyptians. Refuelling under heavy enemy shelling, Bren regrouped his division and prepared to cross the Canal (By 4 pm, while the battle along the Great Bitter Lake was being waged, the pontoon bridge across the Canal was completed). It had been a good day for Bren: he had cleared most of Tirtur and Akavish and had destroyed the 25th Egyptian Armoured Brigade. (Tuvia's brigade was to complete the mopping up on Tirtur.)

At 2.00 in the morning of 17 October, Bren informed Jackie, Sharon's deputy who was responsible for the crossing, that Akavish was open. Jackie ordered the commander of the pontoon convoy to advance along Akavish to Lakekan where he would meet Sharon, who would show him exactly where to launch the pontoons into the Canal. At 7.15 on the morning of 17 October the first pontoon splashed into the water. Jackie saw that Tirtur was not yet opened and that eighteen tanks in addition to bulldozers were tied up with the preconstructed bridge which was under constant artillery fire. Sharon ordered the tanks to leave the bridge and to rejoin Tuvia's brigade, which was fighting in the area of the corridor. At 11 o'clock Jackie reached Matzmed (receiving under command all the forces in the launching area) and by 4 o'clock in the afternoon the pontoon bridge was ready. From 4 o'clock to midnight the bridge was in position and awaiting the arrival of Bren's division, which was now reorganizing after the armoured battle along the Great Bitter Lake.

By 8 o'clock on the morning of 16 October, Matt was in control of the bridgehead as planned, reaching northwards from the Great Bitter Lake some 3 miles. Resistance had been weak and as his forces moved along the Egyptian ramp northwards, they came upon thirty Egyptians manning electronic equipment 1 mile to the north; part of the force was killed and part was taken prisoner. When isolated Egyptian armoured personnel carriers drove along, they were wiped out by the advancing Israeli forces. As they waited in position, the forces facing northwards observed a convoy of seven trucks loaded with 150 troops approaching unsuspectingly. They destroyed it and seized the four main crossings over the sweet-water canal. During the morning, leaving seven tanks to protect Matt's forces, Haim took twenty-one tanks westward on his mission to seek out the surface-to-air missile sites.

On the morning of 17 October – after the Israelis had been on the west bank of the Canal for one full day and two nights – the bridgehead came under artillery fire. Matt's headquarters received a direct hit and his deputy was wounded. From this moment until the cease-fire, the bridgehead and the area of the bridge were under constant heavy artillery fire as guns, mortars and katyushas combined to pour tens of thousands of shells into the area of the crossing. Planes attempted to bomb every afternoon, but large numbers were shot down both by the Israeli Air Force, which was now patrolling over the bridgehead, and by the ground forces. Egyptian helicopters came in on suicide missions to drop barrels of napalm on the bridge and the bridgehead; large numbers were shot down. FROG surface-to-surface missiles were employed, but the Israeli forces soon learnt how to bring them down with anti-aircraft fire.

The last of Haim's forces had crossed on the 16th at 11.30 in the morning and for thirty-seven hours thereafter no more tanks crossed. This fact was to be heavily criticized by Sharon. Soon Matt's northern flank was under heavy attack by Egyptian commando forces, which were driven back by his paratroopers. Meanwhile the intense artillery bombardment continued without let-up – in one case the entire quartermaster staff of brigade headquarters became casualties.

Meanwhile Amnon's brigade had reorganized and on 18 October, under Sharon's orders, attacked the Chinese Farm from the rear. The Egyptian forces had by now been worn down by the intense fighting and this time the Israeli attack was successful. The Chinese Farm fell. Before the eyes of the Israelis there unfolded a picture of a highly organized infantry, anti-tank, defensive locality with very heavy concentrations of anti-tank weapons, anti-tank guns and Sagger missiles abandoned on all sides. Following the fall of this position, Amnon pressed northwards widening the corridor for some 3 miles. In the afternoon the minister of defence arrived on the battlefield with Sharon. As he looked down and saw the scene of destruction and the evidence of the incredibly bitter and cruel battle which had taken place, he was visibly shaken. Amnon said to him,' Look at this valley of death.' Dayan murmured in astonishment, 'What you people have done here!'

16

On the Other Side

THE EGYPTIAN REACTION to the Israeli crossing was one of incredulity and light-hearted dismissal, with the various levels of command so blinded by self-adulation at their initial success that they tended to brush the operation off as a tiresome nuisance which could be dealt with. In any case, they argued, it was designed by the Israelis to boost morale in Israel and, as President Sadat put it, to be a spectacular 'television operation' – no more.

The Egyptian reaction has been reported in numerous post-war statements made by the various Egyptian commanders, by members of the government and also by reports published by correspondents covering the Egyptian side. A reconsideration of the reaction from these sources reveals that the Egyptian Army appreciated that the Israeli forces had crossed the Canal in the area of Deversoir for the first time only in mid-morning of 16 October; none of the reports however estimated the force to be greater than a reconnaissance unit composed of five amphibious tanks, which in their view had crossed the Great Bitter Lake. The Palestinian press, published in Beirut, maintained that it was the Palestinian brigade stationed on the west bank of the Great Bitter Lake that had sounded the alarm and reported that three Israeli tanks were operating on the west bank. But even at this point, when Egyptian reports described the Israeli penetration of the Second Army bridgehead, the descriptions again talked in terms of a limited number of Israeli amphibious tanks on the west of the Canal which were attacking anti-aircraft surface-to-air missile bases.

According to the description of these developments as seen by the Egyptian headquarters, given in post-war interviews and statements by President Sadat and Minister of War Ahmed Ismail, reports from the front-line armies were coupled with a description of the Egyptian commando operations being mounted against the Israeli bridgehead and also of the fact that the 25th Egyptian Armoured Brigade had been ordered to move northwards to attack the Israeli forces which had penetrated the Second Army bridgehead.

One of the basic weaknesses in the Egyptian evaluations – a measure of wishful thinking – becomes evident at this stage. The picture as relayed to the Egyptian High Command continued to repeat the initial stories about small numbers of amphibious tanks, to play down the scope of the Israeli attack, emphasizing that it was designed purely to raise the morale of the Israeli people and army, and to give a general indication that the matter was well in hand and that the Israeli forces would soon be seen off the west bank. An indication of the subconscious attempt by all Egyptian elements that were involved in the reporting to play down the strength and scope of the Israeli move to the west bank emerges from the fact that the Egyptians assumed on the morning of 19 October that the Israeli forces on the west bank numbered only 100–110 tanks.

At this point however a note of desperation is reflected in the Egyptian operational moves. The commander of the Moroccan brigade based on Cairo described how on the afternoon of the 19th he was rushed from Cairo to the Third Army (reports were pouring in of Sharon's move northwards in the area of Serafeum and of Amnon's armoured attack). The Egyptians had not yet appreciated the strategic purpose of the Israeli penetration to the west bank and the danger to the entire Third Army, and only on the 20th after President Sadat had visited the Egyptian headquarters did a clearer Egyptian evaluation of the developments and the dangers become apparent: they now realized that the Israeli purpose was to cut the lines of communications and supplies of the Third Army. Sadat and a number of Egyptian senior commanders describe how they feared a possible amphibious crossing of Lake Timsah as part of Sharon's advance in order to by-pass Ismailia from the north, while Sadat himself reiterated his warning of the possibility of an Israeli landing along the Gulf of Suez. The increasing danger that the Israeli Air Force posed to them was emphasized by the fact that all convoys in the Third Army area began to maintain distances of at least 300 yards between vehicles when travelling by day because of the stepped-up Israeli air activity. An element of panic was beginning to become apparent in the Egyptian reactions to the Israeli moves. Describing the situation at the time in the Egyptian High Command, Heikal admits that 'it had a considerable effect on strained nerves' and goes on to assert 'this was a war against our nerves'.

On 16 October President Sadat addressed a special session of the People's Council in Cairo. As he spoke the Israelis had been in a bridgehead on the west bank for over twelve hours, and Haim's tanks were dashing across the Egyptian countryside with impunity, knocking out surface-to-air missile sites, destroying tanks and ambushing convoys. But Sadat was unaware at the time of these developments because the Egyptian Command had not taken them seriously and had not accurately reported them. During his speech he indicated that Egypt was prepared for a cease-fire based on an immediate and complete withdrawal of Israeli forces from occupied Arab territories to the lines of 5 June 1967; after this total withdrawal he would be willing to attend a peace conference at the United Nations. Indicating his complete ignorance of what was happening along the Canal, he continued, 'We are prepared at this hour, yes even at this moment, to begin clearing the Suez Canal and opening it for international shipping.'

When President Sadat and Gen. Ismail returned from the jubilant and victorious session of the Egyptian Parliament, Sadat went to the operations room to find that a small number of amphibious Israeli tanks had succeeded in crossing the Canal at Deversoir to the west bank. But the local Egyptian Command reported that the destruction of this force was imminent: the Second Army commander had moved a commando battalion against the Israeli intrusion (this was in fact the commando group which launched several attacks on Matt's northern flank on the 17th). According to Gen. Ismail, the information on the Israeli attack came in piecemeal, due to certain changes in areas of responsibility that had occurred at that time in the Egyptian Command. Furthermore, he maintained that the Israeli armour, hidden as it was in the dense foliage of the plantations along the sweet-water canal, did not arouse the reaction which such a force, had it appeared in the open, would normally have aroused. Sadat claimed later that on the afternoon of the 16th he told Shazli to lay siege around the bridgehead, enabling the Israelis to enter it but not to leave, so that the entire Israeli force would fall into their hands. Moreover, he said that he had warned the Egyptian General Staff five days before the war to expect various types of daring Israeli assaults. In his post-war discussion of this event, however, he refused to discuss the developments in the three days following the night of the 16th because he was 'concerned about Shazli's good name'.

What in fact happened was that the debate (whether or not to broaden the Egyptian bridgeheads in the Sinai and move eastwards or not) going on between Sadat and Ismail on the other hand, and Shazli supported by many of the officers on the other, was coming to a head. Sadat saw in the crossing of the Canal a basically limited operation designed to break the political log jam. Ismail, a cautious officer, supported Sadat's view but was opposed by

Shazli, who felt that the Egyptians should have exploited success and pushed on towards the passes. Shazli's view (that had the Egyptian bridgehead been deeper and reached the passes, the Israeli operation at Deversoir would have been impossible) was echoed by many in the Arab world, such as the military editor of *Al Nahar*, the prestigious Beirut newspaper, who wrote that 'had the Egyptian forces advanced in Sinai immediately after the crossing of the Canal and endeavoured to capture the Gidi, Mitla and Bir Gafgafa [Refidim] passes before the arrival of the Israeli reserves, the war in Sinai would not have concluded as it did'.

After the war Ismail explained that they did not move forward because he was waiting to see what the Israeli reaction would be to their crossing and because he was unwilling to move forward without strengthening his armour considerably and without bringing across the Canal the mobile surface-to-air missiles. It is quite clear from his summary of the war that he lived with one main obsession: not to allow the Egyptian Army to advance beyond the missile cover. Indeed, in discussing the armoured battle of 14 October, he explained that it was larger in scope and sooner than planned because of pressures from Syria to draw Israeli forces and the Israeli Air Force from the northern front; only a few days earlier, the Syrians had dispatched one of their highest-ranking officers to Egypt with a message from President Assad pleading for a major Egyptian effort.

At 1 o'clock on the morning of 19 October, Gen. Ismail contacted Sadat urgently with a request to come to the operations room. Here Sadat found Shazli in a state of total collapse, saying, 'The war is over. A catastrophe has occurred. We must withdraw from Sinai.' It was at this point that Sadat activated Soviet Premier Kosygin, who had been in Cairo from the 16th, to convene the Security Council and order a cease-fire. (Sadat decided there and then to dismiss Shazli and to appoint Gamasy in his stead, but he kept the fact of Shazli's relief secret for two months primarily for reasons of morale in the Egyptian forces and for internal considerations.)

Weeks later a well-known Western journalist was seated with Shazli in his home when a messenger arrived informing the commander that he had been relieved of his duties and would be appointed ambassador to the United Kingdom. Shazli burst into tears: 'After all these years, to be dismissed by a messenger.'

At 9 o'clock on the night of the 17th, Bren's division moved along Akavish, with his advanced headquarters leading, followed by Natke's brigade and thereafter by Gaby's brigade. Bren dozed off and was fast asleep in his half-track when he was awakened by one of his officers. There was now bright moonlight;

it was completely quiet and his division was beginning to cross the placid waters of the Suez Canal. As they crossed the bridge, someone produced a bottle of whisky and it was passed round from hand to hand. Haim was on the other side to meet them and lead them to the divisional concentration area at the Deversoir airfield. But as Bren was wondering whether it was advisable to concentrate in this area, suddenly a terrifying artillery barrage descended on them. They moved around trying to avoid the fire and taking shelter by the walls of buildings.

In the middle of all this he was motified by Sharon's deputy, Jackie, that the bridge had been blocked after the third tank of Natke's brigade had crossed. Jackie recommended that the tanks continue to cross on rafts, but in the middle of the Canal the first raft was hit and the tank sank with its crew. Informing Bren that it would take three-quarters of an hour to make up for the break in the pontoon bridge, Jackie proceeded to do so by using a bridging tank from Haim's brigade. All night long Jackie and a group of officers manned the bridge in the open under intense shell fire, supervising the crossing of the tanks; the element of surprise had disappeared and the bridge was now the main target of the enemy artillery fire. But by 4 o'clock on the morning of the 18th, Bren's division – less one brigade – was across the Canal.

Haim is a regular officer who had been forced to fend on his own in a harsh world. As a small boy he had fled to the Soviet Union when the Germans invaded Poland, finally, within the framework of the 'Youth Aliyah' organization, making his way to Palestine via Teheran in 1943. After his force – numbering twenty tanks and seven armoured personnel carriers – had crossed the Canal on the 15th, on Sharon's orders to destroy missile sites it moved along the Test route on the shores of the Great Bitter Lake down to the Sakronut road leading westwards to Cairo. Passing the main crossroads leading due north to Ismailia, they rushed an Egyptian defensive position, known as Tsach, knocking out three tanks and some soft vehicles. Continuing westwards, they passed another locality organized for defence, known as Maktsera; but attacking the missile site at this position, they found it to be empty. Half a mile before the crossroads of the Vadaut road, leading northwards to Abu Suweir, they encountered a large number of Egyptian vehicles and proceeded to knock them out one by one. Haim's force continued on its move westwards, destroying two surface-to-air missile bases by engaging them at a distance of 1,500 yards with tank guns. At 2 o'clock, when the force was already some 15 miles west of the Canal, orders were received to withdraw to the bridges across the sweet-water canal and that night the forces took up positions protecting the bridgehead.

During this foray on the 16th, in which the Egyptians were taken completely

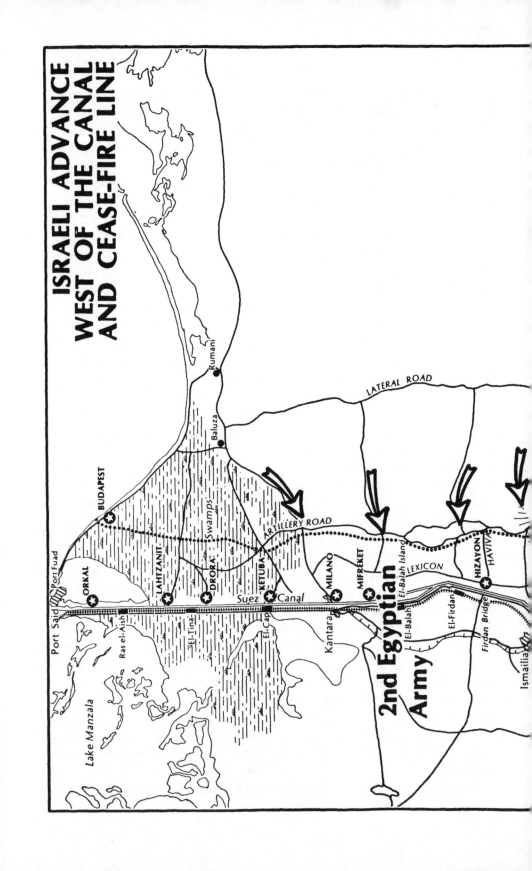

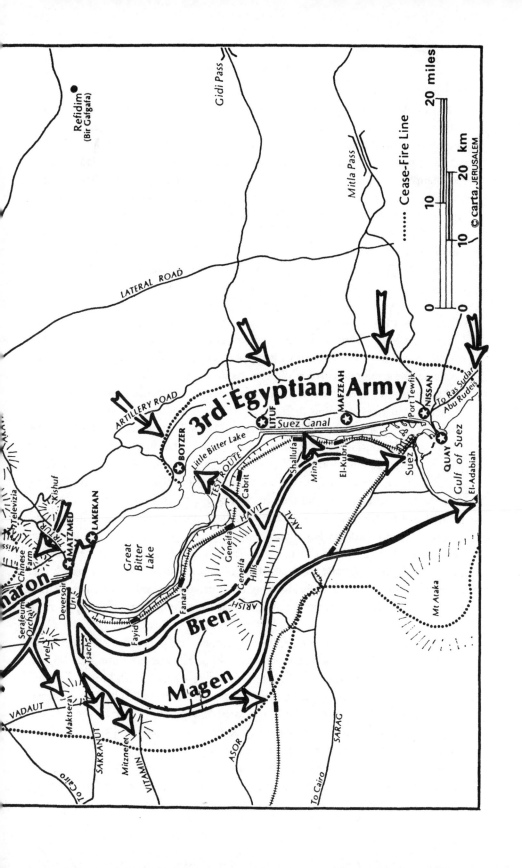

by surprise and in the course of which Haim reported that as far as he could make out the road to Cairo was wide open, his force had moved freely and with impunity, destroying four surface-to-air missile positions, twelve tanks and twenty armoured personnel carriers for the loss of one man wounded. On that morning of the 17th, after an additional battalion of his brigade had crossed, the enemy mounted his first armoured counter-attack against the bridgehead; Haim's brigade suffered casualties, but the counter-attack was broken and the enemy withdrew, leaving ten tanks in the field.

On the 17th the minister of defence visited Sharon and suggested that rather than plan for a wide, deep, flanking movement, it would be better for him to roll up the enemy along the east bank of the Canal. Dayan felt that by two parallel operations on the east and west banks pushing northwards, it would be possible by mutual support from each bank and by the threat each effort created for the enemy flank on the opposite side, to roll up and clear the Canal. Southern Command had been pressing to widen the corridor on the east bank and to take Missouri, thus pushing out of range the Egyptian artillery firing on the bridgehead from the east bank.

At this point another acrimonious argument broke out between Sharon and Gonen, the former wanting to transfer Amnon's brigade into the bridgehead, while Gonen insisted that his forces remain on the east bank and push northwards into Missouri in order to widen the corridor. Sharon appealed to Bar-Lev, who authorized him to transfer Amnon. In the meantime, Sharon, most of whose division was by now on the west bank, went to Bar-Lev again, suggesting that the plan be changed and that instead of his division pushing southwards parallel to Bren's division, he should remain in position, widen the bridgehead and push northwards to Ismailia. Bar-Lev agreed and called Gonen to advise him of the change in plan: Magen's division, instead of remaining responsible for the bridgehead, would push southwards to the west of Bren towards Suez; Sharon would remain in the bridgehead and push northwards. Gonen consented to this proposal, explaining to Bar-Lev that life would be much simpler if he had to manœuvre divisions under Magen and Bren, instead of Sharon. Once the decision had been taken by Bar-Lev, Gonen was overcome by a feeling of relief. The whole war became simpler for him. He was now commanding an advance with commanders who he felt would co-operate with him and whose reservations, if any, would be without personal overtones. The Israeli sweep southwards would, therefore, be in the form of a fan, with Bren to the east and Magen to his west and rear thus giving depth to his attack and creating a firm base in the event of any mishap on his front.

On the morning of 18 October Sharon ordered Jackie to bring the pre-constructed bridge forward. The Egyptians had range of the pontoon bridge and a continuous hail of artillery fire was descending around the area and on the bridgehead; Egyptian helicopters were making repeated attacks with napalm bombs in an attempt to destroy the bridge, and the enemy artillery was taking toll of the vulnerable rafts.

The bridge – an incongruous convoy of a dozen tanks inching forward and towing a 190-yard-long construction on rollers – began to be edged slowly forward under a concentrated artillery barrage with enemy shells landing on all sides. Clearing mines and repairing the Tirtur road, which was pock-marked with shell craters and sown with mines along the shoulders and in the ditches, the unit passed through a ghastly scene. On all sides the carnage of the battle-field unfolded: the dead of war, Egyptian and Israeli, were strewn in unshapely postures alongside the road over which they had fought for days and nights. Enemy planes zoomed in to attack the bridge; Israeli planes swooped in behind them and shot them down. While all around the flashes and explosions of war lit up the scene, the convoy creaked and strained towards the setting sun in the west, finally reaching the crossroads at Lexicon, where Lieut.-Col. Johnny Tanne, the command chief engineer, was killed. He was the man who more than anyone else was familiar with every square yard in the area, and Jackie realized that without him he was now in serious trouble. He himself was only too familiar with the area to know that one false step could bog the entire project down in swampy soil. There was nothing for it but for him to test the strength of the soil personally. He mounted the battalion commander's tank and, together with an armoured personnel carrier, moved slowly forward, testing the firmness of the ground so that the bridge could follow. His improvisation worked and the bridge reached the Canal on the evening of the 18th. Shortly after midnight it was operational; one day later a third bridge made up of pontoons was in position.

The organization under Jackie, with its engineer battalions, anti-aircraft forces and medical evacuation centres, performed heroically. From the moment the Egyptians recovered from their surprise and realized what was happening, the area of the bridges and the 'yard' was under continuous fire; in one night alone forty-one men of Jackie's task force were killed and, in all, over one hundred were killed and many hundreds wounded.

The attack on the west bank now began to develop in earnest. Danny Matt's paratroopers, who had established the bridgehead and had remained almost unchallenged at the outset, now repulsed several Egyptian counter-attacks mounted by commandos thrown into battle. On 18 October a force commanded by Lieut.-Col. Dan moved northwards between the sweet-water canal and the railroad towards Serafeum on the road to Ismailia. It ran into a very heavily fortified Egyptian position and soon found itself in very difficult circumstances;

the battalion commander with thirteen men was cut off from the main body of the force, which was under his second-in-command. Using the cover of the heavy, jungle-type undergrowth in the area, the Egyptians closed in on them, hundreds of them approaching from three directions to within 5–10 yards. The Israeli unit established itself in a single-storied house, while 5 yards away the Egyptians in a two-storied house fired at them from above, lobbed grenades, fired bazooka shells and threatened to destroy them.

For four hours the battle raged. Capt. Asa Kadmoni (who after the war was to be prominent in the protest movements), alone at the critical corner on the northern side of the house, held off with a rifle and grenades hundreds of advancing Egyptians. Two truck-loads more arrived on the scene and moved towards his corner, but before they could disembark he destroyed both, using a LAW anti-tank weapon. The Egyptians brought up artillery and anti-tank weapons, firing over open sights pointblank at the Israeli force from a distance of 100 yards. But help was on the way and two relieving forces (one under command of the second-in-command of the brigade moving along the railroad track and the second moving from Suez Canal eastwards under command of a battalion commander, Lieut.-Col. Zvi) entered the battle. After heavy fighting through the undergrowth and the mango orchards, the relieving forces linked up with the besieged force, which had been cut off most of the day (Kadmoni was down to seven bullets). Israeli casualties were eleven killed and twenty-seven wounded. As darkness fell the entire unit was withdrawn.

On the 19th Amnon was ordered to cross to the west bank of the Canal. Leaving one battalion to support the forces attacking Missouri, he crossed and in the Abu Sultan camps met Sharon, who ordered him to push northwards to the west of Matt's forces at Serafeum and take position Orcha, 4½ miles to the north. Deciding to attack a forward position held by an Egyptian commando platoon from the west, Amnon watched an armoured infantry company attacking and was filled with admiration as he saw the stubborn and very brave battle put up by the Egyptian platoon. Covered by Amnon's tank and some half-tracks, the Israeli company (from one of the elite battalions in the Israeli Army) fought its way forward until there was one Egyptian soldier left alive. As the Israeli forces moved slowly up the hill, this soldier leapfrogged backwards, firing as he went, fighting until he was killed at the summit of the hill. In front was the main Orcha position, but seeing the quality of the troops confronting him, Amnon brought in additional regular paratroopers. They stormed the position in half-tracks, then dismounted and fought through the trenches, cleaning up as they went. The position, a heavily fortified one, had been manned by a battalion of commandos with anti-tank guns, anti-aircraft guns and bazookas. There was a radar station in the position which had underground fortifications and which included a radio intercept unit to monitor Israeli tactical radio traffic (they found an Israeli-built receiver).

The Egyptians fought obstinately as the Israelis moved from one position to another along the trenches until nightfall. When the fighting was over, an incredible scene unfolded before the eyes of the Israeli forces: lying in the trenches of the fortifications were bodies of Egyptians heaped up one on the other; over 300 were counted, testimony to their extremely obstinate and brave stand. The attacking Israeli forces had suffered sixteen killed.

The fall of Orcha caused the complete collapse of the Egyptian defence system in the area, and Amnon's forces advanced slowly through the dense foliage of the agricultural strip. They moved along a number of side roads from west to east, reaching the top of the Egyptian rampart on the Canal, where they fired 'from Africa into Asia' in support of Tuvia's brigade which was attacking Missouri.

By 21 October the paratroopers with Amnon's forces were already on the outskirts of Ismailia. Facing Sharon's forces in the city was an infantry brigade and commando units, while to the west, on the Ismailia–Cairo road, a mechanized division was deployed to defend Cairo. On the morning of the 21st, as they stood on the rampart looking down on the town, they saw large numbers of Egyptian troops fleeing from the east to the west bank near the Monument to the Unknown Soldier to the south of Lake Timsah. Suddenly they saw these withdrawing troops being mown down by intensive fire from an Egyptian position on the west bank.

Sharon pressed for a wide, flanking operation in depth towards Damiette-Balatin on the Mediterranean coast, which would cut off the entire Second Army from Egypt. Southern Command insisted on Missouri being taken, because it was still endangering the corridor to the Israeli bridgehead, and pressed for Sharon to transfer more forces back to the east bank and to push northwards along the Canal. There was to be much recrimination later as to whether or not Sharon had transferred adequate forces to support the attack against Missouri. On the 21st he was ordered to take Missouri, but it was obvious to Southern Command that he was dragging his feet and carrying out this order unwillingly.

The attack began at 3 pm. Gonen heard that it was not going well, but when his deputy tried to speak to Sharon he was informed that the general was busy. In the evening Southern Command ordered Sharon's forces to attack again. Gonen had problems in reaching Sharon. He ordered Sharon to reinforce Tuvia and to attack. Sharon countered that he did not have the force to do this. Bar-Lev then spoke to him and gave him a specific order to transfer forces back to the east bank and to attack. He transferred five tanks back to the east bank, but fifteen minutes later Gen. Tal phoned Gonen to transmit an order from the minister of defence (with whom Sharon had spoken by phone) not to attack Missouri. As a result of the initial attack by Tuvia, during which a bitter and bloody battle was waged over one-third of Missouri had been taken.

On the morning of the 18th, Bren's division attacked along two brigade axes. From now on Bren's forces would be fighting all the way down to Suez against units of an Egyptian mechanized division and the 4th Egyptian Armoured Division. Natke's brigade attacked due westward and took the Orel position. Gaby's brigade to the south ran into heavy Egyptian defences in the area of Uri, incurring losses in tanks. An additional attack by his armoured infantry failed until finally a company of Matt's paratroopers overcame what was an ambush manned by thirty-five Egyptian commandos armed with thirteen RPG bazookas in the undergrowth.

From the south the Egyptians advanced a battalion of tanks along the sweet-water canal road. Gaby moved his tanks along the parallel Test road, endangering the advanced Egyptian battalion on its right flank. The Egyptians accordingly moved towards Gaby's force on the road to the east, but were bogged down in the muddy fields and were an easy prey for his tanks. The entire battalion was wiped out. Meanwhile Natke was trying to move southwards along the main Ismailia–Suez road (Havit) but could not overcome the Egyptian positions at the Tsach crossroads. Haim's brigade was at the same time trying to take the crossroads immediately to the east of Orcha, and ran into an entire brigade of artillery with missiles.

By midday the Israeli forces were blocked in their advance and Bren was ordered to send out raiding parties in strength to destroy surface-to-air missile sites. He instructed both Natke and Gaby to assign a battalion each for this purpose. Natke's force fanned out 15 miles to the west, raided and destroyed two SAM surface-to-air batteries and returned almost without fuel. Gaby's force under Amir slipped out of the bridgehead, moved south 6 miles, engaged enemy tanks and destroyed one anti-aircraft missile base. The raids on the surface-to-air missile batteries were having their effect, and on the morning of the 19th Bren attacked with the full support of the Air Force. With Natke and Arieh fanning out westwards to the west of Tsach, they captured the Fayid landing strip north of Fayid airfield.

Leaving a force to cover the Fayid airfield from the west, Gaby's brigade rushed southwards to the Genefa Hills. He reached the Vadaut road, encountering some forty Egyptian tanks on Mitznefet at ranges of $1\frac{1}{2}$–2 miles. Natke's brigade broke out westwards through Maktsera, stormed an enemy artillery brigade and ran into heavy enemy forces on the main Cairo–Bitter Lake road (Sakronut). Arieh's brigade followed through, moving down and protecting

Gaby's right flank. They continued to attack as many surface-to-air missile sites as they could reach and in these attacks two of Natke's battalion commanders were wounded. Near the Genefa Hills the Egyptians fired a SA2 surface-to-air missile in a flat trajectory over open sites at Gaby's brigade. The missile flew over his force, landing 400 yards from Bren's advanced headquarters.

Bren was now located on the Genefa Hills. Gaby was deployed to the east of Mitznefet and Natke and Arieh were ordered to move along the Genefa Hills. They knocked out a number of surface-to-air missile sites on these heights and reached the secondary Vitamin road leading to the lake. Natke's brigade continued southwards crossing the main road, Asor, and clearing missile sites as they went, while Arieh's brigade continued along the eastern Genefa Hills.

On the 19th Magen's division moved through Bren's division and headed westwards towards Maktsera. Along the main Cairo–Bitter Lake road it overcame the Tsach crossroads position from the rear and moved on to relieve Gaby's forces facing Mitznefet, while Gaby moved eastwards along Vitamin to open the main Ismailia–Suez road (Havit). Heavy Egyptian resistance broke this attack and Gaby's forces sustained losses. Bren received under command a battalion of infantry and a battalion of engineers, which moved down in parallel lines along Test, the sweet-water canal road and Havit. The vital airport of Fayid fell, thus affording the Israeli forces a very important air bridgehead which could now supply the forces on the west bank.

Bren's move in rushing to the Genefa Hills was an important element in guaranteeing the success of the southward dash of the Israeli forces. Had these heights been ignored and been occupied by Egyptian commando units, any further advance by the Israeli forces would have been extremely difficult and very questionable.

Arieh was encountering heavy fighting on the eastern Genefa Hills, while Gaby was moving slowly southwards along the three parallel roads by the lakeside. The Egyptian Third Army moved the 22nd Tank Brigade of the 6th Mechanized Division back to the west bank. Meanwhile on Bren's left flank a task force comprising an armoured battalion, an armoured infantry battalion, a parachute battalion and a battalion of engineers was making its way slowly southwards along Test through the continuous concentrations of army camps, fighting against Egyptian, Palestinian and Kuwaiti forces.

To the west Magen was pushing down as planned towards the Cairo–Suez road, having placed Dan's brigade to protect his west flank at Jebel Um Katib to the south of Mitznefet. By noon on the 19th Dan was 17 miles west of the Canal. On the next day he moved south to Jebel Um Katib and took up positions facing Mitznefet, where for three days his brigade conducted a battle with an Egyptian brigade of tanks, inflicting heavy losses on them.

Meanwhile elements of the 4th Egyptian Armoured Division were fighting back desperately and attacking Natke's brigade south of the Asor road. On the 21st this brigade was already 1 mile north of the main Suez–Cairo road (Sarag) and controlled it by fire. Thus from midday on the 21st the Egyptian Third Army – apart from the southerly road leading south along the Gulf of Suez – was in effect cut off from its rear headquarters and its main supply bases.

On 16 October Soviet Premier Alexei Kosygin arrived in Cairo for two days of talks. He was given an optimistic appraisal of the military situation and tried to agree with the Egyptians on a common policy over the Egyptian peace terms. During the period of the talks the Israeli 'armoured commando raid', as Heikal called it, or 'television operation', as President Sadat described it, was under way. But it was three days before the Egyptians appreciated its full significance and danger.

Kosygin's purpose was to bring about a cease-fire, but so long as the Egyptians were carrying out successful operations, there was no urgency in arranging it. Once the steam had gone out of the Egyptian attack, however, and following the reports of the setback in the armoured battle on the 14th, it was clear to the Soviets that the time had come to halt the fighting and take full advantage of the Egyptian achievements to date. Kosygin assured Sadat that the Soviet Union was prepared, if necessary on its own, to guarantee the cease-fire. Finally they agreed on conditions for a cease-fire and these were presented by Ambassador Dobrynin to Dr Kissinger in New York. Seeing the proposals, which included a total Israeli withdrawal from all territories – including East Jerusalem – Kissinger realized that this could never be a basis for an agreement with Israel. Moreover, he was up to date on the details of the Israeli penetration into Egypt on the west bank of the Suez Canal.

In the meantime the full significance of the deteriorating military situation both on the Syrian front and on the west bank of the Canal had dawned on the Soviet leadership, even though there were still illusions in the Egyptian Command about the situation. The Soviets realized that the entire gamble was at risk and that once again they were in danger of facing a total military Arab collapse. It was clear to them that given a few more days the Egyptian Third Army would be doomed and this in turn could have a direct effect on Sadat's chances of survival. Accordingly Ambassador Dobrynin brought a message from Brezhnev to Kissinger, asking him to fly to Moscow for urgent consultation. During the meeting in Moscow, Kissinger agreed on the necessity for an immediate cease-fire, but insisted that it must, as opposed to previous occasions, be linked to peace talks.

At 9.00 on the evening of 20 October the telephone next to Sadat's chair in the war room rang to advise him that Soviet Ambassador Vladimir Vinogradoff requested an urgent meeting to deliver a message from Brezhnev, meeting at the moment with Kissinger in Moscow. Within half an hour Vinogradoff presented the message to Sadat in which Brezhnev requested him to agree to an immediate cease-fire and attached the proposed resolution which the two super powers were planning to submit to the Security Council which was about to be convened. The note included also a reiteration of the Soviet undertaking to guarantee the cease-fire in the event of Israeli violation. Brezhnev clearly undertook to transfer Soviet troops to Egypt in order to maintain the cease-fire, and hints about this undertaking were made but a few days later both by Sadat and Heikal.

Meanwhile in Israel there was great scepticism about a cease-fire. In fact few believed that one was imminent. Addressing the editors of the press with whom he met every second day during the war, Dayan on 20 October saw no prospect of a cease-fire. Visiting Sharon's division on 21 October Deputy Prime Minister Yigael Allon assured them that they had ample time and that there was no hurry.

Following the agreement on the text of the proposed Security Council resolution to be submitted by the Soviet Union and the United States, Kissinger flew from Moscow to Tel-Aviv and obtained Israel's agreement. The Security Council met at dawn on Monday morning, 22 October, and passed Security Council Resolution No 338 calling for a cease-fire within twelve hours and not later than 6.52 pm on the evening of the 22nd.

Shortly before the cease-fire was to take effect, the weapon whose introduction to the Middle East had led to the final decision to go to war was activated for the first time anywhere in the world. On that day, according to Sadat, a Scud missile was launched against Israel. It landed in the desert of Sinai.

The Israeli push forward was now taking place against the background of urgency following a decision of the Security Council to call a cease-fire for 6.52 pm on the evening of the 22nd and Israel's and Egypt's acceptance thereof. To the north, in Sharon's division, the paratroopers ran into very heavy resistance as they moved northwards, sustaining casualties from infantry and artillery forces. The advance was now taking place along the sweet-water canal and along the main Ismailia–Suez road (Havit) to the west. The mission was to try to take Ismailia, but Egyptian commando resistance blocked the advance. Amnon's brigade lost three tanks at the sewage farm at the outskirts of the town of Ismailia. The bridges on the main road were successfully taken and the forces reached the final bridge across the sweet-water canal. At dusk an infantry battalion commanded by Lieut.-Col. Ephraim moved forward to capture the bridge. But before the mission was accomplished, the cease-fire came into force and Sharon's division remained in place.

On the morning of the 22nd, Moshe Dayan visited Bren and urged him to try to get his forces to the area of Lituf at the confluence of the Little Bitter Lake and the Suez Canal. Bren launched his forces in a pincer movement in order to clear the shores of the lake and the routes running alongside it. Gaby's brigade moved along the Genefa Hills down to the routes along the lake, while Arieh advanced along Asor route to the Havit road in the direction of Lituf. A third southerly prong in the form of Natke's brigade pushed along the main Cairo road (Sarag) in the direction of Suez, turned in a north-easterly direction along the connecting Akal road and headed for Minah, half-way along the Canal between the two lakes and Suez. The Egyptian Third Army was now fighting desperately along the two main routes – Asor and Sarag – leading to Suez from Cairo and mounted counter-attacks against Natke's and Arieh's forces as they advanced. The Israelis enjoyed complete mastery of the air now that the surface-to-air missile danger had been to a great degree removed by the destruction of the sites. The Israeli Air Force joined in the battle, knocking out the tanks which were blocking Natke's and Arieh's advance.

Bar-Lev urged Bren to leave the southern Sarag route and to concentrate the two brigades in the attack on Asor. Finally at noon Bren took his advice and the forces began to move forward. In the afternoon Bren issued orders to his three brigades to storm the enemy forces and reach the Canal before 6 o'clock in the evening. Abandoning caution, the forces charged forward, breaking into the line of military camps along the Little Bitter Lake and reaching the Canal. The Egyptian resistance broke and thousands of their forces withdrew in disorder. One of Arieh's battalions reached the area of Lituf at the southern point of the Little Bitter Lake, mounted the Egyptian rampart and deployed along it. (An Egyptian infantry unit counter-attacked at night with RPG bazookas and grenades, causing casualties and knocking out nine tanks.)

The cease-fire found the Egyptian Third Army with its main supply lines cut, with thousands of troops fleeing in disorder, with entire formations and units cut off and with the forces in the bridgeheads on the east of the Canal in considerable danger. The main army headquarters was cut off from its rear army headquarters. In many parts of the army panic reigned as troops and units tried to flee. In other parts the local commanders organized their units for break-outs. In the 19th Division area the commander transferred units to the west bank and particularly into the town of Suez. Large numbers who had been cut off were fleeing into the town of Suez. Urgent requests were directed to the Egyptian forces pressing from the direction of Cairo to support the forces cut off in the pocket.

The Soviet and Arab propaganda machines were to maintain that the Egyptian Third Army was not cut off at the time of the first cease-fire on 22 October. But it is clear now that the Third Army realized by midday on the 22nd that it was indeed cut off. At that time the commander of the 19th Division informed the Third Army commander that the cutting of the Cairo–Suez road at kilometre 109 by the Israeli forces meant in effect that the army was cut off and isolated. For his part, Gen. Wassel, the Third Army commander, made it clear immediately after to the minister of war that his army was surrounded, cut off from supplies and in danger of complete destruction. He asked for a counter-attack on the besieging Israeli forces, but by this time the Egyptian Command in the field was confused and at a loss.

The situation as seen by the Egyptian commanders in the field at midday on 22 October is best reflected in the following captured records of a conversation recorded in the Third Army. At 12.47 pm the 19th Brigade commander reported to the Third Army commander, 'We emphasize that the cutting [of the Suez–Cairo road] at kilometre 109 has cut off all supplies to you...' A few minutes later at 12.55 the Army commander spoke to Brig. Kabil, saying, 'The Suez road is cut, Kabil. We have to open the Suez road at kilometre 109 where I am locked in and you are on the outside. I tell you, Kabil, that the army is being surrounded. It is not in Arab hands. Open the Suez road for me....'

A few minutes later the Army commander, Gen. Wassel, spoke to Ahmed Ismail, the minister of war, reporting to him that 'Kabil refuses absolutely to co-operate with us....'

Thus, as opposed to the situation along the Egyptian Second Army front, where the cease-fire was being observed, numerous Egyptian units in the Third Army area who had been cut off one from the other were endeavouring either to join up or to break out. As dawn broke those units on the east bank began to engage the Israeli forces facing them from the Egyptian ramparts on the west bank. Fighting broke out along the entire front and as the Egyptian forces attacked, the Israeli forces reacted. Bren ordered his troops to mop up the whole area of the shore of the Bitter Lakes, from the Cabrit Peninsula south to Minah, and to overcome all the pockets in the army camps which had begun to harass his forces. As the news came into Southern Command of Egyptian attacks in every sector of the Third Army front, with heavy fighting going on all the time, Gonen ordered Bren and Magen to deploy their divisions in such a way as to tighten the noose around the Third Army. He set Bren's western limit as the fertilizer plant to the west of the town of Suez, while Magen would move to his west in the direction of the Port of Adabiah.

Bren deployed two brigades, Gaby's and Arieh's, on a 7½-mile front westwards from Minah. At 3 o'clock in the afternoon his forces pushed southwards in a concentrated armoured attack towards the town of Suez. They passed through an area teeming with large numbers of tanks, thousands of infantry, administrative units and supply trains moving around in confusion, numerous anti-tank missile positions and a very heavy concentration of surface-to-air missile batteries. The shock of the armoured punch broke the Egyptian resistance, and Bren's force stormed southwards to the town of Suez, reaching the fertilizer plant and thus cutting off Suez from the Third Army completely. A large number of surface-to-air missile sites were captured, as were thousands of prisoners.

Magen moved down towards Suez along Bren's west flank, leaving a small unit of tanks at the by now famous kilometre 101 on the Cairo–Suez road to protect his west flank in the event of a counter-attack from the direction of Cairo. Gonen ordered him to leave an additional unit of tanks about 8 miles to the east of kilometre 101 in order to support the western flank in the event of an Egyptian counter-attack.

Magen's division, which was by now down to a total of fifty tanks, stormed southwards. Towards evening he moved through Bren's forces along the main Suez road and then around the slopes of Mount Ataka, which dominates the entire area southwards to the Port of Adabiah. Darkness had by now fallen. With his column's lights full on, he charged along the route to the fertilizer plant and thence southwards to Adabiah.

On the 23rd Magen ordered Dan to advance southwards with his brigade, which was now down to seventeen tanks, and to charge through the enemy positions. In the ensuing rapid movement they had on many occasions to pull aside in order to avoid crashing into enemy vehicles. From 2 o'clock in the afternoon to midnight, moving without respite, Dan covered a distance of 30 miles, reaching the Gulf of Suez at Ras Adabiah, where his brigade captured some 800 Egyptian prisoners, including three colonels. As dawn arose they began to mop up and enter the Port of Abadiah. Two torpedo boats raced out of the harbour in a desperate endeavour to escape. Dan's tanks opened fire and sank them.

Feeling very unhappy about the light forces holding the Cairo road, Gonen ordered Magen to hold Adabiah lightly and bring back his main force to the main Cairo–Suez road (Sarag). Magen pulled back and as he moved westwards some 5 miles west of kilometre 101, his tanks ran into an enemy strongpoint which had blocked the main road. All night long his forces fought before they cleared it.

On the morning of the 24th, with the Egyptian forces still fighting, Bren, following advice from Dayan, asked for permission to attack the town of Suez. Gonen's reaction was: 'If it is empty okay. If it is strongly held, no.' Under artillery fire a unit of Gaby's brigade moved forward along the coastal road from the west and occupied the Suez refineries. Arieh's brigade advanced along the main boulevard of the Cairo road into Suez, capturing the army camps on the outskirts of the city. He was followed by a battalion of paratroopers under command of Lieut.-Col. Yossi, and as the tanks moved into the town they were fired on from all the buildings. Within minutes twenty of the twenty-four tank commanders of the column, who were exposed in their turrets, were killed or wounded. The tanks nonetheless continued in their charge forward to the end of the road. The paratroopers came under fire and when some of their vehicles were hit they jumped out and took shelter in the adjoining houses. This had not been envisaged as a major operation against a heavily entrenched enemy, but rather as a routine mopping-up operation against an enemy who was cut off and disintegrating. The troops were therefore psychologically unprepared for such a situation; furthermore they could not even distinguish where the enemy fire was coming from.

All efforts were now concentrated on evacuating the forces cut off in the city. It was very difficult to use artillery or air because the location of the Israeli forces was not clear. Natke's brigade moved down along the agricultural strip from the north, while Gaby's brigade pushed in along the southern coastal road and found the battalion which had broken in at the end of the main boulevard. Gaby evacuated the tank battalion along the coastal road, reaching the refineries by evening. But two groups of paratroopers remained entirely cut off in the centre of the town. Every attempt to reach them cost heavy casualties and was unsuccessful. One unit comprising seventy men managed to slip out under darkness of night and make its way through the dark alleyways and narrow side streets, trying to move without making a sound and carrying the wounded back to the Israeli lines. One of the wounded in this group was the battalion commander himself.

In the second group the battalion commander who had led the force, Lieut.-Col. Yossi, was wounded and semi-conscious. The unit was now under command of a company commander, who did not want to evacuate – the Egyptian forces were on a high adjacent building overlooking him and he felt it would be difficult to move out carrying the wounded. For four hours through the night, in an incredible exchange, Gonen personally coaxed and cajoled the company commander into leaving his position and making a dash for freedom.

At first there was the nerve-racking process of getting the besieged unit to identify on air photographs where it was. After a period of trial and error, Gonen finally identified the actual building. He then planned an artillery box in the centre of which the besieged unit would move until it reached freedom. After hours of planning and urgings on the radio, the company commander finally took the plunge and led the besieged force quietly out, moving from street to street under the directions of Gonen as he read an air photograph, back to the Israeli lines. Suez was a grave error costing some eighty killed.

Early on the 23rd the Soviet Embassy in Washington contacted Secretary of State Kissinger urgently to say that there had been a massive violation of the cease-fire by the Israelis. Kissinger contacted Israeli Ambassador Simcha Dinitz, who maintained that it was the Egyptians who had broken the cease-fire. The Israeli contention was supported by American intelligence experts who confirmed that the Egyptian Third Army commander had, despite orders to the contrary, endeavoured to break out of the Israeli siege. It was clear that the Israeli forces were taking advantage of the Egyptian violation in order to tighten their stranglehold on the Egyptian Third Army. Kissinger now appreciated that rescuing the army could be an important bargaining factor in achieving an ultimate arrangement between the sides with each having a trump card of its own – the Israelis, the besieged Third Army and a presence on the west bank of the Canal; the Egyptians, the bridgeheads on the east bank. Kissinger exerted pressure on Israel through Dinitz and on the 24th a second Security Council resolution was passed again calling for a cease-fire.

Thus on 24 October, with Sharon's division on the outskirts of Ismailia, threatening its links to Cairo; with Bren's and Magen's divisions sealing off completely the Egyptian Third Army; and with Israeli forces holding a corridor on the east bank to the Canal, with three bridges across it, and occupying an area of 1,600 square kilometres inside Egypt down to the Port of Adabiah, the second cease-fire came into effect.

After being caught in circumstances that could well have been fatal, the forces of the Israeli Southern Command had succeeded in turning the tables by carrying out a most daring operation against tremendous odds and in the face of great adversity. They had achieved a major victory by any military standards and had manoeuvred themselves into a position to destroy the Egyptian Army, whose saviour was the Security Council. The Soviet Union had not only made available all the necessary prerequisites for the Egyptian attack, it had also guaranteed against a total débâcle. Indeed, as the Egyptian Third Army turned to Sadat in desperation for supplies, the Soviet Union moved ominously to the brink and readied its airborne divisions for a move to the Middle East.

17

The Air and Naval War

TWO MAIN INFLUENCES combined to fashion Egyptian Air Force thinking about the future air war. The first was the trauma of the three hours on the morning of 5 June 1967, when the Israeli Air Force surprised all the Arab air forces poised to attack Israel – and particularly that of Egypt. Coming in low in a broad sweep from the Mediterranean, the Israelis caught the Egyptian Air Force unprepared even though it had already been in a state of mobilization and stand-to for some three weeks. A highly detailed plan of deception had been evolved by the Israeli Air Force (even to maintaining routine training in the air that morning and planning the strike so that Egyptian officers and pilots were caught *en route* from breakfast in their headquarters to the air bases); the Egyptians were caught comparatively undefended on the ground, in many cases with the aircraft parked in the open – easy prey for the attacking Israeli planes. In three hours the Egyptian Air Force, not to mention the Jordanian and Syrian, ceased to be an element in the battle which was to be waged across the Sinai desert.

A second major factor which guided Egyptian strategy was the paramount influence of Soviet thinking since the so-called Czech arms deal in 1955, when the Soviet Union became the main supplier of arms to Egypt. Over the years hundreds of Egyptian pilots were sent to train in the Soviet Union, and Soviet General Staff officers advised the Egyptian General Staff and participated in Egyptian war games. It is no wonder that gradually the Egyptians, as well as the Syrians, became imbued with Soviet doctrine. But it is relevant to recall here that the air arm has not been the Soviet Union's strong point in war. The Soviet Air Force (unlike those of Great Britain and the United States) was never the outstanding military arm and was never decisive in the major battles which decided World War Two. Furthermore, since that war the Soviets have had no active combat experience: the Egyptian and the other Arab air forces based on Soviet equipment were thus being trained by men with little or no experience of this kind.

The Israeli Air Force in many ways drew its initial experience and traditions from the British Royal Air Force, which marked up a record of combat success and technological advance during World War Two. The predominant element in the Soviet military make-up has invariably been artillery; and the next step from the artillery concept was to that of the missile. The Soviet Union is the only major power in the world in which missilery is organized as an independent arm of service and is therefore a subject that enjoys considerable priority in development and thought.

The experience of the Six Day War had its effect too on the thinking of the Israeli Air Force in its planning for the future. On the eve of that war Arab armies had massed around Israel with a total of 250,000 troops, some 2,000 tanks and some 600–700 first-line planes. Faced with the problem of the lack of strategic depth at the time, the General Staff proposed a pre-emptive attack under conditions of total air superiority (the Air Force was willing to guarantee this superiority provided that it could choose the date and hour of attack and would be permitted to commit its force totally to destroying the Arab air forces). Thus the Israeli attack in the Six Day War was one borne out of a lack of strategic alternative; thereafter, the Air Force operated in direct support of the advancing forces, incurring an accepted average rate of loss (losing 46 planes out of approximately 200 and burying 26 pilots).

In the War of Attrition – from March 1969 to August 1970 – Israeli artillery was greatly outnumbered by Egyptian concentrations, and Israeli casualties along the Canal rose to alarming proportions. An answer to this artillery preponderance had to be produced, and that answer turned out to be the Israeli Air Force. Hitherto it had been reluctant to commit its strength because of the risk of frittering away aircraft in relatively unessential operations, instead of conserving them for a major conflagration. By July 1969, however, air power began to be used as a major factor in security operations, including attacks on encampments of Palestinian terrorists in Jordan, Syria and Lebanon.

There was a school of opinion in the Israeli Air Force that maintained that when the Air Force went into action during the War of Attrition in July 1969, a fatal error was committed: the move was a classic case of the misuse of air power. Furthermore, the comfortable feeling that Israeli air power provided an answer to overwhelming Arab preponderance in artillery soothed any sense of urgency about building Israel's artillery strength. For years the Israeli Command deluded itself into believing that air power was the answer to the problem of the country's weakness in artillery – hence the very unrealistic ratio of forces in artillery during the Yom Kippur War. Worse yet, this error in concept created a disadvantage for the Air Force itself.

The Egyptian defence against the Israeli introduction of air power was a network of SAM 2 missiles along the front. But by the autumn of 1969 the Israeli Air Force had the measure of the SAM 2 surface-to-air missiles and during late September and early October had succeeded in destroying a great part of that system and many radar stations. Indeed, after about six weeks of such operations, the Egyptians were bereft of any air defence potential along the Suez front, apart from their aircraft – which they were unwilling to commit.

The destruction of the Soviet-built anti-aircraft system in Egypt disturbed not only the Egyptians but the Soviet Union as well. It is not surprising, therefore, that when Israel began its deep-penetration air raids into Egypt in January 1970, and Nasser turned to the Soviet Union for aid, the Soviet response was immediate and unhesitating. Indeed, the Soviets seized on Nasser's desperate invitation, as it accorded with their own plans for penetration into the area. By 19 February reports were published in the West announcing the arrival in Egypt of 1,500 Soviet personnel with consignments of SAM 3 missiles. The missiles, with their increased mobility and effectiveness, were manned by Soviets and were sited both in the Canal zone and in depth in Egypt. Soviet units – which reached proportions of 15,000–20,000 troops in air defence, missile and air-force units – assumed responsibility for the protection of Egyptian strategic depth and created a situation whereby an Israeli penetration of Egyptian air space could spell a clash with Soviet forces. (Indeed, on 31 July 1970, an Israeli air patrol encountered what later proved to have been a Soviet-piloted patrol mission in the area of the Suez Canal, and in the ensuing dog fight five Soviet planes were shot down – with no loss to the Israelis.) in mid-April however the Israeli deep-penetration bombing of Egypt ceased.

The decision to bomb Egypt in depth would appear to have been a major error in many respects. Politically the raids failed to achieve their objectives and Nasser's authority was in no way undermined. Although Egypt's surface-to-air defence system was at times in ruins, the Egyptians persevered with their attacks along the Canal, though the scope of Israeli losses was greatly reduced. However, the most important development was a secret visit made by Nasser to Moscow in January 1970. During his visit Nasser presented the military dilemma facing the Egyptians as a result of the Israeli attacks and also the problems which might face his regime if these attacks were to persevere. A very marked escalation in Soviet involvement in the area was in fact in process. Whether this would have been a natural path of events or not is difficult to say. But there is no doubt but that the Israeli decision to bomb Egypt in depth constituted a major turning point in the Middle East and created a situation which led President Nasser to open up Egypt not only to Soviet advisers but also to Soviet combat units.

The war grew in intensity, but diplomatic moves were afoot to bring it to an end. Following the Rogers Plan (proposed by United States Secretary of State William Rogers) a cease-fire between Egypt and Jordan on the one hand and Israel on the other came into effect on 7 August 1970.

The surface-to-air missiles were beginning to take their toll of Israeli planes, however, and the cease-fire came about at a point when a number of questions relating to the issue of planes against missiles remained unanswered. Immediately after the cease-fire went into effect, the Egyptians and Soviets, in breach of an undertaking reached with the United States and Israel, moved the missile system forward towards the Suez Canal under cover of darkness, enabling them to control a strip of air space on its eastern side.

The experience of the Egyptian Air Force in the War of Attrition only strengthened their evaluation that a major factor in their strategy for the next war must be their ability to attack the Israeli Air Force bases in depth. This created a requirement for an attack force of medium-range bombers or fighter bombers. Without planes of this type (such as the Sukhoi 20, the Jaguar, the Mirage or the Phantom) there would be little prospect of winning a war. But in about April 1973, the Soviets convinced their Egyptian clients that the correct use of surface-to-air missiles could enable them to change their basic concept. This change in approach was reflected in the Soviet supply policy, and over a short period in July and August 1973 they also built up the greater part of the missile system protecting Syria in which the new SAM 6 missile constituted three-fifths of the force (the other two-fifths were composed of SAM 2 and SAM 3 missiles).

The concentrated effort to supply the missiles within a short period of time, the 'mix' of the various types of missiles, the timing of the supply, all point to Soviet involvement in the change in concept which enabled the Egyptians to decide to go to war at this early stage. This whole picture of the re-evaluation of Egyptian air policy coupled with the rapid construction of the missile system in Syria can only give added credence to the assumption of Soviet connivance in the planning of the war and the active preparations leading to it.

The Israeli Air Force prepared for the coming war on the assumption that at the outbreak of the conflict it would be given adequate time to concentrate on the missile threat, without being involved in interdiction or close support in the first phase. Apart from the defence of Israeli air space, the Air Force was to enjoy a certain latitude without being obliged to care for the ground forces.

On 13 September 1973 a routine Israeli patrol off the coast of Syria, in the area of Latakia, tangled with Syrian air units, and in the course of the ensuing dog fights the Israeli force shot down thirteen Syrian planes for the loss of one Israeli plane. Gen. Benjamin Peled, the commander of the Israeli Air Force, realized that such a result was bound to bring on a retaliatory Syrian move, such as mass artillery bombardment. And if the Syrians reacted in this way, the problem posed by over thirty Syrian surface-to-air missile batteries of hyper-sensitive SAM 6s would be a very serious one. By Friday, 5 October, the Air Force had been placed on a high level of preparedness, with its combat effectives fully mobilized. Peled ordered his planners to prepare a pre-emptive strike.

Gen. Peled was the first Israeli Air Force commander produced entirely in Israel. A fighter pilot, he had been shot down by ground fire at Sharm el-Sheikh in the 1956 Sinai Campaign and had evaded capture when an Israeli Piper Cub which had landed in the desert literally snatched him from the hands of his would-be captors. An unknown in many ways, he proved himself in the war to be an outstanding commander of an elite force. His restraint, calm confidence and cool-headedness inspired all around him with confidence. He at no time underestimated his adversaries, but neither did he underestimate the force he led. Early in the war he attended an off-the-record briefing given by Minister of Defence Moshe Dayan to the editors of the Israeli press. Peled reported on the air war and mentioned in passing the loss of an Israeli plane that morning of which the crew was missing. While he was speaking a note was passed to him; he read it and commented, 'interesting'. Looking up he reported that the missing pilot and navigator had been recovered by a rescue team and were on their way back to their airfield. At this point Dayan interjected that the pilot was Peled's son. 'Yes,' said Peled, adding with an expressionless look on his face, 'and tonight they will be in action again.'

In the early hours of Saturday morning Peled advised the chief of staff that he was ready to carry out a pre-emptive strike between 11.00 and midday (his plan had to be changed because of low cloud which set in over the Golan Heights). But at 12.30 he was notified by Elazar that such a strike had not been approved by the government. The intelligence information available was that the war would begin at 6.00 in the evening, but this H hour made little sense to Gen. Peled, and he therefore assumed for his own purposes that it would begin closer to 3 o'clock in the afternoon; it did not seem logical to him that the Arabs would launch a war without allowing time for at least two initial air strikes, for which they would require a few hours of daylight.

Although a pre-emptive air strike was rejected, no objection was raised to deterring in the air, and at 1.30 in the afternoon Peled ordered units of the Air Force to patrol at a height so that the Arabs would note that even on Yom Kippur planes were on patrol. But two minutes after two Israeli planes had taken off from the field in Sharm el-Sheikh, twelve Egyptian planes attacked it; the two that had taken off in time however succeeded in shooting down seven of the attackers. At 1.45 there was information from the front that the Syrians were preparing to move. Hurrying to his command post Peled was met with the news that planes were taking off in Syria and in Egypt. He knew that this was war.

As reports poured in indicating a massive crossing of the Canal by five Egyptian divisions, it became clear to Gen. Peled that he must shelve all operational plans designed to deal exclusively with the enemy missile force. He realized quickly that both the Egyptian and the Syrian strategy was to swamp the Israeli defences by sheer weight of numbers, and he was only too aware of the dangerous imbalance of forces giving an overall advantage to the Arab attackers. The developments on the Egyptian front appeared to be particularly dangerous. He committed the Air Force against the forces crossing the Suez Canal along a front of some 100 miles from Port Said in the north to Suez in the south and also against a concentration of small boats at Ras Zafrani in the Gulf of Suez, which was preparing to cross the Gulf with a large commando force. The assumption that a broad, five-division, frontal attack along the entire length of the Suez Canal would oblige the Israelis to spread their air attacks over a wide area, with a resultant loss of effectiveness, was (according to Egyptian Chief of Staff Gen. Shazli) one of the factors favouring such a strategy. The Egyptian assumptions were vindicated.

Four Israeli planes were lost in the first strike. Thereafter the situation can be described only as bedlam, with the Air Force spread to its utmost and with insistent demands for air support pouring in from all along the front – from the hard-pressed fortifications along the Bar-Lev line, from units along the Gulf of Suez as far south as Sharm el-Sheikh, and from units fighting a desperate holding battle in the Golan Heights. All this, while the Air Force also had to ensure that the skies over Israel were kept 'clean'.

The Israeli Air Force fought a desperate battle, flying into the teeth of one of the most concentrated missile systems in the world. But because of the improvised nature of the Israeli response to the surprise attack, it was unable to deal with its main threat – the missile systems of Egypt and Syria – as planned.

There were 150 batteries in Egypt composed of SAM 2 and SAM 3 batteries (with six launching pads per battery) and SAM 6 batteries (each with 12 missiles ready for launching on 4 tanks). Of the 150 batteries, some 50 were concentrated along the Suez Canal front; in Syria most of them were deployed in the area of the front line.

The mobile SAM 6, with an effective range of 22,000 metres, fits into a comprehensive pattern provided by the comparatively static SAM 2 (with a range of 50,000 metres) and the more mobile SAM 3 (30,000 metres). Each of these weapons possesses different electronic guidance characteristics, which complicates the application of electronic counter-measures. The main advantage of the SAM 6 lies in its mobility. It is mounted on a tank chassis and can be moved into action rapidly, requiring only minutes to be folded up before being moved to an alternative site and then another short period to be ready for action again. To seek out a SAM 6 missile, a plane must of necessity enter the range of the SAM 2. If one adds to this formidable interlocked system hundreds of SAM 7, portable, Strela missile launchers organized in platoons in the ground forces, together with conventional anti-aircraft weapons (in particular the multi-barrelled ZSU 23), there is little wonder that the Egyptians and their Soviet advisers were convinced that from the point of view of anti-aircraft defence their forces were well protected.

The attack of the Egyptian Air Force heralded the major onslaught on 6 October. Their attacks were not directed in particular against Israeli formations, but were concentrated rather on airfields, radar installations, headquarters and camps in Sinai, all comparatively close to the front line (the normal depth of their penetration was west of a line passing through Baluza, Refidim, Tasa and the Mitla Pass). The Syrians on the other hand concentrated their attacks on the Israeli combat forces. The very limited depth of penetration by the Arab air force was adhered to throughout, with some exceptions. The deepest penetration was an attempt late in the war by six Egyptian Mirages (supplied by the French to the Libyans) to attack the area of El Arish, flying in from the sea; three of them were shot down over the sea. Other attempts included two Egyptian Tupolev 16 bombers which failed in a mission to reach Eilat, with one crashing near Abu Rudeis; and two Syrian Sukhoi 20 planes bound for the Haifa bay area, one of which crashed over Nahariya while the second fled to Syria. The second Syrian attempt at deep penetration was with four Sukhoi 20s, three of which crashed in the area of Mount Miron in the upper Galilee. The Egyptians tried to make up for their failure to bomb in depth by launching Kelt air-to-surface missiles from over Egyptian territory (in general these missiles were launched from deep inside Egypt). One such missile aimed at Tel Aviv on the afternoon of 6 October was shot out of the air by an Israeli pilot on patrol. Of twenty-five Kelts fired at Israeli targets, it was reported that twenty were shot down by the Israeli Air Force and only two succeeded in causing damage.

The Egyptian and Syrian air efforts were thus concentrated in direct support of their forces in the general area of the front line. The first moves in the war were accompanied by a major attempt to transport heli- copter-borne troops behind the Israeli front lines in order to harass Israeli units moving up to the front and to support advancing Egyptian forces. Some thirty-five Egyptian helicopters, many of them loaded with troops, were destroyed in the first days of the war.

The hard-pressed Israeli Air Force concentrated its attacks in the first hours of the Egyptian crossing in an attempt to help the Israeli regular forces. Its effort was enormous, but to the troops on the ground it appeared to be insig- nificant. On the night of 6–7 October Defence Minister Dayan telephoned Gen. Peled and painted a most depressing picture of the situation on the Syrian front, advising him to transfer all his efforts there. At 7.00 on the morning of the 7th, the Air Force carried out an interdiction flight over Egypt and then moved to a concentrated attack on Syria, which proved to be a tragic one with Israeli planes being shot down. The Israeli forces fighting on the Golan Heights watched in horror as the skies filled with the undulating trails created by dozens of missiles as they streaked up to the Israeli planes. Hard-pressed as they were, they cancelled their calls for air support.

On Monday, 8 October, mindful of a plan to regroup Israeli forces along the main lateral artery in preparation for a counter-attack along the Suez Canal, Gen. Peled ordered the Air Force to concentrate on the Egyptian bridges across the Suez. In the face of the missile danger, which took its toll, the bridges were attacked incessantly and all but one of the fourteen were hit. Despite later disclaimers, Gen. Taha Al Maghdoub, the Egyptian deputy chief of operations, describes in his book *The Ramadan War* the desperate Israeli Air Force attacks, confirming that nearly all the bridges were hit by their air attacks, some of them not less than five times (in one of these attacks, the deputy -commander of Egyptian Army engineers, Gen. Hamdi, was killed). However, the extremely flexible construction of the Soviet bridges enabled them to be repaired rapidly and put into full use under cover of darkness. During daylight many of them were lashed to one of the banks, to be towed out and activated only as darkness fell. Referring to the Israeli air attacks after the war, Gen. Shazli explained that this flexibility allowed for their repair by an exchange of sections 'in a matter, at times, of half an hour to an hour'. Furthermore, des- cribing how they constantly changed their location in order to mislead the Israeli pilots, he maintained that the SAM 7 Strela infantry-operated surface- to-air missile was very effective against the low-flying aircraft attacking the bridges.

In the first phase of the fighting – the holding phase – the Israeli Air Force was unable to attack as planned and was obliged to throw caution to the winds and give close support (a good proportion of the sorties made were in close support of ground forces), without dealing adequately with the missile threat and achieving complete air superiority. Consequently losses were comparatively heavy. But as soon as the holding phase had been completed, it was freer to plan its close support operations in a more selective manner. Thereafter the ratio of losses dropped considerably.

Despite the losses sustained, the Israeli Air Force persevered in its attack and at no point relented. As the Israeli ground forces advanced into Syria and came within artillery range of Damascus, the Air Force succeeded in destroying part of the Syrian missile system and was ranging far and wide into Syria, attacking strategic targets – oil installations, power plants, bridges – and occasioning considerable damage to the Syrian infrastructure. On one day of the battle because of the state of the airfields in the area the Syrian Air Force was reduced to landing on a wide motor route (planned for this purpose) in the vicinity of Damascus. Although the Syrians pressed home a series of hit-and-run attacks against the Israeli-held enclave, flying low with MIG 17s to bomb while MIG 21s patrolled above, and proved to be somewhat better than the Egyptians, the Israelis achieved and maintained complete superiority. (Of 222 Syrian planes lost in the war, 162 were destroyed in air combat.)

On the Egyptian front the Israeli Air Force attacked missile sites and enemy airfields, but above all gave close support. The Egyptians however, although they attacked from time to time, did not press their attacks with any great vigour or determination. This equivocal behaviour in attack was characteristic until, on 18 October, the Egyptian Command at last appreciated the significance of the Israeli crossing on the west bank of the Suez Canal. Here the Egyptian Air Force, defending its homeland, proved to be more daring and more persistent in attack. World War Two-type air encounters were seen again, with forty to fifty planes in the air at times; but again the Israeli planes held the upper hand. Indeed, throughout the war the Egyptians succeeded in downing only 5 Israeli planes in air battle, as against 172 Egyptian planes lost in the same manner, making a total of 334 Arab planes against 5 Israeli planes downed in air-to-air combat (in the Six Day War, 50 Arab planes had been shot down in air-to-air combat against an Israeli loss of 10 planes).

The air battle was waged on, with the Israeli Air Force gaining a freer hand as missile positions on the west bank of the Canal were neutralized or destroyed by the advancing Israeli ground forces. Despite the formidable nature of this missile weapon, the Israeli air attacks nibbled away at it as well. Of a total of some fifty-five to sixty missile batteries in the front-line area in Egypt on 6 October, some forty were hit or destroyed, about twenty-eight of them by Israeli Air

Force attacks and twelve by ground forces. On 9, 10 and 12 October, attacks were mounted against the five missile batteries in Port Said, and by 13 October Port Said air space was open and remained without any missile defence until the end of the war; persistent air attacks against nine missile batteries in the area of Kantara made this area missile-free by 14 October. From 21 October most of the area of the Egyptian Second Army, the whole area of the Egyptian Third Army on the east bank of the Canal and the area of the Gulf of Suez to Ras Adabiah were missile-free. As the main Israeli effort developed on the west bank of the Canal, with the bulk of the Israeli forces committed there, the Israeli forces facing the Second and Third Egyptian Armies on the east bank proved inadequate to take advantage of the fact that missiles no longer protected the Egyptian bridgeheads. At this stage the Israeli Air Force was ranging freely over a wide area of the battlefield, having maintained pressure without let-up on the Arab air forces.

As had occurred with the IDF, so the Air Force did not enter the war according to plan and had to fight against very heavy odds, meeting for the first time in modern warfare the type of surface-to-air missile that will characterize future wars. Nevertheless, the Air Force performed a vital role in the battle Whenever the Egyptian ground forces moved out of the missile umbrella – as they did when their armour moved southwards towards Abu Rudeis – the Israeli Air Force was the major factor in destroying them. At the other end of the front, the Air Force kept Port Said and Port Fuad under constant attack and protected the Budapest fortification. It was instrumental in protecting the area of Sharm el-Sheikh by interdicting the helicopter-borne commando forces. Furthermore, the skies over Israel remained 'clean' throughout the war: not one bomb fell in Israel and the Air Force infrastructure remained unaffected. The maintenance of air superiority also had political implications however. King Hussein explained to his Arab colleagues that a major consideration in Jordan's unwillingness to commit its forces against Israeli territory was Israel's control of the air over the potential battlefield.

According to published figures, the Arab air force entered the war with some 800 first-line planes; creating a ratio of some 3 : 1 in their favour. In addition, during the war they received a total reinforcement of 172 planes from other Arab countries (of which 109 were delivered to Syria and 63 to Egypt). The total losses of the Egyptians and Syrians were 514 planes, some 58 of which were shot down by their own forces; Israeli losses were a total of 102 planes of which according to Minister of Defence Dayan, 50 were lost in the first three days. The bulk of the Israeli losses were caused by missiles and conventional anti-aircraft fire, with the number divided between the two, particularly during close-support missions. Four times as many sorties were made as in 1967. Nevertheless Israeli losses per sortie indicate that despite having to operate within the missile and air-defence environment, the attrition rate was considerably lower in the Yom Kippur War than in the Six Day War.

Air warfare has become a highly involved and complicated affair, but nevertheless, as in all those areas in which human judgement and ability count as in air-to-air combat, the Israeli Air Force maintained its supremacy. The missile had not rendered the aircraft obsolete. Contrary to the general impression gained abroad, the figures reveal that despite these missiles the Israeli Air Force marked up achievements of considerable magnitude. Obviously the whole new generation of stand-off-type air-launched weapons and tactical surface-to-surface missiles, which should enable anti-missile battery operations to be mounted out of the range of the enemy missiles, will change considerably the conditions in the field of battle, while surface-to-air missilery will be based to an increasing degree on highly mobile platforms, such as the SAM 6, the French Crotale or the Franco-German Roland.

The Yom Kippur War will have given additional impetus to the development of anti-missile battery stand-off weapons, and in turn a defensive system will be developed for them. The conflict was a major proving ground from which many will have drawn their lessons. Despite the manner in which the Israeli Air Force acquitted itself in the face of the missiles, there is no doubt but that many of the accepted concepts about air war will have to be re-evaluated. The role of the plane in war has changed, and new strategies and uses of air power will have to be evolved. To a degree air power will obviously not be as influential as it has been and will affect the battlefield less than it did. The proliferation of light, portable missile launchers in the front line means that close support will be the exception to the rule in the future, with the air force being obliged to concentrate on isolating the field of battle, maintaining supremacy in the air and destroying the forces in and near the field of battle.

The Israeli Navy had not experienced a 'good war' in 1967. Indeed the naval command was only too aware of the fact that Israeli equipment was inadequate and could not answer the challenge posed by the Egyptian Navy, one of the most formidable indigenous navies in the Mediterranean. The Six Day War found the Israeli Navy with the right ideas but without the ability to apply them. Specially designed missile boats were under construction in the shipyards of Cherbourg, but none had been delivered.

The Israeli Navy had in many senses been the 'Cinderella' of the IDF, a result of a basic assumption that any war which took place between Israel and the Arab countries had of necessity to be a short one with a decision being achieved only by means of ground operations enjoying air superiority. No one ever assumed that Israel would have to think in terms of a long naval war, including the convoying of a large merchant fleet.

President Nasser on the other hand undertook the construction of a navy early in his regime, and particularly after military support from the Soviet Union became available. But when viewing the naval development of Egypt, sight must not be lost of the fact that President Nasser was obsessed by what he believed to be the danger posed to Egypt by the presence in the Mediterranean of the Western navies. He lived in constant fear and suspicion of the West, believing that some form of agreement existed between Israel and the West guaranteeing Israel's naval defence. The Soviets had been quite happy to supply Egypt with large vessels – such as the Skory destroyers and the W-type ocean-going submarines – not because they had any illusions whatsoever about Egyptian naval prowess, but because they realized that their supply would oblige the Egyptians to create an infrastructure capable of berthing and maintaining vessels of this type, which in turn guaranteed to the Soviet Navy future naval facilities in Egypt, with all the necessary supplies and equipment to maintain Soviet-type ships.

The Egyptians therefore had developed a balanced navy dictated by strategic considerations as they saw them. Their fleet included a sizeable landing-craft force and they were conducting negotiations for missile-carrying destroyers. Then the Six Day War precipitated a crisis: the Western navies were neutralized by the appearance of the Soviet Fifth Fleet in the Mediterranean, while the Israeli danger did not materialize. The Egyptian Navy therefore lost its priority in the Egyptian forces: its development programmes were limited and losses were not made up (indeed, it was not strengthened until 1971–2). By then it had become evident that Israel was quietly building a balanced naval force.

Unlike the ground and air forces of the Israel Defence Forces, the Israeli Navy, after its uninspiring record in the Six Day War, had sustained two tragic losses: the INS destroyer *Eilat* (sunk by missiles off Port Said) and the INS submarine *Dakar* (lost with all hands *en route* from Great Britain to Israel in the east Mediterranean). The construction of a completely new navy was accordingly undertaken. When all twelve of the so-called Cherbourg boats had arrived in Israel by December 1969, they were fitted out with Israeli-built missiles. The Israeli Navy began to develop its own doctrine and to train for the next war: in many ways it was the single element in the IDF that prepared for the next war, without being influenced by the previous one.

The Gabriel missile, with a range of some 12 miles, was developed by Israel as a reply to the destroyers in the Egyptian Navy and, in particular, as an answer to the 5-inch guns mounted on the Soviet-built Skory-type destroyers, with a maximum range of 16,000 yards. But it was also necessary to develop tactics against the Egyptian Styx missiles, with their range of more than 30 miles. The Israeli solution to this problem was reached by intensive development in three fields: electronic warfare, the manœuvrability of their vessels, and the ability of the navy to strike home with missiles while approaching the enemy. In addition the Israeli Navy decided to construct ships in Israel itself and adapt them to the area in which they were due to operate: both the Mediterranean and the Red Sea required a longer-range capability than that available in the Cherbourg boats; indeed, the Israeli-built vessels increased the range two-fold and almost doubled the fire power. A special type of patrol boat for operation against Palestinian terrorist activities and for operations in the Gulf of Suez was also developed.

As the Israeli Navy – based on a fleet of missile boats – grew, the Egyptian naval command realized that the appearance of naval surface-to-surface missiles required a radical change in its own tactics and planning. By 1971–2 the Egyptians found themselves with twelve Osa-type missile boats, in addition to a number of Komar-type boats, facing twelve modern Israeli missile boats. Furthermore, the Egyptians had problems with the Styx missile, which had been developed by the Soviet Union in the late 1950s as a weapon against American task forces of ships the size of destroyer and above. The Egyptians were concerned lest this missile would not be effective against the small targets offered by the Israeli missile boats. Indeed, on 30 May 1970, this concern was vindicated when the Egyptians attacked an Israeli fishing vessel near Lake Bardawil (off the coast of Sinai) with four missiles. Not one of the missiles hit the target (which sank because of a near miss). With concern about the efficacy of the missile thus heightened, they began to improvise and even mounted rocket launchers with a range of 12 miles on their torpedo boats.

In the month before the Yom Kippur War, there was very little change in the deployment of the Egyptian Navy; but there were enough moves to arouse the suspicions of the Israeli naval intelligence, and on 30 September the senior Israeli naval intelligence officer decided that war was imminent. A state of emergency was declared in the Israeli Navy on 1 October, but when GHQ intelligence indicated that this was exaggerated, it was lowered. But Rear Adm. Telem, commander of the Israeli Navy, decided to maintain a higher state of preparedness than normal on the basis of his intelligence officer's estimate, despite the calm at GHQ. And by 5 o'clock on the morning of 6 October the entire naval force was deployed for operation both against the Syrian Navy and against the Egyptian Navy.

On the eve of the war a force of Egyptian submarines was deployed in the central Mediterranean, east of Crete. And for most of the war it prowled about the sea without causing any damage: the sum total of its effectiveness was the sinking of two innocent Greek freighters, one north-west of Alexandria and the second further west in the Mediterranean. When in the later stage of the war Israeli operations began to threaten Egypt, part of this force was withdrawn in order to protect the Egyptian coast.

The war began with the main Egyptian force in the Mediterranean: it consisted of twelve Osa-type missile boats, ten submarines, six advanced-type torpedo boats and some twenty regular torpedo boats, in addition to three destroyers and two frigates, minesweepers, patrol boats and eleven LCT landing craft. The Syrian order of battle included nine missile boats (three Osa-type and six Komar-type), eleven torpedo boats and two minesweepers. Against this combined force, was ranged a force of fourteen Israeli missile boats.

Despite the fact that the Syrian Navy had a very low priority in the armed forces, in the year preceding the war the Soviets began to supply missile boats of the Osa class. The threat of these boats – coupled with the vulnerability of the Syrian coast with its numerous strategic targets – convinced Adm. Telem that a special task force must be available to deal with the Syrian Navy. And so on the night of 6–7 October a force of five Israeli missile boats set out into the darkness to patrol the coast of Syria at a distance of some 200 miles from their base. As the Israeli naval forces moved north past the Lebanese coast and parallel to the Syrian coast opposite Cyprus, a Syrian torpedo boat to the north was identified at 10.28 pm. The Israelis closed in and it turned to withdraw rapidly eastwards towards the Syrian coast. Fire was opened and in the ensuing battle the Syrian torpedo boat sank.

The Israeli force had by now turned eastwards and was sweeping towards the Syrian coast opposite Latakia in two parallel forces, the southern force including the INS *Reshef*. (*Reshef* was the first Israeli designed and constructed naval vessel ever to enter naval combat.) As the force closed in on the coast, it sighted a minesweeper – which was engaged by the *Reshef* with missile fire and sunk. But lying in wait due south of the minesweeper the force now observed a Syrian force of three missile boats – the torpedo boat had been a warning outpost, the minesweeper a form of decoy while the Syrian force was deployed to attack the Israeli vessels from the flank as they were engaging it. The Israelis turned south and joined battle with the missile boats, which fired a volley of missiles at their approach. The Israeli force sailed in parallel columns southwards and manoeuvred so that the Syrian force found itself sandwiched between them. At 11.35 battle was joined: volleys of missiles were fired first by both sides. Within twenty-five minutes the three Syrian vessels had been sunk. The battle of Latakia, the first naval missile battle in history, had been won by the Israeli Navy without sustaining any casualties.

On the same night a second force of missile boats closed in on the area of

THE NAVAL THEATRE

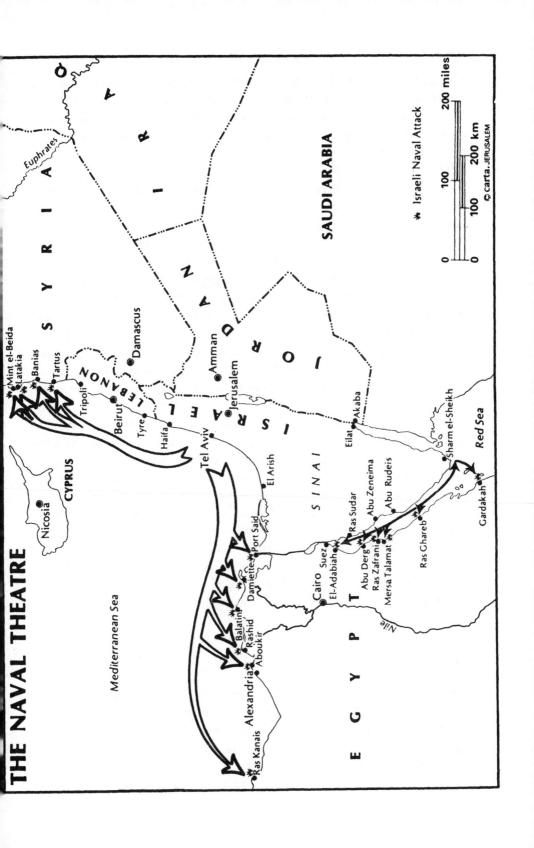

Mediterranean Sea

CYPRUS
Nicosia

SYRIA
Mint el-Beida
Latakia
Banias
Tartus
Damascus
Tripoli
LEBANON
Beirut
Tyre
Haifa
Euphrates
IRAQ

Tel Aviv
El Arish
Jerusalem
Amman
JORDAN

ISRAEL
Akaba
Eilat

SAUDI ARABIA

SINAI

Port Said
Damietta
Balatine
Rashid
Aboukir
Alexandria
Ras Kanais

Cairo
El-Adabiah
Suez
Ras Sudar
Abu Derg
Ras Zafrani
Mersa Talamat
Abu Zeneima
Abu Rudeis

Ras Chareb

Gardakah

Sharm el-Sheikh

Red Sea

Nile

EGYPT

✳ Israeli Naval Attack

0   100   200 miles
0   100   200 km

© carta JERUSALEM

Port Said. (The Egyptians had planned to engage Israeli ground targets with rocket fire from specially equipped rocket-launching torpedo boats). When the Israeli force was sighted, the Egyptians turned and withdrew; the Israelis closed in but this time it was their aircraft which succeeded in sinking one Egyptian missile boat.

The Israeli naval forces persisted in their aggressive action, closing in night after night on the Syrian and Egyptian coasts and obliging both countries to tie down comparatively large forces – armoured and artillery – along the coasts (an entire armoured brigade was deployed to protect the Syrian coast).

The second naval battle of significance, that of Damiette-Balatin on the Mediterranean coast of Egypt, took place on the night of 8–9 October. A force of six Israeli missile boats approached the Egyptian coast to shell the military installations and coastal defences in the area of Daniette. Just on midnight an Egyptian force of four missile boats engaged the Israelis with missile fire. Still outranged, the Israeli force moved in at full speed, and as they observed the Israelis approaching undeterred by the missile fire, the Egyptians turned and began to withdraw. Three of the Israeli boats launched their missiles, and in a matter of forty minutes three Egyptian boats had been sunk, while the fourth disappeared out of range.

A new-found feeling of confidence, daring and *esprit de corps* motivated the Israeli Navy, which now began to harass the enemy naval forces and coasts with ever-increasing daring and initiative. On the night of 10–11 October a missile force attacked the Port of Mint el-Beida (a Syrian naval port near Latakia) and also the oil tank farm at Banias. In the ensuing fighting in which the Israeli force encountered fire from a large concentration of 100 mm and 130 mm radar-operated coastal batteries, two Syrian missile boats were hit and ran aground on the shore. On the next night four Israeli missile boats attacked the Syrian port of Tartus and the oil tank farm north of it. Again a very heavy concentration of artillery engaged the Israeli vessels and again two Syrian missile boats were hit by Israeli missile fire. Most of the tank farms went up in flames.

The ferocity, daring and dash of the Israeli attacks had their effect on the Syrian and Egyptian navies. In the first phase of the war the Syrians engaged the Israeli Navy on the high seas, while the Egyptian Navy attacked targets along the Sinai coast. This phase continued for the first three nights of the war – until the battle of Damiette-Balatin. In the second phase the Arab navies adopted the tactic of making quick sorties from the shelter of harbour, firing their missiles and retiring immediately to take shelter beside the merchant ships in the harbour and behind breakwaters.

As the Israeli pressure mounted, the Arab navies moved into the third phase of activity, where they endeavoured to fire their missiles from the mouth of the harbour without emerging into the open seas, while relying for protection on a very heavy concentration of coastal artillery, strengthened by armoured forces along the coast. Thus on the night of 13–14 October Israeli naval forces shelled Damiette with no Egyptian naval reaction. Again on the night of 19–20 October, when the Israeli forces shelled the same area, Israeli missile boats sailed with impunity along the coast of the Nile delta without encountering interference. On the night of 21–22 October, a force of Israeli missile boats closed in on Aboukir near Alexandria and sank two Egyptian radar boats, taking a number of prisoners. They then engaged and damaged a coastal radar station with missile fire. At this point the Egyptian forces fired four shore-to-sea missiles, but without registering hits. As Israeli harassing operations (which included action by naval commando units against targets in Egyptian ports) increased, the Arab naval reaction became weaker and weaker, although to protect themselves against penetration by the Israeli frogmen, the Egyptians did drop thousands of anti-personnel charges in their ports every night. One such Israeli commando operation in the harbour of Port Said caused the loss of a tank-landing craft, a missile boat and a torpedo boat. Israeli naval commandos were so active in the naval port of Gardaka, for instance, that towards the end of the war the port was evacuated completely by the Egyptian Navy.

With the outbreak of war the Egyptians had declared a naval blockade in the Red Sea, in the area north of the 23rd parallel (they had previously taken steps to base two Skory-type destroyers and some ancillary craft in the port of Aden). A screen of two submarines based itself on Port Sudan and on the morning of 7 October attacked an Israeli-bound oil tanker in full daylight, firing three torpedos but missing the target. Further north, in the Gulf of Suez, the Egyptians took action to blockade the Abu Rudeis-Eilat route used by Israeli chartered tankers carrying oil from the fields of Sinai to the port of Eilat. With the outbreak of hostilities they launched an attack of naval vessels and helicopter-borne commandos against the Israeli-held coast of Sinai on the Gulf of Suez. Missile boats and torpedo boats based on the Egyptian port of Gardaka closed in on Ras Muhamad and Sharm el-Shiekh, engaging Israeli vessels and land-based targets.

Large-scale commando landings from helicopters took place along the route southwards and in depth to prevent any Israeli reinforcements from moving towards the coast. In addition a large fleet of small vessels in anchorages and fishing ports along the Gulf of Suez was to ferry forces and supplies across to the advancing Egyptian forces. On the first night of the war the Israelis identified a concentration of boats in the Bay of Mersa Talamat, south of Ras Zafrani.

Two Israeli patrol boats mounting 20 mm guns attacked and destroyed part of the force, which was just about to sail with Egyptian commandos for Abu Rudeis. The Israeli attack created havoc, and the Egyptian operation was disrupted before it got under way.

On a number of occasions the Egyptians pressed their attack along the Israeli-held Sinai coast, but Israeli pressure developed and within a few days the Israeli Navy was in complete command of the Gulf of Suez. On the night of 8–9 October a battle took place off the Egyptian coast at Ras Sadaat in which an Egyptian de Castro-type patrol boat was sunk despite the support it received from radar-operated land-based 130mm coastal guns. Five nights later a force of five Israeli patrol boats entered the anchorage at Ras Ghareb, where over fifty Egyptian small craft were concentrated to move across the Gulf of Suez. In the ensuing close-range *mêlée* nineteen armed Egyptian fishing boats were sunk.

During the war world attention was directed to the Egyptian blockade of the Straits of Bab el-Mandeb. In fact this blockade had given rise to a counter-blockade on the part of the Israeli forces (based on Sharm el-Sheikh and the Sinai coast in the Gulf of Suez), which affected the Egyptian economy to a greater degree than was generally appreciated. The Morgan oil fields in the Gulf of Suez and those on the Egyptian coast produce some 8 million tons of oil a year (out of a total of 10 million tons produced by Egypt). Part of this production was exported and accounted for 20% of Egypt's foreign currency income; the remainder was shipped to the pipeline at Ras Sadaat and thence to Cairo. To make up for the oil lost as a result of the state of war in the Gulf of Suez, Egypt had to depend on Saudi Arabia and Libya for supplies; but these were not always forthcoming and were in any case debited against Egypt's credit with the two countries. In other words because of the war Egypt was forced into paying for fuel that was readily available on its own soil; a further economic threat was the fact that the Gulf of Suez ports are Egypt's outlet to east Africa and to Asia, no less than the port of Eilat is for Israel. This economic threat had been created because Israel was in a position to operate freely in the Gulf of Suez as a result of positions it held along the Sinai coast, and particularly at Sharm el-Sheikh – a fact frequently ignored by those who argue that the blockade of the Straits at Bab el-Mandeb has rendered Israel's insistence on a presence at Sharm el-Sheikh superfluous.

The Israeli naval planners had given considerable thought and study to Israel's naval problem and had managed to concentrate the maximum fire power feasible in a small vessel (manned by some 40 sailors, the Israeli missile boat proved to be far superior in fire power to any conventional destroyer with a crew of 220). The fast, compact Israeli Navy that suddenly appeared in the arena therefore took the Arab navies by surprise. Its degree of effectiveness can be gauged from the fact that in the course of the war it suffered a total loss of three killed at sea and twenty-four wounded; not a single Israeli vessel sank, despite the fact that the Egyptian and Syrian navies fired a total of some fifty-two missiles at Israeli targets at sea and sustained a confirmed loss (not counting vessels which were damaged and later repaired) of nineteen naval vessels, including ten missile boats. Throughout the war the shipping lanes to and from Israel were kept open (despite the patrolling activities of Egyptian naval units) and the small Israeli Navy enjoyed complete command of the seas both in the Mediterranean approaches and in the Gulf of Suez.

But the naval battles in the Yom Kippur War did not have a decisive influence on its final outcome: the basic Israeli strategic concept had always assumed as much. However the small naval war in the Middle East was to enable naval architects and planners to have a closer look at the sea war of the future. Countries operating in closed seas, such as the Mediterranean, will in future have to base themselves on fast, compact, missile-carrying boats as well as submarines. The nature of the fighting in confined areas requires more concentration on quality than on quantity; navies of the conventional type will become the exclusive province of the major powers, whose forces are required to operate in oceans. The remainder will have to focus on the development of coastal forces attuned to the requirements of closed seas. The experience in the Yom Kippur War shows that naval warfare has entered a new era.

18

Lessons and Implications

THE BASIC ERRORS of the Israelis in the Yom Kippur War grew, paradoxically enough, out of their victory in the Six Day War. It was never properly appreciated that in that war the Israel Defence Forces had attacked a comparatively hastily deployed Egyptian Army – with the result that the Israeli commanders had emerged from it feeling that it was possible to accomplish everything with a tank and a plane and so built their armed forces in an unbalanced manner.

The Egyptians realized that with the outbreak of another war their problem was how to neutralize the tank and the plane and how to slow down the process of growth of the IDF's reserve potential. Their reply was a missile umbrella, a concentrated mass of anti-tank weapons and strategic surprise which would force the IDF to react piecemeal. But the Israelis did not construct their forces as a reply to this concept; they ignored it, adopting a fixed concept of their own based on experience in the previous conflict. For instance, since the half-tracks in use during the Six Day War had been inadequate from the point of view of their desert and cross-country capabilities and could not keep up with the tank, the armoured personnel now tended to discard the infantry in their plans. As a result, while infantry were an integral part of the Egyptian defensive system, Israeli armour stormed enemy positions without infantry and mortars, sometimes in wasteful battles. The Israeli infantry lacked mobility, and its weapons – with a few exceptions – were no match for the Soviet equipment (its anti-tank capabilities had been drastically reduced because the basic assumption made in the IDF was that the best answer to tank is tank).

Furthermore, having suffered for years from Israeli superiority in night fighting, the Arab forces now exploited all the modern technological advances in this area in order to equip themselves. Because Israeli thinking placed the emphasis on the tank and the plane, which are not ideal night-fighting weapons, the subject of night fighting – previously Israel's forte – was neglected, and with few exceptions Israel did little that was spectacular in night fighting in the war. The absence of night-fighting equipment could be explained in part as being the result of a lack of budget. But this cannot explain away the lack of conscious-ness throughout the army about night fighting, and the inadequate use of Israel's superb paratroops and commandos to solve the problems that the armoured forces were called upon to solve. A classic example was the failed attempt (in which heavy casualties were sustained) of the 7th Brigade to take Tel Shams in Syria by frontal armoured assault, while the same position was taken the next night by a parachute battalion with four wounded.

The lessons of the war dictate the conversion of the ground forces into one large, interarm battle team controlled by one headquarters. There should be two types of team: armour being dominant in one, infantry in the other.

Again there was a failure to take into account available intelligence – such as that on the Sagger anti-tank missile – and apply its lessons organizationally and operationally. A more serious example of this failure was the fact that a more or less complete Egyptian plan of attack as it was ultimately carried out on 6 October was known to Israeli intelligence, but no conclusions seemed to have been drawn from this material planning-wise or operationally. Gen. Gonen, GOC Southern Command, was later to insist that he never knew about it.

Again, because the Israeli forces placed so much emphasis on the plane, the artillery arm was neglected. Once it is assumed that close support is not avail-able from the Air Force, increased reliance on artillery becomes self-evident. But because it was assumed that the Air Force could answer most of the problems of close support, the Israeli forces lacked adequate artillery, and above all lacked the necessary transporters, so that the artillery available reached the battlefield in the south only on the third and fourth days of battle.

The war taught the incisive lesson that ground forces must be capable of dealing with all problems without depending in any way on the Air Force. Translated into the terms of the field of battle, this requires a very heavy con-centration of artillery weapons, so that the Air Force can concentrate on main-taining superiority in the air and intervene in the field of battle in a selective manner.

One error in planning led to another. The importance of moving tanks and guns down to the front in Sinai was obviously not overlooked; but what was overlooked was the fact that such a move could not take place at the leisurely pace afforded when there is adequate advance warning. Entire formations had to move across Israel to the north and across Sinai to the south on tracks, with the result that they all left a fair percentage of their tracked vehicles stranded for technical reasons, crowding and blocking the main supply routes at critical periods. In 1967 the Israelis had found a railroad line leading across Sinai to the Suez Canal. Incredibly, instead of developing it and planning to move formations to the front on railway flats, the entire line was uprooted to provide a steel covering for the fortifications in the Bar-Lev line. A cursory and very inexpert look at Israel's transport problem strengthens the belief that the country should have given priority to the rapid development of a railroad system, which for some unknown reason remained the Cinderella of its transport network.

The Israel Defence Forces were again not constructed in a balanced fashion. Tremendous investment was made in air and armour, while below in the field there was a lack of fire power, mortars, flame throwers, night-fighting equipment and adequate mobility. Israeli ground forces – unlike for instance the Air Force, a homogeneous, compact force in which each subject is obliged to adapt its development to that of the others – were still based on arms of service with their loyalties and their pressure groups and their positions in planning conferences. The result was that Israeli GHQ operated through ten arms of service requiring ten compromises with all the resultant weaknesses that that brought about.

Contrary to the hasty conclusions published throughout the world after the Yom Kippur War, the tank still remains a dominant factor on the field of battle, provided that it is part of a well-planned battle team which is capable of answering the problems of modern warfare. Indeed, the results achieved by the Sagger anti-tank missile bore no proportion whatsoever to the publicity accorded it. In fact surveys published indicate that less than 25% of the Israeli tanks damaged were hit by such a missile. It was not a new weapon on the battlefield. It had been encountered in the Six Day War and Gen. Raful Eytan, as chief paratroop and infantry officer, had certainly realized its significance and had trained the forces under his command to deal with the threat. He was one of the few Israeli commanders who entered the war fully conscious of the problem of anti-tank missiles and prepared answers for it, with the result that in his division a minimum of losses from such weapons was sustained. Furthermore, he was to activate the only operation of the Israel Defence Forces behind the enemy lines at night, destroying enemy tanks.

The Israeli infantry did not come into its own in the Yom Kippur War On few occasions was it correctly used or to full advantage. Highly trained infantry, such as the paratroopers, was rushed into battle in an improvised, unprepared manner – as incidentally occurred on a number of occasions in the Six Day war. The Israeli error is highlighted by the fact that in the battle in Sinai the Israel Defence Forces fought exclusively with tanks against five infantry divisions and performed at one and the same time the tasks of defence, holding the front line, and of counter-attack. The fact that they were nevertheless so successful in holding the line only emphasizes the comparatively poor handling of the Arab forces.

In analysing Israel's approach to attack, the impression one gets is that inadequate attention was paid to the possibility of an indirect strategic approach. Israel's borders with the Arabs are some 2,100 miles long, with the armies concentrated along about 250 miles of this length. Little effort was made to create the ability to by-pass these forces and so force the enemy to spread out. In other words, in future every effort must be made to make the forces as versatile and as mobile as possible. Eighty per cent of the Egyptian Army was concentrated along the Canal, either attacking or defending. The answer to this situation must be an indirect operational approach. It is wrong for the Israeli forces to be obliged tactically to attack strongly held defensive positions, such as Missouri or the Chinese Farm. The importance of forcing the enemy to attack well-held and adequately manned defensive positions was emphasized in the battle of 14 October.

Many of the Israeli commanders noted a marked improvement in the standard of fighting of the Arab forces, and particularly of the Egyptian infantry. Because of the rapid and impressive Israeli victories in the past, a number of misconceptions about the Arab forces tended to gain currency. By and large, the Arab forces have invariably been poorly led at the higher level (with the possible exception of the Jordanian Army), but it would be wrong to say that they have not fought well in the past. They never excelled in attack, because this type of warfare calls for an ability to think rapidly, to improvise in the heat of battle, and the willingness of the junior officers to take responsibility and make decisions on the spot. On the other hand, in the defensive type of warfare or in a set-piece attack, they have invariably fought well. In all battles in which the Israelis came up against the Egyptian forces in previously prepared positions fighting a set-piece battle, the Egyptian soldiers fought well. But once the balance and equilibrium of their command had been upset, they tended to break and lose cohesion.

It seems that in their preparation for the Yom Kippur War the Arab armies had learnt these lessons and, accordingly, one of the reasons for the limited plan prepared by the Egyptians was the realization by the command that the development of an involved attack might be beyond their army's capabilities. Because of the emphasis that had been placed on the intellectual ability of the officers and men, the Israeli forces faced an Egyptian Army better led at the tactical level than they had known before. Added to this was a marked increase in the standard of discipline and outward smartness, which very naturally enough reflected itself also in the execution of orders on the battlefield. To this was added the sanction of fear, with orders being issued throughout the army that anybody failing to obey a command or withdrawing under fire was to be shot on the spot. These orders were carried out without hesitation both in the Egyptian Army and in the Syrian Army.

The very detailed orders the Egyptians received for the crossing of the Canal, coupled with at least three years of training for the operation, showed that President Sadat had no illusions whatsoever about his army. This fact was emphasized by Gen. Ismail after the war in explaining why the Egyptian Army had not continued to exploit success towards the line of the passes. The débâcle of the Egyptian Army in the attack on 14 October bears out the fact that apart from a very schematic operation the Egyptian Command is not ripe for the handling of major formations in mobile attack requiring manœuvre.

At the higher level the Egyptian strategy was excellent, combining as it did strategic offensive with tactically defensive operations, for as soon as they were across the Canal they deployed in narrow bridgeheads and waited for the Israeli forces to attack. The wide crossing of the Canal dissipated the force of the Israeli Air Force and the very nature of the attack, which obviously could not be disrupted all along the line, guaranteed them a number of footholds. Since no major operation was developed from the bridgeheads, there was no room for the Israeli forces to exercise their superiority in the war of manœuvre.

One field in which the Egyptians had made great advances was that of military intelligence. After the Six Day War, the Soviet Union had reorganized the Egyptian intelligence system and had provided it with modern, sophisticated equipment for all forms of electronic warfare. Radio interception, electronic surveillance and locating equipment were all introduced and attained a satisfactory standard of operation. And in addition to dispatching agents to operate inside Israel, the Arabs also benefited from Soviet surveillance over Israel by means of electronic intelligence ships and satellites.

It is clear from an evaluation of the very considerable amount of intelligence material that fell into Israeli hands during the war that the Egyptians enjoyed a number of considerable successes in this field. Their initial attack was based on a detailed appreciation of the Israeli plan for the defence of the Canal, and indeed one of the plans for its crossing (prepared in Sharon's division in May 1973) was found in their possession. (The plan called for a crossing north of the area of Deversoir, which the Egyptians fortified heavily, leaving the place where the crossing actually took place lightly held.) Far more serious, perhaps, is the fact that the Israeli code map of Sinai, including the area of the Canal and the west bank, fell into their hands. This code map, prepared in nine copies in 1973, showed all the code names referred to in Israeli radio traffic. The map in its entirety was found during the war translated into Arabic, and this boon was compounded by the fact that Israeli signal security over the radio was extremely lax during the war, leading to a number of tragic situations.

The general consensus was that the Syrians also fought better than they had done in the past because they had been specifically trained for the mission before them and did not deviate from it. In general the Syrian Command revealed a degree of daring not previously seen. The individual Syrian soldier proved to be brave, but the standard of their tank crews was very low. Like all Arab armies, they never departed from the doctrine implanted in them, and when the situations for which they were not prepared arose they proved in general to be at a loss. Their reply to the problems posed by the superiority of the Israeli forces was the scope and strength of their attack. For years before the war they had trained for a set-piece attack on a fixed model, based on wave after wave of tanks advancing regardless of what had happened to the previous wave. Thus the advance never stopped. This was the problem that faced Avigdor in his historic battle.

At most stages in the fighting the Syrian force acted as a well-disciplined army. The withdrawal which they carried out into Syria was orderly and controlled, but sometimes they were over-systematic. Both at Nafekh and in the 7th Brigade sector, the attacks they mounted one after the other were invariably of the same nature. Many of the Israeli forces in the north were surprised by their Sagger anti-tank missiles, although this should not have been the case because Northern Command had faced this problem in the various fire fights that had taken place previously. This highlighted a problem in the Israel Defence Forces – that of failing to apply lessons that should have been learned.

While the Syrians fought well as individuals, there is no justification for the exaggerated degree of praise which was heaped on the Syrian forces after the war, particularly abroad and to a lesser degree in Israel. When they launched their attack all the factors they could have hoped for were in their favour. Because of the nature of the fighting and the piecemeal supply of equipment and units, on no day in the battle did the Israeli Northern Command fight with more than half its tank force. There were days when the total force was much less. Raful's division on no day numbered more than 150 tanks. The Syrians outnumbered the Israeli forces in armour by 12 : 1 at times, fighting against an enemy depleted and disorganized because of the element of surprise and his failure to mobilize reserves in time. They fought under a missile umbrella which limited Israeli air intervention. They had crushing superiority in artillery. They were near success at times, but their armoured forces proved to be completely inadequate in battle against the better-trained and highly flexible Israeli commanders and tank crews.

It must be emphasized that the main element in limiting the scope of the Egyptian operation was the Israeli Air Force. It obliged the Egyptians to concentrate so much on the construction of a surface-to-air missile system to provide an umbrella for their forces. It was the force which dictated the limits of the Egyptian advance and this dictation would have been valid even if the Israeli Air Force had not made one pass over the battlefield. That they had been justified in limiting themselves to the area covered by the missile umbrella was proved to them when the Israeli Air Force twice destroyed their advancing forces pushing southwards along the Gulf of Suez.

In all considerations of future strategy along the Sinai front, Israeli thinking had been coloured very considerably by the War of Attrition. It was this war more than the future Yom Kippur War that the Israeli planners saw in their mind's eye, because of the assumption in the General Staff that the Egyptians would not attempt to cross the Canal until they enjoyed air superiority in Sinai, which would not be achieved till 1975. Herein lay one of the basic errors of Israeli evaluation of Arab strategy – a failure to appreciate that the Egyptians would decide on a limited military solution to their problem based on the missile umbrella, and would accordingly develop a limited strategy. The mistake of the Israeli General Staff was to judge the Arab General Staff by its own standards of military thinking; they did not envisage that the Arabs would come to the conclusion that they could achieve their war aim by a limited strategy under the cover of a missile umbrella.

In 1973 the Israeli doctrine of deterrent had proved to be a failure. The Arabs had analysed the deterrent factors in the Israeli defence posture and had prepared solutions for them, the main one being strategic and operational surprise, after which they planned to utilize the mechanism of international diplomacy in order to take advantage of any situation that would develop in their favour. In this they succeeded. They planned their offensives in such a manner as to ensure that the Israeli forces in the line would be inadequate to smash their attack before the deployment of international political forces. The Israeli post-war explanation of their failure to deter was that from an economic point of view it would have been impossible for Israel to have maintained the IDF fully mobilized along the front lines; the command strategy was based on receiving adequate advance warning, which would guarantee the mobilization of the reserve forces in time. This 'all or nothing' attitude of the Israeli defence and military leadership proved to be a grave error. There were solutions in between which could have been applied according to the developments on the Arab side, as for instance partial mobilizations for different periods to answer different sets of circumstances, such as Arab exercises along the borders. This lack of flexibility was reflected by their behaviour in this respect before the war and was in marked contrast to the steps taken when war threatened in May 1973.

The intensity of the war took the quartermaster staffs by surprise. The expenditure of ammunition was inordinately high, the losses of aircraft were serious, the figures of tanks destroyed were alarming. It was clear that the staff tables on the basis of which equipment and ammunition had been stock-piled over the years required drastic revision. Some weeks later Gen. Dayan was to make an ill-advised public admission that Israeli forces had run out of certain items of ammunition and that but for American supplies the country would have been in a very serious situation. The public was horrified at the revelation of the lack of foresight which such a statement implied.

The Arabs had obviously planned their resupply from the Soviet Union in advance, for but a few days after the outbreak of war a major Soviet airlift was under way as giant Antonov 22 cargo carriers landed at short intervals in Damascus and Cairo. They flew from the Soviet Union, staged in Budapest and thence across Yugoslavia to Cairo and Damascus. Soviet ships loaded with thousands of tons of equipment passed through the Bosphorus Straits on their way to Latakia and Alexandria.

The flow of supplies to Israel however was not so smooth. As the seriousness of the situation became evident to the Israeli staff, particularly in respect of certain medium artillery and tank ammunition, the Israeli ambassador in Washington was shuttling desperately to and fro between the State Department, the White House and the Pentagon in a frantic endeavour to cut the knots of bureaucracy and enable the flow to reach Israel. It was not until Saturday, 13 October, that the first flight of c5 Galaxy planes carrying supplies took off for Israel. During the period of one month from 14 October to 14 November the United States Air Force transported 22,000 tons of arms and ammunition in more than 560 sorties loaded with tanks, artillery, helicopters and many other items. Large quantities also reached Israel by sea.

This airlift was obviously of vital importance militarily to Israel at a critical juncture, but perhaps its major significance was a political one. Its unequivocal nature, as seen by the Soviets and the Arabs, who were unaware of the hesita-tion and foot-dragging that had taken place in Washington for a full and fateful week of fighting, was undoubtedly a major factor in bringing about a cease-fire and in turning the United States into the central figure on the stage of the Middle East in the months subsequent to the war.

An analysis of the events leading up to the Yom Kippur War points to two

major errors. The first was the fatal error in intelligence evaluation and the
failure at the command level and the ministerial level to appreciate the significance of the parallel developments on the Syrian and Egyptian fronts. One
of the incredible facts of the period is that at no stage and at no level, so far
as can be seen or evaluated from available material, did any element link the
Syrian build-up in the north (which had so disturbed the minister of defence
following the warnings of Gen. Hofi) with the unusual Egyptian activity and
concentrations in the south. It was as if the assumption that the Arab armies
could not or would not go to war caused a complete mental black-out. None
of the elements involved can escape responsibility. The dogmatic manner in
which a concept was adhered to influenced all concerned, despite the better
instincts of those who were further removed from the direct task of evaluating
intelligence, such as the minister of defence and the chief of staff. Both had at
various times during 1973 expressed anxiety about Arab preparations and talked
about imminent war, and yet when the indications of such a war abounded they
allowed themselves – because of their erroneous evaluation in April and May,
and perhaps also because of an uncomfortable feeling over mobilizing the
nation during the High Holy Days – to limit preparations to the standing army
only. The interesting element here is that there was no thought of some form
of interim mobilization to provide an additional measure of security along the
borders. The thinking seemed to be in terms of all or nothing. What emerges,
too, is that there was no insistence on mobilization at any level in the General
Staff during the fateful days before the war.

The reason for this laxity lay in the second major error, which was the
stubborn assumption of the Israeli defence and military establishment that the
unrealistic and unfavourable ratio of forces along the borders was adequate to
hold any Egyptian or Syrian attack. This in turn was based on erroneous
readings of developments in the field of war, particularly of the Air Force's
ability to deal with the surface-to-air missile systems, and a failure to appreciate
the significance of various developments, such as the construction of the high
rampart on the Egyptian side of the Canal. The latter was interpreted as a
defensive measure, when in fact it constituted a very important element in the
operation of the Egyptian anti-tank missile system against both the first and
second lines of the Israeli defence. Gen. Gonen – and apparently Gen. Mandler
earlier – had warned about this development and urged counter-measures on the
Israeli side, particularly along the second line of defence, but it was too late.

After the war President Sadat was to describe the elevation of the main
rampart along the Canal as the first practical move in the preparation of its
crossing. 'The Israelis mocked at our building activity saying that the Egyptians
always like to build pyramids,' he said, 'but these ramparts were most important

in exposing the enemy and for military uses to which the enemy paid no attention. . . . Our control of the west bank by means of these ramparts which were completed by the end of February 1973 . . . was complete.'

The Israeli error began with a basic concept about Arab inability or unwillingness to attack. Every new development in the intelligence evaluation was adapted to this concept, instead of being evaluated independently. As a result, Arab preparations were misread. But it must be remembered that, as an additional insurance policy, everybody involved in decision enjoyed a sense of security about the ability of the standing army in the line, together with what was considered to be an adequate number of tanks, to deal with any eventuality and the ability of the Air Force to deal a resounding blow to the enemy. This 'insurance policy', however, was based on a misreading of technological developments and on a misevaluation of the scope of the planned Arab attack both in manpower and in equipment. Although these factors were known arithmetically, they were not translated into operational terms by the Israeli Command. The Israeli thinking also revealed a complete lack of appreciation of the new anti-tank capability within the Arab forces.

From these two errors emerged many of the mistakes which were to be highlighted in the war. The army was ready for an orderly mobilization in seventy-two to ninety-six hours, but the improvised mobilization, which was brilliant, heroic and saved the country, by its very nature caused formations to be thrown piecemeal into battle. This gave rise to a feeling of inadequacy in mobilization, which was unjustified; for the very strength of the system was revealed in exactly the circumstances in which the mobilization was carried out.

At the same time, many weaknesses were revealed. A laxity had grown in the IDF, permitting the retention of semi-trained reservists in the front line along the Suez Canal when the situation was sufficiently serious to warrant the highest degree of alert. There was also a lack of discipline, which had long been expressed in the very high ratio of deaths (hundreds annually) in road accidents and training accidents. Over the past few years there was a tendency for the senior command of the armed forces to slacken on discipline and to accept a state of indiscipline rather than impose its will. The outward appearance of the troops, the high ratio of accidents involving human lives, the state of maintenance of buildings and vehicles, all these should have given an indication of something deeper going on within the armed forces. This writer was a lone voice in drawing public attention to this portent. There was little or no reaction, and to this day such matters make little impression on those bodies responsible for the public supervision of the armed forces. Combat discipline has always been and continues to be superb, but the fact that slackness in administrative discipline invariably increases the casualty rate arouses little comment or reaction in Israel.

Most important, the rapid turnover of senior officers seemed to have become an end in itself so far as the Israeli High Command was concerned. Well-tried and highly experienced officers at the peak of their ability were replaced in order to increase rotation within the higher ranks of the armed forces. The result was that in time of war some potentially able officers lacking experience suddenly found themselves in positions for which they were not completely mature, while highly experienced officers were onlookers.

A Public Commission of Inquiry headed by the President of the Supreme Court of Israel, Shmuel Agranat, spent many months in apportioning responsibility. It had access to all officers and all documents, and therefore no attempt will be made here to compete with it. Yet although the Agranat Commission absolved the minister of defence of all responsibility for the failings that preceded the outbreak of war, it would seem inconceivable to a Western reader that any minister of defence – however able, however brilliant and however effective – could avoid ministerial responsibility for what occurred.

Dayan is a man of unusual ability who preferred to focus on certain aspects of his job and ignore all others. On the other hand, he tended to try to share responsibility with various functionaries – highlighted by his custom of being accompanied to Cabinet meetings by the chief of staff and the director of intelligence – creating a situation in which he could say: 'They said it, I didn't.' He developed the brilliantly successful Israeli policy in the occupied territories, which interested him. He took a direct interest in the front line whenever it erupted and in the army's planning and operations. But as a minister he took little interest in the day-to-day life of the army, impatient of the details which go into the management of the largest single organization in the country. Matters of routine, discipline, training, housekeeping and general administration bored him. He would evince an interest in the number of tanks available, but not in the state of the tanks. He relied entirely on the chief of staff and the General Staff, in addition to his own staff, without appreciating that in a parliamentary democracy the responsibility for these matters fell on him too. Likewise, in all matters of military preparedness and intelligence evaluations, he was responsible to the prime minister and the Cabinet.

The shock of the war caused something to snap in Dayan. The initial Arab onslaught and success threw him into a fit of pessimism, which coloured his evaluations right through the war. He spent a considerable amount of time in the front line, away from the nerve centre, frequently creating an air of pessimism around him and giving advice which, had it been taken, could have changed the course of the war and would have left Israel without the trump cards that proved to be so valuable in the disengagement negotiations. It is difficult to evaluate the logic behind his thinking, issuing a directive in May to prepare for war in late 1973 and then, in the light of all the intelligence in the first week of October and on Yom Kippur morning, opposing the total mobilization demanded by the chief of staff, thus causing the loss of valuable hours of mobilization time. Dayan was repeatedly indecisive. On the morning of Yom Kippur he told Mrs Meir that he was 'against total mobilization but he would not resign'; he left the decision about the attack into Syria on Wednesday 10 October, to her; he declared that he would 'not make a *jihad*' against the crossing of the Suez Canal by the Israeli forces although he opposed it. Had his suggestion on the first day for withdrawal to the line of the passes in Sinai been accepted, the subsequent Israeli crossing of the Canal would have been impossible. He misread the political developments, maintaining all through the war that there would be no cease-fire.

In his favour it should be said that he read the international situation, with particular reference to the Soviet Union, as the political general he is. But militarily he moved from the extreme of complete confidence that the ratio of forces along the fronts was adequate to deal with the Arab attacks to a state of complete depression and a lack of confidence in the same forces a day later. His very cautious nature was unable to stand up to the challenge of bitter reality in time of stress. Formally, he might not be responsible for the mistake of the ratio of forces along the front line and for the preparations along it; but in fact he considered himself as a super-chief of staff, acted as such, and stated as much on many occasions. When Gen. Hofi was unhappy about the situation in the north, Dayan flew to inspect the front line with the chief of staff and decided to reinforce the area with units of the 7th Brigade; his interest and involvement in the line along the Suez Canal should not have been any less. On many occasions his instincts both about appointments and other developments in the armed forces were correct, but strangely enough, and contrary to popular conceptions, he hesitated to impose his will.

This major weakness in his make-up was expressed time and again both before and during the war. The famous Israeli cartoonist, Zeev, perhaps summed him up best of all by invariably portraying him as a Hamletian 'to be or not to be' figure torn by doubts. His very powerful charisma had tended to cover up many basic weaknesses in his character and had helped him overcome situations which other less attractive personalities could never have survived.

After the war Dayan went out of his way to praise Mrs Meir, and justifiably so, because it was to a great degree her strength of character and ability to remain composed in the most difficult circumstances which counteracted Dayan's pessimistic nature and his jeremiads. Mrs Meir's method of government brought about a system whereby there were no checks and balances and no alternative evaluations. Her doctrinaire, inflexible approach to problems and to government was to contribute to the failings of the government before the war. She was very much the overbearing mother who ruled the roost with an iron hand. She had little idea of orderly administration and preferred to work closely with her cronies, creating an *ad hoc* system of government based on what was known as her 'kitchen'. But once war had broken out these very traits proved to be an asset. She was strong and adamant and gave the country the powerful leadership it required both in time of war and in the involved post-war political negotiations. On many occasions she, a woman who had reached seventy-five, found herself thrust into a position where she had to decide between differing military options proposed by professionals. She decided, and invariably decided well, drawing on a large measure of common sense which had stood her in good stead.

David Elazar, like his minister, undoubtedly bears responsibility for the erroneous evaluation, although like his minister not all the intelligence was available to him and they were both misled by the totally mistaken evaluations of Military Intelligence. The fact that others in the General Staff acquiesced in the level of forces held along the borders did not in any way diminish his overall responsibility as commander of the forces. However, once it was clear that war would break out, he acted decisively, calling for an immediate general mobilization; and five very valuable hours were lost because of his argument on this issue with Dayan. It is clear that the process of erosion which had affected the army had not escaped the General Staff. The omissions of the intelligence division have been trumpeted far and wide; but the standard of troops in the front line in Sinai, the state of preparedness of the units, the level of discipline in reporting, and the state of equipment in many of the reserve stores all point an accusing finger at the various divisions of the General Staff. And while the chief of staff bears the responsibility for his staff, there has been a tendency after the war to focus the accusing finger exclusively at Elazar, when an objective analysis of the situation at the General Staff level reveals many faults and omissions.

Once in the war, Gen. Elazar proved himself to have stability and strength of character in the most trying circumstances, never losing his composure and asserting his authority throughout the armed forces. His competent handling of the war was cautious and foresighted, and he finally led his forces to a situation which enabled Israel to enter political negotiations on a better basis than might have been envisaged at the outset of the war. Elazar's decision to direct Peled's division to the north on the morning of Sunday, 7 October, and the decision to move over to counter-attack at a very early stage, were the two major command decisions that saved the northern front. He has been criticized for preoccupying himself on the eve of the war with plans for counter-attack; in fact his preoccupation with mounting such counter-attacks and his ability to think ahead several days during the battle was one of the factors which guided the Israeli forces to victory.

Gen. Gonen was an unfortunate war casualty. His tragedy was that he arrived in Southern Command a year too late and was still in the process of getting to know his command when war broke out. The absurdity of the rotation policy in the IDF is highlighted by the fact that the GOC Command (Sharon) and the divisional commander responsible for the front (Mandler) were both to be relieved within less than three months of each other. It seems that many of the accusations levelled against Gonen were done so with the wisdom of hindsight. According to these accusations, the fact was deprecated that his actions in the fateful weeks before the outbreak of war do not indicate an awareness of the gravity of the situation developing along the Suez Canal. However neither he nor any other senior officer in the armed forces believed that war was imminent. On Thursday 4 October he attended a meeting of the General Staff which was devoted entirely to the problem of discipline in the armed forces. And on Friday he heard an intelligence evaluation that the possibility of war was 'the lowest of the low'. Many of his requests for reinforcements were turned down, a fact which in itself indicated how GHQ viewed possible developments along the borders.

The impression that an outsider obtains from an examination of developments during the war is that he was later unfairly treated publicly. His behaviour before and during the war did not warrant the degree of criticism directed exclusively at him. Like most other senior commanders he bears his share of responsibility for mistakes and errors in judgement, and is entitled to his share of the credit for many good decisions and successful operations. He is a courageous, tough, able and professional officer who was unlucky. Had the war broken out three months earlier, he would probably have emerged with laurel wreaths as a divisional commander, as he had emerged from his previous wars.

Gen. Sharon's outstanding ability as a field commander notwithstanding, the fact that he publicly discredited the chief of staff and his personal representative, Gen. Bar-Lev, the GOC Command and other senior commanders tends to make his views about other officers somewhat suspect and to reflect more on him than on the targets of his criticism. An analysis of many of his arguments with his superiors reveals that he understood his enemy; but in the light of the realities on the battlefield he was at times very unrealistic and tended to take risks which Israel could not afford. His personal leadership, bravery, determination, and inspiration to his men mark him out for what he is – an outstanding field commander. But his attitude towards his colleagues, his public behaviour and his accusations raise a question mark in an evaluation of his character. In the circumstances few commanders would have persevered with the crossing of the Suez Canal as he did so very successfully and with his usual drive and perseverance.

Gen. Chaim Bar-Lev emerges from the war as a sound, solid and able commander, whose personal authority, human approach and command ability were instrumental in controlling a potentially unstable command situation in Southern Command. His quiet and cool handling of it marks him out for what he is, a leader with strong nerves in times of crisis.

In the final analysis, the criticism that has been expressed on the various aspects of the war cannot be allowed to cloud the fact that the Israeli armed forces won the most striking victory in their history. (Had the Israeli forces but been mobilized in time, the Arab attack would have been destroyed at the outset, and all the failings of the Israeli leadership and forces since noted, would have been ignored.) The Arab attack took place in the best possible circumstances. A force roughly equivalent to the total of the NATO European forces launched a surprise attack against a small country with a population unready and with an army unmobilized. On the Israeli forces descended a mass of armour, backed by all the technology that the Soviet Union could make available and with the knowledge that a massive Soviet sea and air lift was ready to move into operation immediately after the outbreak of hostilities. Despite this the people and army of Israel mobilized in one of the most impressive mobilizations in history, rushed from prayer to war, conducted a most heroic defensive battle, and on the third day were moving over to the counter-attack. And while the total mobilization was proceeding apace, by dint of previous organization the country succeeded in continuing to function, with industrial production being maintained at 70% of the pre-war level and with a high degree of normality being observed in the day-to-day life. The skies were free of enemy aircraft.

As Israel fought back against the Soviet-supported Arab armies, the forces of the Western world, who live under the same shadow under which Israel lives, reacted with a few exceptions in a cowardly and selfish manner, giving adequate indications what type of reaction might be expected from them if the Soviet Union were to decide to launch its forces nearer home in Europe. In many ways the Israeli officers and troops were fighting for more than the existence and freedom of Israel alone. Only the United States appreciated the significance of Israel's struggle. Paradoxically enough, the courageous and unequivocal American stand in favour of Israel gave the United States a standing in the Arab world such as it had not known before, and showed the countries of Western Europe in their craven and abject surrender to the Arab sheikhs to be the weak, leaderless and divided community they are.

Those who were at fault cannot escape the blame of history – the price for their omission has not yet been fully paid. Because of these mistakes, Israel lost a unique position of strength in its history from which it could have negotiated for the future. It may well have yet to pay a heavier price.

But it would be wrong not to give those who may bear a share of the blame a share of the credit for the incredible success of the IDF in such unbelievably adverse circumstances. Above all, credit is due to the commanders, the officers and the men who physically blocked the advance of the attacking armies and performed with such unselfish bravery and gallantry, saving a nation and leading an army to victory.

The tragedy of the post-war situation is that the Arab armies, which would have suffered a most humiliating defeat, had the IDF been mobilized and in position, have translated their initial successes into a major victory, when in fact they were saved from total defeat by the intervention of the Soviet Union and the Security Council. The danger is that they will not draw the correct lessons and conclusions from the war, carried away as they are in a euphoria of victory which is imaginary. Such euphoria carries within it the seeds of future conflict, unless a wise leadership can give to the Arab world a new and balanced approach.

Yet the implications of the Yom Kippur War affect a much wider public than just the Egyptians, Syrians and the Israelis. Gen. Dayan once said that the key to war in the Middle East is in the hands of the Soviets, while the key to peace is held by the United States. This evaluation, which was made after the Six Day War, is no less valid to this day. If any point emerges quite clearly from an analysis of the events leading up to the war, and indeed of the years between the Six Day War and the Yom Kippur War, it is that the Soviet Union has played a central role in creating the conditions for war in the Middle East Its purpose was, and is, not so much for or against any given party in the area, but a function of its global strategy. The geopolitical importance of the countries of the Middle East; the Mediterranean, to which Soviet eyes have been directed for centuries; the Suez Canal, affording a potential link between the Mediterranean and the Indian Ocean, which in the context of the Soviet struggle with China has assumed considerable importance; and the oil supplies in the Middle East, and particularly in the Persian Gulf, have combined to make the Middle East of vital importance to the Soviet Union. If one adds to this the fact that the Soviet Union borders on Middle Eastern countries (one of which is a member of NATO) and the experience of the Soviet-encouraged Arab oil blockade exercised during and following the Yom Kippur War, the value of the area to the Soviet Union cannot be overemphasized.

By Nasser's own admission, the Soviet Union played a major part in bringing on the Six Day War and taking advantage of the débâcle to strengthen their hold on the Arab world, advising the Egyptians against any accommodation with Israel and offering full support to reconstruct their armed forces and enable them to go to war again. A student of the developments in the Middle East will invariably note that whenever voices were heard in favour of accommodation and peace, a Soviet delegation would descend on the area and attitudes would again harden. Many such visits were followed by an escalation of the military situation, as in the case of Foreign Minister Gromyko's long visit to Cairo early in 1969 shortly before the War of Attrition began and to Damascus in March 1974 before the Syrian front erupted in a War of Attrition as disengagement talks were about to commence. Over the years the Soviet Union built up the Arab armies for the specific purpose of going to war, pouring the most sophisticated weaponry available into the Middle East, leading from one escalation to another.

It is not really important whether or not at any given point it was convenient for the Soviet Union that the Arabs go to war or whether or not attempts were made to restrain them. The Soviets had become so heavily involved in the Arab world at every level of military preparation that at a certain point their opinion as to whether or not war was desirable became immaterial. In principle, they agreed that the Arabs should be ready for an offensive war, and they made available all that was required to embark on a war of major dimensions. Thus while many in the world were deluding themselves into believing that a new era of détente had dawned, the Soviets formally assumed responsibility for the air defence of Egypt in January 1970. And a month before the Nixon–Brezhnev meeting in May 1972, President Sadat was invited to a meeting in Moscow at which he received the Soviet Union's agreement in principle to go to war. Leonid Brezhnev then blithely proceeded to sign a document known as 'The Basic Principles of Relations Between The United States of America and the Union of Soviet Socialist Republics', which includes the statement that 'the USA and the USSR have a special responsibility to do everything in their power so that conflicts or situations will not arise which would serve to increase international tensions'.

Within a year of the 1972 summit meeting, the Soviet Union was supplying the Egyptian and Syrian armies with the weapons they believed essential in order to go to war. The Soviet decision to supply Scud missiles to Egypt – three months before the 1973 summit meeting – was a conscious act designed to remove any Egyptian hesitation about going to war. Sadat had planned to go to war in May 1973 but he decided on a postponement because as he put it in an interview in *Akhbar El Yom* in August 1974: 'then the Soviets set the date for the Second Summit Meeting with Nixon in Washington for the month of May, and for political reasons which it is not necessary to reveal at this point I decided to postpone the date . . .' At the same time President Assad made a secret visit to Moscow and the result of his visit was the stepped-up supply of a complete surface-to-air missile system which was rushed to Syria in the months of July and August 1973.

While a gullible world – and to a very great degree a highly gullible American administration and people – were being soft-spoken by Mr Brezhnev in his toasts about peace and friendship and his reassertion that both countries would concentrate on keeping international tensions to a minimum, the Soviet Union was consciously and actively preparing the stage for a new confrontation in the Middle East.

There are many indications that in the third week of September 1973 the top echelon in the Soviet Union was fully aware of the Egyptian plan to go to war. On 21 September the Italian Communist Party newspaper, *Unità*, published an item stating that Brezhnev had lengthened his visit to Bulgaria in order to meet President Sadat of Egypt. Despite later Soviet denials of this story, it seems fair to assume that at this meeting Brezhnev and Sadat finalized arrangements for Soviet support and reaction to various aspects of the impending military operation. This story also ties in with reports received in the Italian Foreign Ministry that during this visit Mr Brezhnev co-ordinated arrangements with the Bulgarians for the planned Soviet airlift. In fact on 2 October an English-language release by the Bulgarian Press Agency reported Syrian and Egyptian preparations for an imminent attack. It would appear that this report had come about as a result of a slip-up somewhere because it was immediately suppressed.

During the week before the war, the launching of the Cosmos satellites by the Soviet Union to cover the Israeli front lines in the north and in the south, the departure of Soviet ships from Egyptian ports, the sailing of a Soviet electronic intelligence ship northwards from Egypt and the hurried and hasty departure of the families of the Soviet advisers of Egypt and Syria after the respective Soviet ambassadors had been notified of the imminence of war combine to add credence to a picture of Soviet connivance, and certainly an intimate knowledge of the preparations for war.

Once war had broken out, the massive Soviet airlift to Egypt and Syria moved into operation smoothly without the improvisation and the frantic negotiations that characterized the American airlift to Israel. Soviet ships, which must have been readied in the Black Sea ports before the outbreak of war, loaded equipment prepared in stores before the outbreak of war, and were already unloading in Syrian ports on Thursday, 11 October. This fact, more than any other, testifies to the advance connivance and the careful preparations which had gone into the supply plan of the operation. And during the war when the Syrian capital was threatened by Israeli forces, both Israeli and American intelligence learnt of the alerting of three Soviet airborne divisions.

The bare and grim fact emerges that during all the toasting at the summit meetings between the Soviet Union and the United States, the Soviets were playing a sinister game of deception and flagrant violation of the letter and spirit of the 'Basic Principles' of détente, signed in May 1972 – at their insistence. Seldom have nations been misled in such an open manner. The mirage of détente was avidly pursued by many leaders and statesmen for their respective purposes and expedient reasons. But only the very naïve can continue to believe in the sincerity of the Kremlin. For in fact no détente – or at best a one-sided détente – existed, and the Soviets proceed to make a mockery of practically every word in the 'Basic Principles' agreed to at the 1972 summit. Now, as then, détente is at best a convenient myth, at worst a dangerous illusion.

It is fair to assume that the interest of the Soviet Union in obtaining a cease-fire on the first day of the war (ostensibly because the Syrians had asked them to arrange it, although Sadat maintained that the Syrians denied this) and later the alleged agreement of the Soviet Union to the American initiative of 13 October were guided by the Soviet reading of the possible results if the battle were to continue. They viewed the war free from the euphoria that beclouded the Arab thinking. Throughout the war and immediately after, Soviet actions and reactions were guided by a very clear evaluation of the military situation. They threw their full weight behind a continuation of the war when it seemed to favour the Arabs. They hastened supplies and (as when Brezhnev urged on President Boumedienne of Algeria to be more active) encouraged other Arabs to increase their support and to wield the oil weapon. They moved rapidly to stop the war – even to the point of creating tension that might lead to a nuclear confrontation – only when they realized that the Egyptian Third Army was doomed to collapse because of the tactical situation. It would appear too that the Soviet moves immediately after the war – including their insistence on the stationing of Soviet and American troops in the area and their threat to move seven airborne divisions to Egypt – were further attempts to re-establish their presence, which had been so diminished after the withdrawal of some 20,000 of their troops from Egypt in July 1972.

Through the Geneva talks, the Soviet Union has become a party to the negotiations for a settlement in the Middle East. Its strategy seems to be to allow the United States to occupy the centre of the stage and to extract as much as possible from Israel without having recourse to Soviet pressures. It is quite clear, however, that the Soviet Union will do everything possible to prevent any move that might prejudice its position as the principal supplier of arms to the Arabs. Hence any settlement – either to create a peaceful situation or even just lessen the importance of arms supplies – would appear to be prejudicial to the interests of the Soviet Union. Furthermore the Soviets will use the Palestinian issue and the Palestine Liberation Organization (whose leader, Yasser Arafat, was given a state reception in Moscow in the summer of 1974) in order to endanger the regime of King Hussein in Jordan and as a major element to be manœuvred as they see fit in influencing the direction of negotiations in the Israeli–Arab conflict.

A main strategic interest of the Soviet Union in the region lies in the Persian Gulf. Its main base for the development of operations in the Gulf, both from an expansionist point of view and from that of denying the oil of the Gulf states to the West and Japan, is Iraq. The main supply line from the Soviet Union to Iraq is via the Syrian port of Latakia and across Syria. The Soviets are investing huge sums of money in developing this base and they have attempted to bridge the gap between the two opposing factions of the Baath Party which rule in Syria and in Iraq in order to strengthen their hold on these two countries – for they outflank the eastern extremity of NATO in Turkey and act as a counter-threat to the growing power of the Persian Armed Forces encouraged and supported by the United States.

The Middle East conflict emphasizes a determined and unrelenting Soviet threat to the security of the whole of Europe, a fact which the European countries failed to appreciate and to which they failed in their ignominy to react. For so far as the leaders of the Kremlin were concerned, the war was basically a side show in which their weapons could be tested, Western technology evaluated and Western reactions to such a crisis gauged. The cowardly and pusillanimous European reaction to the Soviet moves must have been the most encouraging aspect of the Middle East war for the Soviet Union, while the unequivocal and forceful United States reaction, including the unexpected arms resupply mounted to Israel, was undoubtedly its least encouraging aspect.

The unprecedented magnitude of Soviet armament can be gauged by the fact that within a matter of months the Soviet Union had resupplied Syria with the number of tanks it had lost in the war – some 1,200 – and added more. This followed vast shipments of tanks to Egypt, Syria, Iraq, Algeria, Somalia, India, Yemen and South Yemen, not to mention many other countries, for a total of thousands of tanks, over the period of one year. Such enormous potential must be seen contrasted with the situation reported by the special subcommittee on the Middle East of the House of Representatives Armed Services Committee in 1974: '. . . There is only one producer of tanks in the United States for the United States Army, and the present production rate is 30 a month, or

360 a year.' The total annual tank production in France is similar – some 300 a year. The size and scope of the Soviet arms production facilities obviously leaves the West frighteningly far behind.

It is against these sombre facts of Soviet involvement in the Middle East war that the West must view its future. The passage of time has not diminished Soviet imperialist aims, but has tended to dull Western awareness of the dangers. There is a vital lesson for the West in the Yom Kippur War, and the countries of Western Europe will remain independent only to the degree that they can appreciate the implications of that bloody confrontation and draw incisive conclusions.

As for the Middle East, it faces not only dangers but great challenges. The basic issue remains as it always had in the past: do the Arabs want peace? Do they recognize Israel's right to exist? The historian will find that Israel has never been the element to block peace moves. Israeli reactions may not always have been the most immediate or sophisticated, but Israel has never once failed to react favourably to the possibility of peace. The basic problem has been and continues to be Arab insistence that Israel has no right to exist. The extreme Arab states such as Syria, Iraq and Libya, not to mention the Palestine Liberation Organization, base themselves on the Palestine Covenant, in which the dismantling of the State of Israel is a basic tenet. The more sophisticated Arabs such as the Egyptians and Jordanians, engage in Arab semantics in order to distinguish between different forms of peace, thus enabling them to prevaricate and avoid a clear answer to the question of whether or not Israel has the right to exist and whether or not they are prepared for a true peace with Israel.

Over the years the Arabs have become more sophisticated in their approach, having realized that an insistence on pushing the Israelis into the sea has prejudiced their propaganda campaign against Israel. Instead they had adopted the theory of stages, with the first stage being the withdrawal of Israel to the 1967 lines. Still, the objective remains the same, as evidenced most recently by Yasser Arafat's speech to the UN General Assembly in November 1974, when he reasserted, in effect, the Arab programme to destroy the Jewish state. Israel has every intention of making a determined effort to reach peace, but it dare not enter the new phase with any illusions about Arab intentions. Only when Arab actions indicate a willingness to modify their attitude to the basic issue of the existence of the State of Israel will it be possible for Israel to make concessions.

In the interim the Israelis have learned their lesson, and it will be a very unwise government and military establishment that allows the first-strike option to remain exclusively in Arab hands. The Middle East is entering a phase of military sophistication that can wreak havoc and chaos to a degree undreamt of hitherto, and extending well beyond the narrow confines of the field of battle.

Civilian populations will be exposed to no less a degree than the military forces in any future war. This situation places upon Israel the burden of inevitably possessing a first-strike option and at the same time, whatever the scope of the attack and nature of the weapons used, a second-strike capability. The intensity of destruction of the weapons available to both sides today can, in itself ultimately act as a deterrent in the Middle East, provided that Israel maintains a very high state of preparedness with all options open. Another hopeful factor is the fact that in the initial successes of the Yom Kippur War the Arabs regained their national honour, and this may ultimately facilitate the development of a dialogue and negotiations between the two sides.

Only time can tell whether or not these negotiations will succeed. That Israel has reached a stage of negotiation with the Arab world at all is due to the incredible military victory gained on the field of battle in the Yom Kippur War. Caught surprised and unaware, and despite the initial reverses and heavy losses, the Israeli people, military command and, above all, fighting men rallied, turned the tide and brought on a victory that saved the nation. Many of the great events in a 4,000-year-old history pale into insignificance beside what was achieved on the battlefield in the Yom Kippur War. Israel has every right to draw courage and faith for the future from its performance in what the Israelis may well remember as their war of atonement.

Index

Aboukir, 267

Abu Dirham, David, 45, 174-6

Abu Rudeis, 182, 257, 260, 267, 268

Abu Seweir, 235

Abu Sultan, 240

Adabiah, Port of, 248, 250

Adan, Avraham (Bren), 5-7, 158, 168-9, 182, 184, 185, 188-91, 199-200, 201, 202-3, 208-9, 222-9, 234-5, 238, 242-3, 246-50

Agheila, Abu, 65

Agranat, Shmuel, 280

Agranat Commission, 42, 46, 51, 280

Akavish, 209-12, 223-9, 234

Al Gezira, 37

Albert, see Mandler

Aleika, 94

Alexandria, 33, 48

Algeria, 289

Allon, Yigael, 49, 53, 245

Almagor, 99

Ami, 222

Amir, 166, 167, 168, 190, 224, 226, 227, 242

Amman, 30

Amnon, 156, 158-9, 160, 182, 193-5, 198, 205, 210-12, 214-16, 219, 221-2, 224, 227-8, 230, 238, 240-1, 245

Amos, 129, 130, 132

Amram, 160, 214

Arab Defence Council, 29

Arab Federation, 28

Arab Foreign Legion, 135

Arab Socialist Union, Supreme Council, 19

Arafat, Yasser, 31, 289, 290

Ardinest, Shlomo, 176-9

Arieh, 175, 184, 185, 188, 190, 226, 228, 242-3, 246, 248, 249

Arik Bridge, 56, 88, 100, 101, 117, 217

Armoured Brigade, 7th, 61, 62, 63, 65-7, 68, 79, 80, 93, 106-15, 117, 129, 130, 139-40, 146, 271, 281

Armoured Brigade, 190th, 189

Ashkenazi, Motti, 179-80

Asor, 243, 244, 246

Assad, Hafez, 22, 29, 30, 33, 48, 79, 135, 234, 287

Assad Republican Guard, 63, 108, 111

Ataka, Mount, 248

Avi, 107, 110-11, 132

Avigdor, 66-7, 80-2, 106-14, 129-30, 132-3

Avital, Mount, 57

Avner, 79

Bab el-Mandeb Straits, 268

'Badr', 33

Baluza, 6, 154, 165, 257

Bambi, 72, 73, 74

Banias, 78, 79

Bar-Lev, Chaim, 5, 6, 7, 51, 54, 116-18, 197-9, 201, 202, 205-6, 210, 221-4, 238, 241, 246, 283, 284

Bar-Lev, Rafi, 214

Bar-Lev line, 7, 8, 11, 12, 148, 170-80, 256, 272

Barak Brigade, 59, 63, 64, 66-8, 80, 82-4, 89, 94, 99, 100, 112, 117, 130

Bardawil, Lake, 263

Bats, 111

Beersheba, 146

Beirut, 16, 31

Ben-Ari, Uri, 65, 227

Ben Gurion, David, 41

Ben Shoham, Yitzhak, 68, 82-3, 84-90, 100, 117

Bernstein, Leonard, 167

Bir Gafgafa, 203, 234

Bnot Ya'akov Bridge, 63, 117, 122

'Booster' ridge, 65, 67, 79, 106, 109, 110, 113

Botzer, 161, 164, 228

Boumedienne, Houari, 136, 288

Bren, see Adan, Avraham

Brezhnev, Leonid, 21, 27, 42, 136, 244–5, 286, 287, 288

Brom, Yoav, 216

Budapest, 151, 171, 172, 179, 206

Buka'a, 109, 110, 126

Bulgaria, 287

Buteiha Valley, 56, 88

Butel, 212

Cabinet, Israeli, 40–1, 49, 50–1, 54, 202, 208, 280

Cabrit Peninsula, 247

Cairo, 17, 19, 20, 24, 28, 30, 31, 48, 232, 244, 250, 268, 286

Caspri, 120

Central Intelligence Collection Agency, 40

Cherbourg boats, 261, 262, 263

China, 285

Chinese Farm, 159–60, 195, 205, 209–15, 221–4, 227, 230, 273

Command and General Staff School, 46, 97

Council of Europe, 48

Dakar, 262

Damascus, 29, 30, 33, 48, 56, 57, 129, 132, 135, 136, 259, 286

Damiette-Balatin, 241, 266–7

Dan, 156, 160–5, 181, 200, 219, 239, 243, 248

Dan River, 56, 78

David, 223–4, 225

Dayan, Moshe, 17, 41, 43, 49, 50, 52–4, 60–1, 97, 99, 116, 118, 128–9, 147, 182–183, 195–7, 202, 205, 224, 227, 230, 238, 245–6, 255, 258, 260, 277, 280–1, 282

De Borchgrave, Arnaud, 18, 20, 25-6, 27

Dera'a, 140

Desberg, 174

Deversoir, 150, 155, 195, 201, 208–30, 231, 233–4, 274

Dinitz, Simcha, 250

Dobrynin, Anatoly, 136, 244

Dov, 68, 82, 84, 88, 92, 94–5, 112-13, 130

Drora, 172, 173

Eban, Abba, 38–9

Egypt and Egyptian forces, 1–54, 128, 129, 135, 146–250; et passim
  Air Force, 15, 180, 251–4, 256–8, 259–60
  Armoured Brigade, 1st, 205
  Armoured Brigade, 3rd, 206
  Armoured Brigade, 14th, 214, 222, 226
  Armoured Brigade, 25th, 155, 156, 227–9, 232
  Armoured Division, 4th, 155, 161, 206, 242, 244
  Armoured Division, 21st, 155, 200, 205, 210, 212, 227
  General Staff, 251
  High Command, 232
  Infantry Brigade, 8th, 149
  Infantry Division, 2nd, 190, 191
  Infantry Division, 7th, 151, 156, 161
  Infantry Division, 8th, 185
  Infantry Division, 16th, 39, 151, 210, 212, 227
  Infantry Division, 18th, 190, 205
  Infantry Division, 19th, 151, 154, 161, 205
  Marine Brigade, 130th, 154, 161–2
  Mechanized Brigade, 113th, 205
  Mechanized Division, 6th, 154, 161, 243
  Mechanized Division, 23rd, 205
  Military Intelligence, 14
  Ministry of Foreign Affairs, 33
  Ministry of Information, 33
  Ministry of War, 33
  Navy, 262–4, 265–8
  People's Council, 233
  Second Army, 151, 155, 183, 212, 260
  Supreme Council, 37
  Tank Brigade, 1st, 206
  Tank Brigade, 22nd, 243
  Third Army, 32, 39, 142, 151, 155, 162, 164, 184, 188, 190, 209, 232, 243, 244, 246–8, 250, 260

Ehud, 212
Eilat, 146, 257, 267, 268
Eilat, INS, 262
Ein Gev, 56, 84
Ein Zivan, 122
El Al, 56, 88, 96, 100, 101, 104, 117, 118
El Arish, 65, 257
El-Balah Island, 12, 35, 158, 160, 165, 185
El Hamma, 56
El Hanut, 126
El Rom, 111
Elazar, David, 12, 29, 42–3, 49–53, 60, 91, 98, 116, 128–9, 134, 157, 183, 192–3, 195, 197–8, 202, 208–9, 227, 255, 282–3
Eliezer, 160
Elisha, 140, 143, 144
Emmanuel, 158
Ephraim, 246
E-tih Desert, 147
Even, Jackie, 224, 229, 235, 238, 239
Eytan, Raful, 58–9, 62–3, 75, 89–91, 93–4, 96, 99, 107–8, 110, 112, 113, 122, 127, 129, 133, 139, 216, 272, 275
Ezra, 175

Fawzi, Mahmoud, 8, 19
Fayid, 242
Feisal, King of Saudi Arabia, 26
Firdan Bridge, 12, 149, 157, 159, 160, 185, 188, 189, 190, 191
Fiyad, Shafiq, 122, 125
Force Schmulik, 212
Foreign Office (Israeli), 40
FROG missiles, 31, 57, 75, 136, 151, 230

Gaby, 156, 157–8, 165–9, 172, 184, 185, 188, 189, 190, 200, 221, 222, 226, 227, 242–3, 246, 248, 249
Galilee, Sea of, 55, 65, 118, 124, 136
Galili, Yisrael, 49, 53
Gamasy, Abdel Chani, 29, 32, 234
Gamla Rise, 56, 84, 88, 96, 100, 101, 112, 118
Gardaka, 267

Gavish, Yeshayahu, 5–6, 148, 200
Gaza Strip, 2, 3, 16, 32
Gedaliah, David, 46–7
Genefa Hills, 242, 243, 246
General Staff (Israeli), 2–3, 4, 51, 61, 98, 128, 148, 150, 280, 282
Geneva, 288
Ghadafi, Colonel, 26
Gidi Pass, 37, 147, 154–6, 157, 161, 162, 188, 203–4, 234
Giladi, Gideon, 214, 215
Giora, 83, 85
Givat Yoav, 56, 118
Glasboro, 15
Golan Heights, 30, 43, 49, 55–144 *passim*, 183, 184, 255, 258
Golani Brigade, 69, 74, 90, 100, 108, 132, 139, 143, 144
Gonen, Shmuel, 45–6, 53, 62, 65, 146, 148–50, 157–8, 182–5, 188, 190–8, 200, 203–5, 221, 223, 224, 238, 241, 247–50, 271, 278, 283
Gorodisch, *see* Gonen, Shmuel
'Granite 2', 32
Great Bitter Lake, 148, 151, 154, 184, 195, 208, 210, 211, 214, 226, 277–8
Great Leja, 137, 141
Greengold, Zvi ('Zwicka'), 84, 85, 86, 88, 91, 92
Gromyko, 286
Guma, Sharawi, 19
Gur, Mordechai, 5, 57

Habad, 64
Hader, 130
Haifa, 46, 50, 257
Haim, 166, 198, 208, 210, 220, 222, 229, 230, 233, 235–8, 242
Hales, 130, 132
Halevi, Gideon, 215, 216
Halil, Abd el Munem, 206
Hamadia, 194
Hamdi, 258
Hamutal, 192, 193, 199, 210
Hanan, 82, 89, 94, 95
Havit, 242, 245
Haviva, 185, 188

Heikal, Mohammed Hassenein, 15, 22, 25, 37, 232, 245
Hermon, Mount, 56, 57, 67, 69–74, 129, 143–4
Hermonit hill, 57, 65, 67, 79, 106, 107, 108
Hezi, 143–4
Hilawi, Rafiq, 132
Hizayon, 149, 159, 160, 184, 189
Hod, Mordechai, 62
Hofi, Yitzhak, 49, 57–60, 62–3, 68, 74, 80, 87, 93, 96, 98, 99, 117, 118, 126–7, 129, 137, 139, 140, 143, 278, 281
Horfa, 132
Huleh Valley, 57
Hushniyah, 80, 83, 85, 89, 101, 104, 118, 121, 123–7
Hussein, King of Jordan, 10, 30, 128, 139–40, 260, 289

Ibrahim, Abdul Laviv, 39
India, 289
India-Pakistan War, 21, 23, 27, 44
Instruction in Moral Guidance for the Training Year in 1969, 34
Iraq and Iraqi forces, 128, 135, 289, 290
    Armoured Brigade, 6th, 138
    Armoured Division, 3rd, 137–9, 142–3
    Mechanized Brigade, 8th, 138
Ismail, Ahmed, 23–9, 32–4, 37, 58, 135, 137, 149, 232–4, 247, 274
Ismail, Hafez, 23, 25, 29
Ismailia, 3, 155, 159, 160, 184, 185, 188, 235, 239, 241, 250
Israeli Air Force, 9, 14, 31, 43, 52, 58, 62, 99, 125, 135, 142, 143, 156, 158, 162, 179–180, 200, 229, 232, 246, 251–61, 271, 276, 278, 279
Israeli Navy, 47, 52, 261–9
Itzik, 225, 226

Jarring, Gunnar, 18–19
Javits, Yaacov, 159
Jebel Ma'ara, 182
Jebel Um Katib, 243
Jebel Yalek, 182
Jehani, Tewfiq, 122, 125
Jerusalem, 3, 50, 65

Jerusalem Reserve Brigade, 70
Jiradi, 65
Joint Military Command, 32
Jordan, 30, 135, 139
    Armoured Brigade, 40th, 139–40, 142
Jordan River, 117, 122, 183
Jordan Valley, 55, 94, 97
Josh, 130
Jubat el-Hashab, 80
Jubata, 130
Juhader, 56, 82, 87, 120

Kabil, 247
Kadmoni, Asa, 240
Kalkilyeh, 2
Kantara, 4, 156, 157, 165, 167, 168, 171, 172, 185, 188, 201, 205
Katana, 61
Katzin, Benny, 82, 88, 90
Keating, Kenneth, 54
Ketuba, 171, 172, 173–4
Kfar Shams, 140, 141
Khan Arnaba, 129, 130, 132, 134
Khouli, Hassan Sabri Al, 30
Kibbutz Beit Hashita, 216
Kibbutz Dan, 79
Kibbutz Geva, 136
Kibbutz Gonen, 56
Kibbutz Hogoshrim, 79
Kibbutz Lochamei Hagetaot, 84
Kibbutz Nirim, 5
Kishuf, 227
Kissinger, Henry, 25–6, 38–9, 136, 244–5, 250
Kiswe, 61, 137
'Kitchen Cabinet', 49, 282
Knaker, 136, 137
Knesset, Foreign Affairs and Security Committee, 41
Kosygin, Alexei, 15, 17, 234, 244
Kreisky, Bruno, 48–9
Kudne, 60, 68, 69, 80, 82, 104
Kultum, 104
Kuneitra, 56, 61, 63–7, 75, 80, 93, 107, 110, 140
Kuwait, 24, 26, 128
Kuzabia, 56, 100

Lahtzanit, 172, 176
Lakekan, 222, 227–9
Laner, Dan, 98–101, 117, 121–3, 127, 129,
  133–4, 136–8, 140
Latakia, 60, 136, 255, 264, 266, 289
Latrun, 65, 66
Lebanon, 68
'Leja' plain, 132–3
Leor, Israel, 54
'Lexicon', 147
Libya, 26, 27, 28, 268, 290
Litani River, 68
Little Bitter Lake, 161, 164, 246
Lituf, 161, 164, 246

Maatz, 132
Machsir, 190, 194
Mafzeah, 161, 164
Magen, Kalman, 46, 165–8, 172, 180, 184,
  185, 204, 206, 208, 209, 228, 238, 243,
  247, 248, 250
Maghdoub, Taha Al, 258
Maktsera, 235, 242
Mamoun, Saad, 206
Mandler, Avraham 'Albert', 45, 46, 53,
  147–8, 150, 157–8, 161, 163, 165, 181,
  182, 198, 200, 203–4, 278, 283
Margal, 225
Masadah, 56, 67, 68, 78
Massad, 40
Matt, Danny, 210, 211, 214, 215, 217–20,
  222, 229–30, 233, 239, 242
Matzmed, 150, 184, 210, 211, 212, 214,
  216, 229
Mayer, 81
Mazrat Beit Jan, 129, 130, 131, 139
Mazrat Kuneitra, 118
Meir, Golda, 18, 48–9, 50, 52–3, 54, 97,
  116, 118, 129, 196, 197, 281–2
Meir, 'Tiger', 81–2, 108–10, 113
Meler, Moshe, 141
Men, Col., 94
Mersa Talamat, Bay of, 267
Mifreket, 157, 165–6, 167, 168, 172
Migdal Haemek, 136
Milano, 166, 168, 172, 180, 181
Military Intelligence (Israeli), 40, 42, 44, 282

Min el-Beida, Port of, 266
Minah, 247
Ministry of Defence (Israeli), 148
Mir, 104, 124–5
Missouri, 209, 211, 212, 222, 227, 238,
  240–2, 273
Mitla Pass, 6, 37, 62, 147, 154, 157, 161,
  162, 164, 188, 206, 217, 234, 257
Mitznefet, 242, 244
Mohr, Charles, 221
Morgan oil fields, 268
Moroccan Expeditionary Force, 78, 130
Morocco, 135, 232
Moscow, 15, 16, 19, 20, 24, 26, 28, 244–5,
  253, 287, 289
Moshe, 101, 104, 138
Mount Hermon, 56, 57, 67, 69–74, 129,
  143–4

Nachliel, David, 73
Nada, Mohammed Mahmoud, 162
Nafekh, 56, 62, 64, 66–8, 82–94, 96, 98,
  99, 104, 121, 122, 275
Nahal Geshur, 118, 120
Nahala, 97
Nahariya, 257
Najh Hamadi, 5, 217
Nasej, 136–9
Nasser, President, 1, 3, 5, 7–10, 13–17,
  19, 26, 253, 263, 286
Nathan, 212, 216
Natke, 184, 185, 188–91, 226–8, 235,
  242–4, 246
Nazareth, 136
Negev, 146
Neot Mordechai, 98
Netanya, 2, 3, 97
New York, 244
Nile Valley, 5
Nixon, Richard, 17, 18, 20, 21, 25, 27, 29,
  42, 286, 287
Nofal, Baha Al Din, 33

Oded, 68, 82–4, 87, 88, 112
Orcha, 240–1, 242
Orel, 242
Ori, 88, 92–3, 121, 122–3, 127, 134

Orkal, 45, 174–6
Orlev, Zevulun, 171, 172–4
Ovida, 166–7

Palestine Liberation Organization, 31,
283, 290
Palestinian terrorists, 30, 48–9, 58, 139, 252
Parachute Brigade, 31st, 133, 140
Pearl Zeev, 160
Peled, Benjamin, 52, 158, 255–6, 258
Peled, Moshe ('Musa'), 97, 117, 118–20,
123–7, 137, 140
Persia, 289
Pinhas, 70
Pinie, 90, 91, 94
Pino, 46, 150, 157
Podgorny, Nikolai, 14–15, 20
Port Fuad, 45, 151, 156, 171, 172, 179–80,
260
Port Said, 3, 4, 48, 260, 267
Port Tewfik, 7, 157, 161, 162, 176
Purkan, 181, 184, 193–4, 195
'Purple Line', 56, 59, 69, 115, 124, 125,
126–7, 128, 130

'Quay' fortification, 176–9

Rabin, Yitzhak, 183
Rafid, 56, 63, 64, 75, 80, 87, 89, 104, 118,
126, 137
Raful, see Eytan
Ramat Magshimim, 56, 82, 84, 87, 96, 101,
104, 120
Ramtania, 123, 127
Ran, 86, 100, 101, 121, 133–4, 140
Ras Adabiah, 248
Ras El-Aish, 4
Ras Ghareb, 268
Ras Masala, 161
Ras Muhamad, 267
Ras Sadaat, 268
Ras Sudar, 154, 158, 182, 183, 200, 206
Ras Zafrani, 256, 267
Raviv, 202
Refidim, 155, 182, 203, 218, 234, 257
Reserve Brigade, 14th, 118, 120–1, 124–6,
141

Reserve Brigade, 17th, 86, 99–100, 101,
104, 121, 123–5, 127, 129, 133, 134,
136–7
Reserve Brigade, 19th, 99, 100, 104,
118–21, 124, 126, 136–42
Reserve Brigade, 20th, 118–20, 124–6,
137, 138, 141–3
Reserve Brigade, 60th, 126
Reserve Brigade, 70th, 118
Reserve Brigade, 79th, 88, 91–3, 95, 121,
122–3, 127, 129, 133–4, 136–8
Reserve Division, 14th, 97–8, 99, 100
Reserve Division, 20th, 140
Reserve Division, 21st, 121, 124, 129
Reshef, 264
Reuven, 70–2
Richardson, Elliot, 17
Rogers, William, 16, 19, 20, 254
Rogers Plan, 16–17, 19, 25, 254
Royal Air Force (British), 252
Ruqqad, 56, 87, 118, 126

Saada, Hasan Abu, 189, 190
Sabri, Ali, 17, 19, 20
Sadat, Anwar, 15–27, 29–32, 37–8, 41–4,
48, 79, 231–4, 244–5, 274, 278, 286, 287
Safed, Mohammed, 27, 113
Saika, 49
Sakronut, 235, 242
Sam, 129
SAM missile, 8, 9, 17, 221, 253, 255, 256–7
Sarag, 246, 248
Sasoon, 209
Sassa, 129, 136
Satan, 172
Saudi Arabia, 23, 26, 31, 128, 135, 139,
268
Schonau Castle, Vienna, 48
Scud missiles, 24–5, 31, 245
Sea of Galilee, 55, 65, 118, 124, 136
Serafeum, 232, 239, 240
Shadwan Island, 9
Shalev, Aryeh, 44, 48, 49
Shalev, Shaul, 158, 193–5
Shanon, 209–11, 214
Shapira, J., 54
Sharef, Zeev, 49

Sharm el-Sheikh, 16, 27, 44, 154, 156, 183, 195, 255, 256, 267, 268

Sharon, Ariel, 6, 11, 146, 158, 160, 182-3, 188, 190, 192, 194-5, 197-9, 200, 201, 206, 208, 217, 222-3, 227, 229, 230, 232, 238, 240-1, 245-6, 250, 283-4

Shaul, 160

Shazli, Saad Al, 29, 34, 37, 149, 156, 206, 233-4, 256, 258

Shmulick, 113, 212

'Shovach Yonim' operation, 46, 53, 150, 159, 161, 171, 172, 179, 181, 183, 204

Sidki, Aziz, 22-3

Sinai Peninsula, 1-55, 146-250 *passim*

Sindiana, 66, 67, 121, 122-3

Sisco, Joseph, 17, 19, 20

Six Day War, 2, 3, 4, 5, 14, 55, 57, 58, 68, 98, 146, 217, 252, 259, 261, 262, 270, 272, 273, 286

Snobar, 122

Somalia, 289

Somekh, Gad, 174, 175

South Yemen, 289

Southern Command (Israeli), 45, 46, 47, 51, 146, 148, 149, 182, 191, 201, 205, 208, 209, 210, 211, 220, 224, 225, 241

Soviet-Egyptian Treaty of Friendship and Co-operation, 20

Soviet Union, 1, 2, 3, 9, 10, 13-17, 19-27, 29, 34-5, 47-8, 50, 57, 74-5, 79, 128, 135-6, 244-5, 250, 252, 253, 254, 262-3, 274, 277, 284-90

'The Spark', 37

Sterner, Michael, 20

Straits of Tiran, 1

Strasbourg, 48

Suez, 3, 32, 142, 201, 247, 248, 249-50

Suez Canal, 3-54, 146-250 *passim*

Syria and Syrian forces, 28, 30, 31, 33, 34, 45, 47-9 52, 55-144 *passim*, 195, 255, 275, 288, 289

Air Force, 57, 132, 143, 257-8, 259

Armoured Brigade, 68th, 130

Armoured Brigade, 81st, 107

Armoured Division, 1st, 87, 89, 100, 104, 122-6

Armoured Division, 3rd, 107, 108, 126

Armoured Division, 7th, 106, 107, 108, 130

Assad Republican Guard, 63, 108, 111

Infantry Brigade, 33rd, 63

Infantry Brigade, 52nd, 63

Infantry Brigade, 61st, 63

Infantry Brigade, 68th, 62-3

Infantry Brigade, 85th, 62-3

Infantry Brigade, 112th, 63

Infantry Division, 5th, 63, 75, 87, 104, 123

Infantry Division, 7th, 62-3, 75, 80

Infantry Division, 9th, 63, 75, 79

Mechanized Brigade, 15th, 126

Mechanized Brigade, 40th, 126

Mechanized Brigade, 42nd, 101

Mechanized Brigade, 91st, 125

Mechanized Brigade, 132nd, 87, 101, 104, 121, 124, 125

Navy, 263, 264, 266

Tank Brigade, 46th, 87, 124, 125

Tank Brigade, 47th, 87, 101-4

Tank Brigade, 48th, 101

Tank Brigade, 51st, 92, 101

Tank Brigade, 78th, 106

'Tahrir 41', 32

Tal, Israel, 6, 11-12, 41, 43, 47-8, 52, 53, 242

Tal, Shimon, 149-50

Tamir, 209-10

Tanenbaum, Yadin, 166

Tanne, Aharun 'Johnny', 223, 239

Tapline route, 56, 80, 82-9, 91-3, 101, 104, 120-3

Tartus, 136, 266

Tasa, 154, 155, 165, 188, 218, 224, 257

Tel, Wasfi, 30

Tel Abu Hanzir, 89

Tel Ahmar, 79, 132

Tel Aksha, 80

Tel Antar, 139, 140, 141, 143

Tel Aviv, 2, 46, 49, 50, 53, 62, 116, 257

Tel Azaziat, 78

Tel Dan, 78

Tel el-Alakieh, 139, 140, 141, 143

Tel el-Hariyen, 81

Tel el-Kadi, 78
Tel el-Mal, 136, 137, 139, 140, 142
Tel Faris, 57, 88, 112, 125, 126
Tel Fazra, 126, 127
Tel Git, 110
Tel Hara, 63, 142
Tel Hashomer, 112
Tel Hazeika, 64, 80
Tel Kudne, 124, 126
Tel Maschara, 136–40, 142
Tel Nasej, 139
Tel Ramtania, 123
Tel Saki, 82, 120
Tel Shaar, 136, 137, 138
Tel Shams, 129, 130, 132–3, 139, 140, 271
Telem, 263, 264
Televizia, 190, 194, 195, 210, 225
Test route, 235
Thant, U, 1
Tiberias, 87
Tiger, see Meir, Tiger
Timsah, Lake, 232
Tirtur, 209–12, 214, 216, 220–2, 224–9, 239
Tito, Josip Broz, 29
Tlas, Mustafa, 30, 33
Tov, Benjamin Siman, 46–7
Tsach, 235, 242
Tulkarm, 2
Turkey, 289
Tuvia, 193, 210, 225–7, 229, 241, 242
Tzemach, 118

Um Butne, 140–1, 142
Um Mahza, 155, 203
Unger, Rafi, 204
United Nations, 44, 56, 233
   Emergency Force, 1
   General Assembly, 39, 290
   Security Council, 18, 27, 145, 196, 234, 245, 250, 285
United States, 10, 15, 17, 19–24, 28, 31, 42, 50, 136, 254, 277, 284, 288, 289

Uri, 242
Uzi, 86, 161, 222, 225

Vadant, 235
Valley of Tears, 106–15
Verbin, Nahum, 176–8
Vinogradoff, Ambassador, 48, 245

Wadi Sudar, 154
War of Attrition, 7–12, 15, 16, 27, 41, 158, 252, 286
War of Independence, 134
Washington, 18, 25, 29, 250, 287
Wassel, 247
Wasset, 56, 66, 106
Watergate affair, 37
Weizman, Ezer, 203, 204
West Bank, of the Jordan, 2, 30

Yadin, 166, 167
Yagouri, Asaf, 188, 189
Yair, 64–5, 67–8, 79–80, 109–10, 114, 130, 225, 226
Yariv, Aharon, 196
Yarmouk River, 57, 63
Yehudia, 56, 101, 117
Yemen, 289
Yisraeli, David, 68, 82, 84, 88, 89, 90, 92
Yomtov, 158, 165, 166, 168
Yossi, Naty, 112, 113, 129, 130, 132, 133 249
Yugoslavia, 29
Yukon, 201

Zayat, Mohammed, 38–9
Zeev, 281
Zeira, Eli, 42, 44, 47–8, 50–3
Zemach, 56
Ziona, 190
Zur, Zvi, 53
Zvi, 217, 240
Zwicka, see Greengold, Zvi